Depression and Aggression in Family Interaction

ADVANCES IN FAMILY RESEARCH

David Reiss, Editor

Consortium for Research on Family Processes and Psychopathology

Patterson: *Depression and Aggression in Family Interaction*

Depression and Aggression
in
Family Interaction

Edited by

GERALD R. PATTERSON
Oregon Social Learning Center

LAWRENCE ERLBAUM ASSOCIATES, PUBLISHERS

1990 Hillsdale, New Jersey   Hove and London

Lawrence Erlbaum Associates, Inc., Publishers
365 Broadway
Hillsdale, New Jersey 07642

Library of Congress Cataloging-in-Publication Data

Depression and aggression in family interaction / edited by Gerald R.
  Patterson.
        p.   cm.
    Proceedings of a conference held 6/86 in Teton Village, Wyoming
  and sponsored by the Family Research Consortium.
    Includes bibliographies and indexes.
    ISBN 0-8058-0137-5
    1. Depression, Mental—Congresses.   2. Aggressiveness
  (Psychology)—Congresses.   3. Family—Mental health—Congresses.
  I. Patterson, Gerald R.   II. Family Research Consortium.
  RC537.D4272   1989
  616.85′27—dc20   89-118
                                                                         CIP

Printed in the United States of America
10 9 8 7 6 5 4 3 2 1

Contents

Preface

Francis Bacon presented in elegant detail his model for a science that would move from "the skirmishings and slight attacks and desultory movements of the intellect . . . to the discovery of many new things of service to the life and state of man" (Bacon, 1620/1947, p. 236). He visualized an interactive process where a consortium of investigators would examine, measure, weigh, and/or carry out experiments. This data base would, in turn, lead to new hypotheses, or axioms in his parlance, and thus create a demand for yet further experiments. "For our road does not lie on the level, but ascends and descends; first ascending to axioms, and then descending to works" (p. 240).

By working cooperatively, Bacon thought that it would be possible to solve problems heretofore open only to philosophical debate. From his perspective, a cooperative effort would soon produce solutions to ancient problems. These products would dot the intellectual landscape like cathedrals, each a monument to the great instauration. Within the social sciences, Bacon's dream has seldom been realized. Many of us work in isolation. Others are elitists who roam their oak forests, bronze sword in hand, protecting hidden treasure from the eyes of all but the initiated. In recent times, however, there have been several currents moving against these two traditions of scholarship. First, the funds for research are more limited now. Second, many of the questions are too complex to be solved by a single investigator. These and other considerations led to a decision by a working committee at NIMH to design a special conference of investigators. Each participant would be productively engaged in empirical studies of families, and all studies would include longitudinal designs. The conference would also include a sprinkling of investigators who are committed to the study of family therapy outcomes and process. The details of the participants and what occurred at the conference are discussed in the opening chapter of this volume.

The planning committee's decision to select such a group reflected a long-standing conviction about the relevance of studies of family process to the field of psychopathology. Such a conviction had, in fact, been entertained for several decades by theorists of disparate persuasions. It persisted despite reviews of the empirical findings, which concluded that there was no consistent relation between family variables and measures of pathology in children or adults (Frank, 1965).

There were several reasons for the planning committee's belief that the tide might have turned. There had been more than a decade of development in both laboratory (Forgatch, 1987; Gottman, 1979; Reiss, 1981; Sigel, McGillicuddy-Delisi, & Johnson, 1980) and field observation (Reid, 1978) techniques designed specifically for the study of families. There had also been more than a decade of development in techniques of statistical analyses that seemed uniquely appropriate for problems in the family that had been difficult to study. For example, the applications of time series analytic techniques to social science data by Gottman (1981) has immediate relevance to the analysis of family interaction patterns, as shown in the powerful application of these techniques in the publication by Levenson and Gottman (1983) and the review of related studies by Margolin (1983). In a similar vein, the application of structural equation modeling techniques to problems in psychology by Bentler (1980) and others seemed promising as a means for examining complex relations among family variables and peer group processes thought to function as determinants for both prosocial and deviant behaviors.

These innovations in statistical analyses paralleled new developments in assessment procedures tailored to family studies. The combination of more powerful statistical tools and more focused measures have been applied with good effect to the problem of antisocial behavior in children. Reviews of the literature showed empirical findings that were consistent across investigators (Loeber & Dishion, 1983; Parke & Slaby, 1983). The fine-grained observation of family interaction patterns implicated the exchange patterns among family members as a critical mechanism in the inadvertent training of the child for antisocial behavior (Patterson, 1982). These studies identified social exchanges as a prime mechanism driving changes in social behaviors over time.

Also, some of the family and peer variables that accounted for variance in measures of antisocial child behavior (Patterson & Bank, 1985; Patterson & Dishion, 1985) also served as focal points in interventions that effectively reduced deviant child behavior (Blechman, 1980; Patterson, Chamberlain, & Reid, 1982). Application of similar measurement and intervention techniques produced significant findings that contributed both to the understanding and the alteration in parenting behavior for parents of abused children (Reid & Kavanagh, 1985; Reid, Patterson, & Loeber, 1982).

More recently, a similar combination of laboratory, field, self-report, and intervention studies has produced a testable formulation for adult depression

(Lewinsohn & Hoberman, 1982). The appropriate field studies demonstrated the impact of the depressed behavior on the interactional behaviors of the spouse (Hautzinger, Linden, & Hoffman, 1982). Like the coercive behavior of the child, depressed behaviors of adults seem functional. Is it the functional impact on other persons that maintains depressed behavior?

These developments were thought to be an encouraging and necessary beginning to the study of antisocial behavior and depression. However promising the beginning, the problem itself constitutes a higher order of complexity than that covered by any of the existing studies. A satisfactory answer would require the concerted effort of a group of investigators. In addition, there was good reason to believe that it would be necessary to include the data from one or more longitudinal studies. The reasons for this lay in the complex nature of the problems of antisocial and depressed behavior.

This volume was the outcome of the first annual summer institute sponsored by the Family Research Consortium in June of 1986. The week-long conference was held for a small, select audience in Teton Village, Wyoming. Each member of the group was actively engaged in investigating some aspect of family interaction. In a very real sense, many members of the participating audience had research careers as well established as the presenters. The exchanges among equals was very much in keeping with the mandate adopted by the consortium: ". . . devoted to increasing the quality of investigation and level of collaboration in the field of family research." The program, entitled "Regulation of Emotion in the Family: Depression and Aggression", was planned by Ross Parke and John Gottman.

Whether or not one has a biological orientation, the basic social environment for most adults and children is the family. To understand the etiology and maintenance of pathologic behaviors, we must begin with an understanding of what goes on in family interactions. In fact, an empirical understanding of the processes that occur in families seems to be a necessary (though not sufficient) condition for treating the full range of human psychopathologies. One may or may not be in full agreement with this strong statement of the Consortium position. Nevertheless, given that all perspectives must in some sense acknowledge this as *one* of the necessary empirical components, then all of us face a common set of questions. How does one go about studying something as complex as the family? What are the key variables? Where are the measuring instruments for the enterprise to be found? In the mid-1960s, reviews of the empirical literature claimed that there was *no* connection between measures of family variables and pathologic outcomes (Frank, 1965)! The Consortium goals seemed distant indeed.

As noted earlier, major advances in family theory, methodology, and measurement have occurred within the last decade. These advances gave the whole enterprise some aura of plausibility. When applied to such a complex phenomenon as depression in families, the nature of the question itself is often altered. The reader will see this process reflected in several chapters in the present volume (cf. chapters by Biglan, Lewin and Hops, and Gottman).

In most of the reports, the emphasis is upon collecting data based on several different levels of assessment, varying from self-report to the more molecular observation coding schemes. Data are still collected in the traditional interview and questionnaire and represent an important component in the data base for almost every chapter in this volume. These continue to be an important source of molar variables reflecting family member perceptions about their own behavior as well as that of others in the family. The present volume makes a strong case for the use of observation data in describing sequences of family interaction. It becomes a key component in four of the chapters (cf. Radke Yarrow, Gottman, Hops, and Patterson and Forgatch). The settings in which the molecular data are collected vary: videotaped family problem solving sequences (Forgatch, 1987), the home (Patterson, 1982), and the laboratory (Reiss, 1981; Sigel, 1982). The chapter by Radke Yarrow is unique in this respect. She has innovated a design for a whole new setting. Families are brought into a specially designed apartment laboratory setting where data can be collected with multiple agents and methods for an entire day.

Sigel's chapter catches the essence of what the volume is about. One gets a sense from his perspective that the volume represents some kind of a new beginning. Several authors struggle to present integrative models that synthesize the relation between sets of hypotheses. Others (e.g., Griffin) outline time series and sequential analytic statistics to these problems as techniques for shoring up the empirical foundation itself. In this welter of activity, several shapes emerge to viewers like Sigel and myself. It seems to us that the volume may serve as a first step in building process models of family life. What are the forces that contribute to stability and change in emotional exchanges among family members? What mechanisms seem to amplify and dampen these processes? The process metaphor should prove to be extremely useful in guiding the next round of studies. We faithfully followed Bacon's injunction, but the best we can do is hand the king no answers and, instead, metamorphize his prior questions.

REFERENCES

Bacon, F. (1620). Aphorisms concerning the interpretation of nature and the kingdom of man. From the *Novum organum* as cited by D. J. Bronstein, Y. H. Kroinkorian, & P. P. Winer (1947), *Basic problems of philosophy*. New York: Prentice-Hall.

Bentler, P. M. (1980). Multivariate analysis with latent variables: Causal modeling. *Annual Review of Psychology, 31,* 419–455.

Blechman, E. A. (1980). Family problem-solving training. *American Journal of Family Therapy, 8,* 3–22.

Forgatch, M. S. (1987). *Longitudinal study of depressed mood in recently separated mothers.* Unpublished manuscript.

Frank, G. H. (1965). The role of the family in the development of psychopathology. *Psychological Bulletin, 64,* 191–205.

Gottman, J. M. (1979). *Marital interaction: Experimental investigations.* New York: Academic.

Gottman, J. M. (1981). *Time series analysis: A comprehensive introduction for social scientists.* New York: Cambridge University Press.

Hautzinger, M., Linden, M., & Hoffmann, N. (1982). Distressed couples with and without a depressed partner: An analysis of their verbal interaction. *Journal of Behavior Therapy and Experimental Psychiatry, 13,* 307–314.

Levenson, R. W., & Gottman, J. M. (1983). Marital interaction: Physiological linkage and affective exchange. *Journal of Personality and Social Psychology, 45,* 587–597.

Lewinsohn, P. M., & Hoberman, H. M. (1982). Depression. In A. S. Bellack, M. Hersen, & A. E. Kazdin (Eds.), *International handbook of behavior modification and therapy* (pp. 173–208). New York: Plenum.

Loeber, R., & Dishion, T. J. (1983). Early predictors of male delinquency: A review. *Psychological Bulletin, 94,* 68–99.

Margolin, G. (1983). An interactional model for the behavioral assessment of marital relationships. *Behavioral Assessment, 5,* 103–127.

Parke, R. D., & Slaby, R. G. (1983). The development of aggression. In P. H. Mussen (Ed.) & E. M. Hetherington (Vol. Ed.), *Handbook of child psychology: IV. Socialization, personality, and social development* (4th ed., pp. 547–641). New York: Wiley.

Patterson, G. R. (1982). *A social learning approach to family intervention: III. Coercive family process.* Eugene, OR: Castalia.

Patterson, G. R., & Bank, L. (1986). Bootstrapping your way in the nomological thicket. *Behavioral Assessment, 8,* 49–73.

Patterson, G. R., Chamberlain, P., & Reid, J. B. (1982). A comparative evaluation of parent training procedures. *Behavior Therapy, 13,* 638–650.

Patterson, G. R., & Dishion, T. J. (1985). Contributions of families and peers to delinquency. *Criminology, 23,* 63–79.

Reid, J. B. (Ed.). (1978). *A social learning approach to family intervention: II. Observation in home settings.* Eugene, OR: Castalia.

Reid, J. B., & Kavanagh, K. (1985). A social interactional approach to child abuse: Risk, prevention, and treatment. In M. Chesney & R. Rosenman (Eds.), *Anger and hostility in cardiovascular and behavioral disorders* (pp. 241–257). New York: Hemisphere/McGraw-Hill.

Reid, J. B., Patterson, G. R., & Loeber, R. (1982). The abused child: Victim, instigator, or innocent bystander? In D. Bernstein (Ed.), *Response structure and organization* (pp. 47–68). Lincoln: University of Nebraska Press.

Reiss, D. (1981). *The family's construction of reality.* Cambridge, MA: Harvard University Press.

Sigel, I. E. (1982). The relationship between parental distancing strategies and the child's cognitive behavior. In L. M. Laosa & I. E. Sigel (Eds.), *Families as learning environments for children* (pp. 47–86). New York: Plenum.

Sigel, I. E., McGillicuddy-DeLisi, A. V., & Johnson, J. E. (1980). *Parental distancing beliefs and children's representational competence within the family context.* (Research report). Princeton, NJ: Educational Testing Service.

1 The Family Research Consortium: At the Crest of a Major Wave?

David Reiss
George Washington University Medical Center

Joy Schulterbrandt
National Institution of Mental Health

The Family Research Consortium can be viewed as itself a small-scale group interaction experiment; when this experiment has run its course it may help to answer four questions:

1. Is it possible for a group of working family scientists to define, accurately and contemporaneously, the major ebbs and flows of their own field. In particular, can they spot a significant wave of scientific advance *before* it crests.

2. Is it possible for such a group to position its work in relationship to that crest, drawing on the wave's increasing momentum and directing and accelerating it further?

3. Is it possible for a group to sustain work of this kind even though it is dispersed to the four corners of a large continent?

4. If work of this kind is possible, what are the social structures, within the group, which work best?

This very brief essay on the Consortium is, perhaps, a fitting opening for the report of the Consortium's first annual Summer Institute. The Institute itself, including the publication of its proceedings, constitutes one of the social structures sustaining the work of the Consortium; part of the group interaction experiment. The Institute was designed to serve two functions simultaneously. First, as intended in the original blueprint for the Consortium, it is an opportunity for the Consortium and its scientific colleagues to contribute to and benefit from an intense week of continuing education in the field of family studies. Second, it is an opportunity for the Consortium and its colleagues to reflect on the progress of the Consortium itself. In fact, these are, presumably, synergistic efforts: the teaching function of the Institute is enhanced by appreciating the larger aims of the Consortium it was designed to serve.

DEVELOPMENT OF THE CONSORTIUM

The Consortium developed partly by design and, in almost equal measure, partly by accident. Its progenitor was convened, in 1983, by Joy Schulterbrandt, then Chief of the Section on Family Process and Mental Health in the National Institute of Mental Health. It was convened as an advisory group to the Section, which itself was a new enterprise; it was the first administrative unit in the NIMH extramural program, the component responsible for giving research grants, to focus exclusively on the family and its relevance for mental health.

Schulterbrandt had three aims in mind for her advisory group. First, she needed advice on priorities in the field of family studies: What were the most promising areas likely to have a clear yield for mental health? Second, she needed to enhance the liaison between her program and the field of family studies. Here, the short term objective was to increase the flow of high quality grant applications but, beyond that, to enhance both programmatic research and training in the field of family studies. Finally, she needed to demonstrate for NIMH skeptics that it was possible to fill a small size conference room with family researchers who were also scientists: who understood, practiced and discussed sound research design.

The skepticism, it is worth pausing to note, was itself born of two important background issues. First, was the rapid emergence of the neurosciences in mental health research. By the time the little family working group was convened, many inside and outside the Institute were looking to the neurosciences as the king of the intellectual disciplines in mental health research, at long last a hard-nosed science which promised to have the biggest payoff for diagnosis and treatment of the major mental disorders. Equally important, family studies was attached to no discipline and had no independent credentials. In contrast, for example, cognitive science was squarely within the scientifically sturdy traditions of experimental psychology; hence, their practitioners were, at least, assumed to have met the basic requirements for a doctoral degree in the behavioral sciences. Who were these practitioners of family studies? Were they professional castoffs who didn't know a chi-square from a centrifuge?

Thus, the group that convened initially was picked with certain criteria in mind. First, with one exception, they all held major NIMH research and/or training grants. Thus, they would know something of the NIMH system and would also have passed muster in front of scientific peers recognized by the NIMH. Second, again with one exception, they were all, shall we say, enjoying the fruits of midlife. They were laboratory or program directors who, in that capacity, represented a number of more junior colleagues, had experience with research training and were well known in the field. Third, they covered a broad—but not, presumably, too broad—spectrum of disciplines: developmental psychology, clinical psychology, psychiatric epidemiology and clinical psychiatry. Notably absent were sociology, history, ethology and animal studies, and anthropology. Fourth, again with one exception, all were heavily engaged in the direct observation and precise measurement of family interaction. As a group they were enthralled by the unanticipated and arresting patterns of interaction behavior when members of the same family were observed together. Fifth, their work centered squarely on mental illness and mental health. More than half were active and committed clinicians and all were doing research on disorders of individuals or relationships of conspicuous clinical relevance.

In 1983, when the group was convened, it would have been possible to fill several small conference rooms with men and women who met these criteria, particularly if the criterion of funded NIMH applications was relaxed. Thus, the Consortium was—in a very important sense—an interesting accident rather than an august, duly constituted college. Moreover, although Schulterbrandt had some hopes from the first, it was also an accident that the group became self-perpetuating. Efforts at self-perpetuation arose from three discoveries the group made about itself as it worked. First, its members were learning from each other and no other group was serving a similar continuing education function for them in this country or abroad. Second, as it surveyed the field, it recognized that many other investigators, were they also in the group, would experience the same thing. Most were self-taught family researchers and had obtained their degrees in some other field. A few academic settings had groups of sophisticated, senior researchers but many more family researchers worked in relative isolation in their institutions—mainly with their own junior colleagues and students. Thus, there was a genuine task to be done: to afford to other investigators some measure of the collective self-education the fledgling Consortium was beginning to enjoy. Third, and most important, the group thought they detected a major confluence of intellectual themes in family studies, the cresting of an intellectual wave. Research and research training could, they predicted, benefit immensely if this confluence could be encouraged. There seemed to be no other agency tending precisely to this chore; thus began the little social experiment of the Consortium. It developed two simultaneous objectives: (1) to identify some of the most promising themes in family research, particularly in relationship to mental health, and encourage their confluence in strong, programmatic research, and (2) to design and maintain novel social forms to achieve those objectives; its first two social experiments are the Summer Institutes and a ten-site, 3-year postdoctoral training program in family process and mental health. Each of these initiatives are currently supported by NIMH grants.

THE CONFLUENCE OF INTELLECTUAL THEMES

As it surveyed the family field, the fledgling Consortium thought it detected several emerging themes. These themes seemed always to have both a methodological and theoretical aspect and either or both could be emphasized.

Perhaps the most central was to recognize that the field of family studies, and those who watched it from outside, had been energized by several findings of enormous theoretical and practical relevance. The first was the growing recognition that the clinical course of some major mental disorders were intimately linked to specific, measurable, and contemporaneous family process. For example, hospitalizations of adults with schizophrenia were closely linked to hostile and intrusive interaction patterns in their families and severe conduct disorders in school age boys were tied, with equal closeness, to patterns of coercive relationships among all members of their families. These data were leading to a reconceptualization of mental illness as not simply a disorder under the skin of single individuals but also as a public reflection of more secluded patterns within the interior of the family group.

These intimate and important associations were buttressed by major advances in the measurement of family interaction process. These advances, in turn, led to the recognition that family interaction processes were intimately tied not only to major psychopathological syndromes but also to variations in normal human development as well. For example, in this country and abroad, a series of detailed studies of marital interaction patterns was particularly fruitful. For example, using precise, direct observations of marital interaction, patterns specific to unhappy marriages were observed: Unhappy marriages were unable to damp down reciprocal, negative exchanges of feelings in the service of efficient information exchange, mutual support and problem solving. These patterns had significant impact on the development of the marital relationship as well as on the psychological and physical well-being of the marital partners themselves.

These major findings suggested both the vitality and importance of the family research field. It encouraged us to conduct an informal survey of this field. We asked, what are the important new intellectual themes and research methods and what further advances would be possible if these underlying developments were identified and encouraged? Four major themes, which can only be alluded to in this brief essay, seemed especially promising: *life-span development in concentric family and community contexts; social and family learning; the temporal form of family relationships,* and the *evolution of social reality in families.*

Life-span Development in Concentric Family and Community Contexts

The Consortium recognized, along with many of its colleagues in the field, that family studies were contributing to a radically new concept of human development. This new concept could be broken down into three components.

First, human development could no longer be seen as being driven simply by some internal engine which prompted the unfolding of human potential in critical phases of childhood and adulthood. Rather, both child and adult development was deeply embedded in contemporaneous family processes. Indeed the family could be understood as a confluence and regulator of simultaneous developmental trajectories of all its members. For example, family-oriented studies of early infancy were recognizing that infancy not only initiates a cascade of developmental process in the newborn family member. Simultaneously the parents' relationships with each other, with their other children, with their own parents, with their friends and places of employment also shifts. The infant's own development remains highly sensitive to major shifts or transformations in any of these other relationships in this broad social context. Furthermore, studies of difficult or disabled infants demonstrated that all these other relationship systems—and the development of individuals within them—are responsive to the vicissitudes of the infant's own development.

A second component of this concept was to recognize that families, as coherent entities, have their own developmental trajectories. They go through expectable developmental crises and changes during the formation and solidification of marriage, through child rearing, and through death and dissolution. Further, important intergenerational processes, linking development in older and younger generations within the same family, could be mapped with increasing precision. More recently, family developmental processes in response to unanticipated events such as divorce and fatal illness could be defined. Recognizable phases of premonitory stress, severe crisis and a kind of family wound healing could be observed. More important, significant maladaptive variations in these sequences of crisis and wound healing, with major implications for mental health, could be measured with increasing precision. An intriguing concept emerging from these studies is that one set of factors may initiate transitions and crises in families and another set shape the family's longer term responses.

Finally, it became increasingly evident that these coordinated processes of development, regulated and mediated within the family, are shaped in major ways by the communities in which families live together. A new discipline of community/family epidemiology was deploying powerful techniques of sampling, measurement and analysis to map variation in family form and functioning within well-defined communities. Data emerging from these studies clarified at least two forms of community influence. First were the impact of variations *within* the community on development in the family. For example, even within the same community dramatic variations in structure and discipline among schools and class rooms play major roles in shaping the lives of children within families. Second, variation *among* communities had equally important impacts. For example, variation in community structure, including levels of employment, have been shown to have a major impact on the control of violence within the family.

Social and Family Learning

A second major theme, noted by the new Consortium, was strong evidence suggesting that the family was a central agency of learning. The powerful techniques of behavioral analyses and learning theory had their origins in laboratory studies of the links between animal behavior and inanimate, reinforcing stimuli. A major transformation of the field occurred when social stimuli—behavior of other individuals—were recognized as reinforcing. This perspective has become expanded and transformed in the study of the family most notably in the study of childhood and adolescent psychopathology and marital conflict. New techniques of laboratory and in-home observation have mapped repetitive sequences of social behavior which serve to both positively and negative reinforce problem behaviors such as destructive aggression. Perhaps the central finding in this tradition is that sequences of family behavior include reinforcers such that a reaction subsequent in the chain serves to reinforce the prior response. In this way behavioral cycles, often quite destructive, become firmly embedded in the texture of family life.

One of the most intriguing mechanisms, emerging from many family studies, is an analog in families of the well-known escape-conditioning learning process. Family members, often through aversive or violent behavior, "escape" from unpleasant social stimuli from others by reducing the frequency of those negative social stimuli. Violence in one member, for example, often leads to appeasement in the other. This "escape" enhances or reinforces the aversive or violent behavior in conspicuously effective ways; extinction becomes most unlikely.

Because of the precision of this behavioral analysis of family process it has been possible to design equally precise interventions to interrupt these destructive behavioral cycles. The therapeutic benefit of many of these programs has already been clearly demonstrated. Perhaps of greater importance, the family learning perspective has generated the greatest impetus for using precisely tailored interventions as true experimental tests of models of family process.

The Temporal Form of Family Relationships

As techniques for microscopic analyses of family behavior have rapidly improved a new conception of family relationships has been shaped. This conception relates changes in the family which unfold on a second-to-second basis with those changes which occur over a span of months or even years.

Three interrelated developments in methods are critical here. First, has been the development of new techniques for measuring communicative intent and affect in family members. These techniques permit careful measurement of the feelings and interpersonal strategies inherent in even very brief interactions. Second have been techniques which permit *simultaneous* measurement of the autonomic nervous system, as well as other physiological control mechanisms, alongside measures of family interaction. The third advance has been statistical and computer methods for storing large amounts of data and examining the physiological and communication data for its sequential patterns.

These powerful new tools have yielded images of relationships unfolding in four broad spans of time. One the most microscopic levels are very brief repeated sequences of interaction—usually containing seven or fewer separate components—and lasting only a few moments. The irritable sequences in unhappy marriages, noted earlier, have now also been observed in mother infant interaction as well interaction between parents and older children. However, interaction also unfolds across longer episodes sometimes lasting from minutes to hours and proceeds through recognizable phases. For example, marital conflict situations can be seen as proceeding through agenda building, arguing and negotiation phases. The patterns of more microscopic interactional sequences changes in each of these three phases. In yet a third span of time, often lasting over days and weeks, are recognizable time-dependent transformations in relationships. These have been studied with particular care in marital as well as friendship dyads; clearly demarcated phases in relationship development are being identified. Finally are changes over months and years, phasic patterns in relationship development, which are only just being demarcated.

Social Reality in Families

A final theme noted by the Consortium, along with other observers of the family field, is concerned not with the analysis of behavior primarily but with meaning and symbols. A broad range of data suggest that the development of interaction patterns and relationships in the family is accompanied by a parallel development of shared systems of meaning: common beliefs, common versions of family history and common constructions about the social world in which the family is embedded. Parents develop concepts of their own efficacy and of their child's development potential. Where there is clear psychopathology, parents develop or reify their own concepts of the pathogenisis of the disorder. Marriages develop their own philosophy of marriage with particular values about the importance of intimacy and conflict resolution. Whole families vary in their beliefs about the danger or safety of their social world and the importance of using collaborative or individualistic strategies to deal with it.

Observational, laboratory, and interview methods have been developed to assess these shared symbolic processes in families. Evidence already suggests they play a major role in child-rearing patterns by parents, and an equally important role in strategies for resolution of marital conflicts in a family's response to a broad range of mental health interventions to medical care.

An intriguing concept emerging from these studies is that these family philosophies or beliefs may shape or regulate some of the more molecular or moment-to-moment interactional patterns. For example, marital partners develop shared beliefs about the importance of interdependence—how much of their daily lives should be closely meshed. These beliefs appear to shape their moment-to-moment sensitivity to each others' changes in feeling states as well as their moment-to-moment patterns of self-disclosure.

PRIORITIES IN THE CONSORTIUM'S WORK

In its early work the Consortium attempted to focus these themes on issues of major mental health relevance. It centered its attention on two of many possible areas. The first were two areas of psychopathology: depression and aggression. The second was factors shaping the family's capacity to respond to severe stress.

Aggression had received a great deal of attention from family research. Two areas had been investigated with particular thoroughness: the development of aggressive syndromes in school age boys and marital and family violence (there is, in fact, considerable overlap between these two areas). Several chapters in this volume summarize work on these topics. Depression had received far less attention from family researchers despite a great deal of preliminary evidence that the family plays a central role in this syndrome.

The choice of these two areas was strategic. In its selection of aggression, the Consortium hoped to encourage research in an area where significant advances had already been made. In this area some of the broad potential of family studies could be more fully probed. For example, data were already in hand to develop not only a family-based concept of the pathogenisis of aggression syndromes in boys but to develop and assess an increasingly refined family-based therapeutic strategy. For depression there was an opportunity to encourage deployment of a broad range of concepts and methods, from those described briefly above, to a major problem in public health.

The focus on the family's response to severe stress was an effort to deploy basic research, in the service of clinical needs, in an entirely different frame. First, it centered attention on the competence and development of the family, considered as a unitary entity, rather than on individually-based psychopathology. Second, it offered a particularly good opportunity to explore the applicability of family-level concepts and methods of measurement such those focussing on family development, community/family epidemiology and shared meaning systems in families. Finally, an understanding of family invulnerability, in the face of stress, promised to be of relevance to a range of clinical issues much broader than one or two psychopathologic syndromes.

THE CONSORTIUM'S SOCIAL EXPERIMENT

Clearly the task was ambitious and certainly would have far exceeded the capacity of any single research group whatever its size and diversity. The ten members of the Consortium, and the large and diverse research groups they represented, came closer to being adequate as a collectivity. But what form would collaboration among these ten groups take? Mullen has recently provided a perceptive analysis of the role of collaborating scientific groups in the forward progress of several areas of biological and social science. The groups Mullen studied, such as the bacteriophage group associated with Woods Hole, engaged in prolonged, innovative, and collaborative scientific work in ways that capitalized on the momentum of a nascent field and which gave energy and direction to its first currents. But these groups tended to have a common site and were often glued together by a senior mentor, sage, or professor and the charismatic impact of this leader on present and former students.

The Consortium recognized from the start that it could not focus on collaborative research across all ten sites (although collaborative links of this kind, on a smaller scale, have been developed). The group was scattered to all four corners of a vast republic and no member has been elected or volunteered for the job of sage. The Consortium, it seemed, would function as *stimulators, provocateurs, and consultants* rather than *collaborating investigators* and would experiment with forms that, while not excluding collaborative research, would not depend on it either. Two possible experiments were suggested: an annual summer institute and a multisite postdoctoral program. There were some models to use for the former, none for the latter.

The Annual Summer Institute

The shaping of this plan helped the Consortium refine its central objective; to *stimulate* research rather than, as a body, to produce it. For well-trained researchers, the Consortium reasoned, there is nothing so intoxicating as some terrific ideas mixed with intriguing and well-developed methods to test them out. The basic plan, then, was to provide an opportunity for intensive teaching of researchers about both new concepts and techniques which would advance their own work in family studies or, if they languished in other fields, to entice them into family research. But, from the start, the Consortium eschewed its own role as the exclusive teacher. They sought to be taught as well as teach and to create an intense intellectual environment where all participants could learn and teach.

The experiment was designed with these procedures. First, invite a very limited number of experienced researchers to join in an annual conference. Second, select an Institute focus which extended one of the basic aims of the Consortium. Third, invite—from within the Consortium and without—people who were especially expert on the selected topic. Fourth, give each of them enough time—up to one full day—to show their wares: theory, methods (in detail), and findings. Fifth, sequester the whole group in a physical setting that would energize the proceedings.

Is this part of the experiment working? The immediate results were very promising. Participants gave the first institute and its format rave reviews. Following the conference a number of new, collaborative links among registrants were developed. But the long-term results (the most important as in any experiment) can't be gauged yet. What important new research might be shaped or influenced by the first or subsequent institutes?

The Ten-Site, Postdoctoral Training Program

Here, the Consortium had no precedent to reply upon. Nonetheless, it felt that the rabble might be roused at a summer institute but die-hard revolutionaries could only be shaped by more prolonged and perhaps more Spartan exposure to a full range of ideas and methods in family studies. The Consortium felt that few if any researchers were being trained to identify and master the broad range of concepts and techniques now available. Consortium members themselves, as we have said, were in their mature years and their own training and experience was shaped and limited, to varying extents, by the field of family studies as it has been. Thus, a training program was born from the most powerful generative motive known to humankind: to create progeny more perfect than oneself. No single Consortium site could mount a training program with sufficient range and depth. Could they be linked together in some pedagogically sensible program?

This experiment is also composed of several straightforward procedures. First, select a group of talented men and women with a burning commitment to a research career (5 were selected into the first class entering the program in 1985; 6 have been selected to enter in the fall of 1987). Second, bring them all together for 1 year to (1) survey, through intense programs of readings and seminars, the major contours of the current family field; (2) become acquainted with the work at all ten sites, and (3) to begin their own investigations. The first year site is the Department of Psychology at the University of Virginia. Third, encourage each fellow to select a second site most consonant with their long-term interests. Fourth, encourage them to take on one or more major research projects at that site with clear-cut requirements for publication. Fifth, instruct them in the completion of a highly competitive grant application to be finished before concluding the program; this artifice would enable them to be independent investigators in whatever positions they were appointed following graduation from the program.

Is this program working? Once again, there is only an uncertain verdict. The short-term results are very encouraging. We have attracted two classes of immensely talented men and women. The first class mastered a great range of material in their first year and completed important research projects the report of which have, in many cases, already been accepted for publication. Further, all of the first year fellows have successfully accomplished the transition to their second site. The future looks rosy not only for these 11 talented fellows but for the field that receives them.

2
Developmental Epidemiological Framework for Family Research on Depression and Aggression

Sheppard G. Kellam, M.D.
Johns Hopkins University

Recent advances in family research have caused investigators to realize the need for theoretical and methodological integrations and a wider interdisciplinary perspective. More limited perspectives have produced fairly high levels of precision in measurement and hypothetical models to explain outcomes, but new problems have arisen based on these successes. Current sampling procedures often leave uncertain the populations of individuals or families for whom research findings pertain. In many family studies the sample is not representative of a defined population. Further, the frequency and distribution of family processes that put children and families at increased risk cannot be measured without defining the population under study. Most important, causal models are frequently limited by not defining the population and including in the model relevant aspects of the environmental contexts with which the family and its members must articulate.

Prior family research has frequently been done on volunteer populations or populations drawn from clinics where the families have sought help for problems. Such samples come from unknown total populations and entail selection bias in the sampling, since those families who seek help are likely to be importantly different from families with similar problems who do not seek such help (Greenley & Mechanic, 1976; Greenley, Mechanic, & Cleary, 1987; Kellam, Branch, Brown, & Russell, 1981). Those who seek help from the church may be quite different from those who seek help from the clinic; many families do not seek help at all. Relying on volunteer subjects has similar problems when they are sought through newspaper or poster advertising; those that respond may not be representative of those that do not. As important, the ecological context is lost to the research when such opportunistic sampling is done; families are mostly viewed in isolation from their societal milieu.

Epidemiology can provide an important conceptual framework for this next stage of family research and addresses the problems described earlier. Epidemiology permits us to formulate questions about whom generalizations can be made, rates and distributions of antecedents and outcomes, and tools and concepts for integrating disciplines into a broader, more ecological perspective. Traditionally, the phrase host/agent/environment is part of the epidemiological lexicon (Morris, 1975). It refers to a way of conceptualizing cause or etiology as involving vulnerability in the person (the host), illness producing conditions in the environment, and a causal process of interaction (the agent) between the individual and the environmental risk conditions.

Research on total cohorts within specified populations can be related through multistage representative sampling to more microanalytic studies on smaller populations that require more frequent measurement and close laboratory control. This link between population based research and the smaller samples required for more microanalytic study shows great promise for the next stage of family research, and is a central theme of this chapter.

We examine epidemiology in this chapter from several perspectives: demographic, transitional, community, developmental, and lastly, experimental. Each of these has distinctive functions in relation to family research. We use data from epidemiological studies in Woodlawn, beginning in the 1960s and still continuing, to illustrate these perspectives, showing demographic aspects of this urban poor, Black, neighborhood, the mobility or transition of the families over the period of 1966 to 1976, antecedents along developmental paths to aggression and depression from 1st grade through midadolescence. We examine epidemiologically within Woodlawn variations in school and classroom environments and in family structure at the time of 1st grade, as well as family evolution through the child rearing cycle.

We then turn to the epidemiological examination of aggression and depression, these being special cases of the more general problem of measuring psychopathology. Measuring variation in the population of behavior, signs and symptoms, syndromes, and diagnoses is discussed and illustrated, using data from the N.I.M.H. Epidemiological Catchment Area (ECA) studies. E.C.A. and U.S. Census Data are also used to illustrate the complementarity between demographic and community epidemiology. Multivariate analyses of changing and stable family and school risk factors, and child psychological and social adaptational risk factors are drawn from Woodlawn studies to illustrate the kinds of inferences that can be drawn from what we term developmental epidemiological family research.

PERSPECTIVES ON EPIDEMIOLOGY

Demographic Epidemiology

Epidemiology involves the study of the occurrence and distribution of health and disease in populations. Nonrandom distribution is of great interest, since it focuses the search for explanations of nonrandomness, in other words the search for causes. However, at a demographic level, epidemiological research is less characterized by the search for explanation than by the description of the condition of the population in relation to the health related characteristics. The prevalence of cancer of a certain kind in the population provides information regarding the condition of society. At this level epidemiological research is closely linked to demography (Sweet, 1977). Demographic epidemiology, over periods in the history of a society, can teach us about trends in family, using such indicators as variation in the standard deviation of age of first marriage, the number of children and their spacing, divorce rates, and so forth. These trends over time provide important insights into the past, current, and coming stages of the structure and function of the family. Kramer illustrates by the following description of recent evolution in the family in the U.S. (Kramer, Brown, Skinner, Anthony, & German, 1987):

- The population of the United States increased from 152 million to 236 million from 1950 to 1984.
- Married couples increased from 34 million to 50 million.
- Male-headed families without spouses increased from 1.2 million to 2 million.
- Female-headed families without spouses increased from 3 million to 9.9 million.
- Divorces increased from 385,000 to 1.2 million by 1984.
- Rates of mental disorder were significantly higher for those living alone or in female-headed families.

Although these data do not explain these trends, they surely present a powerful context for planning family research directed at their causes and consequences.

"The life cycle of the family" is a concept described by Paul Glick in a classic article in 1947 and enlarged upon in the ensuing years (Glick, 1947, 1955, 1977). Complementing the cohort effects noted by Kramer, here we are concerned with the demographic characteristics of the family that evolve as the family proceeds through its course from initiation, to child rearing, to contraction after the offspring move out, to dissolution or generational continuity. Glick points out the higher rates of residential mobility at the time the family begins child rearing, for example, which may effect rearing, behavior monitoring included. Family transitions, including children entering elementary school are associated with residential mobility, according to these demographic data, with their associated loss of neighborhood integration, as families in our society seek more housing space and good schooling.

Transitional Epidemiology

The perspective of transitional epidemiology has recently been described by Soberon, Frenk, and Sepulveda (1986) as the study of the distribution of rates of health or illness in populations undergoing change in environments. The rural/ urban transition in Mexico by many millions of people over the last 2 decades offers an important example of this perspective. Rates of illness, risk factors, and the very structure of the environment itself have undergone dramatic changes only partially understood in the course of this major transition of populations. Migrations to and within the United States in the later half of the 19th century, and migrations of Blacks to urban centers from rural southern states provide many examples of this kind of epidemiology, which is concerned with the nonrandom distribution of health related characteristics in populations undergoing such major environmental transitions.

Community Epidemiology

Community epidemiology is well suited for analytic and explanatory goals, aimed at understanding the etiology and course of disease particularly when there is a partnership with microanalytic laboratories (Kellam, Branch, Agrawal, & Ensminger, 1975; Kellam & Ensminger, 1980). We have used community epidemiology in the Woodlawn research for this purpose. This epidemiological orientation holds constant the macro-characteristics of a population, for example a neighborhood such as Woodlawn—poor, Black, and urban—allowing examination of differences within Woodlawn in the developmental course of children toward good outcomes or toward aggression and/or depression. We can examine diverging developmental paths in the context of variation in small social fields such as family and classroom within Woodlawn. Examination of these social fields, the child's characteristics, and aspects of their interaction, within this single community, has shed light on aspects of the evolution of families as well. This population-based strategy informs us about development in a particular community, and then requires systematic and direct replication in other communities to define the limits of generalizability.

Community epidemiology is a very important part of the next stage of family research in that it allows the broad characteristics of a population to be held constant, while differences within the population can be sought that explain why some individuals develop toward health while others in the same community become maladaptive or ill. Definition of specific total cohorts within the community can be done by birth certificate, or 1st-grade registration, or registrations at later times in the life course of individuals. Alternatively, household sampling can be done, searching out the cohort of interest. Such a defined population allows sampling either for microanalytic studies randomly or stratified by research needs.

Few samples are likely to be complete in the sense of all of the population being constantly available for research, and longitudinal family research is particularly difficult given the migration of families. However, an epidemiological orientation allows us to understand who participates compared to who does not, since we have some information about the total population. In longitudinal research damage from sample loss can often still be reduced by the knowledge available about the total population coupled with that of the earlier measures on the study sample that allows comparisons to be made between those lost and those still in the sample.

Developmental Epidemiology

The term developmental epidemiology as we define it refers to the integration of community epidemiology with that of life course development. Following total populations or representative samples of populations over time and stages of development is the core idea. Developmental epidemiology is intended to allow the mapping of developmental paths within defined populations over significant portions of the life course. Although developmental psychologists and psychiatrists often study smaller populations with more frequent observations, developmental epidemiology involves total cohorts or representative samples often over longer periods of time, often with less frequent points of observations. It supplies both a better definition of population as well as a longer period in the life course for observation, but with less precision and details than is generally possible through more microanalytic methodology. Together in a multistage sampling and measurement design the strengths of each are gained.

Experimental Epidemiology

Experimental epidemiological field trials can be directed at specific antecedents in developmental models and can be an important strategy in both prevention and developmental research. Preventive trials currently being done in Baltimore schools are directed at early behavioral responses of children to school demonstrated in prior research to be risk factors for later aggression and depression. These preventive trials function as tests of the developmental significance of early risk behaviors or conditions, as well as having potential significance as to specific prevention programs. Sometimes called experimental epidemiology (Morris, 1975), this last topic will help integrate population based family research and microanalytic family studies with research on etiology, vulnerability, and prevention.

ILLUSTRATION WITH EPIDEMIOLOGICAL STUDIES FROM WOODLAWN

In what follows we use data from Woodlawn on four total populations of 1st-grade children, particularly the third cohort, which was followed from 1st grade in 1966–1967 through age 16 or 17, to illustrate our perspectives on epidemiology. By restricting the research to a single poor, Black, urban neighborhood, we could look inside Woodlawn and examine variation in the children and in the families, schools, and classrooms in the search for explanations of different child outcomes.

We include a map of the City of Chicago with map tacks indicating the location at 10-year follow-up of the families of 1966–1967 Woodlawn 1st graders. The neighborhood boundaries (seen as black lines defining one neighborhood from another) were originally set by Park, 1925) and their colleagues in sociology at the University of Chicago, who developed the Ecological Theory of Urbanization. Briefly stated the theory points to the ecological function of neighborhood areas in the broader city. Immigrant populations move into the industrial areas near major transportation routes. With upward mobility populations migrate outward along socioethnic as well as geographic lines, toward areas with more space and better housing. The movement of populations within the cities in many parts of the United States follows this pattern of residential transitions, often at times of life course transitions of the individual, and often at times when the family is undergoing change, such as the initiation of child rearing, as Glick has described (1947, 1955, 1977).

The map tacks in Fig 2.1 indicate a great diversity of residential relocation of this 1st grade cohort of families and children over 10 years, and illustrates transitional Epidemiology. They moved to 43 of the 76 neighborhood areas within Chicago. The families who made this transition from 1966–1976, we can hypothesize, are different in important respects from the families that remained within Woodlawn. Woodlawn itself was, during the decade of this population mobility, one of the four most impoverished neighborhoods in Chicago.

From a community epidemiological perspective we can begin to ask about variation in families. Seventy percent moved out of the neighborhood. Eight of ten Woodlawn families that moved went to neighborhoods with more space and better housing, very often stating their reasons for moving as seeking better schools and environments for their children. Those who remained behind in Woodlawn, and those two out of ten who moved but not to better areas, are of

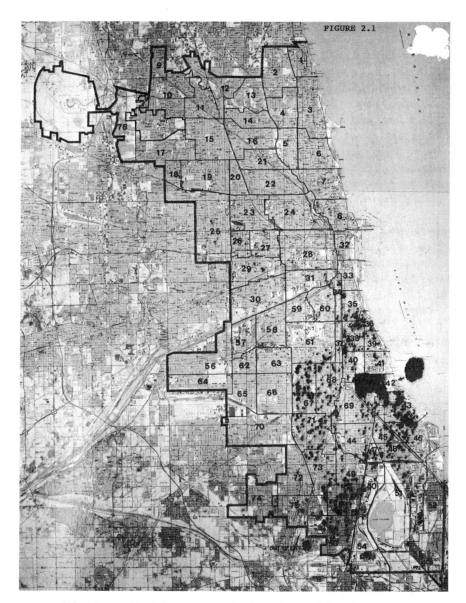

FIG. 2.1.   Residential mobility of Woodlawn 1st-grade families over 10 years.

great importance to compare in regard to family structure and processes to those who were upwardly mobile.

The developmental epidemiological perspective can also be inferred from the map, since the population of families and their 6-year-old 1st graders are shown

10 years later, a significant span in the life course of both the families and the children. To discuss what we mean by this perspective we have found it useful to consider stages of life in relation to the small social fields relevant to each stage, and to look inside these social fields at the social task demands and behavioral responses of individuals in each social field. We have applied this perspective in a set of constructs the first of which is called the *Life Course-Social Field* concept, and the second *Social Adaptation* and *Social Adaptational Status*. These concepts have guided our choice of measures over an important portion of the life course of the children and we believe can provide an important theoretical meaning to the developmental paths these measures have enabled us to study. Adequacy of role performance as discussed by Parsons has very important similarities to social adaptational status (Parsons, 1964). The Life Course-Social Field Concept is based on the theoretical development of Erikson (1959, 1963), Havighurst (1952), Neugarten (1968), and others over the last several decades. In each case, there is a primary concern with the stages of life through which all individuals pass. If the individual's life course is considered from the community standpoint, specific social fields, such as the school, the job, or the family, can be seen to have more or less importance at different stages. Everyone in a community is in one or another stage of life and is functioning in several or all of the social fields relevant to that stage. Each social field requires individuals within its sphere to perform certain social tasks, and there are specific criteria of success and failure.

The *Life Course-Social Field Concept* is illustrated in Figure 2.2. At each stage of life our prototype individual is involved in a few major social fields. The first is that of family of orientation, followed by school and classroom, and quickly thereafter by the peer group. The intimate social field develops through adolescence and becomes the marital social field later in the life course. The work social field develops in importance, as does the social field of the family of procreation of the children. In all there are a fairly small number of such social fields, and these vary in their importance at each stage of life, shown by the variation in width of each bar. Neugarten has pointed out that increasingly in recent years the sequence and timing of moving from one social field to another has itself become far more varied. The age at first marriage, age at child bearing, entrance into the work social field, and other aspects of the life course now reveal considerably more variation from individual to individual (Neugarten, 1979) than in the 1950s, for example.

Measuring Social Adaptational Status and Psychological Well-being

The Woodlawn children who entered 1st grade were confronted by social task demands placed on them by their teacher. Such a process occurs in each social field at each stage of life. Each social field, the parental family, the classroom,

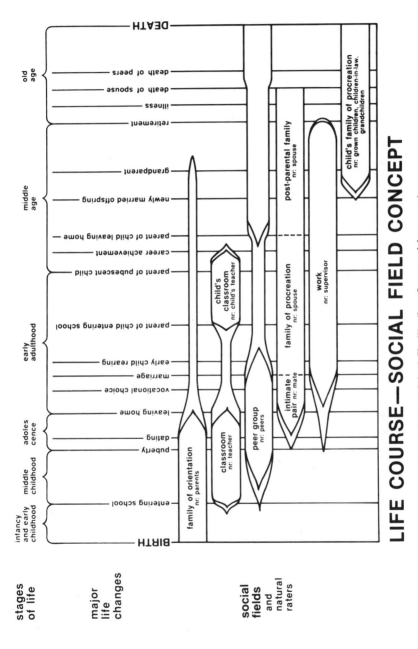

LIFE COURSE—SOCIAL FIELD CONCEPT

Kellam, S.G., et al. (1975). Mental Health and Going to School: The Woodlawn Program of Assessment, Early Intervention, and Evaluation. University of Chicago Press. Revised 1989

FIG. 2.2. Life course—social field concept.

the peer group, the work place, entails a person in authority who defines the social task demands and rates the adequacy of the performance of individuals within that social field. The 1st-grade teachers in Woodlawn defined tasks, graded children as to adequacy of performance, and decided whether the child moved on to 2nd grade or not. Supervisors on the job, spouses in the marital social field, parents in the family social field, are examples of such individuals who define social tasks and rate adequacy of performance. We have termed such people *natural raters*. Chance, idiosyncratic events, the fit of individuals with natural raters and others in the social field all play a role in their ratings. We call this highly interactive demand/response process between natural raters and individuals in specific environments *social adaptation,* and the ratings made by the natural raters *social adaptational status (SAS)* measures (Kellam, Branch, Agrawal, & Ensminger, 1975). We have found this concept of SAS important in mapping the developmental paths leading to later depression and aggression and other specific outcomes, particularly when gender is included in the investigations (Kellam, Brown, Rubin, & Ensminger, 1983; Ensminger, Kellam, & Rubin, 1983).

In addition to SAS which reflects the societal view, in the Woodlawn studies we assessed psychological well-being (PWB) which reflects the individual perspective. The two views taken together comprise a two-dimensional definition of mental health. PWB includes the primary components of the traditional psychiatric view of mental health: how the individual feels in regard to self-esteem, anxiety, depression, and other affects and the status of his or her thought processes. We defined SAS and PWB as separate concepts and measured them independently of each other, so that we might study their long-term interrelationships and the outcomes of each. To illustrate our understanding of developmental epidemiology, we report here on the long-term relations of SAS to adolescent substance use, assault, and psychiatric symptoms, particularly depression (Kellam, Brown, Rubin, & Engminger, 1983; Ensminger, Kellam, & Rubin, 1983).

In four cohorts from 1964–1965 we assessed periodically both the SAS and PWB of the Woodlawn 1st graders. Their teachers rated their SAS in standardized interviews three times in 1st grade and again in 3rd grade. IQ, readiness-for-school, and achievement test scores were used as additional measures of SAS because these tests were SAS tasks the school expected the children to perform. The children themselves, mothers or mother surrogates, as well as clinical raters reported on the children's PWB in the first and third cohort, and the third cohort was followed at age 16 or 17 providing data on outcomes 10 years after initial measures.

We chose the 1st-grade classroom of the child for the measurement of SAS and PWB because we required a total population of students and this was the earliest such school registry. Also we continue to be influenced by the very likely importance of this social field and its natural rater, the teacher, at this major transition in the life course. Our primary instrument, the Teacher's Observation of Classroom Adaptation (TOCA) was developed based on teacher reports of the classroom social tasks they expected children to perform. The final version in 1964–1965 was comprised of six rating scales to measure SAS: social contact (shy behavior), authority acceptance (aggressive behavior), maturation, cognitive achievement, concentration, and an overall global scale of how well the child performed as a student.

Each teacher (all were women) rated all of her students in a standardized interview on a global 4-point scale for each social task, with specific items of behavior provided to illustrate each global scale. The scales ranged from adaptive to severely maladaptive behavior. TOCA ratings were made early in the school year, at midyear, and at its end. (See Kellam, Branch, Agrawal, & Ensminger, 1975, for reliability and validity data regarding these scales.) The original instrument was developed prior to our understanding of multi-item scaling and current psychometric methods, and it is interesting to note the power to predict outcomes ten years later. We believe the early intense investment in the interview process was a major factor in the strength of prediction.

To construct the TOCA scales, we first requested from the 57 Woodlawn 1st-grade teachers of 1964–1965 lists of the ways children demonstrated maladaptation to the classroom. From these lists the social tasks expected of 1st-grade children in this community were inferred. The teachers noted some 450 maladaptive behaviors, which were then grouped independently by two research staff members into five global scales. The following are representative maladaptive items and the five social tasks we inferred from them:

Maladaptive behaviors	*Categories of social tasks*
Shy; timid; alone too much; friendless; aloof	Social participation
Fights too much; steals; lies; resists authority; destructive to others or property; obstinate; disobedient; uncooperative	Authority acceptance
Acts too young physically and/or emotionally; cries too much; has tantrums; sucks thumb; physically poorly coordinated; urinates in class; seeks too much attention	Maturation

Does not learn as well as he is able;   Cognitive achievement
lazy; does not come prepared for work;
underachieves; lacks effort;

Fidgets; does not sit still in classroom;   Concentration
is restless; has short attention span

For the long-term follow-up at age 16 or 17, the target population was the 1242 1st grade students of 1966–1967 who remained in the Woodlawn 1st-grade classrooms that school year and their families.

Following a Cohort of First Graders: Points Along Developmental Paths Leading to Depression, Heavy Substance Use, and Assault

Teacher ratings of SAS toward the end of 1st grade are used in this section to illustrate developmental epidemiological mapping within the Woodlawn neighborhood from entrance to school through age 16 or 17 based on self-reports of teenagers at follow-up. The results we summarize here are drawn from three or four variable loglinear analyses in which certain other possible influences were controlled. Gender was taken into account and was almost always important in developmental course. Family data was included in these analyses and was obtained through interviews with the mothers or surrogates in 1967 and again in 1976.

During 1975–1976 we located and reinterviewed 939 (75%) of the mothers or mother-surrogates of the 1242 families from the 1966–1967 study. The mothers' refusal rate was 5.9%. An additional 18% of mothers were not reinterviewed because either we could not find them, the families had moved from Chicago, or their children included in the study population had died. We asked mothers who consented to the interview for permission to interview their children, now teenagers. If the mother gave her permission, we approached the teenager for reassessment. Of the 939 teenage children of the reinterviewed mothers, 75% (705) participated in the reassessments, 14.5% refused to participate, and 10.4% had moved out of Chicago, had an unknown address, or were unavailable because they were in an institution. The population on whom we report here consists of 705 teenagers whom we assessed.

To study differences between those reassessed and those not we compared three groups from the original population: (a) children who participated in the follow-up as teenagers and all of whose mothers (or mother-surrogates) participated; (b) children who did not participate but whose mothers did; and (c) children who did not participate and whose mothers also did not. Among the three groups, we found no differences in children's or mother's 1966–1967 psychological well-being, family income, kinds of adults at home, or welfare status. The third group was more likely to have begun child rearing during adolescence, had been somewhat more mobile before and during 1st grade, and more likely to have been in parochial schools in 1st grade. It was harder to trace students in parochial schools because these schools did not maintain centralized and computerized records, in contrast to Chicago public schools.

We found significant differences in only 3 of 21 1st-grade measures of the children's SAS. We examined IQ and school readiness test scores, along with a set of teacher ratings of each child's SAS as a student. Only maturity as assessed by teachers early in 1st grade and the grade point averages for both semesters of 1st grade were different. All three differences were small, and the other 18 SAS measures did not provide any indications of important trends. We concluded that the population of teenagers we assessed did not differ substantially for most analyses from the groups we did not assess, except in terms of mother's age at first birth, early mobility, and parochial school enrollment. (For further information on the follow-up methods, see Agrawal, Kellam, Klein, & Turner, 1978; Kellam, Brown, Rubin & Ensminger, 1983). Nevertheless, each analysis on these data requires renewed assessment of relevant aspects of sample loss. That this is an epidemiologically defined population allows us to determine the nature of the sample loss and its relevance to specific analyses.

Our analyses of Woodlawn data gathered in 1st grade and in follow-up 10 years later identified social adaptational and psychological antecedents leading to specific problem outcomes. These included depression and other psychiatric symptoms of distress, delinquency including physical assault, and heavy substance use. Teacher ratings of early aggressive behavior in both the delinquency as well as the substance abuse literature are consistently related to both later heavy substance use and delinquency. In the Woodlawn data among the early shy behaving children in 1st grade, 5% were to be regular smokers 10 years later at age 16 or 17. Among the 1st graders who were aggressive, the rate of regular smoking was 40%, while the rate was 59% among the 1st graders who were rated both shy and aggressive. These were children who did not participate and who sat apart, but also broke rules and fought. These results were only evident for boys.

In the same log linear analyses early readiness-for-school test scores did not interact with the shy and aggressive predictors but independently also predicted heavier substance use by age 16 or 17. Boys as well as girls who were readier for 1st grade as exhibited by their performance on these tests were also apparently readier for trying out drugs 10 years later.

In Fig. 2.3 we show the distribution of males who were rated by teacher as shy, aggressive, both, or neither in 1st grade in relation to their level of self-reported assault behavior at age 16 or 17. The reports were divided into thirds based on the sum scores on a 6-item subscale of the Gold antisocial behavior scale (Gold, 1970). The shy/aggressive males fall in the upper third of self-

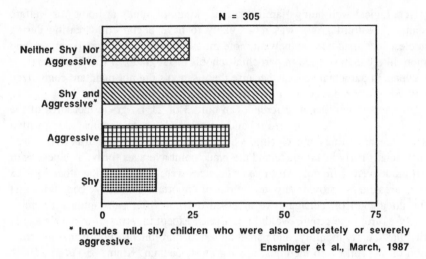

* Includes mild shy children who were also moderately or severely aggressive.

Ensminger et al., March, 1987

FIG. 2.3.   High assault by males age 16–17 who were shy and/or aggressive in first grade.

reports of assaultive behavior at a rate of 47%, compared to 35% for the aggressive 1st graders, 24% for those neither shy nor aggressive, and 15% for those who were shy behaving.

Depressive and other psychiatric symptoms of distress were also predicted from 1st grade teacher ratings and other measures of SAS in the 1st grade classroom. Learning problems as rated by teachers, readiness-for-school, or IQ tests predicted depression ten years later as well as other psychiatric symptoms (Kellam, Brown, Rubin, & Ensminger, 1983). In the case of all these measures the better performing children had much better psychological well-being at age 16 or 17. If we examine the risk of depressive symptoms 10 years later, for example, those rated underachieving by their 1st grade teacher were twice as likely as their 1st grade classmates who were mastering the basic learning tasks.

The following inferences summarize, along with references to other similar results, relevant findings from the Woodlawn developmental epidemiological investigations. These inferences illustrate the kind of developmental mapping possible through such studies. More intensive research over shorter periods of time clearly will augment this kind of strategy and holds promise of revealing the mechanisms by which these predictions are brought about. Microanalytic studies of family processes such as those reported in this volume in our next stage of research can be done on representative subsamples of individuals or families drawn from first stage population-based samples.

1. First-grade problems in learning as rated by teachers and readiness-for-school test performance, are strong predictors of teenage depressive and other

symptoms among males and to a lesser extent among females (see Rutter, Tizard, and Whitmore, 1970; Shaffer et al., 1979; Watt, 1974; Kellam, Brown, Rubin, & Ensminger, 1983). Learning problems did not predict delinquency when aggression was controlled.

2. Psychiatric symptoms in 1st grade proved to be a strong antecedent of teenage psychiatric symptoms in females but not males. If we combine males and females the result is an attenuated prediction due to the gender difference.

3. Shy behavior among 1st-grade males (not females) clearly inhibits delinquency and drug, alcohol, and cigarette use at age 16 or 17. For males early shy behavior also predicts higher levels of teenage anxiety.

4. First-grade aggressive behavior in males (not females) is a strong predictor of increased teenage delinquency and drug, alcohol, and cigarette use. Similar findings have been reported in many studies (Conger & Miller, 1966; Kaplan, 1980; Lefkowitz, Eron, Walden, & Huesman, 1977; Mitchell & Rosa, 1981; Robins, 1973, 1978; Spivak, Marcus, & Swift, 1986; Kellam, Brown, Rubin, & Ensminger, 1983; Farrington, 1987; Ensminger, Brown, & Kellam, 1982).

5. A combination of shy and aggressive behavior in 1st-grade males (not females) was associated with higher levels of both delinquency and substance use than aggressiveness alone. This combination is very much like the DSM-III undersocialized conduct disorder (Kellam, Brown, Rubin, & Ensminger, 1983; Ensminger, Kellam & Rubin, 1983).

6. Children who score higher on readiness-for-school tests in 1st grade are more likely to have tried alcohol, marijuana, and cigarettes by age 16 or 17 and are more likely to be heavier users than their less ready 1st grade classmates (Kellam, Brown, Rubin, & Ensminger, 1983).

7. The social adaptational and psychological predictions do not generally interact with each other in the effects on later delinquency, depression or other psychiatric symptoms, or other outcomes.

8. There are strong differences between males and females in the developmental paths leading to adolescent outcomes. Early behavioral responses to school have strong predictive power for both later social adaptation and psychological well-being among males (points 1, 3, 4, and 5), while early psychological well-being shows clear continuity with later psychological well-being for females (point 2).

These results illustrate the usefulness of distinguishing between social adaptational status and psychological well-being. By studying these two measures both separately and in terms of their interrelationships over time, for instance, developmental gender differences became apparent as noted in the points above. Equally important in terms of interaction with the environment, however, was the emergence of the classroom as a crucially important social field where the teacher, as a natural rater, defines the tasks and grades the behavioral responses of the children as succeeding or failing at these tasks (see also Pedersen, Faucher, & Eaton, 1978; Kellam & Brown, 1986).

MEASURING VARIATION EPIDEMIOLOGICALLY IN SMALL SOCIAL FIELDS

An epidemiological orientation calls attention to variation in the rates of individuals with particular health related conditions across variations in environment. Community and developmental epidemiology call attention to small environments within defined neighborhoods such as the family, school and classroom, peer group, work place, and intimate social fields including the marital field. The relationship of variation in such environments over time to the developmental course of individuals is central to the concept of developmental epidemiology. The long-term predictions we briefly described earlier involved such early social maladaptation as underachieving, shy behavior, aggressive behavior, and the combination of shy and aggressive behavior. The rates of such behavioral responses were distributed nonrandomly, putting it mildly, in the 12 elementary schools and in the classrooms in which the 1966–1967 1st-grade children resided.

Variation in Schools and Classrooms.   Several of the 12 elementary schools had a prevalence of moderately to severely aggressive 1st-grade children of less than 10% while in others such children were 30% or more of the enrollment. If we look inside these schools, however, at the variation across classrooms (Fig. 2.4), we see from a micro-epidemiologic perspective that the variation within many schools is even greater than across schools. Each bar represents the prevalence within a classroom. Within one elementary school, for instance, which has eight 1st-grade classrooms, one has less than 10% moderate to severe aggressive children while another has 65% exhibiting this kind of social maladaptation.

The longitudinal predictions from moderate to severe aggression in 1st grade to heavy substance use and assault 10 years later seemed simple and clear based on early data aggregated across classrooms and schools. We can now see by examining variation in these classroom environments that there is a strong potential for this classroom environment measure itself to interact with the child's own aggressive behavior to enhance or inhibit the risk of the long-term outcome. This point needs to be underscored, since it illustrates a strength of the epidemiological perspective in examining developmental paths.

The remarkable nonrandom distribution of rates of aggression across schools and classrooms is not accidental, but reflects ability grouping or tracking, a deliberate policy in many school districts. Children are assigned to classrooms based on Metropolitan readiness test scores, kindergarten teacher's impression, and the principal's judgment as to the likely behavior and learning by each child on entrance to 1st grade and thereafter. This process sets in motion student

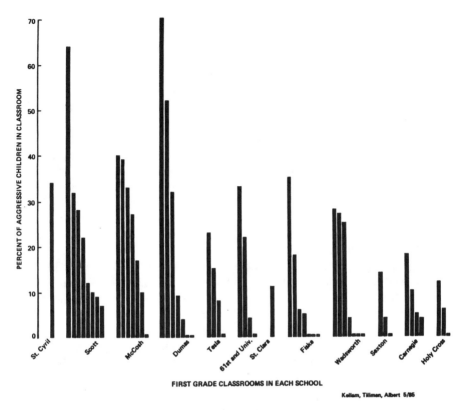

FIG. 2.4.   Prevalence of moderate or severe aggression in each Woodlawn 1st-grade classroom (1966–1967).

tracking within schools in the first few days of 1st grade and possibly throughout
school and even beyond through the life course. The impact of such policies has
begun to be studied in regard to broad SAS and PWB outcomes. Where it has
been examined, there is evidence of the importance of tracking on social stratifi-
cation outcomes (Vanfossen, Jones & Spade, 1987).

There is evidence that early behavioral responses of children may have biological underpinning (Kagan, Clarke, Snidman, & Garcia-Coll, 1984; Suomi,
1987). The ability grouping of the children in school provides social structure
that hypothetically may enhance the biological or earlier learned predisposition
of the child for better or worse. Investigating how these biopsychosocial factors
may be integrated in testable models regarding developmental outcomes is now a
high priority and very possible. By illustrating through a particular kind of
community and its variation in schools and classrooms, we can show how the
epidemiological perspective provides a conceptual framework for drawing models and samples for more intensive research on causal processes.

Variation in Family Types. The families from which the children in the classrooms come can also be examined in regard to variation and evolution. The adults present in the homes of these children provided a basis for taxonomic classification of variation in family structure (Kellam, Ensminger, & Turner, 1977). In the 1964–1965 children and in the 1966–1967 cohort we examined the various combinations of adults present in their homes. The family taxonomy graphic (Fig. 2.5) illustrates this variation in the 1966–1967 cohort.

Adult relatives we found in the homes of the 1st graders are listed along both the left and right margins, ordered by their frequency. Each circle represents a different combination of adults found in that total population. In the upper left is mother alone, occurring in the 1966–1967 cohort in 517 homes. Moving down the left portion of the taxonomy, we see that mother/father alone occurred 483 times. Mother/father/grandmother occurred 10 times. If the next additional adult did not occur in our population we move laterally and downward to the combination that we did find.

Stepping back we can see that there is a group of mother/father families in which mother and father are alone or with various other relatives. Further to the right, if the father is absent we can see mother/grandmother families alone or with others. If both father and grandmother are absent, we see mother and aunt alone or with others, and so on. When the mother is absent, we see the father alone or with others. As we move toward the right portion of the graphic we note that the alternatives to either mother or father are rare, and indeed foster families do not appear frequently in this poor, urban, Black community.

As in the case of variation in classroom environments, this epidemiologic perspective on family variation provides the opportunity to examine family process within very different combinations of family members. Siblings in regard to number and spacing and other relatives can be added, and family types aggregated in various ways for analytic purposes.

When we examined the relationships of these differing kinds of families to how well their children were adapting to classroom task demands, we found that mother alone and mother/stepfather along with certain other family types were far less effective than mother/father. However, mother/grandmother and mother/aunt families were about equally effective to mother/father. The absence of the father appeared less important than the presence of a second stable adult other than a stepfather to the early social adaptation and psychological well-being of the children. We can imagine in the next stage of family research combining this kind of neighborhood family typing with studies of family process. This can be done within and across types of family in relation to child and/or family outcomes.

We have also examined family structure by the age of mother when she gave birth to her first child (Kellam, Adams, Brown, & Engminger, 1982). Figure 2.6 shows the distribution of family types of teenage and older mothers whose first-grade child was either the first or the second born. Rates of mother alone families

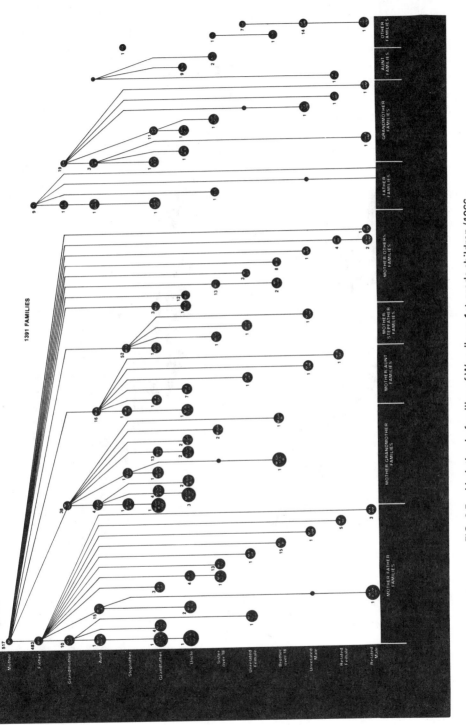

FIG. 2.5.   Variation in families of Woodlawn 1st-grade children (1966–1967).

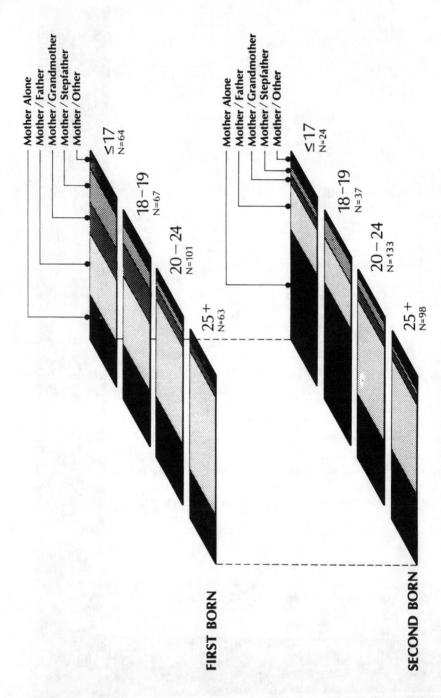

FIG. 2.6. Age of mother at birth of child and family type at 1st grade.

Mother Alone
Mother / Father
Mother / Grandmother
Mother / Stepfather
Mother / Other

≤17
N=64

18–19
N=67

20–24
N=101

25+
N=63

FIRST BORN

Mother Alone
Mother / Father
Mother / Grandmother
Mother / Stepfather
Mother / Other

≤17
N=24

18–19
N=37

20–24
N=133

25+
N=98

SECOND BORN

30

among the first born were fairly consistent at about 20% for each of the four age groups of mothers. Mother/father families were markedly diminished for teenage mothers, where mother/grandmother and mother/stepfather were more frequent as family types. We see a marked shift toward mother-alone families when we look at teenage mothers and their second-born child, however. Mother-alone families now make up two-thirds of the teenage mothered children.

Mother/grandmother families were effective in the child's adaptation to first grade and in promoting the child's psychological well-being in both cohorts of first graders we studied (1964–1965 and 1966–1967). Unfortunately this family type did not survive long, in that the mothers tended to separate from the grandmothers to become mother-alone families, particularly when the mother was herself a teenager. Our evolving family structure studies revealed that over time the mother-alone families remained so throughout the child rearing cycle. Over 80% of those who were mother-alone at the time when the index child was in first grade were still mother-alone when the child was a teenager at age 16 or 17 (Fig. 2.7). Mother/father families can be seen in this figure to demonstrate a divorce rate of over 80% among teenage mothers, but while only 25% among those who began their child bearing later in the mother's life course.

The epidemiological perspective on family first leads us to identify with some precision variation in types of family. Consequently, examination of family variation among teenage and older mothers leads us to further elaboration and understanding of evolving family structure. This definition of family typology provides a vital context for the more microanalytic studies of family process relevant to both depression and aggression.

Population-based study is badly needed of processes within particular types of family and the relationship of the family type and processes to institutions in the community, including schools. Measures would be done on all families (or at least a sufficiently large sample) in stage 1; more intensive observation at stage 2 on representative smaller samples; and a stage 3 stratified sample drawn if necessary for yet more intensive study. At each stage the samples can be representative of the stratum from which they are drawn.

The kinds of inferences that have been drawn from family developmental epidemiologic research on depression and aggression in Woodlawn are described briefly in the following paragraphs. These illustrate both the potential inferences as well as their limits from what we have come to call first stage developmental epidemiological studies.

Family Predictors for Depression

• Among Woodlawn first grade children, the absence of a stable second adult at home was associated with school failure, and this was in turn related to higher risk of later depressive symptoms (Kellam, Ensminger, & Turner, 1977; Kellam,

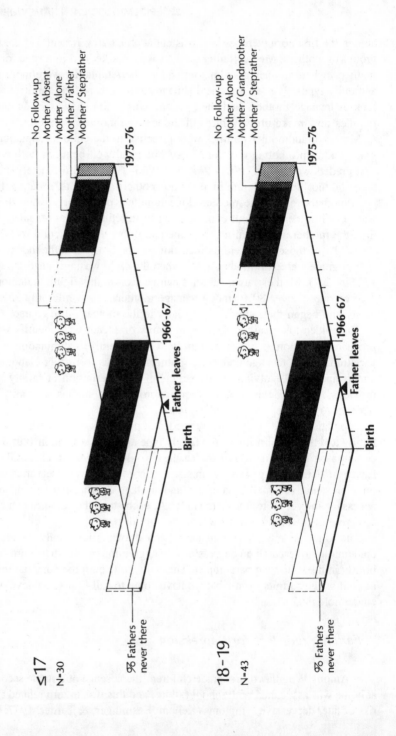

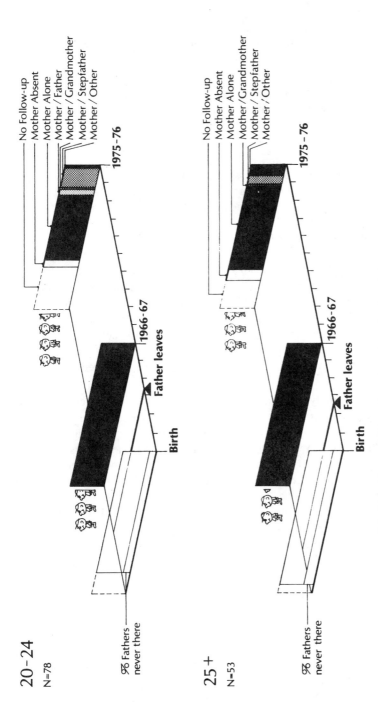

FIG. 2.7. The evolution of mother alone families by age of mother.

33

Brown, Rubin & Ensminger, 1983). The explanations may include genetic transmission, parenting deficits, and/or the experience of failure. The data strongly suggest gender differences in the processes and risks leading to depression.

• Teenage mothering is strongly predictive of loss of the second adult, depression in the mother, and depression in the child through both of these risk factors, particularly when coupled with school failure (Kellam, Adams, Brown, & Ensminger, 1982; Brown, Adams, & Kellam, 1981; Kellam, Simon, & Ensminger, 1980).

• Mother's self-reports of depressive symptoms, her hopes regarding her daughter's future, and her expectations were predictive over the period of 1st grade to age 16 or 17 of daughter's depression.

Family Predictors of Antisocial Behavior

• Lower risk family structure such as mother/father, mother/grandmother, or mother/aunt lead to less aggressive 1st-grade children (Ensminger, Brown, & Kellam, 1982). However, among children from such families who do behave aggressively in the 1st grade classroom there is an increased risk of delinquency later on in adolescence. Thus, family structure appears to be associated with reduced numbers of aggressive children but a higher risk among those fewer children who are aggressive. Again, the explanation may be genetic or rearing deficits or both.

• Higher risk family structure such as mother/alone or mother/stepfather generally lead to more 1st-grade children being aggressive but there is not very much prediction from early aggressiveness to later delinquency. We interpret this finding to mean that in Woodlawn, where aggressive behavior occurs very frequently, the stronger family structure inhibits aggressive behavior over the period of 1st grade to adolescence, while the higher risk family structures do not inhibit aggressive behavior nor protect those not yet aggressive from becoming aggressive later on. Thus, the general prevalence of aggression is high and remains fairly well distributed among children from higher risk families regardless of the child's earlier behavior.

MEASURING AGGRESSION AND DEPRESSION: THE ROLE OF EPIDEMIOLOGY

The distinction between normal and abnormal behavior remains a critical measurement problem in psychopathology. Epidemiology provides the concept of the population base as part of the solution. Variation in the rates of psychiatric symptoms and signs as well as diagnoses can be studied without confounding variables such as the bias introduced by studying volunteers or those who attend clinics. Case control studies in epidemiology allow sampling from the population of those who have a disorder and those who do not in the search for differences that might explain incidence and prevalence. Research on etiology and vulnerability can be done by following cohorts within a defined population over time searching for developmental paths or testing the validity of paths leading to pathological or healthy outcomes. Such research depends upon measuring pathology or health and this involves distinguishing the two states, if they are indeed categorically different. The possibility exists that pathology may be merely quantitatively different rather than different in quality from healthy condition.

A significant issue beyond the question of the distinction of normal and abnormal, then, is the issue of whether either aggression or depression, or for that matter other parameters of psychopathology as well, are on a continuum with healthy states, being at the severe end; or whether they are categorically different with different antecedents and consequences, i.e., different etiologies than the severe end of the healthy. Putting it another way, is great sadness different in its origins and consequences than major depressive disorder? The quantitative versus qualitative problem is inextricably related to that of whether the individual symptoms and signs are to be aggregated to form diagnoses or are most validly maintained as separate measures.

The psychiatric signs and symptoms that are criteria for depressive disorder must be determined empirically to be necessary parts of the diagnosis of major depressive disorder. In the absence of closure on this question, we can do both, maintain measures of the signs and symptoms as well as apply the criteria for the diagnosis. An important strategy consists of examining the distribution of psychiatric signs and symptoms in samples drawn from a defined population. Analyses can be done of whether the symptoms and signs occur with each other more than by chance. Antecedents in the family or other environments, or in biological characteristics predicted to lead to depression or aggression can be studied as to their developmental relation to the diagnosis or to the individual symptoms or signs. Similarly, developmental consequences can be studied as to the role of individual, or smaller clusters of symptoms, or the diagnosis in predicting important outcomes.

The criteria for diagnosis we have applied in Woodlawn data consists of covariation of hypothesized components of a disorder along with interaction among the components over time to produce a psychopathologically definable outcome. This process of searching for the best representation of signs, symptoms, and psychiatric diagnoses can be done only on samples drawn from a defined population. An epidemiologically defined population is necessary for either prospective longitudinal research or case control studies. The selection bias associated with volunteers or clinic attendees makes any other method for sampling and generalization dangerous.

To illustrate these issues in this section we use data from the Baltimore sample of the NIMH Epidemiological Catchment Area (ECA) studies done during the

---

DYSPHORIC MOOD OR LOSS OF INTEREST OR PLEASURE IS REQUIRED PLUS

AT LEAST FOUR OF THE FOLLOWING SYMPTOMS:

    O   APPETITE DISTURBANCE

    O   SLEEP DISTURBANCE

    O   PSYCHOMOTOR AGITATION OR RETARDATION

    O   LOSS OF INTEREST OR PLEASURE

    O   LOSS OF ENERGY

    O   FEELINGS OF WORTHLESSNESS OR GUILT

    O   LOWERED ABILITY TO CONCENTRATE

    O   RECURRENT THOUGHTS OF DEATH OR SUICIDE

NO OTHER DIAGNOSTIC EXPLANATION

FIG. 2.8. Diagnostic criteria for major depressive disorder.

last decade. The criteria for the diagnosis of major depressive disorder are indicated in Fig. 2.8 and are in accord with the DSM-III. Note that four symptoms are required in addition to dysphoric mood in order to make the diagnosis. While experienced clinicians developed these criteria, the next stage of research on depressive disorder must go further and provide an empirical basis for the definition of criteria. Two major possibilities exist in addition to the question of which signs and symptoms are essential in diagnosis. There may not indeed be a single point defining normal from abnormal. As we stated above this determination can only be done by combining studies of covariation and interaction over time among the signs and symptoms, coupled with studies of antecedents and consequences.

We may find that there is no cut point, and that a continuum is the best representation of major depressive disorder. In such a case a set of interval measures of the relevant signs and symptoms would provide a profile representing the disorder not as a category but rather as a set of signs and symptoms each present to a greater or lesser degree in an individual. Alternatively, we may find that there is indeed a cut point and that certain symptoms, or any combination of a set of symptoms at a certain level provides a definitive point beyond which a disorder is diagnosable.

The distribution of the self reports of symptoms in the Baltimore ECA sample is shown in Fig. 2.9 for female respondents age 20–24 and in Fig. 2.10 for those

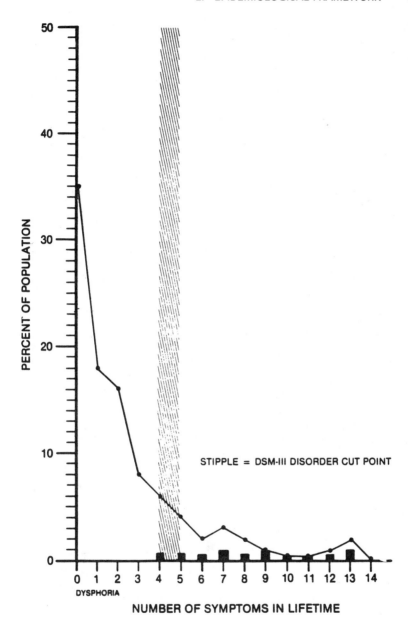

FIG. 2.9.   Depressive symptoms and DSM-III major depressive disorder among 20–24 year-old females in Baltimore (NIMH epidemiologic catchment area project, by D.I.S.)

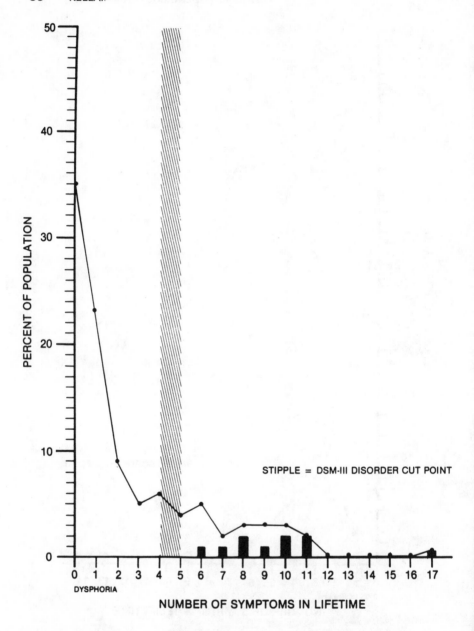

STIPPLE = DSM-III DISORDER CUT POINT

NUMBER OF SYMPTOMS IN LIFETIME

*NIMH EPIDEMIOLOGIC CATCHMENT AREA PROJECT, BY D.I.S.

FIG. 2.10.   Depressive symptoms and DSM-III major depressive disorder among 25–29 year-old females in Baltimore (NIMH epidemiologic
catchment area project, by D.I.S.)

age 25–29. Each of the figures show the number of symptoms by their frequency in the population. Also, the rates of major depressive disorder are shown under the distribution curve in the form of bars. Note that the DSM-III cut point is four symptoms plus dysphoria and is indicated by the stippled bar on each figure.

We can see that it is not obvious where the cut point should be if anywhere, since the curve is fairly continuous through the DSM-III cut point. Through developmental epidemiologic studies we can look at the covariation of the symptoms with each other through following the epidemiological population over time to discover whether there is interaction among the signs and symptoms and whether four symptoms lead to different outcomes than three symptoms, two symptoms, or more than four symptoms.

We can also determine whether a categorical definition of disorder is supported, or whether a more quantitative definition is needed to best represent the data. The latter would be suggested if there is increasing risk of depression and its consequences in longitudinal follow-up in accord with an increasing number of symptoms. Such research on aggression and depression must be a fundamental part of the next stage of family research on psychopathology.

Family research can be a tool itself for understanding psychopathology and its origins and consequences. Already, family aggregation studies have revealed considerable risk to the child of depression among the parents, with the risk rising if both parents are depressed. Family environment studies also suggest that depression may be a consequence of other aspects than purely biological. The integration of family aggregation, parental diagnosis, and family environment would seem to be advantageous for our next stage of family research on psychopathology. These studies should be done on samples drawn from epidemiologically defined populations.

MULTISTAGE SAMPLING AND ASSESSMENT

The developmental epidemiological studies reported in this paper say little regarding the specific developmental and family processes actually accounting for the outcomes described. The strength of this kind of epidemiological orientation is in mapping and modeling potential long-term developmental paths. Microanalytic studies are vital for understanding how these outcomes evolve out of the earlier predictors.

Multistage sampling provides the needed bridge for linking the developmental epidemiology to the studies based on more frequent or precise observations on smaller samples. Probability samples are drawn from a defined followed by a second sample drawn from the first. This second stage sample can be drawn to represent the strata from which it was drawn as well as the total population originally sampled. A third stage sample can be drawn from the second that represents strata from the second and the first. This method allows increasingly intensive assessments to be done on suitably small but representative subsamples.

For the reader interested in more detailed description of methods and application see Deming, W. E., 1977; Duncan-Jones, P., 1977; Duncan-Jones and Henderson, 1978. Of direct relevance to this chapter is an article by Anthony, Folstein, and Romanoski, 1985, in which a second stage sample was drawn from the original Baltimore E.C.A. population for clinical reappraisal. The first stage measure of psychopathology was the Diagnostic Interview Schedule (Anthony, Folstein, & Romanoski, 1985). To understand better the meaning of these data obtained by non-clinically trained interviewers, a more extensive clinical assessment by psychiatrists was needed. The second stage sample was drawn to represent the strata of most interest as well as the original epidemiological sample.

In the Woodlawn studies total populations of children were assessed in regard to family and classroom environments, social adaptational status, and psychological well-being. With these newer methods more intensive studies can be done through representative samples drawn from various strata at the first stage for second stage assessment. A third stage is feasible for even more intensive study on yet smaller samples. Through multistage sampling and assessment we can integrate epidemiological strategies with those more traditionally carried out by developmental psychologists or others interested in frequent observation on small samples.

First stage measures should be both theoretically and empirically related to the more intensive measures of the second or third stages. Teacher ratings and peer nominations are first stage measures currently done in our Baltimore prevention research, coupled with independent observers' time sampling of behavior in classrooms, and self-reports of anxiety and sadness by children. These are being elaborated using a second stage with smaller representative samples. In collaboration with the Laboratory of Psychology and Psychopathology of N.I.M.H. Continuous Performance Tests (CPT) and other more precise attention measures have been done on representative smaller samples to examine the role of specific aspects of attention in relationship to the first stage measures. Our general focus is on vulnerability as marked by early risk behaviors cited earlier, enhanced or inhibited by child or environmental characteristics. Of particular interest is the child's response to the two preventive intervention trials directed at early risk behaviors including attention.

Similar strategies can be used for family research. Behavior monitoring and coercive interaction measures are good candidates, since these have been found to be important processes in the generation of aggressive behavior by children (Patterson, 1986). Our strategy will be in the next stage of such research to develop measures that can be used on larger, first stage population based family samples that would be nested both theoretically and empirically to the more intensive and precise measures at the second and third stages. We should thereby be able to specify for whom or under what conditions a family risk factor applies. We should be able to calculate rates of the risk factor in known populations.

Equally important, we can continue to sample and study the risk factor. And we can experimentally intervene to test its etiologic functions—all on known populations.

EXPERIMENTAL EPIDEMIOLOGY AND ITS ROLE IN RESEARCH ON DEVELOPMENT, VULNERABILITY, AND PREVENTION

The search for developmental paths and the mechanisms that underlie them is supported but not satisfied by the integration of epidemiological and life course developmental orientations. Aggressive behavior in 1st grade or earlier, for example, is a significant predictor of criminal or assaultive behavior in adolescence and adulthood; but its role in etiology remains unclear. Assuming we could reduce early aggressive behavior, we do not know whether changing the early behavior changes the probability of the criminal outcome. The same question arises in the prediction from problems learning to read in elementary school to later depression. These questions require experimentation that is prospective longitudinal and epidemiologically based. In fact, such experimental research is an important kind of prevention research, a kind that tests the etiological and developmental meaning of specific target antecedents. Such preventive trial research can involve biological, social, or psychological interventions and/or targets.

An important strategy, then, in this search for paths and mechanisms involves experimental interventions into those early behavioral responses of children that place them at increased risk of specific problem outcomes later in their life course. Early intervention can be done into family processes hypothesized to increase risk, as in the studies of the Oregon Social Learning Center described in this volume. The goal is to determine whether by changing the antecedent predictor, the risk of the outcome improves. An affirmative answer informs our understanding of the etiological significance of the predictor, whether it is a behavioral response or a family process. Theory-building regarding the role of antecedent predictors is well served by this strategy, as is the need for carefully evaluated prevention programs.

Learning problems and aggressive behavior are good candidates for such a strategy; we will use our current two intervention trials in Baltimore to illustrate. First we should note that learning problems is correlated in 1st grade with both aggressive and shy behavior and the combination (Kellam et al., 1975). It is possible that learning problems leads to aggressive and/or shy behavior; children either rebelling or withdrawing in the face of academic failure. It is equally plausible that shy and/or aggressive behavior are predispositions the child brings to the classroom that lead to learning problems. The third possibility is that some other factors not yet known account for their intercorrelation.

Our strategy has been to mount two interventions in 1st and 2nd grade for entire classrooms, one directed at improving reading scores, the other at improving shy and aggressive behavior. The first is a version of Mastery Learning (Block & Burns, 1976; Dolan, 1986; Guskey, 1985), the other a version of the Good Behavior Game (Barrish, Saunders, & Wolf, 1969; Robinson & Swanton, 1980).

Nineteen Baltimore City Public Schools are participating with the strong endorsement of the Board of School Commissioners and the Superintendent, Ms. Alice Pinderhughes. Parents and community organizations have been involved and their support solicited at each stage. In each of five quite different urban area schools were matched and designated at random to be either a Mastery Learning school, a Good Behavior school, or a control school. Within each intervention school children were randomly assigned to the intervention or a control classroom. The version of Mastery Learning was developed at the specific request of the superintendent by Professor Lawrence Dolan of our faculty in collaboration with the curriculum leadership of the Baltimore City Public Schools, particularly Ms. Carla Ford. The second intervention, the Good Behavior Game, was developed by them and others also with strong collaboration across public education, public mental health, parents, and community organizations.

The results of 2 years of intervention for the first cohort of 1200 children and almost 2 years for the second brings us to the analytic stage, with early results indicating that reading scores have improved for cohort one, and so have classmate nominations of aggressive behavior. These have only been examined through 1st grade, however. Assuming these short-term results are confirmed in both cohorts, we then must follow the children to determine the slopes of impact over the next period of their life course, to examine possible impact on the risk of the problem outcomes as well as the specificity and developmental course of impact. The results should be useful in addressing the question of whether aggressive and/or shy behavior are in response to failure to learn, or the opposite direction is more in keeping with the trial results, or whether the two antecedent targets operate independently from each other.

Experimental epidemiological research can be done with biological, psychological, or social interventions. Coupled with multistage sampling, it provides a strong bridge from basic studies on causal processes to understanding of the distribution of such processes in the populations under study, the conditions governing generalizability, and the role of ecological factors in the causal processes.

FROM CONCEPTS TO APPLICATION

The structure of science is most often out of the awareness of the investigator as long as he or she does not wander afield in search of new approaches to solve unexpected or sudden obstacles. The ideas we have discussed are part of the next stage of integrations necessary to advance family research along with other related developmental and epidemiological investigation, particularly psychopathology and its prevention and treatment. On one level the problems include the need to broaden the expertise and understanding of grant review groups, as well as the reviewers of science journal articles. On another level the problems are more related to actual research under the new perspective and methods we are describing.

On the epidemiological side there is the issue of defining the population in ways that allow study of the role of the physical and social environment. At the same time there is the new and far from trivial need to relate to the population and its institutions in a manner that allows the investigation to proceed and promotes its success. Gaining support from the leadership of the Baltimore City Public Schools, the parents in each of the school catchment areas, the local community organizations are all part of the process of engaging the population in the investigation.

Many times we have heard our colleagues who are expert at small sample micro-analytic studies express their concern that such collaboration with community organizations and institutions is either not possible or potentially dangerous to scientific independence. Public health research has much to inform us in this regard. Placing chlorine in our drinking water clearly is invasive as is vaccination with live bacteria or virus, yet we take these for granted even though they are accomplished by strenuous efforts at the very same kind of community and institutional sanction building. Careful diagnosis of the political structure and sensitive follow through, with meetings in the living rooms and offices of the leadership will reward the mental health investigator with necessary support, given that dignity and mutual self-interests accrue to the population and its leaders.

An important tool is the community advisory board comprised of the leaders of the community citizen organizations (Kellam & Branch, 1971; Kellam, Branch, Agrawal, & Grabill, 1972). The school board is another vital group requiring engagement and from whom continuing support is often available if the quid pro quo is appropriate in the view of the leaders of the community or institution with whom one is negotiating.

In constructing such boards several important caveats may be essential. First, the members must be chosen out of the existing organizational leadership itself, not appointed by the investigator, who is often an outsider. Community organizations have their own ways of choosing leaders and these must be respected. The Catholic Church has one way of choosing their minister, the local Methodist Church another. The investigator can request help in forming a structure for a priori consultation and for advice and consent. He or she will need the participation of the leaders no matter how they are chosen by their constituents.

Our research is well-served by this process, since enlisting such support means less sample loss, more access to the private and public environments needed in our research, and help from our population (subjects) in formulating our research. In Woodlawn it was our community board who first alerted us to the great variation in families raising children and also pointed out the fundamental difference between psychological well-being and social adaptational status. They did not accept readily the assumption that their children's learning or behavior stemmed from the children's mental status alone, and wanted us to measure mental well-being and teacher ratings of behavior and learning separately, so that we could study their interrelationships and ultimately develop prevention programs.

The reader should recall that Woodlawn was and is a very poor neighborhood, and yet the wisdom offered us over the many years of our collaboration causes us to seek such collaboration with our populations each time we start anew the process of longitudinal research into development and prevention. Besides, in public health research the result of not developing such a partnership is very often "tar and feathers," or rapid exile from the community rather than simply losing a subject or two. Such is the price of focusing on the total population and its social and political environment. For those of us who have tried it, there is no greater satisfaction in research than that derived from a good collaborative relationship with our partners and their social institutions, the subjects of our studies.

Defining the population can efficiently be done by discussion with social and political leaders and through reference to census data. The latter can be misleading, however, since census data does not necessarily define tracts or urban areas by taking into account the history and common beliefs regarding where a neighborhood boundary truly belongs. The community board can be extremely useful in identifying people and sources for such decisions. Institutional boundaries such as school catchment areas or church parishes are all important possible sources for such decisions.

Birth certificate, registration for school, social security, draft registration are ways of finding populations within neighborhoods, cities, or other geographic areas. Household sampling often is the method used for defining the specific families or individuals for assessment. Birth certificate and 1st-grade registration are both required by law in our society and thus provide a good method. The infant or child registered is part of a sibship, either the first or last or in the middle somewhere. Therefore the rest of the sibship and family can be traced through the child's registration. Periodic follow-up can be done using the school information system and their assigned student number, as we described earlier.

The more writing on this subject we do the more detailed the discourse becomes, with tricks of the trade, ways of solving technical problems such as what the dress code should be that most protects the trust issue from coming unraveled in the partnership, who to consult as to where to place the offices when we need to be near the subjects with equipment for assessments, how to develop trust for moving children to farther away laboratories, and so on. It is enough in this chapter to try to define the integrations needed, point out some of the concepts, illustrate their application in family and developmental epidemiological research, and point toward core areas of application that will allow the new structure of our science to succeed.

ACKNOWLEDGMENTS

The Woodlawn developmental epidemiological studies began in 1963 and continue to the present. The research contained in this paper depended upon the strong collaborative support of the community organizations of Woodlawn, the public education and health institutions, as well as the parents and children themselves of the several thousand families with whom we were involved over this 25 year period. The Woodlawn Mental Health Center was the base for our research and was a City of Chicago Department of Health agency. The Board of the Center was the formal structure in which leaders of the community organizations interpreted the community's values and aspirations to the investigators and clinicians, and in turn explained the mutually agreed upon research and service programs to their constituencies. The board was formed of the leaders of the major community organizations, including welfare unions, churches, businesses, and block clubs.

Ms. Jeanette Branch was for many years Director of the Woodlawn Mental Health Center and played a major role in all aspects of the research reported here. She led the development particularly of the standardized interviews with teachers from which much of the prediction reported here was gained. Margaret Ensminger, Ph.D. and Hendricks Brown, Ph.D., both long time colleagues in Chicago and now here at the School of Hygiene and Public Health at The Johns Hopkins University, played major roles in the development and reporting of this research. Ensminger led much of the field assessment in the long-term follow-up and the analyses related particularly to delinquency and sexual activity. She brought sociological perspectives to this work. Brown led our design and use of biostatistical models and methods. He continues to lead our data analytic work in Baltimore including the development of new biostatistical methods for modeling missing data, stochastic methods for analyses, sampling designs, and other aspects essential to the interpretation of developmental epidemiological and preventive intervention research. Dr. James Anthony, in the Department of Mental Hygiene, is a major collaborator in the Baltimore studies and is responsible for the analyses of ECA data and much of the discussion of multi-stage sampling reported here. Dr. Lawrence Dolan, also a major collaborator from our department, has led the development and implementation of the preventive interventions. We are grateful to the other faculty and staff of the Department of Mental Hygiene and the Prevention Research Center for their strong support of the research we report here. Beth Van Fossen of S.U.N.Y. Brockport read the entire manuscript and contributed to the section on school tracking.

Our partners in the Baltimore City Public Schools have been incredibly available and truly collaborative in the development and use of multi-stage measures and in the design and implementation of the interventions we are testing here in Baltimore. Mrs. Alice Pinderhughes, Superintendent of the Baltimore City Public Schools (B.C.P.S.), has been strongly supportive and always ready to solve research problems in the best ways for both the design and the children. Dr. Leonard Wheeler, B.C.P.S. Executive Director of District B, has devoted a great portion of his time to the leadership and implementation of the Baltimore prevention research program. Ms. Carla Ford (B.C.P.S.) working closely with Dr. Dolan of our faculty and Ms. Vera Newton (B.C.P.S.) have all collaborated in the development of the interventions and the maintenance of our research design. Dr. Lisa Werthamer-Larsson of our department has been the important leader of our field operations and of the development of the newly revised teacher interview and other assessment measures.

From all of this it should be obvious that developmental epidemiology is never done by a single investigator alone in a small laboratory. Such longitudinal research programs as reported here develop by combinations of scientific and lay interests and prosper when done on a strong base of community and institutional base-building. Mutual interests among all constituencies must be served for the long-term purposes to be served. This paper represents the collaborative efforts of many people across many institutions in many parts of the world, but particularly those in Chicago and in Baltimore.

REFERENCES

Agrawal, K. C., Kellam, S. G., Klein, Z. E., & Turner, J. (1978). The Woodlawn mental health studies: Tracking children and families for long-term follow-up. *American Journal of Public Health, 68,* 139–142.

Anthony, J. C., Folstein, M., Romanoski, A. J., et al. (1985). Comparison of the Lay Diagnostic Interview Schedule and a Standardized Psychiatric Diagnosis. *Archives of General Psychiatry, 42,* 667–675.

Barrish, H. H., Saunders, M., & Wolfe, M. D. (1969). Good behavior game: Effects of individual contingencies for group consequences and disruptive behavior in a classroom. *Journal of Applied Behavior Analysis, 2,* 119–124.

Block, J., & Burns, R. (1976). Mastery learning. In L. Shuelman (Ed.), *Review of research in education,* (Vol IV). Itasca, IL: F. E. Peacock.

Conger, J. J., & Miller, W. C. (1966). *Personality, social class, and delinquency.* New York: Wiley.

Deming, W. E. (1977). An essay on screening, or on two-phase sampling, applied to surveys of a community. *International Statistical Review, 45,* 29–37.

Dolan, L. (1986). Mastery learning as a preventive strategy. *Outcomes, 5*(2), 20–27.

Duncan-Jones, P. (1977). Planning and piloting a two-phase psychiatric community survey. *Bulletin of the International Statistical Institute, 47* (Book 4, pp. 160–163).

Duncan-Jones, P., & Henderson, S. (1978). The use of a two-phase design in a prevalence survey. *Social Psychiatry, 13,* 231–237.

Ensminger, M. E., Brown, C. H., & Kellam, S. G. (1982). Sex differences in antecedents of substance use among adolescents. *Journal of Social Issues, 38*(2), 25–42.

Ensminger, M. E., Kellam, S. G., & Rubin, B. R. (1983). School and family origins of delinquency: Comparisons by sex. In K. T. Van Dusen & S. A. Mednick (Eds.), *Prospective studies of crime and delinquency* (pp. 73–97). Boston: Kluwer-Nijhoff.

Erikson, E. H. (1959). Identity and life cycle, selected papers. In G. S. Kleim (Ed.), *Psychological issues*. New York: International Universities Press.

Erikson, E. G. (1963). *Childhood and society*. Rev. ed. New York: Norton.

Farrington, D. P. (1987). Early precursors of frequent offending. In J. Q. Wilson & G. C. Loury (Eds.), *From children to citizens (Volume 3). Families, schools and delinquency prevention* (pp. 27–49).

Glick, P. C. (1947). The family cycle. *American Sociological Review, 12,* 164–179.

Glick, P. C. (1955). The life cycle of the family. *Marriage and Family Living, 17*(1), 3–9.

Glick, P. C. (1977). Updating the life cycle of the family. *Journal of Marriage and the Family,* February, 5–13.

Gold, M. (1970). *Delinquent behavior in an American city*. Belmont, CA: Brooks/Cole.

Greenley, J. R., & Mechanic, D. (1976). Social selection in seeking help for psychological problems. *Health and Social Behavior, 17,* 249–262.

Greenley, J. R., Mechanic, D., & Cleary, P. (1987). Seeking help for psychological problems: A replication and an extension. *Medical Care, 25*(12).

Guskey, T. (1985). *Implementing mastery learning*. Belmont, CA: Wadsworth.

Kagan, J., Reznick, J. S., Clarke, C., Snidman, N., & Garcia-Coll, C. (1984). Behavioral inhibition to the unfamiliar. *Child Development, 55,* 2212–2225.

Kaplan, H. B. (1980). *Deviant behavior in defense of self*. New York: Academic Press.

Kellam, S. G., Adams, R. G., Brown, C. H., & Ensminger, M. E. (1982). The long-term evolution of the family structure of teenage and older mothers. *Journal of Marriage and the Family,* 539–554.

Kellam, S. G., & Branch, J. D. (1971). An approach to community mental health: Analysis of basic problems. In *Seminars in Psychiatry, Vol. 3,* No. 2.

Kellam, S. G., Branch, J. D., Agrawal, K. C., & Ensminger, M. E. (1975). *Mental health and going to school: The Woodlawn program of assessment, early intervention, and evaluation*. Chicago: University of Chicago Press.

Kellam, S. G., Branch, J. D., Agrawal, C., & Grabill, M. E. (1972). Woodlawn mental health. In S. E. Golann & C. Eisdorfer (Eds.), *Handbook of community mental health* (Vol. 36, pp. 711–727). New York: Appleton-Century-Crofts.

Kellam, S. G., Branch, J. D., Brown, C. H., & Russell, G. (1981). Why teenagers come for treatment: A ten year prospective epidemiological study in Woodlawn. *Journal of the American Academy of Child Psychiatry, 20,* 477–495.

Kellam, S. G., & Brown, C. H. (1986). Social adaptational and psychological antecedents in first grade of adolescent psychopathology ten years later. In G. L. Klerman (Ed.), *Suicide & depression among adolescents & young adults* (pp. 147–183). Washington, DC: American Psychiatric Press.

Kellam, S. G., Brown, C. H., & Fleming, J. P. (1982). The prevention of teenage substance use: Longitudinal research strategy. In T. J. Coates, A. L. Petersen, & C. Perry (Eds.), *Promoting adolescent health: A dialogue on research and practice* (pp. 171–200). New York: Academic Press.

Kellam, S. G., Brown, C. H., Rubin, B. R., & Ensminger, M. E. (1983). Paths leading to teenage psychiatric symptoms and substance use: Developmental epidemiological studies in Woodlawn. In S. B. Guze, F. J. Earls, & J. E. Barrett (Eds.), *Childhood psychopathology and development* (pp. 17–51). New York: Raven Press.

Kellam, S. G., & Ensminger, M. E. (1982, June). *Prevention research strategy and structure*. Paper presented at the National Institute of Mental Health Center for the Study of Prevention, Rockville, MD.

Kellam, S. G., Ensminger, M. E., & Turner, R. J. (1977). Family structure and the mental health of children: Concurrent and longitudinal community-wide studies. *Archives of General Psychiatry, 34,* 1012–1022.

Kramer, M., Brown, H., Skinner, A., Anthony, J., & German, P. (1987). Changing living arrangements in the population and their potential effect on the prevalence of mental disorder: Findings of the Eastern Baltimore Mental Health Survey. In B. Cooper (Ed.), *Psychiatric epidemiology, progress and prospects,* London and Sydney: Croom Helm.

Lefkowitz, M. M., Eron, L. D., Walden, L. O., & Huesmann, L. R. (1977). *Growing up to be violent.* New York: Pergamon Press.

Mitchell, S., & Rosa, P. (1981). Boyhood behavior problems as precursors of criminality: A fifteen-year follow-up study. *Journal of Child Psychology, 22,* 19–33.

Morris, J. N. (1975). *Uses of epidemiology.* (Third Ed.). New York: Churchill Livingstone.

Neugarten, B. L. (1979). Time, age and life cycle. *American Journal of Psychiatry, 136,* 887–894.

Park, R. E. (1925). *The city.* Chicago: University of Chicago Press.

Parsons, T. (1964). Social structure and personality. New York: Free Press.

Patterson, G. R. (1986). Performance models for anti-social boys. *American Psychologist, 41,* 432.

Pedersen, E., & Fauchter, T. A., with Eaton, W. (1978). New perspective on the effects of first-grade teachers on children's subsequent adult status. *Harvard Educational Review, 48*(1), 131.

Robins, L. N. (1973). *A follow-up of Vietnam drug users.* Special Action Office Monograph, Series A, No. 1, Special Action Office for Drug Abuse Prevention, Washington, D.C.

Robins, L. N. (1978). *Sturdy childhood predictors of adult outcomes: Replications from longitudinal studies.* Paul Hoch award lecture. Presented at the American Psychopathological Association Meeting, Boston.

Robinson, V., & Swanton, C. (1980). The generalization of behavioral teacher training. *Review of Educational Research, 50*(3), 486–498.

Rutter, M. L., Tizard, J., & Whitmore, K. (Eds.). (1970). *Education, health and behavior: Psychological and medical study of childhood development.* New York: Wiley.

Shaffer, D., Stokman, C., O'Connor, P. A., Shafer, S., Barmack, J. E., Hess, S., & Spaulten, D. (1979, November). *Early soft neurological signs and later psychopathological development.* Paper presented at the annual meeting of the Society for Life History Research in Psychopathology and Society for the Study of Social Biology, New York.

Soberon, G., Frenk, J., & Sepulveda, J. (1986). Commentary—The health care reform in Mexico: Before and after the 1985 earthquake. *American Journal of Public Health, 76*(6), 673–680.

Spivak, G., Marcus, J., & Swift, M. (1986). Early classroom behaviors and later misconduct. *Developmental Psychology, 22,* 124–131.

Suomi, S. J. (1987). Genetic and maternal contributions to individual differences in rhesus monkey biobehavioral development. In N. Krasnagor, M. Hofer, & W. Smotherman (Eds.), *Perinatal development: Psychological perspectives* (pp. 397–420). New York: Academic Press.

Sweet, J. A. (1977). Demography and the family. *Annual Review of Sociology, 3,* 363–405.

Vanfossen, B. E., Jones, James D., & Spade, J. Z. (1987). Curriculum tracking and status maintenance. *Sociology of Education,* Vol. 60 (April), 104–122.

Watt, N. F. (1974). Childhood and adolescent routes to schizophrenia. In D. F. Ricks, A. Thomas, & M. Roff (Eds.), *Life history research in psychopathology* (Vol. 3, pp. 194–211). Minneapolis, University of Minnesota Press.

3 Methodological Issues in the Study of Family Violence

Richard J. Gelles
University of Rhode Island

A review of the table of contents of social science journals published prior to 1970 would uncover virtually no articles on family violence. Readers would be left convinced that family violence was not a significant social problem. The reports of child abuse or occasional wife abuse that were tucked away in the middle pages of newspapers, emblazoned on the front pages of *The National Enquirer,* or presented as clinical case studies in social service and medical journals appeared to be rare aberrations which most certainly were the product of the mental illness of the offenders.

Today we know that violence in the home is a significant social problem with an estimated incidence far greater than the risk of experiencing violence on the streets. Research points to a problem that is not confined to a few mentally ill or emotionally disturbed individuals. Battered wives are not the cause of their victimization, nor are those who remain in violent homes masochists.

With the vision of hindsight we now assemble historical records and uncover centuries of violence and abuse between family members (see for example, Bakan, 1971; DeMause, 1974, 1975; Radbill, 1980; and Shorter, 1975). Additional research reveals that the pattern of violent family relationships cuts across cultures (Gelles & Cornell, 1983; Korbin, 1981; Taylor & Newberger, 1979). Finally, research finds violence in virtually all family relations—victims not only include children and women, but young and elderly parents, siblings, and dating partners.

That there has been an explosion of research on all facets of family violence is obvious even to a casual consumer of the professional literature. Although there is an abundance of research, the collected body of knowledge is diverse, often contradictory; and frequently the data collected, and even published, fail to meet stringent standards of empirical evidence. The uninformed conventional wisdoms of the 1960s and 1970s have been replaced with semiinformed and ill-informed conventional wisdoms of the 1980s.

This chapter reviews methodological issues in the study of family violence. Our review covers the standard issues of research design—conceptual issues, sources of data, sampling, and measurement. Although the issues are the same as those that confront any social scientist, the context of research is unique. The family is a private and intimate social institution. As a unique social group, the family presents special challenges and constraints for social scientists. Add to this the fact that violence, like mental illness, suicide, and sexuality, is a taboo topic that is infrequently discussed in private, let alone with strangers. Finally, and perhaps an equally salient methodological issue, the study of family violence is often governed more by the heart than the head. Emotions run high among those who have responsibility for serving, treating, protecting, or understanding victims of violence and abuse. Because there is so much tragedy, anger, frustration, and ultimately cynicism involved in working with violent families, rational thought and logic—the very foundation of research design—are often left behind.

MAJOR QUESTIONS IN THE STUDY OF FAMILY VIOLENCE

In the first decade of research on domestic violence, questions about the extent of the problem dominated the research and policy agenda. Answering the questions with scientific data was aimed at exploding the myth that violence in the home is rare. Another goal was to convince policy makers, opinion leaders, and the public that the various forms of domestic violence were extensive enough to be considered legitimate social problems—especially since one part of the definition of a social problem is that a behavior is found harmful to a *significant* number of people (Merton & Nisbet, 1976). Finally, social scientists required data on the incidence of family violence in order to plan social survey research.

A second question focused on identifying the correlates of family violence. Here too, answers were needed to deflate the conventional wisdom that violent family members and abusers suffered from some form of personality disorder or psychopathology. A third dominant question concerned the causes of violence in the home.

In the third decade of research on family violence two additional questions have been added to the list of research concerns. One question focuses on the consequences of experiencing and observing domestic violence. The statement that abused children grow up to be abusers is reported so often in the professional and lay literature that it is considered by many to be a deterministic truism. Yet, precious little high quality empirical evidence has actually been collected on the relationship between experiencing violence as a child and later violent behavior as an adult. Similarly, many researchers, clinicians, and the public in general presume that experiencing violence produces lifelong psychic and social scars. Yet, again, although this seems to be a reasonable theory, there is very little scientific evidence to support such a belief.

Finally, a recent concern has turned to the effectiveness of various forms of intervention and treatment. Researchers and clinicians alike are interested in the effectiveness and impact of the various intervention and treatment strategies that were developed once family violence was placed on the public agenda as a major social problem.

This chapter does not attempt to answer these questions. Our concern is not with *what* we know about family violence, but with *how we know about it*. We shall, however, review some of research on family violence as a means of illustrating some of the methodological issues in the field.

ISSUES OF DEFINITION

Thus far we have used the terms *violence, abuse, domestic violence, intimate violence,* and *family violence* interchangeably, without defining any of the conceptual terms. One of the major problems that confronts investigators who attempt to study domestic violence has been the quagmire of conceptual dilemmas encountered. The terms *violence* and *abuse* are often used interchangeably by those who study domestic violence. These concepts, however, are not conceptually equivalent. Moreover, there is considerable variation in how each concept is nominally defined.

Defining Abuse

The first form of family violence that was uncovered and recognized as a problem was child abuse, or the battered child syndrome. The first widely disseminated article defined the battered child syndrome as a clinical condition (with diagnosable physical and medical symptoms) having to do with those (children) who have been deliberately injured by physical assault by a parent or caretaker (Kempe et al., 1962). The term "battered child syndrome" quickly gave way to terms such as child abuse and neglect, and child maltreatment. The term abuse was not only applied to physical assault, but also to malnutrition, failure to thrive, sexual exploitation, educational neglect, medical neglect, and mental abuse. The official federal definition of child abuse, stated in the Child Abuse Prevention and Treatment Act of 1974 (PL 93-237) was:

> . . . the physical or mental injury, negligent treatment, or maltreatment of a child under the age of eighteen by a person who is responsible for the child's welfare

under circumstances which would indicate that the child's health or welfare is harmed or threatened thereby.

This definition is consequential to methodologists because it became the model for state definitions, which are in turn the basis for state statutes that require the reporting of suspected cases of child abuse and neglect. This, in turn is consequential (as we see later) because the vast majority of investigations of child abuse begin by operationally defining child abuse as those cases that are reported to official agencies and are determined to be valid cases of abuse. Also, the federally financed national incidence surveys of officially reported child abuse and neglect (Burgdorf, 1980; National Center on Child Abuse and Neglect, 1988) employed this as the nominal definition of abuse. Thus, most official report data, which are the data used in the majority of studies of child abuse, are influenced, to one degree or another, by the federal definition.

It would be a mistake, however, to assume that because there is a federal definition, there is uniformity in how child abuse is nominally defined by researchers. In point of fact, most studies of child abuse and violence towards children cannot be compared to one another because of the wide variation of nominal definitions employed by investigators. While some researchers study violence towards children (see for example, Gelles, 1978), others examine the full range of acts of commission and omission (see for example Newberger et al., 1977). As a result, reports of incidence, correlations, causes, and consequences vary from study to study for many reasons, one being that researchers infrequently define child abuse the same way.

To a lesser extent, the same definitional problems that have plagued the study of child abuse and violence towards children have been part of the development of research on violence towards women. Initial definitions of wife abuse focused on acts of damaging physical violence directed toward women by their spouses or partners (see for example, Gelles, 1974; Martin, 1976). As wife abuse became recognized as a social problem, the definition of abuse was broadened to include sexual abuse, marital rape, and even pornography (London, 1978).

Defining Violence

Violence has also proven to be a concept that is not easily defined. First, *violence* has frequently been used interchangeably with the term *aggression*. Whereas violence refers to a physical act, aggression refers to any malevolent act that is intended to hurt another person. The hurt may not be only physical, but may be emotional injury or material deprivation. Second, because of the negative connotation of the term violence, some investigators have tried to differentiate between hurtful violence and more legitimate acts. Thus, Goode (1971) tried to distinguish between legitimate acts of force and illegitimate acts of violence.

Spanking a child who runs into the street might be considered force, while beating the same child would be violence. Attempts to clarify the concept of violence have demonstrated the difficulty of distinguishing between legitimate and illegitimate acts. Offenders, victims, bystanders, and agents of social control often accept and tolerate many acts between family members that would be considered illegitimate if committed by strangers (Gelles, 1974; Steinmetz, 1971; Straus, Gelles, & Steinmetz, 1980).

Additional theoretical and ideological concerns influence the ways in which the concept of violence is defined. Violence is frequently a political concept used to attract attention to undesirable behaviors or situations. Thus, some members of the political left define various federal programs, such as Aid to Families with Dependent Children, as violent. Members of the political right will likewise claim that abortion is a violent act.

One frequently used nominal definition of violence, proposed by Gelles and Straus (1979), defines violence as "an act carried out with the intention or perceived intention of physically hurting another person." The *hurt* can range from the slight pain caused by a slap or a spanking to harm that results in severe injury or even death.

Defining Family

Weis (1989) notes that there is a third conceptual concern in the study of family violence. Not only are there difficulties in defining abuse and violence, but, as Weis notes, there is a need for conceptual clarity in determining who are the participants in acts referred to as family violence. Weis identified three possible relationships that could come under the heading of family or domestic violence. First there are instances when victims and offenders share *kin relationships*—those who are related through birth or marriage. Kin relationship violence refers to the classic forms of violence towards wives or children, sibling violence, and violence towards parents. A second category is *intimate relationships*. These include relationships where the participants know each other in a close and personal way—such as violence between dating partners. Finally, violence can occur between those who share a *domestic relationship* by virtue of sharing the same household.

SOURCES OF DATA

Data on child abuse, wife abuse, and family violence come from three major sources. Each source has certain advantages and specific weaknesses that influence both the nature and generalizability of the findings derived from the research.

Clinical Samples

The most frequent source of data on family violence are clinical studies carried out by psychiatrists, psychologists, and counselors. This is primarily due to the fact that these investigators have the most direct access to cases of family violence. The combination of the taboo nature of the topic and the relatively low base rate (even though the base rate of nearly 40 per 1000 is considered high for violent behavior, it is low by most standards of social research) makes access to cases of family violence difficult for nonclinicians. The clinical setting (including hospital emergency rooms and battered wife shelters) provides access to extensive in-depth information about particular cases of violence. The pioneer studies of child abuse were almost exclusively based on such clinical samples (see for example, Galdston, 1965; Kempe et al., 1962; Steele & Pollock, 1968).

Such studies, although important for breaking new ground and rich in qualitative data, cannot be used to generalize information on incidence or the frequency and strength of factors associated with violence. Such samples are never representative, and few investigators gathering data from clinical samples employ comparison groups.

Studies of wife abuse and violence towards women have relied heavily on samples of women who seek help at battered wife shelters (Dobash & Dobash, 1979; Giles-Sims, 1983; Pagelow, 1981; Walker, 1979). Such samples are important because they are the best, and sometimes the only, way of obtaining detailed data on the most severely battered women. Such data are also necessary to study the impact of intervention programs. However, these data are not generalizable to all women who experience violence; and the study designs (see, for example, Walker, 1979) frequently fail to employ comparison groups.

Official Statistics

One of the major responses to the discovery (or rediscovery) of child abuse in the early 1960s was the effort to write and implement mandatory child abuse reporting statutes. Between 1963 and 1967 every state and the District of Columbia passed some form of child abuse reporting law.

The establishment of mandatory reporting laws for suspected cases of child abuse and neglect made case-level and aggregate-level data on abuse available to researchers. Each year the American Association for Protecting Children (a division of the American Humane Association) collects data from each state on officially reported child abuse and neglect (American Association for Protecting Children, 1985; American Humane Association, 1982, 1983). The Federal government sponsored two national surveys of officially reported child maltreatment (Burgdorf, 1980; National Center on Child Abuse and Neglect, 1988).

There has not been a tradition of officially reporting spouse abuse. Until recently there were few localities or states that recorded instances of spouse abuse. An exception is the state of Kentucky, which instituted an adult protection statute in 1976 that mandates the reporting of any individual known or suspected of adult abuse, neglect, or exploitation. The statute was amended in 1978 to specifically include spouse abuse. Today, three states collect such data.

Official report data provide information on an extremely large number of cases. But these cases are limited only to those known by service providers. Incidence rates based on these data are likely to be lower than the true rates, and the data are biased in a number of ways (Finkelhor & Hotaling, 1984). A major problem with all official report data is the selective, biased sample of offenders, victims, and violent acts that is produced. As with many other types of official records of deviant behavior, the poor are overrepresented in official records of child abuse, as are ethnic and racial minorities (Gelles, 1975; Newberger et al., 1977). Turbett and O'Toole (1980) conducted an experiment, the results of which demonstrate the biases inherent in official statistics. The researchers presented sample medical records to groups of physicians and nurses. The files contained descriptions of injuries suffered by the child. One trial varied the socioeconomic status of the father of the child described in the medical record while holding all other variables, including the nature of the physical condition of the child, constant. The second trial held all variables constant, but varied the race of the father. Subjects were more likely to define a case as child abuse if the father was described as having a working class occupation. Furthermore, the clinicians stated that the child of the working class father should be reported as a victim of child abuse. Similarly, injuries to the Black child elicited greater definitions of abuse and more inclination to officially report than the case of the White child.

Biases in official data also arise in the process of validation of child abuse reports. A comparison of reports of child abuse which were ruled valid or invalid by a child protection agency indicated that the status of the person making the report, not the nature of the reported injury, influenced whether the report would be found valid. If the reporter was a professional, such as a physician, a report was much more likely to be found valid, even controlling for the nature of the injury to the child or the social status of the alleged abuser (Carr, 1979).

Social Surveys

As we said earlier, the low base rate of most forms of abuse and family violence and the sensitive and taboo nature of the topic poses constraints for those who desire to apply standard survey research methods to studying family violence. A major problem is to locate a sufficient number of individuals who are involved as offenders or victims in incidents of family violence.

Some investigators cope with the problem of the low base rate by employing purposive or nonrepresentative sampling techniques to identify cases. We have drawn samples of abused women from police records or cases from private social work agencies (Gelles, 1974). A second approach has been to use available large groups of subjects. Murray Straus's first research studies of family violence collected data by distributing questionnaires to undergraduate students enrolled in introductory sociology courses (Straus, 1974). Similarly, David Finkelhor's (1979) first research project on sexual victimization of children collected data from undergraduate students.

Self-report surveys of college students or purposive samples provide considerable descriptive data on the extent and nature of violence in families. However, such surveys are still limited by the nonrepresentative nature of the sample. One cannot generalize about the incidence of family violence, the correlates, causes, or consequences from samples of White, middle-class college students, or from those individuals who either sought help from social service agencies or the police. In order to develop a generalizable knowledge base it is necessary to derive data from representative samples of families.

INCIDENCE DATA: VARIOUS DATA FROM VARIOUS SOURCES

The varying estimates of the incidence and prevalence of child abuse provide an excellent illustration of the impact of source of data on the data actually collected.

Incidence Estimates

Clinical Guesstimates.   Clinical studies do not attempt to gather data on the extent of child abuse. However, clinicians, based on their clinical experience, have presented their own estimates (or guesstimates) of the extent of the abuse of children. DeFrancis (1973), testifying before the U.S. Senate in 1973 estimated that there were 30,000 to 40,000 truly abused children in the United States. Kempe (1971) set the figure at 60,000 while Vincent Fontana (1973) placed the figure at 1.5 million children.

Official Report Data.   Data from official statistics yielded higher incidence figures than the clinical estimates. Cohen and Sussman (1975) obtained evidence on officially reported data from the 10 most popular states and projected 41,104 confirmed cases of child abuse in 1973. Nagi (1975) attempted to compensate for the shortcomings of estimates of child abuse based on official report records by surveying a national sample of community agencies and agency personnel. Nagi estimates that there were 167,000 cases of abuse reported annually, while an additional 97,000 cases go unreported.

One of the most detailed attempts to record officially reported cases of child abuse is conducted annually by the American Association for the Protection of

Children, a division of the American Humane Association. Beginning in 1974 the agency has collected data on officially reported cases of child abuse from child protection agencies nationwide.

Data are collected from each of the 50 states and the District of Columbia, with evidence based exclusively on cases that were identified and reported to the state agency designated by the state child abuse reporting law.

The most recent data available are for 1984 (American Association for Protecting Children, 1985). During 1984 1,727,000 child abuse and neglect reports were received by state agencies, or 27.3 reports per 1000 children in the United States. Physical abuse alone constituted a little more than a third of the reports—33.5% or 578,545 children while 16.3% of reports involved abuse and neglect. Thus, there were 860,046 reports involving physical abuse in 1984.

A second source of data on the national incidence of child abuse are the two National Studies of the Incidence and Severity of Child Maltreatment conducted for the National Center on Child Abuse and Neglect by Westat (Burgdorf, 1980; National Center on Child Abuse and Neglect, 1988). The surveys assessed how many cases of child maltreatment were known to investigatory agencies (including the protective service agencies used in the American Humane Association census) as well as other agencies such as schools, hospitals, other social agencies, and the police.

Table 3.1 presents the results of the 1980 national incidence survey. A total of 652,000 maltreated children were known by agencies surveyed in the study (Burgdorf, 1980). Stated in terms of incidence rates, it was estimated that 10.5 children per 1000 are abused and neglected annually; 5.7 children per 1000 (351,000) are physically abused.

The 1986 national incidence survey found a total of 1,025,900 countable cases of child maltreatment (National Center on Child Abuse and Neglect, 1988). Stated in terms of incidence rates 16.3 children per 1000 were abused and neglected in 1986; 9.2 per 1000 (580,400) were physically abused.

Surveys.   Gelles and Straus have conducted two national surveys of physical violence in families (the sample, measurement, and other methodological aspects of these surveys are described in detail in the following section). The first survey, conducted in 1975, used the Conflict Tactics Scales (Straus, 1979) to measure physical violence in 2146 households. One part of the study involved measuring violence towards children in the 1143 homes with children at home between the ages of 3 and 17.[1] Nearly 40 parents in 1000 (3.6%) engaged in one

---

[1]The sample of households which contained children in the First National Family Violence Survey was limited to those homes where their was at least one child aged 3- to 17-years-of-age. This was done because one of the goals of the First National Family Violence Survey was to measure violence between siblings. It was assumed that violence initiated by a child under the age of 3-years-old would not be meaningful in the same sense as violence initiated by a child 3-years-of-age or older.

TABLE 3.1
Estimated Number of Recognized In-Scope Children (Per 1000 Per Year)[a]

Form of Maltreatment and Severity of Injury/Impairment	Number In-Scope Children	Incidence Rate[c] (per 1000)
Form of Maltreatment[b]		
Total, all maltreated children	652,000	10.5
Total, all abused children	351,100	5.7
Physical assault	207,600	3.4
Sexual exploitation	44,700	0.7
Emotional abuse	138,400	2.2
Total, all neglected children	329,000	5.3
Physical neglect	108,000	1.7
Educational neglect	181,500	2.9
Emotional neglect	59,400	1.0
Severity of Child's Injury/Impairment		
Fatal	1,000	0.02
Serious	136,900	2.2
Moderate	410,300	6.6
Probable	101,700	1.6

[a]National incidence estimates by major form of maltreatment and by severity of maltreatment-related injury or impairments.

[b]Totals may be lower than sum of categories, since a child may have experienced more than one in-scope category of maltreatment.

[c]Numerator = estimated number of recognized in-scope children; denominator = 61,900, the estimated total number (in thousands) of children under 18 in the United States in December, 1979.

From Burgdorf (1980). Recognition and Reporting of Child Maltreatment. Findings from the National Study of the Indicence and Severity of Child Abuse and Neglect. National Center on Child Abuse and Neglect, 1980, p. 37. Reproduced by permission of the author.

act of abusive violence during the year prior to the survey. Projecting this rate to all children 3- to 17-years-of-age who lived at home in 1975 means that 1.4 million children experience acts of abusive violence each year (Gelles & Straus, 1987; Straus, Gelles, & Steinmetz, 1980). The detailed breakdown of the data are found in Table 3.2.

Because two groups of high risk children, children under 3-years-of-age and children of single parents, were excluded from the survey, the study findings are considered to be underestimates of the true rate of physical abuse.

Even with the underestimate, the results of the First National Family Violence Survey confirm Burgdorf's notion that only about one-third of child maltreatment incidents are reported to official agencies.

Estimates of the Changing Rates of Child Abuse

A second, and more dramatic comparison of data collected by varying methods, is a comparison of data that address the question of whether the rate of child abuse is increasing, decreasing, or remaining the same.

TABLE 3.2
Frequency of Parental Violence Toward Children

Violent Behavior	Percentage of Occurrences in Past Year				Percentage of Occurrence Ever Reported
	Once	Twice	More Than Twice	Total	
Threw something	1.3	1.8	2.3	5.4	9.6
Pushed, grabbed or shoved	4.3	9.0	18.5	31.8	46.4
Slapped or spanked	5.2	9.4	43.6	58.2	71.0
Kicked, bit or hit with fist	0.7	0.8	1.7	3.2	7.7
Hit or tried to hit with something	1.0	2.6	9.8	13.4	20.0
Beat up	0.4	0.3	0.6	1.3	4.2
Threatened with knife or gun	0.1	0.0	0.0	0.1	2.8
Used a knife or gun	0.1	0.0	0.0	0.1	2.9

From Gelles (1978).

Data collected by the American Human Association find that, overall, there has been a 212% increase in child maltreatment reporting between 1976 and 1986. The largest yearly increase was from the first year of the study (1976) to the next—an increase of 24.2%.

A comparison of the two national incidence surveys of the incidence and prevalence of child abuse and neglect conducted by the National Center on Child Abuse and Neglect found that a 66% increase in the rate of child maltreatment between 1980 and 1986 and a 73% increase in the rate of child abuse (National Center on Child Abuse and Neglect, 1988).

The Second National Family Violence Survey found that parent reports of physical child abuse had *declined* 47% between 1975 and 1985, from 3.6% to 1.9% (Gelles & Straus, 1987; Straus & Gelles, 1986). See Table 3.3.

Clearly, different methods of data collecting produce different data. Clinical estimates of child abuse have been the most conservative. Official report data, while producing higher estimates than clinical data, are still subject to biases of underreporting and selective reporting. Survey data produce the highest estimates of incidence, even with some methodologically imposed biases that lead to underreporting.

The greatest differences between data sources are estimates of changing rates. Increased funding for public awareness campaigns and staffing child protection agencies both increased the capacity of agencies to accept and investigate reports and the willingness of professionals and the public to make child abuse reports. Given the expansion of child abuse reporting laws, public awareness, and professional services, it would have been surprising if official reports had not increased each year. That two social surveys would find a decrease in personal reporting of violence towards children was a surprise. The methodological biases of the two surveys were such that methodological artifacts would have produced increased, not decreased reports of physical abuse (see Gelles & Straus, 1987 and Straus & Gelles, 1986 for a complete discussion of the methodology of the two surveys). The two plausible rival explanations for the decrease in parental admissions of severe violence towards children is that parents are less willing today than 10 years ago to report use of violence or that the use of violence towards children has indeed declined in the last decade.

RANDOM SAMPLE SURVEYS: QUESTIONNAIRES, IN-PERSON INTERVIEWS, AND TELEPHONE INTERVIEWS

Random sample surveys offer the advantage of large sample size, efficiency of data collection, standardization of measurement instruments, and generalizability to a general or specific population. However, as with all forms of data collection, fielding a random sample survey on the topic of family violence involves a series of logical decisions and compromises. The first is the choice

TABLE 3.3
Parent to Child Violence: A Comparison of Rates in 1975 and 1985[a]

Type of Violence	Rate Per 1000 Children Aged 3 Through 17[a]		
	1975 (N = 1, 146)[b]	1985 (N = 1, 428)[c]	t for 1975-1985 Differences
1. Threw something	54	27	3.41***
2. Pushed, grabbed, or shoved	318	307	0.54
3. Slapped or spanked	582	549	1.68
4. Kicked, bit or hit with fist	32	13	3.17**
5. Hit or tried to hit with something	134	97	2.91**
6. Beat up	13	6	0.26
7. Burned or scalded	N/A	5	N/A
8. Threatened with gun or knife	1	2	0.69
9. Used gun or knife	1	2	0.69
Overall Violence (1-6; 8-9)	630	620	0.52
Severe Violence (4-6; 8-9)	140	107	2.56**
Very Severe Violence (4; 6; 8-9)	36	19	4.25***

[a]For two caretaker households with at least one child 3- to 17- years-of-age at home.
[b]On some items, there were a few responses omitted, but figures for all incidents represent at least 1140 families.
[c]On some items, there were a few responses omitted, but figures for all indidents represent at least 1148 families

* $p < .05$
** $p < .01$ } two tailed tests
*** $p < .001$
From Gelles and Straus (1987).

between sample size and instrument length. The choice arises because investigators with a limit on funding must choose between how many subjects or families from whom they will collect data, and how much data will be collected.

Sample Size.   We note again that the low base rate of family violence impinges upon the collection of data using a random sample survey. The results of the First National Family Violence Survey (Straus et al., 1980) are an example. When that survey was designed in 1975, estimates of the incidence of physical child abuse ranged from one-half of 1% to perhaps 3 or 4%. There were no estimates of the extent of wife abuse available other than from our own exploratory sample surveys. We opted for a sample size of some 2000 households. Children under the age of 18-years-old live in about half of the households in the United States. Thus, a national sample of houses would yield about 1000 homes containing children under 18. If 40 children in 1000 are victims of severe physical violence at the hands of their parents each year, then we would expect to find 40 victims of physical abuse in our national sample. That is barely enough cases to conduct cross-tabular and correlational analysis. However, if one wants to control for the impact of income on the relationship between race and abuse, there would be an insufficient number of cases for the analysis.

Thus, even a sample of 2000 homes proved to be too small for some of forms of multivariate analysis. The obvious solution would be to expand the sample size. This was done in our Second National Family Violence Survey: the sample for that survey was 6000 households. However, by increasing the sample size we placed constraints on how much data we could collect.

Instrument Length.   Our First National Family Violence Survey collected data by in-person interview. Interviewers traveled to the homes of the 2000 subjects and conducted interviews that lasted, on average, 60 min. However, by expanding our sample size to 6000 households for the second survey, it would have been extremely expensive to conduct 1-hour, in-person interviews. Our estimate was that the interviewing alone would cost in excess of 1 million dollars in 1985. Thus, by opting for more subjects, we needed to choose a cost-efficient data collection method. We chose to collect data by using telephone interviews. We shall compare the advantages and disadvantages of in-person vs. telephone interviewing in the following section. A major disadvantage of telephone interviewing is that telephone interviews do not necessitate keeping subjects on the telephone for much more than 35 min. Interviews that last longer than 35 min tend to produce lower completion rates and data that are inferior in reliability and validity to data collected from shorter interviews.

In summary, investigators of low base rate behavior, such as child abuse, wife abuse, elder abuse, and marital rape face tradeoffs of larger sample sizes and smaller amounts of data collected vs. smaller samples sizes and the ability to collect richer and more detailed information.

DATA COLLECTION TECHNIQUES: QUESTIONNAIRES, IN-PERSON INTERVIEWS, AND TELEPHONE INTERVIEWS

Survey researchers can choose from three data collection techniques: questionnaires, in-person interviews, and telephone interviews. After a brief discussion of questionnaires we turn our attention to a comparison between in-person and telephone interviewing.

Questionnaires are the backbone of survey research. They are cost-effective and easy to administer to captive audiences such as college students, clients of social service agencies, and other natural groupings. However, once an investigator is required to mail out the questionnaires, the efficiency must be measured against some important limitations. The first limitation is that a subject must be functionally literate to complete a questionnaire. Although this typically is not a problem in a college classroom, it is a major problem with representative samples. Estimates are that nearly 10% of the United States population may be functionally illiterate. Response rate would be further limited by mailing English language questionnaires to homes in which the subjects do not speak English.

Mailed questionnaires have the lowest response rate of any form of random sample survey. Even with a sophisticated follow-up system, mailed questionnaires elicit completion rates between 50 and 60% (Babbie, 1983).

In-person interviews, although more expensive, solve the problem of literacy and language (assuming multilingual interviewers are hired), and consequently have higher completion rates than questionnaires. In-person interviews generally have completion rates between 70 and 80%. However, we have found that when the subject is family violence, the completion rate is more modest. The First National Family Violence Survey had an overall completion rate of 65%, varying from a low of 60% in metropolitan areas to a high of 72.3% in other areas.

Because of the cost of interviewing 6000 subjects and our desire to improve upon the completion rate of the First National Family Violence Survey, we chose to collect data in the second survey using telephone interviews. The advantages of telephone surveys have been documented by Groves and Kahn (1979), Marcus and Crane (1986), Miller, Rollins, and Thomas (1982), and Klecka and Tuchfarber (1978). In brief, the advantages include: ease of administration, lower cost than in-person interviewing, more rapid completion of the survey, and better access to hard to reach households. The drawbacks of telephone surveys include less than 100% coverage of households, the biases of the telephone sampling frame, and the impact of the telephone itself on reliability and validity.

Groves and Kahn (1979) have demonstrated that telephone surveys are about one-fourth the cost of in-person interviews because of the shorter length of interviewing and the absence of travel costs involved in locating and interviewing respondents. Whereas Groves and Kahn found that the response rate of telephone interviews was about 5% lower than that of in-person interviews, our experience is just the opposite. While the in-person First National Family Violence Survey had a completion rate of 65%, the telephone survey used in the Second National Survey had a completion rate of 85%. A telephone survey of spouse abuse in the state of Kentucky had a completion rate of 91% (Harris and Associates, 1979).

Not only does the flexibility and anonymity of the telephone lead to higher response rates in research on sensitive topics, but there is some reason to believe that the attributes of the telephone interviewing technique yield data that are equivalent in reliability and validity to face-to-face interviews. Researchers have found statistically insignificant differences in surveys of sensitive topics between face-to-face interviews and telephone interviews (Bradburn, Sudman, and Associates, 1979; Hochstim, 1977). Telephone interviews provide greater protection of respondent privacy. The interviewer does not come from the same community as the respondent, and the respondent does not physically see the interviewer. The respondent does not have to worry that information divulged in the interview will become known to others in the community. The worst instance of in-person interviews—that the interviewer and subject know each other or some of the same people—cannot happen over the telephone. Another advantage of telephone surveys for a study of violence is that the study directors and the supervisors can maintain closer contact with the interviewers and help them deal with difficult situations, apparent lack of privacy, and referrals to sources of help. Another advantage is that well trained telephone interviewers can increase response rate by rescheduling interviews for more convenient times, otherwise converting would be refusals or incomplete interviews.

The current technology of telephone survey sampling frames is a final advantage of the technique. Sampling frames for in-person interviews are typically clustered—that is, four to six households within close proximity of each other will be selected for the sampling frame. Clustering is designed for cost efficiency. Clustered sampling allows individual interviewers to conduct more interviews without long-distance travel. Because there is no travel involved in telephone interviewing, sampling frames are unclustered, thus eliminating possible biases introduced by clustered sampling units.

MEASUREMENT ISSUES

A number of scholars are wary of applying survey research to the study of abuse and violence because they assume that subjects will not provide either reliable or valid answers (Pelton, 1979). Although the number of random sample surveys of domestic violence is small (see for example, Gelles & Straus, 1987, 1988; Harris and Associates 1979; Steinmetz, 1977; Straus et al., 1980, Straus & Gelles, 1986), there have been successful efforts made to study domestic violence using this method.

Self-report research on deviant or taboo behavior has always been subject to

criticism. The basic criticism offered is the question, "Assuming they can remember, why would people tell the truth about deviant, illegal, or embarrassing
behavior?" Thus, the major threats to validity in self-report research on family
violence are inaccurate recall, conscious or unconscious distortion, and differential interpretation of the questions and terms (Weis, 1987). For example, suppose
the question is "Have you ever abused your child?" The subject's definition of
the term *abuse* may well be quite different from the investigator's definition.
Other threats to validity include whether or not another family member is present
during the interview. Choosing to interview one member of a family can also
produce distortion. Szinovacz (1983) used the "Conflict Tactics Scales" with
couples as respondents. She found that husbands tended to underreport both
victimization and their own offenses.

At present, our solution to the problem of measuring family violence is the
Conflict Tactics Scales, which measure violence using a series of items that
assess the ways in which families deal with conflict among themselves. There are
three general means of conflict tactics that the scales measure:

1. The use of rational discussion and agreement (e.g., we discussed the issue
calmly; got information to back my side up; brought in or tried to bring in
someone to help settle things);

2. the use of verbal or nonverbal expressions of anger or hostility (e.g.,
insulted or swore; sulked or refused to talk; stomped out of the room or house;
did something to spite the other person; threatened to hit or throw something;
threw, smashed, or hit something); or,

3. the use of physical force or violence (e.g., threw something at the other
person; pushed, grabbed, or shoved; slapped or spanked; kicked, bit, or hit with
a fist; hit or tried to hit with something; beat up; choked; threatened or used a
knife or gun.)

Abusive violence were those items that have the high probability of injuring
the victim. Thus, we measured abuse by focusing on the most extreme acts in the
scale—kicking, biting, punching, hitting or trying to hit with objects, choking,
beating, and using weapons.

The administration of the Conflict Tactics Scales begins by stating:

No matter how well a couple (or parents and children) get along, there are times
when they disagree, get annoyed with the other person or just have spats or fights
because they've in a bad mood or tired or for some other reason. They also use
many different ways of trying to settle their differences. I'm going to read some
things that you and your (partner or child) might do when you have an argument. I
would like you to tell me how many times in the past 12 months that you. . . . .

The limitations of this measure are obvious. First, the list of acts of violence is
not exhaustive. Parents and partners engage a much wider range of violent acts

than are listed in the scales. Second, the referent period is 1 year, thus posing the possibility that some violent events can not be recalled by respondents. A third problem is that the scales measure only violent acts and not consequences. Thus, the seriousness of the act is measured only by the *a priori* classification of what might cause injury. Finally, the scales do not provide an insight into the context in which the violence occurs. No information is gleaned as to who initiated the violence, the motives or emotions involved, or whether alcohol or drugs were involved, etc.

Straus (1979, 1989) has reported on both the reliability and validity of the scales. Item analysis and ALPHA coefficient analysis provide data on the adequate reliability of the scales. The mean item–total correlation is .83 for the Husband-to-Wife Violence Index, .82 for the Wife-to-Husband Violence Index, and .88 for the Couple Violence Index. Straus also presents evidence for the concurrent and construct validity of the scales.

Barling and his colleagues (Barling et al., 1987) have also examined the construct validity of the Conflict Tactics Scales. A factor analysis produced two consistent factors from the scales—physical and psychological aggression—emerged in separate samples of 187 couples seeking therapy for marital problems and 398 nonclinic couples in beginning marriages.

A Summary of Validity Problems

Each of the major data sources has unique threats to validity. Official report data suffer from variations of definitions and biases introduced in the reporting and recording procedures. Operationally defining child or wife abuse as those cases that come to public attention, or are seen in a clinical setting, introduces biases in terms of types of violence reported, who is reported as offenders and victims, and who initiates the reports. Surveys of victims, such as those conducted by the U.S. Department of Justice (1980, 1984) can be biased by interviewing only the offender. Self-report surveys, such as those using the Conflict Tactics Scales are biased by problems or recall, under reporting, and biased reporting.

Unlike the research tradition in juvenile delinquency, which does find overlap between self-reports of delinquency and official records, to date no validation studies have been conducted that relate self-reported use of violence towards family members with official reports of abusive family violence (e.g., official child abuse reports).

RESEARCH DESIGNS: CROSS-SECTIONAL AND LONGITUDINAL DESIGNS

The nonexperimental, cross-sectional design has been the most frequently employed research design in the study of family violence. In part, this is because the studies based either on clinical data or official report data have been the most common form of research.

There are a number of inherent weaknesses in the nonexperimental, cross-sectional design. These weaknesses are often exacerbated by the sampling and data collection techniques employed by many students of family violence.

Cross-sectional designs limit the investigator's ability to determine the time order of the variables studied. For example, in our most recent survey of family violence, we asked respondents to list the kinds of trouble and difficulty that their children had encountered in the previous year. We found substantial associations between experiencing violence and various forms of delinquent behavior; including vandalism, drug use, stealing, alcohol abuse, and getting arrested. Further, children who experienced violence were also reported as having more school problems as well as problems with violent behaviors in and out of the home (Gelles & Straus, 1988). Although it was tempting to conclude that violence had led to the troublesome behaviors, it was just as plausible that the children had gotten into trouble and had been physically punished as a result. Even if we had asked the respondents to identify time order, our ability to infer time order would have been limited by the reliability and validity of the respondents' recall. Long-term memory can be faulty, and there is always the threat to validity of the respondents "telescoping" behaviors from the past into the present.

Longitudinal design, especially a panel design, is a means of resolving the issues of temporal ordering and change of behavior. However, longitudinal research on domestic violence is limited by the low base rate of domestic violence and the need to follow subjects over a long period of time. Take for example the question about the intergenerational transmission of violence. The hypothesis of the intergenerational transmission of violence cannot be adequately tested using a cross-sectional design. Yet, there are significant limits on fielding an appropriate longitudinal study that would test the hypothesis. To begin with, the study ought to begin with children as subjects. The first measures would be aimed at assessing how much violence the children experience. The children ought to be than followed until they are adults with children of their own. Given that the estimated incidence of severe violence towards children is about 4%, and the estimate that half of abused children grow up to be abusive (Straus et al., 1980), the initial sample size to be followed might well need to be more than 10,000. The expense and complexity of such a survey would be overwhelming. A second approach might be to retrospectively assess violence experience among young adults and follow these subjects through the birth and rearing of their own children. This would limit the time needed to follow subjects. The sample size would still need to be substantial, however, and the study design would not control for the threat to validity of faulty recall.

A third approach would be to prospectively follow a population that has been defined as high risk for family violence. This approach has been used by Egeland and his colleagues (see, for example, Egeland, Breitenbucher, & Rosenberg,

1980; Egeland & Sroufe, 1981; and Egeland, Jacobvitz, & Papatola, 1987). Starting in 1975 Egeland and his research group began enrolling a sample of 267 mothers who were in their last trimester of pregnancy. The mothers were patients at the Minnesota Public Health Clinics and were considered at high risk for caretaking problems due to their low socioeconomic status, and a number of other factors, such as young age (mean 20 years). Sixty-two percent of the mothers were unwed at the time of the birth and 86% of the pregnancies were unplanned. Many of the mothers encountered a high number of life stress events and lacked support from a husband/boyfriend, family, or friends. Within the high risk group there were 44 cases of child maltreatment, which included 24 cases of physical abuse, 24 cases of neglect, and 19 cases of hostile/rejecting behavior. Egeland and his group have followed these mothers for over 12 years. Among the mothers who had been abused as children, 70% have mistreated their own children. Egeland and his colleagues have not only examined the pattern of continuity of abuse across generations, but also have looked at discontinuity— instances where abused mothers did not maltreat their children. Although one can generalize from Egeland's sample only with considerable caution, his study is an example of a cost-efficient use of a longitudinal design to study a fundamental question in the field of family violence.

Weis (1989) notes that the few prospective longitudinal studies of family violence that have been conducted, have focused almost exclusively on examining the notion of the cycle or intergenerational transmission of violence or the likelihood of early abuse leading to later juvenile delinquency. The majority of these studies begin by defining child abuse as those cases that have been officially reported to public or private agencies. Many of these studies fail to employ any kind of control or comparison group, thus threatening the external validity of the study. If a control group is used, the typical one is a group made up of children from similar social backgrounds but who have not been reported for abuse. These longitudinal studies are typically flawed from the outset. The investigators who choose to operationalize child abuse as those cases reported to official agencies fail to obtain an adequate baseline measure of violence and/or maltreatment experienced by the child. The design presumes that the control children have not been abused, yet virtually all students of family violence recognize that abuse is underreported to official agencies. Thus, the study design inevitably includes children in the control group who may well have been abused, but who have not been officially recognized. If the number of abused-but-not-reported children is substantial (even a small number would be substantial if the overall sample size is low), the investigation runs the serious risk of falsely accepting the null hypothesis.

Other methodological issues threaten the validity of prospective longitudinal studies. Investigators frequently fail to select measures with adequate reliability. Thus, what changes they report may well be due to measurement error. The typical prospective study collects data at but two points in time. As a result, the investigator is often unable to rule out regression artifacts as a threat to the validity of the survey. A number of prospective studies collect data from samples that are too small to allow the investigator to statistically rule out major plausible rival explanations to the findings reported.

In the end, the cost and effort of conducting prospective longitudinal research on an issue with a base rate as low as family violence poses a major obstacle to fielding such research. The issues of funding and management are so overwhelming that many investigators conclude that cross-sectional research, even with its inherent limitations, produces a far greater yield for the time and energy expended than would longitudinal research.

A Note On Experimental Designs

This section on research design has not mentioned experimental design. Most of the experimental research on domestic violence has focused on the relationship between child abuse and aggressive behavior of the children (from Weis, 1989; see Bousha & Twentyman, 1984; Herrenkohl, Herronkohl, Toedler, & Yanushefski, 1984; Kinard, 1980). Given the sensitive and dangerous nature of family violence, many forms of experimental research would be considered unethical. This would include designs where abuse was the dependent variable as well as evaluation studies where victims and/or offenders would be randomly assigned to treatments. One exception is the Minneapolis Police Experiment (Sherman & Berk, 1984). The design of this study involved the random assignment of an intervention strategy to cases of misdemeanor domestic violence. Police officers in Minneapolis were randomly assigned one of three strategies prior to arriving at the scene of the violence. The strategies included arrest, offering advice or mediation, or ordering the offender from the home. The investigators report that arrest produced significantly less violence than the other two forms of intervention.

On the surface, the Minneapolis Police Experiment is an impressive example of a field experiment. Beneath the surface are some troubling threats to validity. The investigators admit they had no way of monitoring whether the officers actually followed the randomly assigned instructions. In addition, a majority of the cases in the study were contributed by a handful of police officers. Finally, a significant amount of missing data forced the investigators to statistically substitute for missing data, thus raising the possibility that the significant findings were a statistical artifact. The Minneapolis Police Experiment is now being replicated in a number of cities. Methodological problems notwithstanding, it remains an example of a creative and ingenious approach to the ethical and practical constraints of applying experimental methods to the study of domestic violence. We do not, however, expect to see a widespread application of the method. Randomly assigning police intervention is possible; but many researchers, and even more policy makers and social service personnel, resist designs that would withhold services from a control group, including the establishment of "wait list controls" for overcrowded services such as battered wife shelters.

CONCLUSIONS: TOWARDS IMPROVED RESEARCH ON FAMILY VIOLENCE

The Benefits of the Survey Design

The explosion of interest in the topic of domestic violence has been accompanied by tremendous growth in research and publication on the various aspects of violence in the home. Unfortunately, although the amount of data collected in the past 25 years is impressive—at least compared to the dearth of data collected prior to 1962—the knowledge base is still far from solid. By and large, the reason for the lack of a well-developed knowledge base is the rather brief period of time the topic of family violence has been studied. In addition, the knowledge base has been built through exploratory and descriptive research. Such research can is useful for generating hypotheses, but cannot test those hypotheses. Furthermore, even well designed exploratory and descriptive research is subject to innumerable plausible rival explanations for the findings.

Although few researchers, clinicians, or policy makers held out much hope that useful data on family violence could be collected using survey research techniques, the skepticism has turned out to be unwarranted. Survey research on violence between family members has yielded estimates of the incidence and prevalence of violence in the home not confounded by the biases of official reports. Furthermore, survey data that examines associations between individual and social factors and family violence is also not confounded by the biases inherent in using clinical or official report data. The large samples used in survey research have provided opportunities to test hypotheses about various aspects of violence in the home. When the surveys employ representative samples, investigators have been able to break the confines of small, limited samples, and generalize their results to larger populations.

An unintended benefit of survey research on family violence is that those using the survey method have been forced to rigorously develop replicable nominal and operational definitions. Whereas studies based on clinical or official report data can simply define violence and abuse as those cases in the clinical or official records, survey researchers were forced to develop reliable and valid measurement technique to tap violence between family members.

Obviously, survey research is not the panacea for the problems and constraints inherent in studying, understanding, and explaining family violence. The biases of clinical and official report data have been replaced by the biases that are part of any project which depends on self-report and recall to measure human behavior. The advantages of large sample sizes and resulting statistical power are weighed against the disadvantages of the limit on how much data can be collected using in-person or telephone data collection procedures. Although it is possible to collect contextual data on family violence using social surveys, it is much more difficult to collect these data with a survey instrument than by other means. Surveys tend to be unable to adaquately collect data from members of the lowest socioeconomic groups. Because the base rate of the severest forms of violence is so low, surveys also fail to locate adequate numbers of family members experiencing the most injurious or life threatening abuse.

Towards Improved Research on Family Violence

There is no question that if we are to improve our understanding of family violence, there are many research issues and problems that need to be overcome and solved. First and foremost, the field of family violence must continue to improve upon the definitions of abuse, violence, and the family. Until such time as the majority of investigators are employing similar definitions for the central concepts in the field, confusion and contradiction will dominate the study of family violence.

More research studies need to be based on larger and more representative samples. There is a compelling need to collect data which can be generalized to larger populations. Survey research is a means of generating a general causal model of family violence. Such a model could then be subjected to more intensive investigation using smaller samples and more intensive assessment with psychometrically sound measures.

Although the problems of fielding adequate longitudinal designs are many, there is a need to employ more of these designs. Change and time order should not exclusively be inferred from cross-sectional data. Panel and cohort studies are a necessity if knowledge of family violence is to be advanced.

Students of family violence need to attend to the major measurement issues in the study of violence and aggression. The field has been well served by the Conflict Tactics Scales, but a single scale is not a solution to measurement problems. Weis (1987) points out that there is not one validation study of family violence yet published. An experimental design which compares measures on the same sample is imperative.

The field must move beyond accepting conventional wisdoms and *post hoc* conclusions as theory. For the study of family violence to be truly advanced, programs of research must begin to test the various notions, hypotheses, and propositions which have been developed over the past 25 years.

ACKNOWLEDGMENTS

This paper is part of the Family Violence Research Program at the University of Rhode Island. The program is funded by a grant from the National Institute of

Mental Health, MH 40027. A complete list of books and articles is available upon request.

REFERENCES

American Association for Protecting Childen. (1985). *Highlights of official child neglect and abuse reporting, 1983*. Denver: American Humane Association.

American Humane Association. (1982). *National analysis of official child neglect and abuse reporting, 1980*. Denver: American Humane Association.

American Humane Association. (1983). *Highlights of official child neglect and abuse reporting, 1981*. Denver: American Humane Association.

Babbie, E. R. (1983). *The practice of social research* (2nd ed.). Belmont, CA: Wadsworth.

Bakan, D. (1971). *Slaughter of the innocents: A study of the battered child phenomenon*. Boston: Beacon Press.

Barling, J., O'Leary, K. D., Jouriles, E. N., Vivian, D., & Macewen, K. E. (1987). Factor similarity of the conflict tactics scales across samples and sites: Issues and Implications. *Journal of Family Violence, 2*, 37–54.

Bousha, D. M., & Twentyman, C. T. (1984). Mother-child interactional style in abuse, neglect, and control groups: Naturalistic observations in the home. *Journal of Abnormal Psychology, 93*, 106–114.

Bradburn, Sudman, and Associates. (1979). *Improving interview method and questionnaire design*. San Francisco: Jossey-Bass.

Burgdorf, K. (1980). *Recognition and reporting of child maltreatment*. Rockville, MD: Westat.

Cohen, S., & Sussman, A. (1975). *The incidence of child abuse in the United States*. Unpublished manuscript.

Carr, A. (1979). *Reported child maltreatment in Florida: The operation of public child protective service systems*. A Report Submitted to the Administration on Children, Youth and Families, National Center on Child Abuse and Neglect, Department of Health, Education, and Welfare. Kingston, Rhode Island. (mimeo)

Defrancis, V. (1973). *Testimony at the hearing before the subcommittee on children and youth of the committee on labor and public welfare*. United States Senate, 93rd Congress, First Session. On S.1191 Child Abuse Prevention and Treatment Act, 1973. U.S. Government Printing Office.

De Mause, L. (Ed.). (1974). *The history of childhood*. New York: Psychohistory Press.

De Mause, L. (1975). Our forbearers made childhood a nightmare. *Psychology Today, 8*, 85–87.

Dobash, R. E., & Dobash, R. (1979). *Violence against wives*. New York: Free Press.

Egeland, B., Breitenbucher, M., & Rosenberg, D. (1980). Prospective study of the significance of life stress in the etiology of child abuse. *Journal of Consulting and Clinical Psychology, 48*, 195–205.

Egeland, B., & Sroufe, L. A. (1981). Development sequelae of maltreatment in infancy. In R. Rizley & D. Cicchetti (Eds.), *New directions for child development: Developmental perspectives in child maltreatment*. San Francisco, CA: Jossey-Bass.

Egeland, B., Jadobvitz, D., & Papatola, K. (1987). Intergenerational continuity of abuse. In R. Gelles & J. Lancaster (Eds.), *Child abuse and neglect: Biosocial dimensions*. Hawthorne, NY: Aldine deGruyter.

Finkelhor, D. (1979). *Sexually victimized children*. New York: Free Press.

Finkelhor, D., & Hotaling, G. (1984). Sexual abuse in the national incidence study of child abuse and neglect: An appraisal. *Child Abuse Neglect: The International Journal, 8*, 23–33.

Fontana, V. (1973). *Somewhere a child is crying: Maltreatment-causes and prevention*. New York: Macmillan.

Galdston, R. (1965). Observations of children who have been physically abused by their parents. *American Journal of Psychiatry, 122,* 440–443.

Gelles, R. J. (1974). *The violent home: A study of physical aggression between husbands and wives.* Beverly Hills: Sage.

Gelles, R. J. (1975). The social construction of child abuse. *American Journal of Orthopsychiatry, 45,* 363–371.

Gelles, R. J. (1978). Violence towards children in the United States. *American Journal of Orthopsychiatry, 48,* 580–592.

Gelles, R. J., & Cornell, C. (Eds.). (1983). *International perspectives on family violence.* Lexington, MA: Lexington Books.

Gelles, R. J., & Straus, M. (1979). Determinants of violence in the family: Toward a theoretical integration. In W. Burr, R. Hill, F. I. Nye, & I. Reiss (Eds.), *Contemporary theories about the family* (Vol. 1). New York: Free Press.

Gelles, R. J., & Straus, M. (1988). *Intimate violence.* New York: Simon and Schuster, 1988.

Gelles, R. J., & Straus, M. (1987). Is violence towards children increasing? A comparison of 1975 and 1985 national survey rates. *Journal of Interpersonal Violence, 2,* 212–222.

Giles-Sims, J. (1983). *Wife-battering: A systems theory approach.* New York: Guilford.

Goode, W. (1971). Force and violence in the family. *Journal of Marriage and the Family, 33,* 624–636.

Groves, R., & Kahn, R. (1979). *Surveys by telephone: A national comparison with personal interviews.* New York: Academic Press.

Harris, L., & Associates. (1979). *A survey of spousal abuse against women in Kentucky.* New York: Harris & Associates.

Herrenkohl, E. C., Herrenkohl, R. C., Toedler, L. J., & Yanushefski, A. M. (1984). Parent-child interactions in abusive and non-abusive families. *Journal of the American Academy of Child Psychiatry, 23,* 641–648.

Hochstim, J. R. (1977). A critical comparison of three strategies of collecting data from households. *Journal of the American Statistical Association, 62,* 976–989.

Kempe, C. H. (1971). Pediatric implications of the battered baby syndrome. *Archives of Disease in Children, 46,* 28–37.

Kempe, C. H. et al. (1962). The battered-child syndrome. *Journal of American Medical Association, 181,* 17–24.

Kinard, E. M. (1980). Emotional development in physically abused children. *American Journal of Orthopsychiatry, 50,* 606–696.

Klecka, W. R., & Tuchefarber, A. J. (1978). Random digit dialing: A comparison to personal surveys. *Public Opinion Quarterly, 42,* 105–114.

Korbin, J. (1981). *Child abuse and neglect: Cross-cultural perspectives.* Berkeley: University of California Press.

London, J. (1978). Images of violence against women. *Victimology, 2,* 510–524.

Marcus, A. C., & Crane, L. A. (1986). Telephone surveys in public health research. *Medical Care, 24,* 97–112.

Martin, D. (1976). *Battered wives.* San Francisco: Glide.

Merton, R., & Nisbet, R. (1976). *Contemporary social problems* (4th edition). New York: Harcourt Brace Jovanovich.

Miller, B., Rollins, B., & Thomas, D. L. (1982). On methods of studying marriages and families. *Journal of Marriage and the Family, 44,* 851–873.

Nagi, S. (1975). Child abuse and neglect programs: A national overview. *Children Today, 4,* 13–17.

National Center on Child Abuse and Neglect. *Study findings: Study of national incidence and prevalence of child abuse and neglect: 1988.* Washington, DC: U.S. Department of Health and Human Services.

Newberger, E. et al. (1977). Pediatric social illness: Toward an etiologic classification. *Pediatrics*, 1977, *60*, 178–185.

Pagelow, M. (1981). *Woman-battering: Victims and their experiences*. Beverly Hills, CA: Sage.

Pelton, L. G. (1979). Interpreting family violence data. *American Journal of Orthopsychiatry, 49*, 194.

Radbill, S. (1980). A history of child abuse and infanticide, In R. Helfer & C. Kempe (Eds.). *The battered child* (3rd ed.), Chicago: University of Chicago Press.

Sherman, L. W., & Berk, R. A. (1984). Deterrent effects of arrest for domestic violence. *American Sociological Review, 49*, 633–644.

Shorter, E. (1975). *The making of the modern family*. New York: Basic Books.

Steele, B., & Pollock, C. (1968). A psychiatric study of parents who abuse infants and small children, In R. Helfer & C. Kempe (Eds.), *The battered child*. Chicago: University of Chicago Press.

Steinmetz, S. (1971). Occupation and physical punishment: A response to Straus. *Journal of Marriage and the Family, 33*, 664–666.

Steinmetz, S. (1977). *The cycle of violence: Assertive, aggressive, and abusive family interaction*. New York: Praeger.

Straus, M. (1974). Leveling, civility, and violence in the family. *Journal of Marriage and the Family, 36*, 13–29. (Plus addendum in August, 1974 issue)

Straus, M. (1979). Measuring intrafamily conflict and violence: The conflict tactics (CT) scales. *Journal of Marriage and the Family, 41*, 75–88.

Straus, M., & Gelles, R. (1986). Societal change and family violence from 1975 to 1985 as revealed by two national surveys. *Journal of Marriage and the Family, 48*, 465–479.

Straus, M., Gelles, R., & Steinmetz, S. (1980). *Behind closed doors: Violence in the American family*. New York: Doubleday/Anchor.

Taylor, L., & Newberger, E. H. (1979). Child abuse in the International Year of the Child. *New England Journal of Medicine, 301*, 1205–1212.

Turbett, J. P., & O'Toole, R. (1980). *Physician's Recognition of Child Abuse*. Paper presented at Annual Meetings of the American Sociological Association, New York.

U.S. Department of Justice. (1980). *Intimate victims: A study of violence among friends and relatives*. Washington, DC: U.S. Government Printing Office.

U.S. Department of Justice. (1984). *Family violence*. Washington, DC: Bureau of Justice Statistics.

U.S. Senate. (1973). *Hearing before the subcommittee on children and youth of the Committee on Labor and Public Welfare*. United States Senate, 93rd Congress, First Session on S.1191 Child Abuse Prevention Act. Washington, DC: U.S. Government Printing Office.

Walker, L. (1979). *The battered woman*. New York: Harper and Row.

Weis, J. G. (1989). Issues in family violence research methodology and design. In M. Tonry & L. Ohlin (Eds.), *Crime and justice: An annual review of research*. Chicago: University of Chicago Press.

4 How Marriages Change

John M. Gottman
University of Washington

In this chapter I present a theory about the mechanisms through which marital relationships change over time. The theory explains both the improvement and the deterioration of marriages. I share my own thinking here, for there is no direct guide for the mostly biological and empirical grounds that I employ. My supposition has some implications for the study of depression and aggression through the relationship of negative affect blends and one of the major constructs of the theory, Diffuse Physiological Arousal (DPA). The link here can be made theoretically through the Henry and Stephens (1977) model.

OUTLINE OF THE THEORY

Goals

The theory I have constructed is designed to have cross-cultural universality and to pertain to the wide variety of marriages that are found in various cultures. To accomplish such a feat, it is necessary to tap into those processes that are basic to marriage among our species. For this purpose, I have selected as the domains of variables for investigation the interface between social processes (particularly those that have to do with emotion and the regulation of emotion) and physiological processes (particularly those that have to do with the expenditure or storage of energy in the body and the readiness of the body for emergencies). The selection of these domains was really motivated by past research I and others have done on marital interaction in which we have found that emotional processes are able to account for a good portion of the variance in marital satisfaction.

The Criteria. I am predicting four kinds of criterion variables: (1) changes in marital satisfaction over time; (2) changes in marital interaction patterns over time; (3) changes in health and other measures of immunological functioning; and (4) whether or not a couple will divorce.

The Predictor Variables. There are several domains of variables that are active in the theoretical model that I propose in this chapter. The first domain is marital interaction and the couple's perception of the interaction. These are clearly not always the same thing or we could avoid observing couples. In this area of *marital interaction and the couple's perceptions of the interaction,* first, we (Krokoff, Gottman, & Roy, 1988) have recently found it important to distinguish couples in terms of whether their marital contract is designed to engage in or to avoid conflict. Conflict avoiding couples do not have an interactive view of marriage, nor do they spend much time in conversation. These kinds of couples are not difficult to incorporate into the theory, but it is useful to treat them separately. Next, I consider the nature of conflict itself. I discuss what we have found to be crucial in previous work with couples, particularly clinical work, namely, whether the conflict occurs or does not occur within the context of unresolved "hidden agendas," which have to do with whether or not the spouses feel loved and respected by their partners. In this discussion I review our (Gottman & Krokoff, 1989) recent finding that different interaction patterns predict the longitudinal improvement of a marriage than predict concurrent variation in marital satisfaction. In particular, we have found that a specific interaction pattern, which I will call "Pattern-X" is predictive of longitudinal deterioration in a marriage, but that anger and disagreement, by itself, is longitudinally functional for a marriage.

In the domain of *physiology,* I discuss the concept of Diffuse Physiological Arousal (DPA), which we believe has implications for understanding why certain conflictual marital interactions escalate negatively while others do not; the concept of DPA is also useful in predicting the longitudinal course of the relationship. In this discussion a brief excursion into physiology is necessary for theoretical purposes.

In the interface between physiology and interaction/perception, there are some additional variables that make sense as intervening variables in creating theoretical linkages, and these are *perceived threat* and *loneliness.*

DATA BASES

I draw primarily from two longitudinal studies. The first began in 1980 in collaboration with Robert Levenson and the second began in 1981 in collaboration with Lowell Krokoff. The two studies were extensions of my previous work. The study with Krokoff extended previous work whose goal was to describe how satisfied and dissatisfied marriages differed in interaction patterns and the couple's perception of the interaction. This early work was summarized in Gottman 1979).

Blue Collar marriages.   The study I conducted with Lowell Krokoff was an extension of the work reported in Gottman (1979) in several ways. Previous research (Komarovsky, 1962; Rubin, 1976) painted a picture of the blue collar marriage as distressed, noncompanionate, and not *able* (presumably because of less education than white collar couples) to discuss events in a psychological fashion and to problem solve marital disagreements. In fact, Rubin's book is titled "Worlds of Pain" to reflect this conclusion. Krokoff and I were troubled by this conclusion for several reasons. First, we thought that the conclusion was unwarranted because the research on blue-collar couples had been done so poorly. Neither study employed statistical analyses; neither study paid attention to sampling issues; neither study assessed marital satisfaction in an acceptable way. Also, the interview techniques, which formed the basis of the data, often seemed biased. For example, Rubin always interviewed the husband after she interviewed the wife; then Rubin presented the wife's complaints to the husband for his response. The reverse procedure was never employed. Clearly this picture of the blue-collar marriage was in need of challenge. This was especially true because sociological researchers appeared to accept these and other more objectionable pejoratives as true of working class couples. In fact, researchers were inclined to dismiss more careful observational data on marital interaction in favor of this methodologically inadequate work by Komarovsky and Rubin. Finally, we objected to the research conclusions because we thought they were untrue; they certainly did not fit our experience with working class marriages.

Krokoff and I collected a representative sample of couples from the Champaign-Urbana Illinois community, filling the cells of a 2×2 factorial design; one factor of the design was social class (blue or white collar) and the other factor of the design was marital satisfaction (happily or unhappily married). Also in this study we began expanding our study of the couple's perception of their marriage, investigating the couple's philosophy and expectations of marriage with some new questionnaires and with a new oral history interview. Our interest in studying the couple's philosophy of marriage came from an important book in the marriage field by Raush, Barry, Hertel, and Swain (1974). In many ways we saw this book as Raush et al.'s struggle with the conflict-avoiding couple; they seemed to find that the conflict-avoiding dimension was orthogonal to marital satisfaction. This was striking because almost all the research on couples and families began by investigating dimensions related to the resolution of conflict. Our own research backs up their speculations that the two dimensions are orthogonal.

The Social Psychophysiology of Marriage.   The second extension of earlier work has involved the application of social psychophysiology to the study of emotion in marriages. Robert Levenson and I collected physiological data from couples as they interacted and as they individually watched their videotape and provided a continuous self-report recall rating of the positivity of their own feelings. The self-report and physiological data were synchronized to the video time code. This study was designed to investigate the role of emotional expression and regulation in marital interaction by employing data from all the major measurement domains available to us at this time, observational, self-report, and physiological.

THE MAJOR CRITERION VARIABLE: MARITAL SATISFACTION

In both studies we obtained 3-year followup data. The criterion variable is marital satisfaction and its change over time, although I also talk about the couple's health in this chapter as an additional criterion variable that we think we can predict. Marital satisfaction is a reasonable criterion from a scientific standpoint. Its measurement has a nearly 50 year history and it has proven itself psychometrically. Poor measures and ineffective items have been eliminated in a series of longitudinal and cross-sectional studies (for a review see Burgess, Locke, & Thomas, 1971). In the 1950s Burgess recommended that most marital researchers were measuring the same construct because their questionnaires correlated in the high 80s and low 90s. This has remained true today. For example, the Spanier (1976) scale correlated 0.83 with the Locke and Wallace (1959) scale. In fact, if one selects a sample with sufficient range in marital happiness, it is difficult to measure anything other that marital satisfaction that involves the couple's perception of their relationship. This is also true if the items involve an assessment of the spouse's personality. The robustness and domain-sampling reliability of marital satisfaction measures is probably due to two halo effects. First, whatever one asks that *could* be wrong with the marriage or partner will tend to be endorsed by the unhappily married couple. Second, there is an analogous, but not so powerful, positive halo in happily married couples. Furthermore, in attributional research with marriages (Jacobson, McDonald, Follette, & Berley, 1985), these halo effects can be elaborated further by adding two facts. Unhappily married couples attribute positive marital events to temporary situational factors and negative marital events to lasting traits of their spouses; happily married couples do the reverse, namely, they attribute positive events to lasting traits and negative events to temporary situational factors. To summarize, in general, marital satisfaction tends to be unidimensional with high internal consistency reliability, test-retest reliability, construct validity, and moderate levels of predictive validity. It has also been robust to secular trends and to other biasing factors such as traditionality.

Although, not well understood from a psychological perspective, marital satisfaction is one of the only variables in the family literature that has proven itself worthy from a psychometric standpoint, and hence it is reasonable as a criterion variable. Because of the ubiquity of some types of studies, it is important to note that marital satisfaction cannot be understood, nor can its variability be explained with variables derived from similar measurement operations. Common method variance is so powerful in this type of assessment that the easy path to understanding (one large questionnaire or survey study) must be considered invalid from a scientific standpoint. This fact has yet to be reflected in most research in marriage.

I now focus primarily on the results that have emerged from the program of research that I have conducted with Robert Levenson.

PARADIGM

In the first study Levenson and I conducted in 1980, 30 couples were recruited by advertisements and paid a $30 subject fee for participating. The couples interacted in two discussions. First, they talked about the events of their day for 15 minutes, after a 5-minute preconversation period. Couples had been separated for at least 8 hours prior to this conversation. Second, after an interview identifying the major problem issue in their marriage, they tried to resolve the issue for 15 minutes, once again after a 5-minute preconversation period. I focus here on the conflict discussion. Each spouse returned to the laboratory on a separate occasion to view the videotape of these interactions and to provide a continuous self-rating of his or her own affect on a rating dial that utilized a "positive-neutral-negative" scale. During both sessions we measured four physiological variables: heart rate, pulse transit time to the finger, skin conductance, and general somatic activity. All physiological, self-report, and video data were synchronized to the same time base (for full details on these procedures, see Levenson & Gottman, 1983).

Three years later 21 of the 30 couples were recontacted and marital satisfaction data were again obtained for 19 of the 21. Parenthetically, since then we have improved our followup procedures, and in 1984 were able to engage the participation of 89% of the couples who participated in the Gottman-Krokoff study.

Selected Findings with this Paradigm

In this section I describe selected results that we have obtained from this study. A replication and extension of this study is currently in progress. We have collected 4-year followup data from a new sample of 79 couples we initially studied in 1983.

1. *Validity of the self-report of affect procedures.* To assess the validity of this self-report of affect procedure, we devised five tests. The first three were: (a) the measure should be able to discriminate between high conflict and low conflict interactions; (b) the measure should be able to discriminate between satisfied and dissatisfied couples, and (c) spouses' ratings of the same interaction should show evidence of statistical coherence. (d) The fourth test required agreement between the self-reports of affect and the ratings of objective coders (we used our Specific Affect Coding System, called SPAFF, to code all of the videotapes in terms of specific affects and then collapsed these ratings into positive and negative affect codes). (e) The fifth and final test was designed to assess the power of the video recall procedure itself. We reasoned that if subjects experienced the same sequence of emotions when viewing the videotapes as they had experienced during the actual interaction, then we should see indication of similar patterns of ANS activity in the video recall session as had occurred in the interaction session.

The self-report of affect procedure passed all five of these tests (see Gottman & Levenson, 1985, for a full reporting of these results). We think that one reason it passed the first four tests, was because it passed the fifth test, which we have termed "physiological reliving." We assessed this by computing the coherence between the interaction session and the video recall session for each of the 30 couples for each of the four physiological measures (e.g., interaction session heart rate vs. recall session heart rate). We found that the spouses could be said to be reliving the original physiological experience as they watched and rated the videotapes. Not only were these two sets of responses strongly correlated, but the time series were usually in-phase. This means that when a spouse watched the tape of the interaction, sweating, changes in cardiovascular functioning, and changes in movement all occurred at the same times as they had occurred when he or she was in the actual interaction.

2.*The followup study.* We computed a simple change score that indicated the amount and direction of change in marital satisfaction that had occurred between 1980 and 1983. Using partial correlations (to control for initial levels of marital satisfaction), we determined which of the affective and physiological variables measured in 1980 were predictive of changes in marital satisfaction that had occurred during the ensuing 3 years. A major finding that emerged (see Levenson & Gottman, 1985, for a complete report of these findings) was that physiological arousal (in all measures) was highly predictive of declines in levels of marital satisfaction. We reported that physiological arousal during conflict interaction predicted deterioration in marital satisfaction over three years, controlling the initial level of marital satisfaction. The best three predictors were the husband's heart rate ($r = 0.92$, HIBI, measured as the interval between R-waves of the electrocardiogram), the husband's skin conductance level ($r = -0.48$; HSCL), and the wife's skin conductance level ($r = -0.76$; WSCL). The three predictors are independent, except for the husband's and the wife's SCL ($r =$

0.41, $p < 0.05$). The sizes of these correlations were surprisingly high; for example, the correlation between the husband's heart rate during the conflict discussion and decline in marital satisfaction was .92. A multiple regression showed that the physiological variables were not collinear, and, in fact, the regression accounted almost 90% of the variance in the change in marital satisfaction over three years.

3. *Rating Dial as a Predictor.*   Negative affect reciprocity (computed from the rating dial measure) and the wife's self-report of affect data also predicted changes in marital satisfaction over 3 years.

4. *Interpreting the Rating Dial Data.*   Obviously, we have learned to have a great deal of respect for the rating dial data collected in conjunction with our video recall procedure. However, we did not actually understand the rating dial measure. We can understand the meaning of the self-report of affect data by employing the SPAFF codes. Gottman and Levenson (1985) had reported that the self-report of affect data: (a) discriminated high-conflict from low-conflict interaction; (b) correlated significantly with concurrent marital satisfaction; (c) were coherent between husband and wife; (d) were significantly related to observer's coding of the positivity of the couples' affect (using SPAFF codes summed into positive, negative, and neutral affect categories). They also suggested that during the self-report session couples were physiologically reliving the marital interaction. They suggested that couples sweat more, moved more, their hearts beat faster, and their blood flowed faster at the same time points while viewing the tape as in the original interaction.

To gain insight into the potential the meaning of the rating dial, for this chapter I performed multiple regression analyses to predict the mean ratings from unconditional probabilities of specific affects. In predicting the husband's mean rating, his anger was stepped in first ($R = 0.61$, $F = 16.45$, $p < .001$), with no huge gain in prediction by other affects (SPAFF coding). In predicting the wife's mean rating, which is the salient longitudinal predictor, once again the husband's anger was stepped in first. ($R = 0.71$, $F = 28.22$, $p < 0.001$), with no major gain from stepping in the other variables. Based on these results and those reported by Gottman and Levenson (1985), I propose that the rating dial data should be renamed "subjective upset" and that it be viewed as couples' monitoring the anger-related "hotness" of the interaction, particularly tapping into the husband's anger.

Flowchart of the Theory

Figure 4.1 is a flowchart of the theory of this chapter. The remainder of the chapter is an explanation of this flowchart.

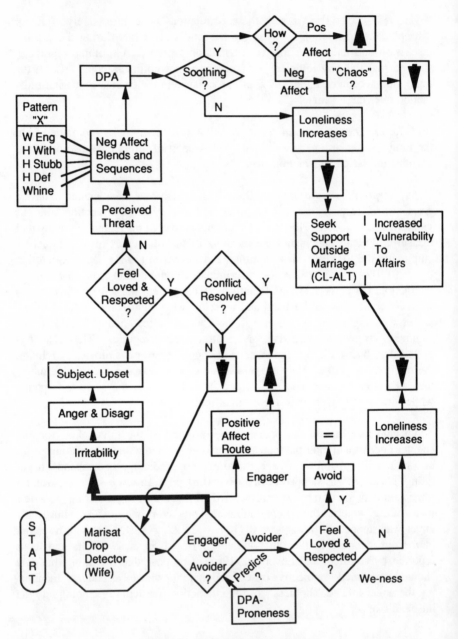

FIG. 4.1.   Flowchart of the theory.

Entry. The entry point for the flowchart is not arbitrarily chosen. As I suggest in the section entitled "Marital interaction patterns that predict change," the wife in our culture is usually the one who monitors intimacy and gets both people to confront issues and disagreements.

First Choice Point: Engager or Avoider? The first question is whether the couple's implicit marital contract is designed to avoid conflict. Conflict avoiders follow a different path because their marriage is set up to avoid conflict entirely. The risks are:

1. that it is possible for people in this kind of marriage to become increasingly lonely, which could make them vulnerable to extramarital affairs, and,

2. it is not always possible to avoid dealing with stresses and problems together, and, if this becomes necessary (either through normative life events such as the death of a parent or nonnormative events such as a chronically ill child) the couple will not have developed the necessary conflict-resolution skills to deal with the problem.

The Positive Affect Route. Conflict-engaging couples often deal with drops in marital satisfaction through the positive affect route. This means that they will cope with drops in marital satisfaction by reinstating those things that they enjoy doing together and those things that bring them closer. Regarding this pathway through the theory we have the least amount of data. We suspect that it is important, but it has not been adequately studied. By and large the data in the field of marital interaction have been collected during conflictual interaction; in general, we have found that when we do study more positive interaction, the correlation between our interaction variables and marital satisfaction is less than when we study conflict. Nonetheless, the positive affect pathway is in the theory.

The Conflict Pathway. As irritability builds and anger and disagreement increase, *subjective upset* increases. If people feel loved and respected and the conflict is resolved, they will feel closer to one another and marital satisfaction will improve. Unresolved conflict will continue to create irritability, anger, and disagreement. If there are "hidden agenda" issues of love or respect, the conflict interactions will engender perceived threat and negative affect blends; later, I refer to the Henry and Stephens model that relates blends of two specific negative affects, *depression* and *aggression* (*or anger/hostility*) to specific kinds of physiological activations involving the adrenal glands; these blends also are related to what I am calling "Interaction Pattern X." This pattern of interaction predicted the deterioration of marital satisfaction over time.

The Physiological Pathway. These negative affect blends and sequences are excellent candidates for inducing Diffuse Physiological Arousal, a construct that is central in the theory for the prediction of change in the marital relationship. In the following two sections I discuss this next major construct of the proposed theory. To do this, I need to review a bit of the psychophysiology of the autonomic nervous system.

REVIEW OF BASIC PHYSIOLOGY NECESSARY
FOR THE THEORY

Overview of the Autonomic Measures

Our physiological measures were selected as a compromise of two considerations: (1) we wanted to sample from a reasonably wide range of physiological responses, and (2) we wanted to minimally encumber our subjects. We measured heart rate as the interval between R-waves of the electrocardiogram (EKG), pulse transit time to the middle finger of the nondominant hand as the time between the R-spike and the arrival of blood volume in the finger as measured by the finger photoplethysmograph (using a photoplethysmograph that passes a cool red light through the finger), skin conductance using a constant voltage method from the middle phalanges of the first and third finger of the nondominant hand, and gross motor movement using a highly sensitive jiggleometer in the base of the subject's chair that measures movement in all three planes. These measures were amplified with an 8-channel Lafayette polygraph, synchronized to the video time code, and averaged over 10 second intervals with a DEC LSI 11/23 laboratory microcomputer.

Anatomy.   These peripheral physiological measures were selected to provide various information about the autonomic nervous system (ANS), which has two anatomically and functionally distinct subsystems, the parasympathetic branch (PNS) and the sympathetic branch (SNS). Both subsystems are characterized by a two-neuron linkage from the brain or spinal cord. The first preganglionic neuron is joined to a second neuron that innervates the target organ. In the SNS the neural fibers leave the spinal cord from the chest and saddle regions (thoracolumbar) and in the PNS the fibers leave the spinal cord from the brain stem and tail regions (craniosacral). In the SNS the two-neuron chain is short preganglioic and long postganglionic, whereas in the PNS the anatomy is reversed—long fibers from the spinal cord to the vicinity of the target organ, and then short fibers into the target organ. In the SNS the short preganglionic fibers go from the spinal cord to a chain (called the sympathetic ganglia) that runs alongside the spinal cord. One implication of these different anatomical features is that there is lots of potential for the mixing of sympathetic ganglia and possibly more "cross talk," which implies that the SNS is capable of diffuse action. For the PNS, on the other hand, the anatomy appears to be designed for little mixing and thus fairly specific action.

Although there are no main SNS nerves due to the amount of SNS mixing, there are two main nerves of the PNS and the organs it serves. The first is the *vagus nerve* (Xth cranial nerve), which serves the heart, bronchioles of the lung, stomach, small intestine, liver, pancreas, and the large intestine. The second is the pelvic (Sacral nerves 2, 3, and 4), which serves the colon, kidney, bladder, the sex organs, and the exterior genitalia. PNS fibers are also found in the following cranial nerves: oculomotor (III), facial (VII), and glossopharyngeal IX).

Chemistry.   The stimulation chemistry of the two branches of the ANS are also different. Preganglionic fibers in both systems stimulate postganglionic targets using *acetylcholine* (ACh) released at the synapse. However, in the SNS the primary neurotransmitter from postganglionic fibers to target organs is *norepinephrine* (NE), whereas in the PNS it is *acetylcholine.* Two exceptions are: (1) the SNS innervation of the adrenal medulla, which is stimulated by SNS *pre*ganglionic fibers and hence ACh and, (2) the sweat glands, which are stimulated by SNS postganglionic fibers, but the neurotransmitter is ACh. Hence, sweat gland activity, which in the emotionally responsive *eccrine* glands is still SNS innervated has a different stimulation chemistry that, for example, SNS innervation of the heart.

Function.   The two branches of the ANS usually act in reciprocal and contrasting fashion throughout the body. However, there are a few well-established gross functional differences that can be described, albeit with some qualifications:

1. The SNS is a fight/flight system and it acts in an energy-expending or *catabolic* fashion, while the PNS acts in an energy conserving, or *anabolic* fashion. For example, while the SNS is responsible for converting the carbohydrate glycogen stored in the liver to glucose for energy, the PNS is responsible for the conversion of glucose to glycogen.

2. The SNS generally acts *diffusely,* while the action of the PNS is usually *specific.*

3. The SNS has a slow onset of the order of 2 seconds, while the PNS has a more rapid onset, of the order of 0.5 seconds.

4. The action of the SNS is longer lasting than the action of the PNS because NE is not degraded as readily by body tissue, whereas ACh is. The time for recovery of some effects of the SNS (for example on left ventricle contractility, see Berne & Levy, 1981) can be long, for example of the order of 2 to 3 minutes.

5. In the cardiovascular system the main effect of the PNS is on heart rate, while the main effect of the SNS is on myocardial contractility (actually both branches affect both aspects of cardiac function; see, for example, Levy, 1983).

These general contrasts have to be qualified in some major ways. First, the effects of the two branches of the ANS are usually reciprocal, so that, for example, it is tricky to tell whether a heart rate increase resulted from less PNS activity or more SNS activity. This problem holds throughout. Second, the SNS is quite capable of *specific* functioning. For example, in the human sexual response there is a temporal orchestration of PNS and SNS responding. The excitement phases that regulate the engorgement and lubrication of sexual tissue are usually controlled by the PNS; SNS activation during these phases of the sexual response will result in sexual dysfunction. However, orgasm and ejaculation are regulated by the SNS. It is as if the SNS were the cymbalist who came in at the conductor's signal only at the crescendo and in very specific fashion. Another example concerns the functioning of the PNS and SNS during pure emotions (Ekman, Levenson, & Friesen, 1983). Nonetheless, these general and gross contrasts are useful.

Diffuse Physiological Arousal (DPA)

It is important to have a viewpoint about the nervous system so I propose one organizing variable called Diffuse Physiological Arousal. To describe this variable, consider an ordinal pattern of ANS activation, arranged from high to low:

1. *Emotion specific patterning.* I have already noted that both branches of the ANS are potentially able to function with great specificity. The form of action most important to building a theory of marriage is the specificity that results from specific patterns of emotional responding of the kind described by Ekman et al. (1983).

2. *Multiple Negative Emotions in Close Temporal Sequence, Constrained Emotions, Negative Emotion Blends.* Here activation in terms of physiology is likely to be more diffuse, so that the specific profiles Ekman et al. found are likely to produce a more general elevation of autonomic activity.

3. *SNS Global Discharge.* This kind of general activation of the SNS is the kind that Cannon (1927) described as part of the fight or flight syndrome.

4. *SNS and PNS Discharge.* There is some evidence that the PNS is activated as a negative feedback mechanism to regulate SNS the effects of discharge; for example, vagal action can reduce SNS effects on myocardial contractility (Levy, 1983).

5. *Chronic Adrenal Involvement.* When the adrenal medulla is activated by the SNS, there is a general increase of systemic levels of stress-related hormones, epinephrine, and NE. There is also evidence that the pituitary-adrenocortical axis is important as a second axis in relation to the body's response to stress (Selye, 1975).

It is reasonable to suggest that DPA is a highly unpleasant and aversive subjective bodily state. The evidence for this contention is weak, but some support comes from the work of Pennebaker (1982) on the psychology of physical symptoms.

Henry and Stephens' Model

There is some evidence beyond our own results to suggest that the DPA construct is useful. For example, Henry and Stephens (1977), suggested that the two adrenal endocrine processes associated with stress are connected to specific emotional states. They reviewed a great deal of human and animal research that supported the notion that the sympathetic-adrenomedullary system (which results in the increased secretion of the catecholamines) is related to anger, hostility, and active coping, whereas the pituitary-adrenocortical system (which results in the increased secretion of cortisol) is related to depression, passive coping, and helplessness. Taggart and Carruthers (1971) found that plaque formation in arteries was predicted by both catecholamine secretion (which increases the amount of free fatty acids in the blood) and cortisol secretion. Thus, we may have a fairly interesting emotion-based theory of myocardial infarction due to atherosclerosis, namely that it is related to *chronic* life situations that generate blends or temporal sequences of both states (anger, hostility, active coping *and* sadness, depression, and helplessness). As we will see, unfortunately distressed marriages provide a rich resource for this kind of configuration. This central notion of the activation of both axes of the Henry and Stephens model with negative affect blends and sequences, which predict DPA is part of the flowchart (Fig. 4.1).

HYPOTHESES ABOUT THE IMPLICATION OF DPA FOR SOCIAL INTERACTION

The following hypotheses show why a biologically based theory of marital functioning contributes knowledge that can not be obtained from a study of social behavior alone. I suggest that the state of DPA has powerful implications for cognitive and social behavior.

1. *DPA reduces the ability to process information.* This distinction is one that is akin to the Lacey (see Coles, Jennings, & Stern, 1984) and Sokolov (1963) stimulus intake/rejection hypothesis in psychophysiology. This hypothesis in psychophysiology has linked the intake of stimuli to cardiac deceleration and the rejection of stimuli to cardiac acceleration (see also Obrist, 1981).

2. *DPA makes overlearned behaviors and cognitions more likely than newly*

acquired behaviors and cognitions.   If this hypothesis were true, it would explain why it was difficult for marital therapy clients to have access to new learnings during times of heated controversy that resulted in DPA.

3. *DPA increases the likelihood of the same behaviors that are engaged during fight or flight, that is, withdrawal and aggression.*   This would make sense as having been the result of past emotional conditioning; it states that, in effect, emotions that result in DPA become linked to the primitive fight or flight diffuse SNS response.

4. *Sex differences exist in recovery time from DPA: Males take longer than females.*   There are clear cut implications of this hypothesis, which are spelled out in Gottman and Levenson (1988). These are that males will be more likely than females to manage the level of negative affect in marital interaction and to take steps to keep it from escalating. In particular, males are more likely than females to inhibit the expression of emotion, to appeal to rationality and compromise (see Raush et al. (1974).

What Mediates Between Subjective Upset and DPA?: Perceived Threat

In this section we discuss marital interaction patterns that predict change in marital satisfaction over time, and then attempt to integrate these findings with those processes that predict concurrent autonomic arousal. This discussion is then summarized in one hypothesis.

Marital Interaction Patterns that Predict Change.   Gottman and Krokoff (1989) reported the results of two longitudinal studies of marital interaction. The first study was coded with several coding systems, including the Marital Interaction Coding System (MICS) and the Specific Affect Coding System (SPAFF). In this section I summarize the conclusions of that paper.

The most striking result was that a different pattern of results predicted *concurrent* marital satisfaction and concurrent negative affect at home (particularly the husband's) than predicted *change* in marital satisfaction over time. In particular, positive verbal behavior and compliance expressed by wives were functional in the short run, but problematic in the long run. The opposite was true for both partners' Conflict Engagement, which predicted concurrent dissatisfaction with the marriage, but improvement over time. On the other hand, some codes were dysfunctional in both concurrent and longitudinal terms (Interaction Pattern X), namely, Defensiveness, Stubbornness, and Withdrawal from Interaction. Thus, conflict engagement of a specific kind was functional longitudinally, but conflict that was indicative of defensiveness, stubbornness and withdrawal were dysfunctional longitudinally. When specific affects were examined, the *wife's* expression of contempt and anger showed the pattern of negative correlation with concurrent marital satisfaction and positive correlation with change in her (and only her) marital satisfaction. The wife's fear predicted deterioration in her marital satisfaction, while her sadness predicted deterioration of both partners' marital satisfaction. The husband's whining predicted deterioration in his marital satisfaction.

To summarize, the major finding was that conflict engagement of a specific kind was functional for a marriage longitudinally, but conflict that is indicative of defensiveness, stubbornness, and withdrawal (particularly on the part of husbands) was dysfunctional longitudinally. It is clear that we cannot assume that the correlation of interaction patterns with *concurrent* relationship satisfaction is adequate for labeling these interaction patterns as "functional" or "dysfunctional." It is possible that couples who engage in conflict may pay a price in terms of concurrent dissatisfaction and negative affect at home, but the strife may pay off in the long run, provided that the conflict does not invoke stubbornness, defensiveness, or withdrawal from interaction.

There were also interesting spouse differences in the results. Wives who were positive and compliant fared better in terms of their husbands' concurrent negative affect at home and concurrent marital satisfaction, but the marital satisfaction of these couples deteriorated over time. On the other hand, the stubbornness and withdrawal of husbands was most harmful to the longitudinal course of marital satisfaction. In terms of specific emotions, the marital satisfaction of wives improved over time if wives expressed anger and contempt during conflict discussions, but declined if the wives expressed sadness or fear. For husbands, only whining predicted change in marital satisfaction over time, and it predicted the deterioration of both partners' marital satisfaction. Thus, we may not be able to say that the same negative affects are equally positive or negative, in a longitudinal sense, for husbands and wives.

What are we to take from these longitudinal results? Several studies suggest that wives are more likely than husbands to confront disagreements in their marriage (e.g., Burke, Weier, & Harrison, 1976; Huston & Ashmore, 1986; Wills, Weiss, & Patterson, 1974). In our data, we have generally noticed that in most conflict discussions either the wife begins by stating the issues, or the husband begins and quickly defers to his wife for elaboration. However, there is another pattern in the marital research literature. In interview and questionnaire-based research, in unhappy marriages wives are described as conflict-engaging, whereas husbands are described as withdrawn. For example, there is a consistent spouse difference in marital complaints: Unhappily married women complain about their husbands being too withdrawn, whereas unhappily married men complain about their wives being too conflict engaging (Locke, 1951; Terman et al., 1938). Komarovsky (1962) reported that blue collar husbands are self-disclosing in happy marriages but withdrawn in unhappy marriages. Rubin's (1979) interviews with married couples suggest that these unhappily married husbands may have withdrawn from intense negative affect. In research based on observational methods, these differences are mirrored. For example, when discussing disagreements, wives act in ways designed to confront the issue and enforce their feelings about it, whereas husbands rely on more conciliatory and factual explanations (Margolin & Wampold, 1982; Raush et al., 1974). When our results are added to this picture, they suggest the hypothesis that the wife, as the manager of marital disagreements, has to manage a complex dialectic.

Gottman and Krokoff suggested that this dialectic is as follows. If the wife is to introduce and elaborate disagreements in marriages, the data suggest that, for the sake of long-term improvement in marital satisfaction, she may need to do this by getting her husband to confront areas of disagreement and to openly vent disagreement and anger. This much is likely to be functional for the longitudinal course of relationship satisfaction, but only if the interaction does not also result in his whining, his stubbornness, his withdrawal from interaction, or the defensiveness of both partners. These interaction patterns of whining, stubbornness, and withdrawal in a marriage, we suggest, are more deleterious if they are characteristic of husbands. Although this hypothesis is asymmetric with respect to gender, and is likely to be controversial, it does organize a vast quantity of marital interaction data. The actual picture may be mediated by the intensity of the conflict. In fact, Gottman (1979) reported that men in satisfied marriages de-escalate negative affect in low-conflict discussions whereas women in satisfied marriages de-escalate negative affect in high-conflict discussions; both spouses relinquish the de-escalation role in unsatisfied marriages.

This hypothesis is consistent with our review of other research on marriage. Several studies suggest that wives are more likely than husbands to confront disagreements in their marriage. Wives appear to be more sensitive to the negative qualities of their interactions (e.g., Burke et al., 1976; Huston & Ashmore, 1986; Wills et al., 1974). They are more likely to express their dissatisfactions, and to do so earlier than males (Burgess & Wallin, 1953; Hagestad & Smyer, 1982; Harvey, Wells, & Alvarez, 1978). When discussing disagreements, wives act in ways designed to confront the issue and enforce their feelings about it, whereas husbands rely on more conciliatory and factual explanations (Margolin & Wampold, 1982; Raush et al., 1974). These gender (or spousal) differences appear to be augmented in unhappy marriages, where the wives escalate their negative affect and the husbands withdraw from conflict. Komarovsky (1962) reported that blue collar husbands are self-disclosing in happy marriages but withdrawn in unhappy marriages. Rubin's (1979) interviews with married couples suggest that these unhappily married husbands may have withdrawn from intense negative affect. This is consistent with a pervasive and consistent spouse difference in marital complaints: Unhappily married women complain about their husbands being too withdrawn, whereas unhappily married men complain about their wives being too conflict engaging (Locke, 1951; Terman et al., 1938).

As Gilligan (1982) noted, women tend to be socialized to take care of relationships. Elder's (1984) work on the rearing of children of the Great Depression supports the notion that girls are socialized to remain close to the family and be concerned with social relationships, whereas boys are encouraged to leave the family, be independent of it, and achieve. Raush et al. (1974) speculated that wives base their feelings of well-being more than husbands do on the quality of their marriage, and hence, have a greater need to deal with any marital shortcomings. When our results are added to this picture, they suggest the hypothesis that the wife, as the traditional manager of relationship quality in our culture, may have to manage a complex dialectic. It is functional for the relationship in the long run that she express her actual disagreements with her husband rather than being overly agreeable, but not functional for her to employ commands and negative solutions. These latter actions may be related to increased general defensiveness of both spouses, but it is particularly important if husbands become stubborn, defensive (the excuse code) or withdraw from interaction.

Marital Interaction and Autonomic Arousal

The relationship between physiological arousal and decline in marital satisfaction provides a theoretical basis for understanding the pattern of results between marital interaction and change in marital satisfaction. DPA is probably a subjectively upsetting state. Yet, it is not possible to predict DPA just from the rating dial variables. Thus, it makes sense to ask what kinds of marital interaction patterns, when coupled with subjective upset, will lead to DPA. Since DPA appears to be a construct closely related to decline in marital satisfaction, we can generate hypotheses about which behaviors lead to DPA by asking which marital interaction patterns lead to decline in marital satisfaction.

If we assume that autonomic arousal is an aversive state (Pennebaker, 1982) in which people are not very likely to be effective problem solvers and are likely to rely on fight or flight behaviors, then the dimensions of defensiveness and withdrawal are the interactive analogues of this classic fight or flight pattern first described by Cannon (1927).

Soothing and Escape Conditioning

Another phenomenon Gottman and Levenson (1986) sought to explain is the greater rigidity, predictability, and stereotypy of behavior in dissatisfied marriages as compared to satisfied marriages. In their efforts to explain this phenomenon they developed an *escape conditioning model* of marriages, which links the reduction of physiological arousal with the reinforcement of behavioral sequences. This model may be able to explain both how marriages become either more or less satisfying over time.

Escape conditioning moments during marital interaction are defined as occurring when both spouse's make the transition from high levels of DPA to low levels of DPA. We expect that the behavior patterns that accompany these escape moments will be reinforced and increase both in unconditional probability and in conditional probability (i.e., given ANS arousal). As an example of this kind of analysis, they considered one married couple. In general, they found that the percentages of each category of negative affect that occurred during the escape moments were similar to those that occurred during the rest of the interaction, *with one exception*. The wife, who was hardly ever angry or contemptuous (6.7% in the nonescape moments), was angry or contemptuous in 53% of the escape moments. For this couple, the wife's expression of anger was associated with the reduction in physiological arousal. Thus, according to the escape conditioning hypothesis, over time this couple's interactions should become increasingly more predictable; whenever the level of upset becomes great, the wife will resort to the expression of anger, and calm will be restored. However, this is a double-edged sword, because escape conditioning theory predicts that the base rate of her anger will increase. What are the consequences of this change? In the case of this couple, we can predict that they will be severe. We make this prediction by performing a sequential analysis of the marital interaction and it turns out that her anger results, almost invariably, in an increase of his anger or contempt above his baseline (unconditional) level, which leads eventually to her sadness, fear and self-deprecation. Hence, it is possible that increases in her anger could lead this particular couple back to DPA, and thus, there could be a positive feedback loop that predicts a highly negative interaction for this couple.

This may be the mechanism by which marriages change over time, and these moments may be natural change moments in marriages. The escape conditioning model can also be used as a model for how relationships could improve over time. What makes people feel better and restores calm could just as easily be an empathic, loving response as the anger response seen in the previous example. Then, according to the model, this empathic, loving response should become more likely in the couple's repertoire as the response to upset. We do not know if this is what happens in couples whose marital satisfaction increases over time, but we are investigating this possibility.

Self-soothing is perhaps also an important dimension to study as well. We are investigating specific moments called "stonewalling moments." We have become interested not only in expressed emotion during marital interaction but also in attempts at controlling emotion. We are currently exploring a pattern of emotional control that we call "stonewalling." Stonewalling is a way of dealing with being emotionally aroused or upset by inhibiting facial action, and minimizing gaze and listener backchannels (Duncan & Fiske, 1977). We believe that the inhibition of certain emotions may in itself be autonomically arousing. We also have a bit of evidence to suggest that some stonewalling moments may be accompanied by self-soothing. In a new video recall interview that we are experimenting with, we have detected moments that appear to meet the criteria for stonewalling, but in which autonomic arousal decreases. In these moments people report feeling empathetic with their spouse's feelings and saying such things as they "identify with the pain behind the anger," or that they feel love despite the negative affect being directed at them and do not take the negative affect personally. This contrasts with stonewalling moments that lead to increased autonomic arousal in which spouses report thinking such things as "this isn't fair," and "I don't have to take this," and "I'm getting out of this relationship."

Specific Emotions and ANS Arousal: Further Exploration

To continue exploring the relationship between specific affects and autonomic arousal, some additional statistical analyses were conducted for this chapter. The statistical association between autonomic arousal and change in relationship satisfaction was so strong (Levenson & Gottman, 1985) that the three autonomic arousal variables can be considered as the Time 1 psychometric equivalent of the same dimension as change in marital satisfaction over 3 years. These analyses should be considered tentative. We are currently replicating the experiment conducted in 1980 and should be able to test the generality of the hypotheses we generate here within a few years. Because the three physiological variables are relatively independent, a stringent test would be to be able to account for variation in more than one autonomic variable with the marital interaction process variables we select. Nonetheless, the analyses presented here should be viewed as tentative.

I reasoned as follows in thinking about the relation between behavior and autonomic arousal. Perhaps this dimension of autonomic arousal underlies these dimensions of the husband's defensiveness and withdrawal from interaction reported by Gottman and Krokoff (1989). Since anger predicted improvement in marital satisfaction, the wife's anger and the husbands anger should *not* predict the three autonomic arousal variables that Levenson and Gottman (1985) found would predict change in marital satisfaction. However, when we add the variables of subjective upset, whining and sadness, and those sequences related to following whining and sadness with anger, we *should* be able to predict the three indices of autonomic arousal. More detailed rationale for the selection of these interaction variables can be found in Gottman and Krokoff (1989); there is not adequate space in this chapter to repeat the discussion and analyses that formed the basis for the selection of these variables. Nonetheless, I present Table 4.1 as a summary of these analyses relating marital interaction to our selected measures of physiology that predict change in marital satisfaction. Step I of these analyses showed that, as predicted, husband anger and wife anger did not predict arousal on any of the three indices. However, for all three indices of autonomic arousal the variables of subjective upset and/or sadness, whining, and sequences with anger as a consequent code following sadness or whining significantly predicted autonomic arousal.

Hypothesis. It thus seems to be the case that what mediates between subjective upset and DPA is a variable that might be called *Perceived Threat.* The

TABLE 4.1
Prediction of Autonomic Arousal From Interaction and Subjective Upset

	Husband's Interbeat Interval (HIBI)		Husband's Skin Conductance Level (HSCL)		Wife's Skin Conductance Level (WSCL)	
	R	F	R	F	R	F
1. Anger						
Husb Anger (HAN)	.18	.97	.28	2.37	.09	.21
Wife Anger (WAN)	.29	.08	.30	1.30	.12	.18

Conclusion: Anger, by itself does not predict DPA

II. Adding Subjective Upset and specific interaction variables related
to whining and sadness and anger following whining and sadness

A. Predicting HIBI	R	F
Steps in forward regression		
1. Husband's subjective upset	.47	8.13**
2. Husband sadness → wife anger	.54	5.56**
3. Husband sadness	.58	4.45*
4. Husband whining	.59	3.37*
5. Wife sadness	.60	2.69*

B. Predicting HSCL	R	F
Steps in forward regression		
1. Wife Whining → Husb Anger	.47	7.81**
2. Wife subjective upset	.55	5.86**
3. Husband sadness → Wife Anger	.60	4.95*
4. Wife sadness → Husb Anger	.63	4.18*
5. Wife whining	.65	3.46*
6. Husband whining → Wife Anger	.65	2.85*

C. Predicting WSCL	R	F
Steps in forward regression		
1. Husb whining	.39	4.53*
2. Husb sadness	.49	3.88*
3. Wife whining → Husb Anger	.53	3.17*

*$p < .05$
**$p < .01$

behaviors that seem to mediate between subjective upset and DPA are precisely
those variables that could be considered the marital interactive analogues of fight
and flight.

What Leads to Perceived Threat?

We can now ask the question, which dimensions of marriage are related to
perceived threat? I propose that there are two dimensions of threat, one that is
intrapersonal and one that is interpersonal. The intrapersonal dimension has to do
with the security and self-confidence of each marital partner as an individual. For

each partner, no matter how secure, there will be areas of insecurity, areas in which each person, because of past social learning, will be easily threatened. The interpersonal dimension is addressed by the notion of *hidden agendas* originally introduced by Gottman, Notarius, Gonso, and Markman (1976). The "hidden agenda" is defined as a cognitive filter that listeners have that makes the listener feel unloved or unrespected. For example, if a person has a respect hidden agenda, he or she is always sensitive to put-downs and insults. It would make sense to predict that contempt communications should relate to a respect hidden agendas.

Power and Threat. Power and dominance have always been fascinating variables in the study of marital and family interaction. In general, I have concluded that these dimensions have tended to be relatively orthogonal to marital satisfaction (see Gottman, 1979; cf. Huston, 1983). I suspect that one thing that is compelling about asymmetry in power in a marriage is that some researchers have found it to be common in satisfied and fairly traditional marriages (e.g., Fitzpatrick, 1984; Komarovsky, 1962), while other researchers have found it to be common among very conflictual marriages (e.g., marriages that are abusive; e.g., Walker, 1984). What may make the difference is the affect that surrounds what might be called power or dominance interaction. Komarovsky (1962) described one happily married couple she called The Kings, who had a very clear male-dominance structure, but one in which the wife was extremely influential and respected, and her husband was quite tender and emotionally responsive to her. This contrasted with another, unhappily married couple in her book, called The Clarks, in which the dominance pattern was the same as in the Kings' marriage, but in which the wife was depressed and not respected and in which the husband was cold, distant, and contemptuous of her.

What makes the difference in these two marriages, based on Komarovsky's own anecdotal descriptions, was the nature of the emotional communication. Hence, I propose that concepts such as power and dominance can be subsumed within this theory. Sequences such as Dominant Person's Contempt → Subordinate's Fear or Dominant Person's Contempt → Subordinate's Sadness characterize a marriage in which perceived threat is very likely. Power, although it remains an interesting construct, need not (it seems to me) be added to the theory.

In this version of our theory, we have integrated a number of dimensions we have been discussing into the theory. Thus, the conflict avoider/engager dimension, the perceived threat dimension, and the hidden agendas have been incorporated into the model. We have also added a dimension that is relatively new in our research, namely *loneliness*. We think that loneliness will be an index of partners drifting apart emotionally and that it will be a lead indicator of whether or not the couple stays together. In this theory we have posited relationships between anger and subjective upset, specific interaction patterns (e.g., defensiveness, withdrawal from interaction, stubbornness and whining) and perceived threat, DPA and interaction, and soothing and escape conditioning and change in the criteria.

HOW THE THEORY WORKS

Figure 4.1 is a summary of the theory that explains how marital relationships change over time. Despite the fact that this theory is based entirely on the analysis of marital interaction in high conflict situations, the variables derived from the theory are able to account for a great deal of the variance in the change in marital satisfaction over time. However, the challenge of building a theory is not just to predict, but to understand. The theory in Fig. 4.1 provides such an explanation. It is a dynamic theory, not only of relationship deterioration, but also of relationship improvement over time.

What is difficult to draw is that low levels of DPA lead to relationship improvement over time. We have begun to examine the patterns of escape conditioning moments among couples whose relationships improve over time. It appears that they are more likely to employ behaviors such as humor and affection to soothe, instead of negative affects, which, for some reason (perhaps as limit setting events) also can soothe. It may be the case that these moments of extreme upset and diffuse autonomic arousal are opportunities for improving a relationships as well as destroying it. Also, anger and subjective upset without threat and DPA will lead to the improvement of a marital relationship over time. The path to improving a relationship over time lies in feeling safe even when handling disagreement, which I have suggested concerns feeling loved and respected.

The path to deterioration of the marriage over time lies in the opposite state. Disagreement in such a relationship entails threat. The ''marital group'' is a very special group in many ways. One that concerns the theory proposed here has to do with gender differences with respect to emotion and especially with respect to DPA. These differences were recently explicated by Gottman and Levenson (1988), and they are not reviewed here. Coser (1964) asked the question, Under what conditions is group conflict functional? His answer was that if the group could resolve the conflict by referring to shared basic beliefs, then the result of the conflict would be increased cohesion. However, if every conflict leads to a reexamination of shared beliefs, then conflict will lead to decreased cohesion. A similar process is suggested by this theory.

Expanding the Criteria

We have restricted this discussion to predicting change in marital satisfaction over time. However, inherent in the escape conditioning portion of the model is the basis for expanding the criterion to two criteria: marital interaction and health.

Marital Interaction. The hypothesis is simple. Whatever behaviors accompany the escape conditioning moments will become: (1) more likely in the couple's repertoire, and, (2) more likely in response to DPA.

Health. Another criterion variable is health. The reactivity of the ANS has been considered an important variable in the functioning of the endocrine system and from the endocrine system to the immune system (Jemmott & Locke, 1984; Korneva, Klimenko, & Shkhinek, 1985). Stress can have a deleterious effect on health. Kiecolt-Glaser et al. (1987) employed direct in vitro assessments of immune system functioning in a sample of 38 married women and 38 separated/divorced women. They found that immune system functioning was suppressed: (a) in recently divorced or separated women compared to married women; (b) in dissatisfied married women compared to satisfied married women; and (c) in recently divorced or separated women who maintained a strong attachment to the ex-partner compared to those who did not maintain a strong attachment. Recent research by Kiecolt-Glaser et al. (in press) shows that some of the basic results she found with women also generalize to men.

It is well known that social relationships are crucial factors in predicting health and illness (for a review see House, 1981). Berkman and Syme (1979), in a 9-year longitudinal study of 2229 men and 2496 women, reported that the likelihood of a person dying could be predicted by the presence or absence of four kinds of social ties: (a) marriage; (b) contact with friends; (c) church membership; and (d) formal or informal group associations.

There are a number of lines of evidence linking negative affect to health. Bereavement following loss of a loved one has been associated with diminished immune system response, increased somatic illness, and increased risk for mortality (see Van Dyke & Kaufman, 1983, for a review). Anger, hostility, and suppressed rage have been shown to be related to hypertension and coronary heart disease (see Appel, Holroyd, & Gorkin, 1983, for a review). The Type A coronary prone personality profile, which is thought to be related to heightened risk for coronary heart disease, is associated with a life style characterized by negative affects such as hostility, contempt, and anger (Dembroski, Mac-Dougall, Eliot, & Buell, 1983).

Conflict Avoiding Couples

The extension Krokoff, Gottman, and Roy (1988) have been led to make in their study of blue and white collar couples is that social class is far less important in describing marriage than the couple's philosophy of and expectations about marriage. We propose the hypothesis that the major distinction to make is a conflict-avoiding versus a conflict-engaging distinction. Although still untested, we believe that the conflict avoiding couple is also a couple who:

1. do not expect each other to be companions or best friends;

2. do not tend to talk to each other a lot, for example, about the events of their day;

3. do not see each other as resources for getting over blue moods (a dimension first identified by Komarovsky, 1962);

4. engage in very little sharing of roles, but instead have strong sex-role stereotyped definitions of marital roles;

5. endorse items that state that it is better to work out personal problems on your own instead of talking them over with people.

We have found that when we have these couples engage in conflict resolution tasks in the laboratory or at home, their interaction is hard to understand; for example, it tends to be highly negative affectively (particularly the wife's behavior), independent of marital satisfaction.

How would the theory proposed apply to these couples? We do not know at the moment, but it would seem to apply well. I propose that it may be the case that *these couples have selected an interactional style that is consistent with an exceptional vulnerability to experience DPA, even in the face of milder kinds of disagreements than is currently reflected by our data.* Whether this greater permeability to states of DPA is conditioned or biologically based, or both, is unclear. I tend to think it is biologically based, although its roots may have led to cultural inventions that amplify biological processes.

This speculation implies that for these couples the theory would have to be altered to include additional links from behavior and subjective upset to perceived threat. Anger and disagreement itself might be adequate to trigger perceived threat for the conflict avoiding couple. Perhaps this is the origin of their philosophical orientation toward disagreements, to "agree to disagree," that is, to recognize that they are not in agreement on an issue but to agree never to bring it up for discussion.

In longitudinal terms, according to the theory, these couples are not at risk for deterioration on the criteria if their environment remains stable, particularly if they remain successful at avoiding conflict. However, we may make the prediction that these marriages are somewhat brittle, should their lives change either through normative or nonnormative events. They have not developed social interactive patterns that might buffer them from problems that are difficult to solve alone. These may be the marriages that appear to suddenly break up and to outsiders seem to make a transition from happy to divorced with no intermediate state of conflict or distress. We have seen this pattern on occasion in our data.

How to Expand a Theory: Aesthetics

There are at least two approaches one can take to the construction of a theory. It is possible to attempt to construct the most encompassing theory one can think of by making the measurement domain sufficiently rich. To some extent one always pursues this course in designing a study. However, within the context of programmatic research, another approach is possible, and that is the one I prefer from an aesthetic sense. This approach is to expand the theory only when forced to by the data. To some degree this is the well known criterion of parsimony. However, one person's parsimony is another's clutter, so building a theory is a matter of taste. The issue of how to build a theory is not unlike the issue of how to best build a candy store. Successful candy store owners will often tell you that you should be forced to expand by business itself. Don't start big and then try to cut the inventory.

My goal is to build a certain kind of theory, one that will hold as fairly robust with respect to cultural and secular variation. In other words, the appeal to the interface between emotional and biological processes is not accidental. I believe that there are laws of close relationships in our species; we are fundamentally social animals, as are bees, although considerably more complex. Nonetheless, the goal of this new theory is to discover these laws.

The notable gap in this work, in my view, is that it emerges only from the study of conflict. That is fine, because one of the phenomena in this family field that has held up to replication might be called the *Primacy of Negative over Positive Affect*. Variables related to negative affect are the ones that do the work for us in predicting and understanding variation. However, I believe that we will be led to the more positive aspects of family life through an understanding of the limitations of our current variables.

We do not understand conflict very well. It clearly occurs as a common phenomenon of close relationships, and it undoubtedly has many functions. In a marriage the negotiation of disagreement may preserve intimacy, assuming it is handled well. In one of Sam Vuchinich's tapes (personal communication, 1984) I was struck by the fact that we were seeing a slice of a father's issue with what he sees as his daughter's irresponsibility. He started the fight at dinner. It was not resolved at dinner. Perhaps this argument is enormously prosocial in a long-term developmental sense. Perhaps when this daughter is out on her own she will recall some of her father's words and think that the Old Man wasn't so dumb after all. The longitudinal time course of the resolution of this issue may be of the order of decades. Clearly our brief glimpses of family life are but a beginning. Hopefully the candy story will grow, but it should be forced to grow by the business itself.

ACKNOWLEDGMENT

This research was supported by NIMH Research Career Development Award K00257 and by PHS Grant MH29910.

REFERENCES

Appel, M. A., Holroyd, K. A., & Gorkin, L. (1983). Anger and the etiology and progression of physical illness. In L. Temoshok, C. van Dyke, & L. S. Zegans (Eds.), *Emotions in health and illness: Theoretical and research foundations.* New York: Grune and Stratton.

Berkman, L. F., & Syme, S. L. (1979). Social networks, host resistance, and mortality: A nine-year follow-up study of Alameda County residents. *American Journal of Epidemiology, 109,* 186–204.

Berne, R. M., & Levy, M. N. (1981). *Cardiovascular physiology.* St. Louis: C. V. Mosby.

Burgess, E. W., Locke, H. J., & Thomas, M. M. (1971). *The family.* New York: Van Nostrand Reinhold.

Burgess, E., & Wallin, P. (1953). *Engagement and marriage.* Philadelphia: Lippincott.

Burke, R. J., Weier, T., & Harrison, D. (1976). Disclosure of problems and tensions experienced by marital problems. *Psychological Reports, 38,* 531–542.

Cannon, W. B. (1927). The James-Lange theory of emotion: A critical examination and an alternative theory. *American Journal of Psychology, 39,* 106–124.

Coles, M. G. H., Jennings, J. R., & Stern, J. A. (Eds.). (1984). *Psychophysiological perspectives: Festschrift for Beatrice and John Lacey.* New York: Van Nostrand Reinhold.

Coser, L. A. (1964). *The functions of social conflict.* Glencoe, IL: Free Press.

Dembroski, T. M., MacDougall, J. M., Eliot, R. S., & Buell, J. C. (1983). Stress, emotions, behavior, and cardiovascular disease. In L. Temoshok, C. Van Dyke, and L. S. Zegans (Eds.) *Emotions in health and illness: Theoretical and Research Foundations.* New York: Grune and Stratton.

Duncan, S. D., Jr., & Fiske, D. W. (1977). *Face-to-face interaction: Research, methods and theory.* Hillsdale, NJ: Lawrence Erlbaum Associates.

Ekman, P., Levenson, R. W., & Friesen, W. V. (1983). Autonomic nervous system activity distinguishes among emotions. *Science,* ^S221^S, 1208–1210.

Elder, G. H., Jr. (1984). *Children of the great depression.* Illinois: University of Chicago Press.

Fitzpatrick, M. A. (1984). A typological approach to marital interaction: Recent theory and research. *Advances in Experimental Social Psychology, 18,* 1–47.

Gilligan, C. (1982). *In a different voice.* Cambridge, MA.: Harvard University Press.

Gottman, J. M. (1979). *Marital interaction: Experimental investigations.* New York: Academic Press.

Gottman, J. M., & Krokoff, L. J. (in press). Marital interaction and satisfaction: A longitudinal view *Journal of Consulting and Clinical Psychology.*

Gottman, J. M., & Levenson, R. W. (1985). A valid procedure for obtaining self-report of affect in marital interaction. *Journal of Consulting and Clinical Psychology, 53,* 151–160.

Gottman, J. M., & Levenson, R. W. (1986). Assessing the role of emotion in marriage. *Behavioral Assessment, 8,* 31–48.

Gottman, J. M., & Levenson, R. W. (in press). The social psychophysiology of marriage. In P. Noller & M. A. Fitzpatrick (Eds.), *Perspectives on marital interaction.* San Diego, CA: College Hill Press.

Gottman, J. M., Notarius, C., Gonso, J., & Markman, H. (1976). *A couples guide to communication.* Champaign, IL: Research Press.

Hagestad, G. O., & Smyer, M. A. (1982). Dissolving long-term relationships: Patterns of divorcing in middle age. In S. Duck (Ed.), *Personal Relationships, 4: Dissolving Relationships* (pp. 155–188). New York: Academic Press.

Harvey, J. H., Wells, G. L., & Alvarez, M. D. (1978). Attribution in the context of conflict and separation in close relationships. In J. H. Harvey, W. Ickes, & R. F. Kidd (Eds.), *New directions in attribution research.* Hillsdale, NJ: Lawrence Erlbaum Associates.

Henry, J. P., & Stephens, P. M. (1977). *Stress, health, and the social environment.* New York: Springer-Verlag.

House, J. S. (1981). *Work, stress, and social support.* Reading, MA: Addison-Wesley.

Huston, T. L. (1983). Power. In H. L. Kelley, E. Berscheid, A. Christensen, J. H. Harvey, T. L. Huston, G. Levinger, E. McClintock, L. A. Peplau, & D. Peterson (Eds.), *Close relationships.* New York: W. H. Freeman.

Huston, T. L., & Ashmore, R. D. (1986). Women and men in personal relationships. In R. D. Ashmare & F. Del Boco (Eds.), *The social psychology of female-male relations* (pp. 167–210). New York: Academic Press.

Jacobson, N. S., McDonald, D. W., Follette, W. C., & Berley, R. A. (1985). Attributional processes in distressed and nondistressed married couples. *Cognitive Therapy and Research, 9,* 35–50.

Jemmott, III, J. B., & Locke, S. E. (1984). Psychosocial factors, immunologic mediation, and human susceptibility to infectious diseases: How much do we know? *Psychological Bulletin, 95,* 78–108.

Kiecolt-Glaser, J. K., Fisher, L. D., Ogrocki, P., Stout, J. C., Speicher, C. E., & Glaser, R. (in press). Marital quality, marital disruption, and immune function. *Psychosomatic Medicine.*

Komarovsky, M. (1962). *Blue-collar marriage.* New York: Random House.

Korneva, E. A., Klimenko, V. M., & Shkhinek, E. K. (1985). *Neurohumoral maintenance of immune homeostasis.* Illinois: University of Chicago Press.

Krokoff, L. J., Gottman, J. M., & Roy, A. K. (1988). Blue-collar marital interaction and a companionate philosophy of marriage. *Journal of Personal and Social Relationships.*

Levenson, R. W., & Gottman, J. M. (1983). Marital interaction: Physiological linkage and affective exchange. *Journal of Personality and Social Psychology, 45,* 587–597.

Levenson, R. W., & Gottman, J. M. (1985). Physiological and affective predictors of change in relationship satisfaction. *Journal of Personality of Social Psychology, 49,* 85–94.

Levy, M. N. (1983). Hunting the wild vagus. *The Physiologist, 26,* 115–118.

Locke, H. J. (1951). *Predicting adjustments in marriage: A comparison of a divorced and a happily married group.* New York: Henry Holt.

Locke, H. J., & Wallace, K. M. (1959). Short marital-adjustment and prediction tests: Their reliability and validity. *Marriage and Family Living, 21,* 251–255.

Margolin, G., & Wampold, B. E. (1982). Sequential analysis of conflict and accord in distressed and nondistressed marital partners. *Journal of Consulting and Clinical Psychology, 49,* 554–567.

Obrist, P. A. (1981). *Cardiovascular psychophysiology.* New York: Plenum Press.

Pennebaker, J. W. (1982). *The psychology of physical symptoms.* New York: Springer-Verlag.

Raush, H. L., Barry, W. A., Hertel, R. K., & Swain, M. A. (1974). *Communication, conflict, and marriage.* San Francisco: Jossey-Bass.

Rubin, L. (1976). *Worlds of pain.* New York: Basic Books.

Rubin, L. B. (1979). *Worlds of pain.* New York: Basic Books.

Selye, H. (1975). *The stress of life.* New York: McGraw Hill.

Sokolov, E. N. (1963). *Perception and the conditioned reflex.* Oxford: Pergamon Press.

Spanier, G. B. (1976). A new measure for assessing the quality of marriage and similar dyads. *Journal of Marriage and the Family, 38,* 15–28.

Taggart, P., & Carruthers, M. (1971). Endogenous hyperlipidaemia induced by emotional stress of racing driving. *Lancet, 1,* 363–366.

Terman, L. M., Buttenweiser, P., Ferguson, L. W., Johnson, W. B., & Wilson, D. P. (1938). *Psychological factors in marital happiness.* New York: McGraw Hill.

Van Dyke, C., & Kaufman, I. C. (1983). Psychobiology of bereavement. In L. Temoshok, C. van Dyke, & L. S. Zegans (Eds.), *Emotions in health and illness: Theoretical and research foundations.* New York: Grune and Stratton.

Walker, L. E. (1984). Battered women, psychology, and public policy. *American Psychologist, 39,* 1178.

Wills, T. A., Weiss, R. L., & Patterson, G. R. (1974). A behavioral analysis of the determinants of marital satisfaction. *Journal of Consulting and Clinical Psychology, 42,* 802–811.

5 A Contextual Approach to the Problem of Aversive Practices in Families

Anthony Biglan
Lewis Lewin
Hyman Hops
Oregon Research Institute

Aversive behavior is a cardinal feature of most family problems. It is not hard to see the central role of such practices when considering the related problems of child and spouse abuse (e.g., Straus & Hotaling, 1980). However, aversive control practices are also the chief problem in nonabusive families where there is marital discord or problems with aggressive or noncompliant children. Aversive behavior is found in families where the mother is depressed, families in which there are multiply handicapped children, and families where a member is in chronic pain. Moreover, it is becoming clear that families that use aversive control practices are the crucible for later societal problems, in that children growing up in them are likely to have difficulties in work, social, and familial roles in later life (Elder, Caspi, & Downey, 1986). Thus, the control of aversive practices in families must be a fundamental goal for those interested in improving the welfare of families. Such control cannot be ignored by persons who have a primary interest in a productive society in which the costs of social dislocation are minimized.

The aversive behavior of individual family members can only be understood in the context of the social and nonsocial contingencies for that behavior. The most salient fact about that context is that it, too, is aversive. We therefore analyze the contingencies for the aversive behavior of individual family members in terms of experimentally derived principles of the effects of aversive events on behavior. These principles appear to encompass the most important ways in which aversive behavior is established and maintained in families. However, by itself such an analysis is incomplete. It does not address the ways in which the larger cultural context affects aversive practices in families. We therefore discuss the effects of the larger context on families' aversive practices using the framework provided by Harris' (1979) theory of cultural materialism.

103

THE NATURE OF AVERSIVE EVENTS

Aversiveness is usually defined in terms of functional effects. An event is considered to be aversive if its contingent removal reinforces a class of behaviors or if its contingent application reduces the probability of a class of behaviors (Hineline, 1984). One could argue that an event should only be labeled *aversive* if one or the other of these effects is experimentally demonstrated. However, it is heuristic to consider many events in the family as aversive, even though a direct experimental demonstration is unavailable. Interpreting family processes in terms of findings made in experimental studies of aversive events may suggest important determinants of family interactions that would not otherwise be identified.

Events that might be aversive in families have typically been identified in one of two ways. First, many coding systems have designated certain events as *negative* on the basis of clinical experience and informal input from family members about behaviors that are displeasing to them (e.g., Gottman, 1979; Patterson, 1982). Although such an approach may overlook important behaviors and may obscure a good deal of intersubject variability, it is not unreasonable given the cost of experimentally assessing aversiveness for each subject. Moreover, a good deal of indirect evidence supports the a priori designation of coded behaviors as aversive. At least some of the events included in these coding systems have been empirically demonstrated to be aversive in the sense that they suppress ongoing prosocial interaction (Patterson, 1982). In addition, family members' ratings of how annoying each behavior is correspond well to the a priori designations (Hoffman, 1983). In one study, Patterson (personal communication) found that parents' ratings of the aversiveness of a specific behavior correlated .48 with the degree to which it suppressed ongoing prosocial behavior in directly observed interactions.

A second method of studying aversive events in families consists of asking subjects to complete checklists of items that are rated in terms of their positiveness or negativeness (Grosscup & Lewinsohn, 1980; Jacobson, Follette, & McDonald, 1982; Weiss & Perry, 1979). As the evidence just described indicates, people can label at least some of the events that they find aversive with some accuracy. Presumably a verbal repertoire descriptive of aversive events is reinforced when people escape or avoid those events as a result of their labeling them. (For example, "Stop that, it is annoying me.")

To reject these methods of identifying aversive events because they are not experimental would either discourage further study of aversive processes in families (Marr, 1984) or ignore the rich implications of experimental studies of aversive events for reducing aversive exchanges in families. We will review the evidence regarding the role of aversive events in family interaction, while at the same time acknowledging that (a) some of the events studied thus far might prove not to be aversive if experimental analyses were conducted, and (b) other events may occur in these families that are aversive, yet have not been identified through the methods that have been used thus far.

Two Types of Aversive Social Behavior

It is important to distinguish two types of aversive social behavior that appear to have different functions and thus may not be ameliorated via the same therapeutic interventions. When we speak of aversive social behavior, we are accustomed to thinking of directly aggressive behavior which is likely to stimulate counterattacks and is unlikely to prompt others to be supportive. Our coding system (Arthur, Hops, & Biglan, 1982; Biglan et al., 1986), includes in this category verbal statements that involve humiliating the other, disapproving, threatening, arguing, refusing requests, physical aggression, and ignoring others' initiations (Biglan et al., 1986). Nonverbal behavior is included in this category if it conveys "anger, displeasure, or harsh/cold detachment or when the person mocks or is sarcastic" (Biglan et al., 1986). We have labeled this type of behavior "aggressive," a label that appears consistent with others' use of the term (Patterson, 1982).

A perhaps more subtle form of aversive behavior suggests that the person is distressed but not angry. In our coding system, self-denigration and complaints about oneself, any object, or anyone other than the person being addressed are included in this behavior class as well as any nonverbal behavior that suggests sadness, despondency, or depression. We have labeled this type of behavior "depressive" in previous publications (Biglan et al., 1985, Biglan, Hops, & Sherman, 1987; Hops et al., 1987). However, that designation may be misleading, as the behavior is also displayed by people who are not clinically depressed (Biglan & Thorsen, 1986). We now propose the label "distressed" for this type of behavior, in order to clarify that the behavior may occur in families with various types of problems.

These two types of behavior may have made distinct contributions to survival. The tendency to attack has obvious survival value, especially when the attack occurs in response to aversive stimulation (e.g., Ulrich & Azrin, 1962). Behavior that suggests that an organism is hurt or weak would contribute to survival if it made it more likely that other members of the species would provide help or would stop attacking.

There is converging evidence in support of the distinction between aggressive and distressed behavior. First, in our study of family interactions of depressed women, we found that the functional effects of these two kinds of behaviors are different (Biglan et al., 1985; Hops et al., 1987). For example, when women who were maritally distressed and depressed directed distressed behavior toward their husbands, it was associated with a reduced probability that their husbands would be aggressive in response (Biglan et al., 1985). This tendency was significantly different from that for nondepressed women or women who were depressed but not maritally distressed.

A second indication that these behaviors should be distinguished is the fact that their rates are not correlated. In two studies of problem-solving interactions of married couples, the rates of aggressive and distressed behaviors were not correlated for either husbands or wives (Biglan et al., 1985; Biglan & Thorsen, 1986). The spouse who emitted high rates of aggressive behavior did not necessarily emit high rates of distressed behavior.

Third, Gottman and Levenson (1986) showed that the conclusions one reaches in analyzing conditional responding of husbands and wives are different depending on whether all negative affective behaviors are lumped together or treated separately. For example, when all negative affects are grouped together, there can appear to be a high probability that one spouse will reciprocate the negative affect of the other. However, when different negative affect codes are distinguished, apparent reciprocity may be found to involve one person displaying anger and the other responding with emotions such as sadness, whining, and fear. Finally, evidence that these behaviors are functionally distinct comes from two studies we recently completed of married couples' ratings of the impact of each of these types of behavior (Biglan, Rothlind, Sherman, & Hops, 1987). In one study, 48 married couples rated verbal descriptions of five types of social behavior: self-denigration, complaint (about anything other than the person speaking and the person being addressed), aggression, neutral, and facilitative. Subjects were asked to rate how they would feel and act if their partners behaved in each of these ways and how they would perceive their partners to be feeling. The results are consistent with the hypothesis that self-denigrating and complaining behaviors are aversive to others; subjects said they would feel more sad, anxious, irritated, angry, and defiant in response to these behaviors than in response to neutral or facilitative behavior. However, unlike aggressive behavior, self-denigrations and complaints prompt sympathetic, caring, and supportive feelings and reactions and less counterattack. In the second experiment, members of 43 marital dyads rated videotaped examples of possible spousal behavior that varied in both verbal and nonverbal content. Both sad affect and angry affect were depicted. These affects were crossed with aggressive versus self-denigrating content. These four behavior types were compared to neutral talk with neutral affect. The results indicated that behaviors having aggressive or self-degrading content and either sad or angry affect were rated as producing more negative and fewer positive feelings in the recipient and generally more hostile and angry reactions than was true for neutral talk with neutral affect. In this study as well, the self-denigrating verbal content and sad nonverbal behavior were more likely than aggressive content or angry affect to produce feelings of caring, sympathy, and support and were less likely to produce feelings of irritation, anger, sadness, and defiance. Self-denigrating content and dysphoric affective behavior were rated as more likely to produce comforting and supportive reactions and less likely to produce hostile and argumentative reactions.

THE PROBLEM OF AVERSIVE BEHAVIOR IN FAMILIES

This section summarizes evidence that aversive interactions are a central feature of the interactions of families with diverse problems.

Child and Spouse Abuse

Perhaps the most serious type of aversive practice in families involves physical aggression against children and spouses. Such abuse is common. A nationwide random sample survey conducted in 1985 indicated that 62% of children had been victims of some form of physical violence during the previous year and 10.7% had been the victim of a severe violent act such as being hit with something or being beaten up (Straus & Gelles, 1986). Among married couples, 11% of the husband were reported to have directed violence toward their wives and 12% of the wives directed violence toward their husbands (Straus & Gelles, 1986). There is evidence that families in which child abuse occurs are also characterized by higher rates of aversive behavior on the part of the victim as well as the parents (Burgess & Richardson, 1984).

Marital Discord

Even where physical aggression does not take place between spouses, the most salient feature of marital discord is the high rate of negative behavior of both partners (Jacobson & Moore, 1981) and the high likelihood that such behavior will be reciprocated (Gottman, 1979; Margolin & Wampold, 1981; Revenstorf, Vogel, Wegener, Hahlweg, & Schindler, 1980). Noted negative behaviors include nonverbal behavior suggesting anger and verbal content including criticism and arguing. Distressed couples' ratings of their partners' behavior during discussions of problems are more negative than those of nondistressed couples (Gottman, 1979). Such ratings are predictive of marital satisfaction as much as 2½ years later (Markman, 1979).

Aggressive Behavior of Children

One of the most common and important problems among children involves their aggressive behavior. Patterson (1982) cites research by Achenbach (1978) suggesting that the following behaviors could usefully be included under this rubric: arguing, tantruming, disobeying, fighting, cruelty to others, teasing, showing off, being loud, screaming, and swearing. Patterson (1982) has shown that it is not only the identified child who is aggressive in these families; other family members both initiate and reciprocate aggressive behavior in their interactions with the child they have labeled as too aggressive. Among the patterns of coercive behavior that Patterson (1982) has identified as likely in families of aggressive children are

(a) "punishment acceleration," in which parental reprimands, rather than suppressing aggressive behavior, actually accelerate it,

(b) crossover, in which one family member responds to positive behavior of another with negative behavior,

(c) counterattacks, in which negative behavior of one family member is responded to with negative behavior by another family member, and

(d) continuance, in which family members keep behaving in a negative way regardless of how the other person behaves.

Depression

Patterns of aversive behavior have also been identified in families with problems that have not traditionally been seen as involving aversiveness. Elsewhere, we have reviewed the evidence of aversive interactions between depressed people and their family members (Biglan, Hops, & Sherman, 1987). Depressed people who are married are more likely to experience marital discord than nondepressed persons. Both spouses and children of depressed people direct negative behavior toward them. For example, in our home observations of the interactions of depressed mothers and their families, we found that children of depressed mothers emit more irritable affect than do children of normal, nondepressed mothers (Hops et al., 1987). In problem-solving interactions between depressed women and their husbands, the husbands tended ($p < .10$) to emit more aggressive behavior than husbands of nondepressed women (Biglan et al., 1985).

At the same time, there is evidence that depressed people are, themselves, behaving aversively. Indirect evidence comes from studies showing that depressed people have a negative impact on persons with whom they interact (Coyne, 1976; Gotlib & Robinson, 1982; Hammen & Peters, 1978; Howes & Hokanson, 1979; Strack & Coyne, 1983). Although these studies did not involve family interactions, Arkowitz, Holliday, and Hutter (1982) did find that spouses of depressed partners rated themselves as more anxious and hostile than did spouses of nondepressed partners. Direct evidence of the aversive behavior of depressed people comes from our studies of depressed mothers' interactions with their families. They emitted more dysphoric affective behavior in home interactions (Hops et al., 1987) and tended to emit more aggressive behavior than normal women in problem-solving interactions with their husbands (Biglan et al., 1985). In the problem-solving interactions, depressed women who were dissatisfied with their marriages also emitted more distressed behavior than did normals or women who were depressed but not maritally dissatisfied. Others' studies of spousal interactions involving depressed people have also shown that depressed people behave in negative ways (Hautzinger, Linden, & Hoffman, 1982; Hinchliffe, Hooper, Roberts, & Vaughan, 1975).

Chronic Pain

There is some evidence that elevated rates of aversive interaction occur between women who are experiencing chronic pain and their husbands. Biglan and Thorsen (1986) found that both members of these couples displayed more aggressive and distressed behavior than did comparison normal dyads. These differences held even when differences between the groups that were associated with the Beck Depression Inventory were removed through covariance. Aversive interactions in families with chronic pain are also suggested by the fact that these families are likely to have at least two other problems that are associated with aversive interactions: marital distress (Maruta, Osborne, Swanson, & Halling, 1981) and depression (Romano & Turner, 1985).

Families with Handicapped Children

It appears that aversive behavior is more likely among families of multiply handicapped children than among families with nonhandicapped children. Parents are more likely to be physically abusive (Schilling & Kirkham, 1985) and the handicapped child is more likely than nonhandicapped children to engage in self-abuse as well as fighting and irritable behavior (Rutter & Hemming, 1970), behaviors which have been reported by professionals to lead to institutionalization (Scheerenberger, 1981). The apparently higher rate of emotional and marital distress in these families (Breslau & Davis, 1986) also suggests that higher rates of aversive behavior are occurring in them.

Conclusion

Although meaningful distinctions can be made among these different problems, all involve family members having to deal with others' aversive behavior. What is needed are general strategies for ameliorating these painful and harmful processes, which could be applied across the broad range of family difficulties. The remainder of this chapter sketches the general shape of a contextual analysis that could contribute to such amelioration, and explicates a strategy for reducing and preventing aversive exchanges in families.

A CONTEXTUAL APPROACH TO AVERSIVE BEHAVIOR
IN FAMILIES

Two types of contextual analyses appear useful for understanding and affecting aversive behavior in families: (a) an analysis of the context for individual family members' aversive behavior, and (b) an analysis of the larger cultural context for the aversive practices of families. Contextual analysis is a systematic approach to scientific research that is coming into increasing use. The key features of such analyses are the examination of the event or phenomenon of interest in relation to its context and the evaluation of the merits of the analysis in terms of its usefulness for achieving a specified goal (Hayes & Brownstein, 1986; Hayes, Parrott, & Reese, in press; Pepper, 1942). Both the contextual focus and the pragmatic emphasis on goal achievement seem important for the present problem. Intuitively, and on empirical grounds, it seems that family members' aversive behavior is a function of both its personal and cultural context. However, even if we restrict our focus to the relationships between the context and aversive family interactions, an enormous number of relationships might be identified. Evaluating alternative analyses in terms of their likely contribution to amelioration of aversive family interactions provides a practical criterion for selecting among them.

Contextualism provides a systematic, yet flexible framework for integrating the research of diverse disciplines. The critical issue is the identification of variables that contribute to the control of the target phenomenon—regardless of the *level* or discipline with which those variables are identified. Integration across disciplines is essential for further progress. We now know a lot about how microsocial processes affect family members' aversive behavior (Patterson, 1982). Developing a coherent account of how the larger cultural context affects those processes will lead to more effective strategies for amelioration—strategies that may reach more families at less expense than clinical interventions.

The Context for the Aversive Behavior of Individual
Family Members

The aversive behavior of any given family member occurs in the context of (a) aversive behavior of other family members, (b) aversive behavior of people outside the family, and (c) nonsocial aversive events such as pain and illness. Patterson (e.g., 1982), Wahler, Leske, and Rogers (e.g., 1979) and Gottman (1979) have made particularly valuable contributions to understanding the effects of the aversive social behavior of others. Much of their theorizing has drawn on evidence from experimental analysis of the effects of aversive events. However, a systematic exposition of the implications of experimental results for understanding aversive processes in families is not available. Therefore, we will frame the discussion of the context for aversive behavior of individuals in terms of the

TABLE 5.1
Major Findings of Experimental Studies of Aversive Events

Negative Reinforcement

A class of behaviors is negatively reinforced when the
removal, reduction, or prevention of some set of events
makes that class of behaviors more likely in later similar
circumstances (Hineline, 1977). The following arrangements
of aversive events have been shown to be negatively reinforcing:

  Reduction in the frequency of aversive events
  Delay of aversive events
  Deletion of aversive events at the end of an experimental
    session
  A signal correlated with the periods of no aversive events

Punishment

The response-contingent presentation of a stimulus that reduces
the long-term future probability of responding. The effectiveness of punishment is affected by the following:

  The manner of introduction of the punishing stimulus--
    sudden introduction of high-intensity stimuli was more
    effective than gradual introduction of low-intensity
    punishers that were slowly increased in intensity (Azrin
    & Holz, 1967).
  Immediacy with which the punishing stimulus follows the
    behavior
  Continuous as opposed to intermittent punishment
  The schedule of reinforcement maintaining the behavior

Aggression as a By-Product of Aversive Control

Noncontingent aversive stimulation increases the probability
of aggressive behavior (Ulrich & Azrin, 1962) and of behavior
that is reinforced by the opportunity to engage in aggressive
behavior (Azrin, Hutchinson, & Hake, 1966).

The Relative Rate of Reinforcement and Punishment

Behavior is a function of the consequences for alternative
behaviors as well as the consequences for the behavior in
question.

---

major principles that have been developed in well-controlled experimental studies of aversive events. Such an exposition could have a salutary effect on both
family research and experimental analysis. Family researchers might be guided
to study variables that have thus far been overlooked, and those doing basic
experimental research on aversive control could be prompted to analyze problems that are suggested by studies of family interaction.

Experimentally derived principles of aversive control can be organized into
four categories: negative reinforcement, aggression as a by-product of aversive
control, punishment, and the effects of the relative rate of reinforcement and
punishment for the behavior of interest versus other behaviors. Table 5.1 lists
these categories and summarizes the major relationships that appear to be well-
established in each category. A more detailed discussion of this literature and its
implications for family interactions is available (Lewin & Biglan, 1987).

Negative Reinforcement. Negative reinforcement of a class of behaviors occurs when the contingent removal, reduction, or prevention of some class of events increases the probability of that class of behaviors (Hineline, 1977). Patterson's (1982) analysis of interactional sequences in families of aggressive children suggests that aggressive behavior is frequently negatively reinforced by reduction in the probability of other family members' aggressive behavior. Our own research on the interactions of depressed women and their families suggests that the distressed behavior of depressed women is also maintained by negative reinforcement involving reductions in the probability of other family members' aversive behavior (Biglan, Hops, & Sherman, 1987). Direct observations of interactions in the home indicated that, when depressed mothers emitted dysphoric affective behavior, their husbands and children were less likely to emit aggressive affective behavior than was true in families in which the mother was not depressed (Hops et al., 1987). Observations of problem-solving interactions between husbands and wives indicated that when the woman was both depressed and maritally distressed her distressed social behavior was less likely to be followed by aggressive behavior by her husband than was true for normals or couples where the wife was depressed but there was no marital distress (Biglan et al., 1985).

Analysis of the conditional responding of chronic pain patients and their husbands (Biglan & Thorsen, 1986) also indicated that negative reinforcement may maintain distressed and aggressive behavior. When the women with chronic pain displayed distressed or aggressive behavior, the probability of their husbands' aggressive behavior was reduced more than was true for women who were not experiencing pain. Moreover, distressed and aggressive behavior of the husbands in these dyads was associated with a reduced likelihood of their wives emitting distressed behavior.

All of the tests of negative reinforcement in families just described were limited to lag sequential analysis of events immediately following the behavior of interest. However, experimental studies point to other negatively reinforcing contingencies that need to be considered. First, if a response simply reduces the *frequency* of an aversive event, the response will be reinforced. For example, Herrnstein and Hineline (1966) found that a response that switched rats from a condition in which they received 9 shocks per minute to one in which they received 6 shocks per minute was reinforced by this change in the rate of shocks. Thus, a father's yelling could be reinforced if the rate of his children's annoying behavior simply occurred less frequently, even though it continued to occur. Second, delays in the occurrence of aversive events are reinforcing. Hineline (1970) showed that if a response delayed the occurrence of a shock it was reinforcing, even if the total frequency of shocks was unaffected by the response. Complaining could often function in this way. As our own research indicates, describing some annoying thing that has happened makes it less likely that the other person will be aversive, at least immediately (Biglan, Rothlind, Sherman,

& Hops, 1987). This could maintain complaining, even though the complaining did not reduce the overall amount of aversive behavior from others. Third, it has been shown that responses can be reinforced if they lead to the deletion of aversive events long after the response occurs. For example, a lever press of a rat that postponed shock and deleted 1 minute from the duration of a 2.5 hour avoidance conditioning session occurred at a higher rate than an alternative response that simply postponed shock (Mellitz, Hineline, Whitehouse, & Laurence, 1983). Currently available methods of analyzing family interactions would not allow us to detect such a subtle relationship. For example, a mother's explosive behavior might have the effect of shortening the period of time during which her child engaged in irritable behavior, *even if it had no immediate effect on the child's behavior.* Given the brevity of typical home observations and the statistical limitations of current analytic methods, it would not be possible to detect the effect of this contingency.

Stimuli that are correlated with the occurrence of aversive events also affect behavior. Badia and his colleagues (Badia, Coker, & Harsh, 1973; Badia & Culbertson, 1972; Badia, Culbertson, & Lewis, 1971) found that shock preceded by brief signal cues was preferred to unsignaled shock. Badia, Harsh, Coker, and Abbott (1976) manipulated the dependability with which the signal for shock indicated the onset of shock. Their results suggested that signaled shock is preferred because it makes the periods during which no shock occurs more discernible. In a finding consistent with this research, Wahler and Dumas (1986) presented evidence suggesting that some children's aversive behavior is maintained by their mothers' higher-rate, albeit more predictable, aversive behavior.

Thus, there are a number of ways in which the responding of individual family members could be maintained by the avoidance of aversive behavior of others. Indeed, given the variety of ways in which the avoidance of aversive events has been shown to maintain behavior in experimental studies and the fact that only the most straightforward arrangement of negative reinforcement has been investigated in families, it seems quite likely that negative reinforcement plays an even larger role in maintaining aversive behavior in families than currently available family studies suggest. Strategies for reducing aversive interactions in families must, therefore, assist family members in coping with or avoiding aversive events without behaving aversively themselves and must attempt to reduce the amount of aversiveness that is intruding on them. The successes of treatment programs for aggressive child behavior (Patterson & Fleischman, 1979) and marital discord (Jacobson & Margolin, 1979) can be seen as due to just such strategies.

By-Products of Aversive Stimulation

Aversive stimulation has been shown to produce aggressive responses toward animate and inanimate objects in the absence of any reinforcement (Azrin,

Hutchinson, & Hake, 1966; Kelly & Hake, 1970; Ulrich & Azrin, 1962). The aversive events shown to have this effect include shock and the absence of reinforcement. Such stimulation makes the opportunity for aggressive responding reinforcing. Azrin, Hutchinson, and McLaughlin (1965) showed that, when monkeys are being noncontingently shocked, they will be reinforced by the opportunity to get access to an inanimate object they can attack. There appears to be no experimental evidence regarding the possibility that the other form of aversive behavior we have identified—distressed behavior—is made more likely by aversive stimulation, but this idea seems worth exploring.

The importance of aversively stimulated aggressive behavior in families appears to have been largely overlooked. Aversive stimulation impinging on a family member from any source could increase the probability that he or she will direct aggressive behavior toward family members, *even in the absence of reinforcement for the behavior*. For example, Wahler (1980) has shown that mothers of aggressive children are more likely to behave aggressively towards their children on days when they have aversive interactions with people outside the family.

This principle may be quite broadly applicable and may provide a more straightforward account of some well-established relationships. For example, the effect of stressful events in increasing aversive interactions can be understood as an example of aggression stimulated by aversive events.

The principle of aversively stimulated aggression implies that *any* reduction in aversive stimulation of family members could contribute to the reduction of aversive family interactions. These could include reductions of the aversive behavior of other family members, reductions in aversive exchanges with persons outside the family (e.g., Panaccione & Wahler, 1986), and reductions in nonsocial aversive events intruding on family members.

Punishment

Punishment has been defined as the response-contingent presentation of a stimulus that reduces the long-term probability of a response (Azrin & Holz, 1966). Thus, one effect of aversive events in family interactions may be to suppress the ongoing behavior of the person to whom the aversive event was directed. It is more likely that aversive events suppress prosocial and neutral behavior than aggressive behavior since, as just described, aversive events also tend to stimulate aggressive behavior. Indeed, Patterson (1982) has found that prosocial behavior is suppressed by behaviors coded as aversive, but no such effect has been found for aggressive responding.

In experimental studies with nonhumans, Azrin and Holz (1966) have examined the major parameters of punishment. The sudden introduction of high-intensity punishers had the greatest effect in suppressing behavior. Immediate punishment had a greater effect than delayed punishment. Similarly, providing a punisher following each response is more effective than intermittent punishment. Finally, the effect of a punisher also depends on the schedule of reinforcement that is maintaining the behavior.

Events are not inherently punishing, however. Azrin and Holz (1966) showed that, although contingently delivered shock is usually a punisher, it can be made to function as a reinforcer if it is discriminative for food reinforcement. A mother who reprimands her child, but then *relents* and provides reinforcers such as food or cuddling, may be establishing her reprimanding as a reinforcer. It has been experimentally demonstrated that a situation which functions as a punisher in most situations, i.e., time-out from opportunity to gain reinforcement, can function as a reinforcer if certain reinforcing behaviors are allowed to occur (Plummer, Baer, & LeBlanc, 1977).

On the basis of these findings, one would infer that the suppressive effect of aversive behavior in families depends on the behavior's intensity, the extent to which it consistently occurs immediately following the behavior of interest, and the degree to which that behavior is not being reinforced. It is unlikely that all of these parameters are optimal in most family interactions. For example, many of the child behaviors to which parents respond aversively also receive a good deal of reinforcement (Patterson, 1982). Moreover, as Patterson (1982) has pointed out, punishment and negative reinforcement effects are intermixed in ongoing family interactions. If one member's aversive behavior suppresses another's, this punishing effect will negatively reinforce the first person's aversive behavior. If the punishing behavior of the first person is intermittent, the effect on suppressing the behavior of the second person may be incomplete and aversive behavior will continue to occur. In addition, the effects of these aversive events in stimulating aggressive behavior has to be considered. Thus, most aversive events in families probably have multiple effects; they suppress some behavior, negatively reinforce behavior that avoids them, and stimulate aggressive behavior.

The principles of punishment have contributed to amelioration of aversive family interactions with children. They imply that, if punishing stimuli are going to be used to reduce other aversive behavior, the punisher should be applied consistently and the target behavior should not be reinforced. In addition, the punishing event should be one that elicits as little aggressive responding as possible. Time out is just such a stimulus, and it has been firmly established as a method of reducing the aggressive behavior of children (Zeilberger, Sampen, & Sloane, 1968). Moreover, there is clear evidence that such behavior cannot be reduced solely through the use of positive consequences for nonaggressive behavior (Wahler, 1969).

Matching

The rate of a behavior is not only a function of the consequences for that behavior; it is also affected by the consequences for alternative behaviors. Herrnstein (1974) originally formulated this relationship for positive reinforcement situations. The "matching law" states that, when two responses (1 and 2) are available, the relative rate of each response (R1/R2) and the relative time spent in each response (T1/T2) are a function of the relative rate of reinforcement for the two responses. This relationship has since been found to hold for negative reinforcement (Baum, 1973; Hutton, Gardner, & Lewis, 1978; Logue & DeVilliers, 1978). Moreover, it has been shown that rates of behavior are affected by the relative rates of punishment (Deluty, 1976). The matching law has also been shown to hold for humans when one behavior was maintained on positive reinforcement and the other was maintained by negative reinforcement (Ruddle, Bradshaw, Szabadi, & Foster, 1982).

These findings indicate that family members will engage in more aversive behavior, the less reinforcement is available for nonaversive behavior (McDowell, 1982). We can promote nonaversive styles of family interaction by increasing the degree to which prosocial behavior is reinforced in families as well as by reducing tendencies of family members to reinforce aversive behavior and increasing their appropriate use of punishment for aversive behavior.

The Verbal Context for Interactions

Although the account given so far suggests a parsimonious approach to diverse family problems, it fails to make contact with the more traditional conception of these problems in terms of the thoughts, beliefs, and feelings of the people involved. Typically, our sense is that people behave aversively because of how they feel and what they believe. Is what people think and feel important for understanding aversive family interactions? We feel that such events are very important, but that their importance is itself a function of the social environment.

Space does not permit a detailed discussion of this issue, but the achievement of ameliorative strategies requires that we address two points. First, based on emerging analyses of equivalence classes (e.g., Wulfert & Hayes, 1987), it is likely that most of our behavior is, in part, under the control of the verbal stimuli that are associated with the events to which we are responding. For example, the probability that a husband will respond to his wife's assertive behavior with violence appears to be, in part, a function of the degree to which he subscribes to the view that men should have the power and authority in the home (Allen & Straus, 1980; Carroll, 1980; LaRossa, 1980; Straus, 1980a, 1980b). A very different example is of a person's own wish to avoid feeling upset. Hayes (1987) has discussed how a variety of psychological difficulties seem to involve the person responding to his or her own distress in accordance with rules such as "I must avoid being anxious at all costs." Zettle and Hayes (1982) have shown that an analysis of this type gives a good account of the effects of different treatments for depression.

The second point is that effects of verbal stimuli are themselves a function of the social context (Biglan, 1987). For example, the effects of norms involving sex roles (e.g., "Men don't do housework") are a function of the consequences for behaving consistently with that norm and related verbal stimuli. Husbands may respond consistently with the norm because of prior consequences for behaving "like a man"; women may do so because of aversive consequences from their husbands if they fail to and because of a more general history of punishment for "being too aggressive." Evidence that such norms are important for aversive family practices comes from a study by Straus, Gelles, and Steinmetz (1976) who found that the rate of spouse abuse (both husband to wife and wife to husband) was highest in families that were characterized as male-dominant.

The implications of these points are that (a) we will have to assess the verbal context of norms, beliefs, thoughts, and feelings that helps to determine which events are aversive; and (b) efforts to reduce aversive practices in families will need to change the consequences for behaving in accordance with the norms, beliefs, and feelings that favor aversive family practices as well as the consequences for the norms, beliefs, and feelings that might foster more pacific family interactions.

THE LARGER CONTEXT FOR AVERSIVE BEHAVIOR IN FAMILIES

Thus far, we have characterized aversive behavior in families as an attempt to cope with the aversive behavior of others and with events from outside the family. If our goal is to ameliorate such patterns of aversive behavior, however, we also need to consider how the larger context affects the likelihood that family members will behave aversively.

Cultural materialism (Harris, 1979) provides a framework for examining this problem. Harris (1979) argues that cultural practices, such as the way in which families are organized and interact, are shaped by the requirements of the productive and reproductive systems of the society, which are referred to as the infrastructure. Within the limits set by these systems, family practices are also affected by other aspects of the culture, such as the organization of schools, government, the health care system, mass media, and scientific research. This framework has guided our thinking about how the content of the larger culture affects aversive practices in families.

The Infrastructure and Aversive Family Practices

There are a number of facets of the productive and economic processes of our society that appear to have particular influence on aversive family practices. Poverty may be the single most important cultural factor affecting the prevalence of aversive family practices. Elder et al. (1986) found that income loss was associated with increased punitive behavior of fathers and increased marital dissatisfaction among mothers. The incidence of wife battering is significantly higher among men who are unemployed or only partially employed than it is among fully employed husbands (Gelles & Cornell, 1985). Money problems have been found to predict depressive problems 9 years later (Kaplan, Roberts, Camacho-Dickey, & Coyne, 1987).

Although the strength of the relationships between poverty and aversive practices may be no greater than the relationships for many other variables, the extent of poverty in the United States means that dealing with problems of poverty could have a substantial ameliorative effect on the use of aversive control in families. Unlike most other industrialized nations, there is considerable poverty among U.S. citizens. Rodgers (1982) estimated that, in 1980, there were between 18 and 38 million people living below the poverty line. Poverty is especially likely in families with children under 18 (Moynihan, 1986). Twenty percent of children under 18 have been estimated to be living in poverty—a figure three times the rate for adults (Harris, 1987).

Harris (1981) has delineated additional characteristics of the means of production that are relevant to aversive practices of families. Since the advent of the industrial revolution, there has been a trend toward having fewer children. We have shifted from a farm economy in which children quickly became productive members of the nuclear family to an urban society in which it is expensive to raise children and, thanks to social security and Medicare, they are less needed for our well-being in later life. As the birth rate has dropped, women have become available for employment outside the home. At least over the last 20 years, the increasing cost of living has made it useful for some women and imperative for others to enter the labor market. Given these circumstances, it has proven profitable to develop the service sector of the economy, because well-educated women are available in large numbers to work for relatively low wages—usually in part-time jobs that suit both employers and employees. These changing patterns of production and employment have directly affected families. As women have gone to work, they have apparently been less willing to accept male dominance in the home.[1] Allen and Straus (1980) found that, among working-class couples with little money, when the husband had the decision-making power but limited financial and educational resources, he was more likely to abuse his spouse. The increasing divorce rate may be in part a function of these increased tensions. The divorce rate is also facilitated by the fact that women are able to earn their own—albeit often inadequate—wages. Divorce in turn has direct effects on families. Hetherington and her associates have shown a relationship between divorce and child adjustment problems (Hetherington, 1977; Hetherington, Cox, & Cox, 1978).

Divorce also means single parenting. Single parenting is much more likely

---

[1]For an account of the extent of male dominance and its origin in warfare and attempts to control population, see Harris (1974).

now than it was 20 years ago. Seventeen percent of children live in single-parent families at any one time, and it is estimated that 40% of children will be in such families sometime before the age of 18 (Harris, 1981). Nearly all single parents (95%) are women (Rodgers, 1982). Because, on average, women earn much less than men (58% of what men earn according to Harris, 1987), one concomitant of single parenting is poverty which, as we have just seen, is associated with aversive family interactions.

Another facet of current family organization that has resulted from these trends is teenage motherhood. Teenaged girls are becoming pregnant at younger ages than they once did and they are much more likely to keep their babies and to remain unmarried (Harper, 1983). Teenage motherhood is associated with a variety of problems, many of which involve aversive interactions. Teenage mothers and fathers are more likely than those who postpone parenting to engage in child abuse, to have marital discord, to divorce, and to have children with behavior problems (Schinke, Gilchrist, & Blythe, 1980).

Among Blacks, the high rate of single parenting has been fostered by the high rate of unemployment among males, coupled with welfare policies that penalize poor families in which the father is living in the home (Moynihan, 1986; Rodgers, 1982). The rate of teenage motherhood among Whites has also been increasing (Harper, 1983), however, and here too welfare policies undoubtedly contribute. We believe that this trend is also a function of the context of the teenage subculture that has developed over the last 30 years. This subculture, which promotes myriad activities that were once considered precocious, may also be seen as a product of changes in the means of production. Increasing urbanization, longer periods of schooling for children, and the decreased availability of parents associated with women moving into the labor force (and the absence of alternative childcare) have made it possible for such a culture to arise. Given the lack of sex education for young people (Harris, 1987), the increasing sexual activity that has developed within this subculture virtually guarantees increasing pregnancy rates.

Other Cultural Influences

Familial Socialization to Aversive Practices. A major contributor to aversive family practices in the next generation of families is the existence of those practices in the present generation. Elder et al. (1986) have shown across four generations of the Berkeley Guidance Study that families in which there are high levels of marital discord and parent-child hostility are more likely to produce children who go on to have problems in their relationships with their own spouses and children.

Mass Media. Mass media also appear to influence family practices. The immediate effects of television depictions of aggressive behavior in inducing aggressive behavior are well established (National Institute of Mental Health,

1982). Television may also affect family members' beliefs regarding appropriate sex roles. There is suggestive evidence that norms for male dominance increase the likelihood of certain types of aversive interactions in families (Straus, 1980b). Analyses of the content of television depictions of sex roles suggest that this medium supports just such norms. Greenberg (1982) has provided a useful review of the evidence. Male television characters have been found to outnumber females by as much as 3 to 1, although recently women have more major roles than they did (Greenberg, 1982). Men are less likely to be portrayed as family members and are more likely to have jobs and to be professionals. With respect to typical activities, women are more likely to be depicted entertaining, preparing food, and doing housework, while men are more likely to be shown drinking, smoking, using firearms, and engaging in athletic activities. Compared to women, men are shown as more rational, powerful, stable, tolerant, and intelligent, while women are depicted as more attractive, happier, warmer, more sociable, more peaceful, and fairer. Saturday morning cartoons depict five times as many males as females and females are generally younger than the males. Busby's (1974) comparison of Saturday morning male characters showed that the married men were overweight, less helpful, less intelligent, less logical, more quarrelsome, and less patient than men portrayed as heroes. Among elementary school children, the frequency of watching family dramas or shows featuring small children (e.g., The Waltons) is correlated with the belief that real-life families are cooperative, helping, and sharing. The frequency of watching shows featuring broken families were connected with beliefs that real families are antagonistic, verbally aggressive, and punitive. Both boys and girls tend to nominate male TV personalities as people they would like to be like.

There are a number of other facets of the culture that undoubtedly have a bearing on family practices. However, they are probably best discussed in terms of how they can be used to ameliorate these family problems.

A COMPREHENSIVE APPROACH TO AVERSIVE BEHAVIOR IN FAMILIES

The primary focus of attempts to ameliorate aversive behavior problems in families thus far has been on the provision of therapeutic services to individual families or even individual family members (e.g., Beach & O'Leary, 1986; Jacobson & Margolin, 1979; Patterson & Fleischman, 1979). However, even the best therapeutic services are ineffective when the context for family life undermines compliance with treatment (Dumas & Albin, 1986) or is itself aversive (e.g., Wahler, 1980; Wahler & Dumas, 1986). In what follows we outline areas in which interventions should be empirically tested. The approach is guided by Harris's (1979, 1981) analysis and by research currently under way to reduce tobacco use (Pechacek et al., 1987) and cardiovascular risk in communities

(Jacobs et al., 1986). The latter efforts provide models for how clinical approaches to individual families might be supplemented by programs that target larger social units.

Addressing the Problem of Poverty

We do not claim to be experts on the problem of poverty, but the evidence cited earlier has convinced us that this problem needs to be addressed. Unfortunately, experimental evaluations have shown that guaranteed annual income increases the likelihood of marital dissolution (at least among couples with nonworking wives) and, for some subgroups, it increases distress (Thoits & Hannan, 1980). (The former outcome may not be problematic, since it may reflect women leaving particularly aversive situations.) Any further research on such plans should document their impact on actual family interactions. Both Rodgers (1982) and Moynihan (1986) have stressed the need for programs that would make it more possible for poor, single mothers to work. Rodgers (1982) points to the need for child care for these families, and Moynihan (1986) cites evidence that job training has a beneficial effect.

School-Based Prevention Programs

Given the evidence that cigarette smoking can be deterred through school-based prevention curricula (Flay, 1985; 1986a), it seems appropriate to experimentally evaluate whether the schools could contribute to the alteration of aversive family practices. Schools already have responsibility to report child abuse, but there are a number of additional things they might do. First, school-based programs have shown promise in changing teenagers' contraceptive use (e.g., Schinke, Blythe, & Gilchrist, 1981), and their effects on the incidence of teenage pregnancy should be evaluated. Second, programs to encourage women to develop job skills could reduce the likelihood that they would wind up as poor single mothers. Third, school programs to provide direct instruction regarding nonaversive styles of family interaction could have an effect on family practices in both the families in which teenagers live and the ones they will form. In particular, programs to teach parenting skills to teenagers could reduce the likelihood that they will use aversive control techniques as parents.

The Influence of Health Care Providers

There is growing evidence that physicians can influence smokers to quit through brief discussions (e.g., Russell, Wilson, Taylor, & Baker, 1979). It is worth exploring whether physicians could affect family interactions through brief discussions, perhaps supplemented by videotaped materials. There is already suggestive evidence that the increased role of physicians in detecting and responding to evidence of child abuse has contributed to a lower incidence of the most severe forms of abuse (Straus & Gelles, 1986). Systematic efforts to alert health care practitioners to spouse abuse and milder forms of aversive control and efforts to provide information, models, and support for the development of more nonaversive styles of family interaction could make a difference. It may be thought that such interventions would have a very small impact. But as Russell et al. (1979) have argued with respect to the reduction of tobacco use, even a very small impact could have a significant effect on the prevalence of these practices if such interventions were implemented by all health care providers.

Mass Media

The use of mass media to change family practices has been little explored. Straus and Gelles (1986) reported that the rate of severe child abuse in the United States dropped 47% during the period from 1975 to 1985. They suggest that the drop may be due to the increased public discussion of the problem. Empirical studies of the effects of media campaigns to encourage smoking cessation and prevention campaigns have shown that such programs do have an effect (Flay, 1986b). The effects of TV programs and spots on reducing aversive interactions in families and inducing people to seek other forms of help should also be evaluated.

In light of the evidence suggesting that television does affect aggressive behavior and norms regarding sex roles, steps might be taken to influence the entertainment media to change their depictions of family interactions (with due regard for freedom of expression). Breed and DeFoe (1982) have described a promising method of influencing TV and movie producers.

The Worksite

There is evidence that smoking cessation can be promoted at worksites (Glasgow, 1987). The possibility that aversive family practices could be influenced through the worksite should be explored. Initially, simply getting employers to recognize the value of encouraging nonaversive family practices would be required. This might be done by explaining the role of such practices in the diverse problems cited earlier. Employers' efforts to try to influence their employees could begin with informational campaigns directed toward employees and making sure that health care providers and employee assistance programs had this issue on their "agendas."

Community Intervention Trials

Each of the efforts just discussed might have limited impact by itself. However, community-wide coordination could enhance the effectiveness of each separate facet of the campaign. NCI has begun an experimental evaluation of a community intervention trial that combines all of the just-discussed efforts to deter tobacco use. Preliminary evidence from the evaluation of a community-wide campaign to affect cardiovascular fitness indicates that such programs can have a beneficial impact (Perry, personal communication). A key feature of the latter campaign is its focus on getting community leaders to adopt the goals of the campaign as their own. Such formal placement of these issues on the *agenda* of the community probably enhances the effectiveness of each part of the campaign. For example, efforts to get health care providers to encourage nonaversive family practices may be aided if the social context for the providers includes a good deal of public discussion about the importance of positive family interactions and evidence that other individuals and agencies are working toward the same goal.

CONCLUSION

Aversive practices are a critical feature of most family problems. A good deal of progress has been made in understanding how to ameliorate aversive exchanges through modification of the context for individual family members. However, efforts to change the context for entire families have been limited primarily to interventions by therapists. Analysis of the larger context for family aversive practices suggests that the impact and scope of these efforts could be enhanced through programs in other facets of the context for families, such as government, schools, health care agencies, community service agencies, and the media. Only careful evaluation of the effects of such interventions will tell if they can, in fact, add to our ability to ameliorate these harmful interactions. The task is certainly formidable, since such interventions will be more costly than clinical work with individual families and substantial methodological problems will need to be overcome. However, interventions of this sort have the potential to affect more people than clinical interventions and will affect them in ways that might not be possible in therapeutic interventions. Given the scope and importance of the problem and what we already know, the time has come to take this next step.

Is it reasonable for society to fund such an undertaking? We have tried to show that it is. However, from a contextual point of view, research itself may be seen as a cultural activity occurring in a context. According to Harris (1979), activities such as scientific research will have an impact on other aspects of the culture only to the extent that they are congruent with the requirements for production and reproduction. If research on ways to reduce aversive practices in families is going to be supported by the society and is going to affect actual practices, it will be important to articulate the ways it could contribute to the productive processes. There are several ways in which such a contribution could occur. First, we may be able to reduce the costs associated with aversive family interactions. For example, Elder et al. (1986) have documented that males who come from homes high in aversive interactions are more likely to have erratic patterns of work in which they move from job to job, are unemployed, or shift from one line of work to another. Second, Patterson (1982) reports evidence that children with aggressive behavior problems at home achieve less in school. Thus, it is likely that homes which are more nurturing and less aversive will produce better socialized children who will be more likely to succeed in school and more likely to contribute to the society. Third, as Elder's work suggests, lower levels of conflict in the home could contribute to lower levels of conflict in work settings, which might increase productivity.

ACKNOWLEDGEMENTS

The authors would like to thank Tara Budinger, Steven C. Hayes, Jerry Patterson, and George Singer for feedback on earlier drafts of this chapter. Data used in this chapter were collected thanks to a grant from the National Institute of Mental Health (MH34517).

REFERENCES

Achenbach, T. M. (1978). The child behavior profile: I. Boys ages 6–11. *Journal of Consulting and Clinical Psychology, 46,* 478–488.

Allen, C. M., & Straus, M. A. (1980). Resources, power, and husband-wife violence. In M. A. Straus & G. T. Hotaling (Eds.), *The social causes of husband-wife violence,* Minneapolis: University of Minnesota Press.

Arkowitz, H., Holliday, S., & Hutter, M. (1982, October). *Depressed women and their husbands: A study of marital interaction and adjustment.* Paper presented at the annual meeting of the Association for the Advancement of Behavior Therapy, Los Angeles.

Arthur, J. A., Hops, H., & Biglan, A. (1982). *LIFE (Living In Familial Environments) coding system.* Unpublished manuscript. Oregon Research Institute, Eugene, OR.

Azrin, N. H., & Holz, W. C. (1966). Punishment. In W. K. Honig (Ed.), *Operant behavior: Areas of research and application.* New York: Appleton-Century-Crofts.

Azrin, N. H., Hutchinson, R. R., & Hake, D. F. (1966). Extinction-induced aggression. *Journal of Experimental Analysis of Behavior, 9,* 191–200.

Azrin, N. H., Hutchinson, R. R., & McLaughlin, R. (1965). The opportunity for aggression as an operant reinforcer during aversive stimulation. *Journal of the Experimental Analysis of Behavior, 8*(3), 171–180.

Badia, P., Coker, C., & Harsh, J. (1973). Choice of higher density signalled shock over lower density unsignalled shock. *Journal of the Experimental Analysis of Behavior, 20,* 47–56.

Badia, P., & Culbertson, S. (1972). The relative aversiveness of signalled vs unsignalled escapable and inescapable shock. *Journal of the Experimental Analysis of Behavior, 17,* 463–471.

Badia, P., Culbertson, S., & Lewis, P. (1971). The relative aversiveness of signalled vs. unsignalled avoidance. *Journal of the Experimental Analysis of Behavior, 16,* 115–121.

Badia, P., Harsh, J., Coker, C. C., & Abbott, B. (1976). Choice and the dependability of stimuli that predict shock and safety. *Journal of the Experimental Analysis of Behavior, 26,* 95–111.

Baum, W. M. (1973). The correlation-based law of effect. *Journal of Experimental Analysis of Behavior, 20*, 137.

Beach, S. R. H., & O'Leary, K. D. (1986). Treatment of depression with cognitive therapy or marital therapy. *Behavior Therapy, 17*, 43–49.

Biglan, A. (1987). A behavior-analytic critique of Bandura's self-efficacy theory. *Behavior Analyst, 10*, 1–16.

Biglan, A., Hops, H., Sherman, L., Friedman, L., Arthur, J., & Osteen, V. (1985). Problem-solving interactions of depressed women and their husbands. *Behavior Therapy, 16*, 431–451.

Biglan, A., Hops, H., & Sherman, L. (1987). Coercive family processes and maternal depression. In R. DeV. Peters & R. J. McMahon (Eds.), *Marriages and families: Behavioral-systems approaches*. New York: Brunner-Mazel.

Biglan, Hops, Sherman, Arthur, Warner, Oostenink, Holcomb, & Osteen. (1986). *Living In Familial Environments (LIFE) coding system*. Unpublished manuscript. Oregon Research Institute, Eugene, Oregon.

Biglan, A., Rothlind, J., Sherman, L., Hops, H. (1988). *The impact of presumed aversive behaviors*. Manuscript in preparation.

Biglan, A., & Thorsen, C. (1986). *The interactive behavior of women with chronic pain*. Unpublished manuscript. Oregon Research Institute, Eugene, Oregon.

Breed, W., & DeFoe, J. R. (1982). Effecting media change: The role of cooperative consultation on alcohol topics. *Journal of Communication, 32*(2), 88–99.

Breslau, N., & Davis, G. C. (1986). Chronic stress and major depressive disorder. *Archives of General Psychiatry, 43*, 309–314.

Burgess, R. L., & Richardson, R. A. (1984). Child abuse during adolescence. In R. M. Lerner & N. L. Galambos (Eds.), *Experiencing adolescence*, (pp. 119–161). New York: Garland.

Busby, L. (1974). Defining the sex role standard in commercial network television programs directed toward children. *Journalism Quarterly, 51*, 690–696.

Carroll, J. (1980). A cultural-consistency theory of family violence in Mexican-American and Jewish-ethnic groups. In M. A. Straus & G. T. Hotaling (Eds.), *The social causes of husband-wife violence*. Minneapolis: University of Minnesota Press.

Coyne, J. C. (1976). Depression and the response of other. *Journal of Abnormal Psychology, 85*, 186–193.

Deluty, M. Z. (1976). Choice and the rate of punishment in concurrent schedules. *Journal of the Experimental Analysis of Behavior, 25*, 75–80.

Dumas, J. E., & Albin, J. B. (1986). Parent training outcome: Does active parental involvement matter? *Behavioral research therapy, 24*(2), 227–230.

Elder, G. H., Caspi, A., & Downey, G. (1986). Problem behavior and family relationships: Life course and intergenerational themes. In A. B. Sorensen, F. E. Weinert, & L. R. Sherrod (Eds.), *Human development and the life course: Multidisciplinary perspective*. Hillsdale, NJ: Lawrence Erlbaum Associates.

Flay, B. R. (1985). Psychosocial approaches to smoking prevention: A review of findings. *Health Psychology, 4*(5), 449–488.

Flay, B. R. (1986a). Efficacy and effectiveness trials (and other phases of research) with development of health promotion programs. *Preventive Medicine, 15*(5), 451–474.

Flay, B. R. (1986b). Mass media linkages with school-based programs for drug abuse prevention. *Journal of School Health, 56*(9), 402–406.

Gelles, R. J., & Cornell, C. P. (1985). *Intimate violence in families*. London, England: Sage Publication.

Glasgow, R. E. (1987). Worksite smoking cessation: Current progress and future directions. *Canadian Journal of Public Health, 78*(6), S21–S27.

Gotlib, I. H., & Robinson, L. A. (1982). Responses to depressed individuals: Discrepancies between self-report and observed-related behavior. *Journal of Abnormal Psychology, 91*, 231–240.

Gottman, J. M. (1979). *Marital interaction: Experimental investigations.* New York: Academic Press.

Gottman, J. M., & Levenson, R. W. (1986). Assessing the role of emotion in marriage. *Behavioral Assessment, 8,* 31–48.

Greenberg, B. S. (1982). Television and role socialization: An overview. In E. Pearl, L. Bouthilet, & J. Lazar (Eds.), *Television and behavior: Ten years of scientific progress and implications for the eighties* (Vol. 2, Technical Reviews). Rockville, MD: U.S.D.H.H.S.

Grosscup, S. J., & Lewinsohn, P. M. (1980). Pleasant and unpleasant events and mood. *Journal of Clinical Psychology, 36,* 252–254.

Hammen, C. L., & Peters, S. D. (1978). Interpersonal consequences of depression: Responses to men and women enacting a depressed role. *Journal of Abnormal Psychology, 87,* 322–332.

Harper, A. E. (1983). Coronary heart disease—an epidemic related to diet? *American Journal of Clinical Nutrition, 37,* 669–681.

Harris, L. (1987). *Inside America.* New York: Random House.

Harris, M. (1974). *Cows, pigs, wars, and witches.* New York: Random House.

Harris, M. (1979). *Cultural materialism: The struggle for a science of culture.* New York: Simon & Schuster.

Harris, M. (1981). *Why nothing works: The anthropology of daily life.* New York: Simon & Schuster.

Hautzinger, M., Linden, M., & Hoffman, N. (1982). Distressed couples with and without a depressed partner: An analysis of their verbal interaction. *Journal of Behavior Therapy and Experimental Psychiatry, 13,* 307–314.

Hayes, S. C. (1987). A contextual approach to therapeutic change. In N. Jacobson (Ed.), *Cognitive and behavior therapies in clinical practice.* New York: Guilford.

Hayes, S. C., & Brownstein, A. J. (1986). Mentalism, behavior-behavior relations, and a behavior-analytic view of the purposes of science. *The Behavior Analyst, 9,* 175–190.

Hayes, S. C., Parrott, L. J., & Reese, H. W. (in press). Finding the philosophical core: A review of Steven C. Pepper's *World hypothesis: A study in evidence. Journal of the Experimental Analysis of Behavior.*

Herrnstein, R. J. (1974). Formal properties of the matching law. *Journal of the Experimental Analysis of Behavior, 21,* 159–164.

Herrnstein, R. J., & Hineline, P. N. (1966). Negative reinforcement as shock-frequency reduction. *Journal of the Experimental Analysis of Behavior, 9,* 421–430.

Hetherington, E. M. (1977). Effects of father abuse on personality development in adolescent daughters. *Developmental Psychology, 7,* 313–326.

Hetherington, E. M., Cox, M., & Cox, R. (1978). The aftermath of divorce. In J. H. Stevens & M. Mathews (Eds.), *Mother/child father/child relationships.* Washington, D.C.: National Association for the Education of Young Children.

Hinchliffe, M., Hooper, D., Roberts, F. J., & Vaughan, P. W. (1975). A study of the interaction between depressed patients and their spouses. *British Journal of Psychiatry, 126,* 164–172.

Hineline, P.N. (1970). Negative reinforcement without shock reduction. *Journal of the Experimental Analysis of Behavior, 14,* 259–268.

Hineline, P. N. (1977). Negative reinforcement and avoidance. In W. K. Honig & J. E. R. Staddon (Eds.), *Handbook of operant behavior* (pp. 364–414). Englewood Cliffs, NJ: Prentice Hall.

Hineline, P. N. (1984). Aversive control: A separate domain? *Journal of the Experimental Analysis of Behavior, 42,* 495–509.

Hoffman, D. A. (1983). *Parents rate the family interaction coding system: Comparisons of the family interaction of problem and nonproblem boys with parent-derived composites of behavior.* Unpublished doctoral dissertation, University of Oregon.

Hops, H., Biglan, A., Sherman, L., Arthur, J., Friedman, L., & Osteen, V. (1987). Home observations of family interactions of depressed women. *Journal of Consulting and Clinical Psychologist, 55*(3), 341–346.

Howes, M. J., & Hokanson, J. E. (1979). Conversational and social responses to depressive interpersonal behavior. *Journal of Abnormal Psychology, 88,* 625–634.

Hutton, L., Gardner, E. T., & Lewis, P. (1978). Matching with a key-peck response in concurrent negative reinforcement schedules. *Journal of the Experimental Analysis of Behavior, 30,* 225–230.

Jacobs, Jr., D. R., Luepker, R. V., Mittelmark, M. B., Folsom, A. R., Pirie, P. L., Mascioli, S. R., Hannan, P. J., Pechacek, T. F., Bracht, N. F., Carlaw, R. W., Kline, & Blackburn, A. (1986). Community-wide prevention strategies: Evaluation design of the Minnesota Heart Health Program. *Journal of Chronic Disorders, 39*(10), 775–788.

Jacobson, N. S., Follette, W. C., & McDonald, D. W. (1982). Reactivity to positive and negative behavior in distressed and nondistressed married couples. *Journal of Consulting and Clinical Psychology, 50,* 706–714.

Jacobson, N. S., & Margolin, G. (1979). *Marital therapy: Strategies based on social learning and behavior exchange principles.* New York: Brunner/Mazel.

Jacobson, N. S., & Moore, D. (1981). Spouses as observers of the events in their relationship. *Journal of Consulting and Clinical Psychology, 49*(2), 269–277.

Kaplan, G. A., Roberts, R. E., Camacho-Dickey, T. C., & Coyne, J. C. (1987). Psychosocial predictors of depression: Prospective evidence from the human population laboratory studies. *American Journal of Epidemiology, 125,* 206–220.

Kelly, J. F., & Hake, D. F. (1970). An extinction-induced increase in an aggressive response with humans. *Journal of the Experimental Analysis of Behavior, 14,* 153–164.

LaRossa, R. (1980). "And we haven't had any problems since": Conjugal violence and the politics of marriage. In M.A. Straus & G. T. Hotaling (Eds.), *The social causes of husband-wife violence,* Minneapolis: University of Minnesota Press.

Lewin, L., & Biglan, A. (1987). *Implications of experimental analyses of aversive control for the study of family interactions.* Unpublished manuscript.

Logue, A. W., & DeVilliers, P. A. (1978). Matching in concurrent variable-interval avoidance schedules. *Journal of the Experimental Analysis of Behavior, 29,* 61–66.

Margolin, G., & Wampold, B. E. (1981). Sequential analysis of conflict and accord in distressed and nondistressed marital partners. *Journal of Consulting and Clinical Psychology, 49,* 554–567.

Markman, H. J. (1979). The application of a behavioral model of marriage in predicting relationship satisfaction for couples planning marriage. *Journal of Consulting and Clinical Psychology, 4,* 743–749.

Marr, M. J. (1984). Conceptual approaches and issues. *Journal of the Experimental Analysis of Behavior, 42*(3), 353–362.

Maruta, T., Osborne, D., Swanson, D. W., & Halling, J. M. (1981). Chronic pain patients and spouses: Marital and sexual adjustment. *Mayo Clinic Procedures, 56*(5), 307–310.

McDowell, J. J. (1982). The importance of Herrnstein's mathematical statement of the law of effect for behavior therapy. *American Psychologist, 37,* 771–779.

Mellitz, M., Hineline, P. N., Whitehouse, W. G., & Laurence, M.T. (1983). Duration-reduction of avoidance sessions as negative reinforcement. *Journal of the Experimental Analysis of Behavior, 40,* 57–67.

Moynihan, (1986). *Family and nation.* Orlando, FL: Harcourt Brace Jovanovich.

National Institute of Mental Health (1982). *Television and Behavior: Ten years of scientific progress and implications for the eighties* (Vol. 1: Summary Report). Rockville: Health and Human Services.

Panaccione, V. F., & Wahler, R. G. (1986). Child behavior, maternal depression, and social coercion as factors in the quality of child care. *Journal of Abnormal Child Psychology, 14*(2), 263–278.

Patterson, G. R. (1982). *Coercive family processes.* Eugene, OR: Castilia.

Patterson, G. R. (1987). Personal communication.

Patterson, G. R., & Fleischman, M. J. (1979). Maintenance of treatment effects: Some considerations concerning family systems and follow-up data. *Behavior Therapy, 10,* 168–185.

Patterson, G. R. (1982). *A social learning approach to family intervention: Vol. 3, Coercive family process.* Eugene, OR: Castilia.

Pechacek, T. F., et al. (1987, November). *A randomized community trial for smoking cessation.* Paper presented at the Sixth World Conference on Smoking and Health, Tokyo, Japan.

Pepper, S. C. (1942). *World hypotheses.* England: Cambridge University Press.

Perry, C.L. (1986). Personal communication.

Plummer, S., Baer, D. M., & LeBlanc, J. M. (1977). Functional considerations in the use of procedural timeout and an effective alternative. *Journal of Applied Behavior Analysis, 10,* 689–705.

Revenstorf, D., Vogel, B., Wegener, C., Hahlweg, K., & Schindler, L. (1980). Escalation phenomena in interaction sequences: An empirical comparison of distressed and nondistressed couples. *Behavioral Analysis and Modification, 4,* 97–115.

Rodgers, H. R. (1982). *The cost of human neglect: America's welfare failure.* New York: M. E. Sharpe.

Romano, J. M., & Turner, J. A. (1985). Chronic pain and depression: Does the evidence support a relationship? *Psychological Bulletin, 97*(1), 18–34.

Ruddle, H. V., Bradshaw, C. M., Szabadi, E., & Foster, T. M. (1982). Performance of humans in concurrent avoidance/positive-reinforcement schedules. *Journal of the Experimental Analysis of Behavior, 38,* 51–61.

Russell, M. A. H., Wilson, C., Taylor, C., & Baker, C. D. (1979). Effect of general practitioners' advice against smoking. *British Medical Journal, 2,* 231–235.

Rutter, M., & Hemming, M. (1970). Individual items of deviant behavior: Their prevalence and clinical significance. In M. Rutter, J. Tizard, & K. Witmore (Eds.), *Education, health, and behavior.* London: Longman.

Scheerenberger, R. C. (1981). Deinstitutionalization: Trends and difficulties. In R. H. Bruininks, C. E. Meyers, B. B. Sigford, & K. C. Lakin (Eds.), *Deinstitutionalization and adjustment of mentally retarded people.* Washington, D.C.: Monograph of the American Association of Mental Deficiency, Number 4.

Schilling, R. F., & Kirkham, M. A. (1985). Preventing maltreatment of handicapped children. In L. D. Gilchrist & S. P. Schinke (Eds.), *Preventing social and health problems through life skills training* (Center for Social Welfare Research Monograph No. 3). Seattle: University of Washington.

Schinke, S. P., Blythe, B. J., & Gilchrist, L. D. (1981). Cognitive-behavioral prevention of adolescent pregnancy. *Journal of Counseling Psychology, 28*(5), 451–454.

Schinke, S. P., Gilchrist, L. D., & Blythe, B. J. (1980). Role of communication in the prevention of teenage pregnancy. *Health and Social Work, 5*(3), 54–59.

Strack, S., & Coyne, J. C. (1983). Social confirmation of dysphoria: Shared and private reactions. *Journal of Personality and Social Psychology, 44,* 798–806.

Straus, M. A. (1980a). The marriage license as a hitting license: Evidence from popular culture, law, and social science. In M. A. Straus & G. T. Hotaling (Eds.), *The social causes of husband-wife violence.* Minneapolis: University of Minnesota Press.

Straus, M. A. (1980b). Sexual inequality and wife beating. In M. A. Straus & G. T. Hotaling (Eds.), *The social causes of husband-wife violence.* Minneapolis: University of Minnesota Press.

Straus, M. A., & Gelles, R. J. (1986). Societal change and change in family violence from 1975 to 1985 as revealed by two national surveys. *Journal of Marriage and the Family, 48,* 465–479.

Straus, M. A., Gelles, R., & Steinmetz, S. K. (1976). *Violence in the family: An assessment of knowledge and research needs.* Paper presented to the American Association for the Advancement of Science, Boston.

Straus, M. A., & Hotaling, G. T. (Eds.) (1980). *The social causes of husband-wife violence.* Minneapolis: University of Minnesota Press.

Thoits, P., & Hannan, M. T. (1980). Income and psychological distress. In P. K. Robins, R. G. Spiegelman, S. Weiner, & J. G. Bell (Eds.), *A guaranteed annual income: Evidence from a social experiment* (pp. 183–205). New York: Academic Press.

Ulrich, R. E., & Azrin, N. H. (1962). Reflexive fighting in response to aversive stimulation. *Journal of the Experimental Analysis of Behavior, 5*(4), 511–520.

Wahler, R. G. (1969). Oppositional children: A quest for parental reinforcement control. *Journal of Applied Behavior Analysis, 2,* 159–170.

Wahler, R. G. (1980). The insular mother: Her problems in parent-child treatment. *Journal of Applied Behavior Analysis, 13,* 207–219.

Wahler, R. G., & Dumas, J. E. (1986). Maintenance factors in coercive mother-child interactions: The compliance and predictability hypotheses. *Journal of Applied Behavior Analysis, 19,* 13–22.

Wahler, R. G., Leske, G., & Rogers, E. S. (1979). The insular family: A deviance support system for oppositional children. In L. S. Hamerlynck (Ed.), *Behavioral systems for the developmentally disabled: I. School and family environments* (pp. 102–127). New York: Brunner/Mazel.

Weiss, R. L., & Perry, B. A. (1979). *Assessment and treatment of marital dysfunction.* Eugene, OR: Oregon Marital Studies Program.

Wulfert, E., & Hayes, S. L. (1987). *The transfer of a conditional ordering response through conditional equivalence classes: A behavior analytic model of semantics and syntax.* Unpublished manuscript, University of Nevada at Reno.

Zeilberger, J., Sampen, S. E., & Sloane, H. N. Jr. (1968). Modification of a child's problem behaviors in the home with the mother as therapist. *Journal of Applied Behavior Analysis, 1,* 47–53.

Zettle, R. D., & Hayes, S. C. (1982). Rule-governed behavior: A potential theoretical framework for cognitive-behavioral therapy. In P. C. Kendall (Ed.), *Advances in cognitive-behavioral research and therapy* (Vol. 1). New York: Academic Press.

6
Statistical Methods for Analyzing Family Interaction

William A. Griffin
John M. Gottman
University of Washington

As evidenced by this volume, investigators are extending their search for factors associated with the etiology and maintenance of depression and aggression beyond the individual, into the realm of interpersonal interaction. Obviously, the hope is that this focus on interpersonal rather than intrapersonal factors will reveal some consistent behavioral parameters that might help explain, and predict the emergence of these dysfunctional behaviors. By taking a social interactional perspective in analyzing aggression, depression, and marital conflict, this text implies that pathological behaviors are generated in the context of ongoing social interaction. Hence it is necessary to collect sequential data.

It is interesting to note that this social-interactional perspective, and its emphasis on sequential ordering, fully blossomed (in the scientific sense) only about 25 years ago with the work of Roger Barker and his colleagues (1963), and Harold Raush (1965). The analytic roots of this perspective, however, had been established earlier. In the late 1940s Shannon and Weaver (1949) introduced the concept that the information transmitted within a channel of communication could be quantified. This idea was immediately brought to the attention of psychologists by Miller and Frick (1949), and later by Attneave (1959). However, these writers focused on individuals, and not social interaction. Then in 1965, Stuart Altmann, an ethologist, published a classic paper on the stochastics of social communication. In this paper he developed the rationale for, and illustrated the use of, sequential contingencies as a means of gaining information (or reducing uncertainty) about the probable behaviors of social interactants. Although Altmann's paper addressed the communication patterns in rhesus monkeys, its application to any social group, including families, was quickly recognized. By the early 1970s, the concept of, and analysis for, sequential connection was a common theme among investigators interested in dyadic interaction, either parent-child (Patterson, 1974) or marital (Raush, Barry, Hertel, & Swain, 1974).

In the decade since these initial studies the focus of social interaction research has evolved from an approach utilizing a somewhat singular perspective (e.g., looking at the interaction patterns in distressed couples, or mother-infant reciprocity) to an approach extending its arena of inquiry into the *ripple effect* of social interaction. For example, it's now common to see interaction studies that attempt to examine the hypothesized relationship between marital interaction, parent–child interaction, and child–peer interaction. As the breath of the social interactional approach has widened, so has the number of appropriate data analytic methods. In the late 1970s, four influential texts laid the methodological and analytic foundation for most of the social interaction studies that followed; they were: (1) Sackett's (1978) *Observing Behavior: Vol. II,* (2) Cairns's (1979) *The Analysis of Social Interactions,* (3) Gottman's (1979) *Marital Interaction,* and (4) Lamb, Suomi, and Stephenson's (1979) *Social Interaction Analysis.* Since the publication of these books, some old analytic methods have been refined and some new ones introduced. This chapter reviews three well-documented methods for analyzing social interaction data. The methods are: lag-sequential, log-linear, and time-series.

We first discuss lag-sequential analysis—a method for coding categorical data that has been available for a decade (Sackett, 1974, 1979), and yet, has not become widely used. Lag-sequential analysis is a simple method of examining sequential connection. From lag-sequential analysis it is possible to derive a Z score used to indicate the degree of connectedness within a data stream. By using this analytic approach, it is possible to determine if a particular data sequence occurred greater or less than would be expected by chance. A relevant example might be, "Does an aggressive act by the child increase or decrease the likelihood of eliciting a depressive behavior by the mother?"

A second method, the log-linear approach, became particularly evident and accessible in the mid-70s with the publication of Bishop, Fienberg and Holland's (1975) "Discrete multivariate analysis." Similar to lag-sequential analysis, an investigator using the log-linear approach addresses questions of sequential connection, but uses pooled data. These pooled data are subjected to a variety of powerful techniques useful in determining how exogenous variables affect the observed sequences. This ability to assess a variable's influence on a specified behavioral sequence makes the log-linear approach a powerful analytic tool.

And finally, the third method, time-series analysis, has a long history of application in the physical sciences. Yet, in the behavioral sciences, time-series analysis is an infrequently used analytic technique. This analytic method, however, can be very useful in family interaction research because it permits the investigator to track behaviors over time. This, in turn, allows the investigator to determine if and how behaviors change, and whether the change can be attributed to a specified event, or the behavior of another interactant.

Each method is presented with a minimum of equations, and a maximum of illustrations. It is hoped that this format will encourage a thorough reading of each section, and give the reader an appreciation of the appropriateness of these techniques for family interaction data.

LAG-SEQUENTIAL ANALYSIS

When an investigator has collected sequential categorical data, one of the initial decisions is whether or not the data will be pooled. If there are ample data, the investigator has the option of analyzing unit-by-unit (e.g., family-by-family) or collapsing across subjects. Several things influence this decision, for example, the frequency of relevant events, or the number of subjects. Lag-sequential analysis is appropriate if there are enough data within each family for a family-by-family sequential analysis. If there are not enough data points, pooled data should be analyzed using log-linear models.

Several basic concepts of sequential connection need to be reviewed. To obtain information from social interaction data, it must first be put into a form that (1) reflects and maintains its temporal sequence, and (2) can be analyzed using methods developed for extracting relevant sequential information. Social interaction data are coded into long sequences of behavior. Imagine viewing behavior through a sliding window, where the window allows you to look at X events simultaneously (X equals the number of temporally joined events). Using a two-event sequence, for example, as the window slides to the right, one event drops from the windows as a new event is picked up. Suppose letters represent coded behaviors, then the process can be illustrated as follows:

A(BC)ABCABCABCABC
AB(CA)BCABCABCABC
ABC(AB)CABCABCABC

or if you were interested in three-event sequences (triples) the window would move as follows:

A(BCA)BCABCABCABC
AB(CAB)CABCABCBAC
ABC(ABC)ABCABCABC

Behavior conceptualized in this fashion is consistent with the manner in which data are analyzed using the methods presented below. In essence, the objective is to determine what information there is in the temporal structure of the behavioral string.

Forms of Probability

In any form of sequential analysis the basic component used in deciphering this structure is the *simple probability* of a event. Simple probability reflects the probability that an event occurs; it reflects the distribution of the event over the period of observation, relative to all coded behaviors. The notation for simple probability is **p(A),** where A is the particular event of interest. To estimate the simple probability you divide the number of occurrences of the specific event by the total number of all events. For example, if the event of interest was open handed hitting by males during playground activities and it occurred 14 times during the 107 observed behaviors, an estimate of the simple (unconditional) probability would be .13 (14/107 = .13); or stated differently, 13% of the observed behaviors were open handed hitting.

If you were to widen the behavior window to include two events simultaneously, it would be possible to construct a two-event simple probability. Conceptually, this is the same as a simple single event probability. The notation is the same except that it reflects two joined behaviors, **p(AB),** where AB is the particular two-event sequence of interest. Moreover, the formula for deriving a two-event simple probability is the same except that the denominator is the total number of all two-event sequences (which will be 1 less than the number of single events, or $N_2 = N_1 - 1$).

A different, yet related concept, is *conditional probability*. Conditional probability, like simple probability, reflects the likelihood of a given event, except that it reflects the event's probability conditioned on another behavior. In other words, it reports the likelihood of a specific combination of events.

To understand this better, two terms need to be introduced. First, the behavior on which the probability is conditioned is called the **given** or antecedent behavior. Second, the consequence behavior, or the behavior that occurs given that the conditioned behavior has occurred, is called the **target** behavior. Assume A was the given behavior and B the target, written as **p(B|A),** this combination is stated as the probability of B, given A. The formula is:

$$p(B|A) = \frac{f(AB)}{f(A)} \qquad (1)$$

where f(AB) is the frequency of joint occurrences of AB (i.e., the number of AB pairs), and f(A) is the total number of As. There are 5 AB pairs in example 1 and A occurred 5 times, so p(B|A) is 5/5, or 1.00. This means that, of the 5 times A occurred, B occurred after it 5 times.

As noted, the conditional probability reflects the likelihood of a combination of events, usually consisting of contiguous events. However if the events are not contiguous, and if the lag (displacement) is specified, the conditional probability can be calculated. This is called the *transitional probability*. For lags greater than 1, events occurring between the specific target and the given behavior are ignored. The formula for transitional probability is the same as conditional probability, but in the notation the lag is specified (e.g., $p_1(B|A)$ indicates a lag $= 1$), and the analysis is called "lag-sequential analysis." For example, consider the sliding window:

> AB(CB)CABCBCABCBC
> ABCBCAB(CB)CABCBC
> ABCBCABCBCAB(CB)C

where parentheses indicate the occurrence of a CB. These occurrences are used to determine the conditional probability $p(B|C)$ or the transitional probability $p_1(B|C)$; if, however, if you were interested in $p_2(B|C)$ or the probability of B, given C as two previous behaviors, the window would look like this:

> ABCB(CXB)CXBCBCXBC
> ABCBCXB(CXB)CBCXBC
> ABCBCXBCXBCB(CXB)C

where X is the ignored behavior. Depending on the hypothesized connectedness between behaviors, this displacement (or lag) can be extended to 4 or 5, or even more places. However, it is seldom profitable to go beyond lag 5 or 6.

Note that we have introduced three similar types of probabilities: the simple two event—$p(AB)$, the conditional—$p(B|A)$ and the transitional—$p_1(B|A)$. The difference between the simple two event and the conditional (and transitional) is that a two-event sequence is just the simple probability of that particular sequence relative to all two-event sequences, whereas the conditional probability is the likelihood that a specific behavior will occur given that another specified behavior has occurred at a specified time. And while they may appear similar, each yields a different type of information. Conceptually, this difference is not difficult to grasp, and it is illustrated in the example that follows.

Determining Pattern

Before an example is given, two questions need to be addressed. First, what is the objective of sequential analysis? Simply put, the objective of lag-sequential analysis is to determine if the data has structure beyond randomness; in essence, to determine if the data are connected in some way. Consider, for example, maternal depression. Does the mother's affect change as a function of the child's behavior? If it does not, and no other discriminative stimulus is apparent, then the behavior is considered random. If however, the mother's affect varies depending on the child's behavior, then we might postulate that the two are sequentially connected. In effect, then, the objective of lag-sequential analysis is to determine if, and how, the behaviors of the mother and child are connected.

This leads us to the second question: How does lag-sequential analysis determine sequential connection? The lag-sequential analysis method first derives expected values for what would occur if the behavior sequences were random. It then takes the expected values, compares them to the realized (actual) values and determines if the difference in values is greater than expected by chance. To generate expected values, a model is used. Typically, the most useful model is called the first-order model (or first-order Markov approximation; see Altmann, 1965). It assumes that the occurrence of events are not random, but that event order is (Bakeman & Gottman, 1986).

To derive the expected value of a two-event sequence the following formula is used:

$$p(AB) = p(A) \cdot p(B) \qquad (2)$$

where—

$$p(A) = f(A)/N$$

and

$$p(B) = f(B)/(N - f(A))^1$$

where N = total number of all events, and f = frequency. A simpler overall formula for Equation (2) may be:

$$p(AB) = \frac{f(A)}{N} \cdot \frac{f(B)}{N - f(A)} \qquad (3)$$

The basic measure for sequential connection is the binomial Z statistic, which has been modified by Gottman (1980) and (Allison & Liker, 1982), written as:

$$Z = \frac{f(g,t) - f(g)p(t)}{\sqrt{f(g)p(t) [1 - p(t)][1 - p(g)]}} \qquad (4)$$

where—

$f(g,t)$ = frequency with which the target event t occurred at a particular lag before or after the given event, g.

$p(t)$ = probability of the target event; matrix column total divided by the total # of sequences minus the # of given, where—

$$p(t) = \frac{f(t)}{N_2 - f(g)}$$

---

[1]Note: p(B) is the frequency of B divided by the number of events minus A events—this is because A cannot follow itself. If codes are permitted to follow themselves then p(B) = f(B)/N.

and

$$f(g) = \text{frequency of given; matrix row total}$$

and

$$p(g) = \text{probability of given, where---}$$

$$p(g) = \frac{f(g)}{N_2}$$

Note that N_2 in this case is the number of two-event sequences, not the total number of events.

Example

This example uses data collected from a single couple, at home, attempting to resolve a marital conflict issue (Krokoff, Gottman, & Roy, 1987). For this interaction 6 codes are used: Husband positive ($+$), neutral ($\bigcirc$), and negative ($-$), and Wife positive ($+$), neutral ($\bigcirc$), and negative ($-$). A series of two-event matrices are used to summarize the interaction. First, in Table 6.1 an observed frequency matrix is given. Notice that on the left margin time at t represents the given or antecedent behavior, and time $+1$, on top, represents the target or consequence behavior. Table 6.2 gives the simple two event probability matrix. Each cell valve is derived by dividing the cell by the total number of 2 event sequences. Finally, Table 6.3 shows the lag 1 transitional probabilities for this couple. Each cell value is the raw frequency divided by the row total (rows must sum to 1.00).

The foregoing matrices provide sufficient information to answer questions about specific transitions relevant to the research at hand. For example, suppose

TABLE 6.1
Observed Frequencies for Two-Event Sequences
(N = 268)

		t + 1						
		H+	Ho	H-	W+	Wo	W-	
	H+	0	0	0	0	2	2	
	Ho	0	10	5	5	60	20	
	H-	0	9	2	1	3	0	
t	W+	0	3	0	1	5	0	
	Wo	3	54	6	2	24	8	
	W-	1	24	2	1	3	12	43
				15				268

TABLE 6.2
Simple Probabilities for Two-Event Sequences
(See Table 6.1)

		t + 1					
		H+	Ho	H−	W+	Wo	W−
	H+	0	0	0	0	.0074	.0074
	Ho	0	.0373	.0186	.0186	.2238	.0746
t	H−	0	.0335	.0074	.0037	.0119	0
	W+	0	.0119	0	.0037	.0186	0
	Wo	.0119	.2014	.0223	.0074	.0895	.0298
	W−	.0037	.0895	.0074	.0037	.0119	.0447

we were interested in knowing if the husband was likely to respond to the wife's negative affect (W− at t) with negative affect (H− at t + 1). To get an idea of the likelihood of this occurrence we can look at the lag 1 transitional probability in Table 6.3. It is 0.47—not very high, but its significance can be tested using the binomial Z score. Note that for this example, codes may follow themselves, this is important in calculating the correct Z score. It would be calculated as follows:

frequency of wife's negative statements:

$$f(W-) = 43$$

thus

$$p(W-) = \frac{43}{268} = .1604$$

and the frequency of husband's negative statements:

$$f(H-) = 15$$

TABLE 6.3
Lag I Transitional Probabilities for Two-Event Sequences

		t + 1					
		H+	Ho	H−	W+	Wo	W−
	H+	0	0	0	0	.5000	.5000
	Ho	0	.1000	.0500	.0500	.6000	.2000
t	H−	0	.6000	.1330	.0670	.2000	0
	W+	0	.3330	0	.1110	.5560	0
	Wo	.0310	.5570	.0620	.0210	.2470	.0820
	W−	.0230	.5580	.0470	.0230	.0700	.2790

thus

$$p(H-) = \frac{15}{268} = .0557$$

hence—

$$Z = \frac{2 - 43 \cdot .0557}{\sqrt{43 \cdot .0557 \, [.9440][.8396]}}$$

$$= \frac{-.406}{1.377}$$

$$Z = -.294$$

Z needs to be > 1.96 for the difference between conditional and unconditional probabilities (the numerator) to be significantly different from chance at alpha $= .05$. With a Z score of $-.29$ it appears that for this particular couple that the Husband was not more likely than expected by chance to respond to the Wife's negative affect with additional negative affect. Had the Z score been significant (> 1.96), the next step would have been to determine if there were enough transitions to warrant confidence in stating that the event combination exceeded chance. Examples of how this value can be estimated can be found elsewhere (Bakeman & Gottman, 1986; Siegel, 1956). As an aside, additional inspection of the tables (see Table 6.3) suggests that the Husband was likely to respond to the Wife's negative affect with a neutral response (transitional probability $= .558$); in fact, the Z score for this transition was significant $(Z = 2.74, p < .05)$.

Once a Z score has been calculated, its use depends on the investigator choosing one of several options. First, if there are sufficient data points (Siegel, 1956), and if the within subject serial dependency is low (Gardner & Hartmann, 1984), and the general research question is framed as "is the observed frequency for a particular sequence significantly different from expected?", then the Z score can be interpreted as such. That is, the investigator can state with confidence that the likelihood of the specified sequence exceeds chance, and thus provides information about the interaction. The use of a Z score in this manner is useful in the initial stages of sequence identification and hypothesis building.

A Z score can also be used simply as a score. For example, in the case where a Z score is calculated for a particular behavior sequence or numerous sequences collected over multiple subjects, the scores can be pooled and used in standard parametric statistical procedures such the analysis of variance (Bakeman & Gottman, 1986; Gottman & Bakeman, 1979).

Creative Approaches

The previous example of lag sequential analysis illustrates how inferences about the sequence structure of data can be determined. From the simple method shown above, numerous researchers have developed some creative approaches for using this technique to get more information from the data. Some examples are:

Lagged Probability Profile Analysis.   As implied by its title, this technique constructs a profile of extended sequences of behaviors. It allows the investigator to develop a hypothesized behavioral sequence consisting multiple discrete events. The progression toward a couple conflict, for example, may consist of 3 or 4 separate events ordered in a predictable manner. The ordering of these events can be determined by the lagged probability profile procedure.

Each profile is developed over a series of analytic steps. First, a criterion (given) and a target variable are selected, and transitional probabilities are estimated for a specified number of lags. This procedure is repeated for multiple target variables. The highest transitional probabilities at each lag (across multiple targets) form an hypothesized behavior sequence. To verify this sequence, the investigator then selects the target variable with the highest transitional probability at lag 1, and it becomes the criterion. Again, transitional probabilities for multiple target variables are computed for various lags; this procedure is systematically done until the remaining target variable has become the criterion variable. If the hypothesized sequence is accurate, the pattern should show up again in the moving criterion method. Two notable examples can be found in the literature: Sackett's (1974, 1979) examination of mother–infant interaction in Macaque monkeys, and the work of Gottman, Markman, and Notarius (1977) in their study of marital communication. This latter work is examined as an example of this technique.

Gottman, Markman, and Notarius (1977) coded the sequential utterances of nondistressed and distressed couples discussing marital problems. These investigators were curious about what pattern characterized couple interaction after the husbands complained about a marital problem. With Husband Complaint as the criterion code, they computed lagged transitional probabilities for a number of target codes, including Wife Agreement, Wife Complaint, Husband Agreement, and Husband Complaint. Although 24 codes were defined, the aforementioned codes always included the highest Z scores.

An interesting difference was noted between nondistressed and distressed couples. For nondistressed couples, significant scores occurred only when Wife Agreement (at lags 1, 3 and 5) and Husband Complaint (at lags 2 and 4) served as targets. Conversely, for distressed couples, significant Z scores occurred only when Wife Complaint (at lags 1 and 3) and Husband Complaint (at lags 2, 4 and 6) served as targets. Gottman et al. (1977) referred to this latter behavior among distressed couples as "cross-complaining" and to the process of cycling between Husband Complain and Wife Agreement for nondistressed couples as "validation." Lagged probability profiles for these results are presented in Figs. 6.1a and 6.1b.

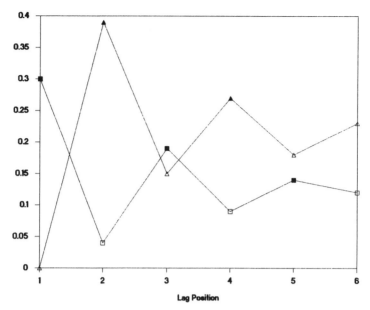

FIG. 6.1a. A lagged profile for nondistressed couples for Husband Complaint at lag (0). Each filled triangle or square represents a significance transitional probability (Z score, $p < .05$) for Husband Complaint or Wife Agree, respectively, at the specified lag.

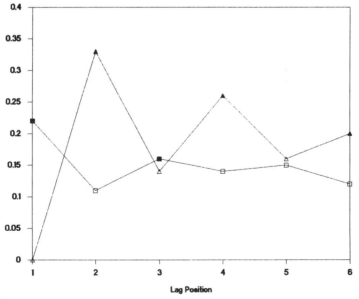

FIG. 6.1b. A lagged probability profile for distressed couples for Husband Complaint at lag (0). Again, each filled triangle or square indicate a significant Z score for Husband Complaint and Wife Complaint, respectively, at the specified lag.

141

Building from Micro to Macro Analyses.   Sequential analysis provides a means of detecting patterns. These patterns can themselves be used as codes. By using patterns as codes, the investigator can construct a macro picture of the interaction. This reduces the number and complexity of data bits, in turn producing a larger, more interpretable perspective of the interaction. There are several examples of this method of data reduction in the literature. Recently, Gottman (1983) used this method to analyze conversations of unacquainted children. He identified a set of sequences that indexed social processes of interest, and then designed a macro coding system that coded for these longer chains.

Similarly, Patterson and Moore (1979) initially used a micro coding system to code family interaction, then changed the unit of interaction and reexamined the interaction at a macro level. They analyzed the interactions of one child, Tina, with her family. By graphing the frequency of Tina's aversive responses for 50 consecutive 1-min intervals, they determined that Tina's aversive behaviors were orderly, occurring every 25 minutes. Moreover, they found that Tina's aversive behavior was displayed in bursts, and that her *complaining* and *arguing* were the most common initiators of extended coercive interchanges. They then used lag-sequential analysis (Sackett, 1979) and found that the mother tended to reward Tina's complaining. They wrote:

> Mother's reaction to Tina's individual "Complain" behaviors (97 isolated events) suggested strongly that Tina's complaining significantly increased the probability that the mother would subsequently react positively towards her. Forty-five percent of the reactions by others to these "Complaints" were prosocial. . . . If Tina ran off two "Complaints" in a row, the mother reacted by providing positive consequences 67 of the time. . . . The data strongly suggest Tina's first "Complain" was often not effective in removing the mother's aversive intrusion, but produced another aversive intrusion which finally produced a positive response from the mother, i.e., an exemplar of negative reinforcement for complain patterns. . . . It seemed likely that if Tina had stopped after her first complain (CP) she should have received an aversive antecedent plus an aversive consequence. However, going on to a third or fourth CP appeared to produce a more favorable outcome. (pp. 88–90)

By using this approach, Patterson and Moore were able to describe the interaction using extended, two- and three-event chains.

The Trick of Lag-Sequential Analysis and the "Full Solution"

One of the unique features of lag-sequential analysis is that it is possible to illuminate sequences of more than two events, and yet require less data that simple probability methods would. To illustrate, first consider that the number of events necessary to examine extended sequences (e.g., 3 or 4) using the simple probability method increases rapidly with each additional event in the sequence.

For example, Bakeman and Gottman (1986) show that for a 5-code coding system, to extend the event sequence from two to three, the necessary data points increase from 189 for two-event sequences to 647 in the case of three-event sequences.

On the other hand, using lag-sequential analysis, the investigator can examine extended sequences by defining the antecedent event (given) as a nonadjacent event where the lag (plus or minus) can be several events from the target event— hence, the extended sequence involves multiple events yet requires no additional data. This is the *trick* of lag-sequential analysis and was illustrated in the previous section on lagged probability profiles. Yet, there is a problem with this approach—specifically, it is not consistent with the full Markov analysis. A "full solution" Markov analysis examining extended sequences requires that the antecedent be a pair or triple (or more) of contiguous events; however, like the simple probability method, this requires a large number of data points. Still, the *trick* approach is useful in the early stages of data exploration, or for developing initial hypotheses. But for confirmation, the investigator needs to employ the full solution.

The techniques of lag-sequential analysis described in this section are only a portion of those available. Additional information on conceptual and analytic issues (e.g., necessary data points, type 1 error), and analytic methods are provided in detail elsewhere (Bakeman & Gottman, 1986; Gottman & Roy, in press).

LOG-LINEAR MODELS

The previous section on sequential analysis dealt with the unit-by-unit analysis of categorical data, the present section deals with the analysis of pooled data using log-linear models. As noted, lag-sequential analysis is a excellent method for developing some ideas about important sequences. Once their sequences are specified, an obvious next step would be to determine how the sequence of interest is affected by exogenous variables. Log-linear models permit an analysis of this influence by reducing the observed behavior to a linear function of the exogenous variables. Before reviewing this approach several relevant facets of handling pooled data are discussed.

Pooling Data Across Subjects

Often the decision is made to pool data across subjects. Pooled data offer several advantages. First, rare, but important, events cannot be studied on a subject-by-subject basis; by pooling, the investigator has greater statistical power, and more analytic options. Second, some of the current coding systems employ a large number of codes, and pooling may deal with problems of relatively low frequencies of certain codes. This provides greater stability across codes, and more options to compare codes.

Basic Formula

Log-linear analyses use basically one formula, it is the Likelihood ratio chi-square (LRχ^2) (Goodman, 1983), written as

$$LR\chi^2 = 2 \sum O_i \ln(O_i/E_i) \qquad (5)$$

where O_i represents the observed cell frequencies and E_i the expected cell frequencies for the ith cell. The LRχ^2 statistic is sometimes referred to as G^2, for Goodman (1972, 1983)—a major innovator in the analysis of cross-tabulated data. A versatile statistical test, the LRχ^2 is used to determine the fit of a model in log-linear analysis as well as the difference between models, and it is used to assess the significance of order, homogeneity, and stationarity in the data. In fact, these latter data parameters—order, homogeneity, and stationarity need to be briefly introduced before discussing log-linear models.

Issues in Pooling Subjects

When subjects are pooled three issues need to be addressed: (1) **Order**—information about how long the interaction chains go back into the past; (2) **Homogeneity**—information about whether or not the pooled subjects have similar transition probabilities; and (3) **Stationarity**—information about whether the transition probabilities are the same over the observation period. These are Markov assumptions about the structure of the data set. The information provided by each assumption is necessary before the investigator can confidently discuss the results from pooled data. Significance for each issue is determined by the LRχ^2 (Equation 5), developed by Anderson and Goodman (1957). Detailed information on computation can be found in Gottman and Roy (in press). These tests can be run by using existing Log-linear programs in major statistical programs (e.g., BMDP); also, Arundale (1982) has developed a computer program that can test these parameters. Each assumption is reviewed below.

Homogeneity. This assumption requires that each individual (or member of a subpopulation) have the same transitional probability structure. In other words, the overall transition probability matrix for the sample should be representative of each member of that sample (Hewes, 1980). A typical use of the test of homogeneity is illustrated by Ting-Toomey (1983) whereby the LRχ^2 for homogeneity was computed across two discussions of marital problems generated by two separate tasks. The likelihood ratio comparing the two discussions was not significant. Because she found no significant difference, this means that the two conversations could be pooled and analyzed as a single interaction.

A slightly different approach was taken by Krokoff et al. (1987). The authors reported the ratio of the chi-square statistic to the degrees of freedom as a function of grouping the subjects in the cells designated by the experimental design. For both variables (occupational status, marital satisfaction) grouping according to designation increased the ratio; this implies that the cells of the experimental design provided significant gain in the homogeneity of the transition frequency matrices.

Order.   This assumption refers to the number of prior states needed for prediction of the state of occupancy. For example, first-order means that only the immediately prior state and the transition matrix representing the dynamics of the system need to be taken into account. A second-order model states that additional gain in information is obtained by going back in the past two time units. In essence, order tells the investigator how far back in the behavioral sequence relevant behaviors occur. It is necessary for investigators to test for independence (zero order), then test for first order. After first-order, second-order, and higher-order chains can be tested for, yet most data are first- and second-order (see Manderscheid, Rae, McCarrick, & Silbergeld, 1982; Vuchinich, 1984).

An example of the application of this test can again be found in the study reported by Ting-Toomey (1983). In comparing a zero-order model (independence) to a first-order model, she found that the likelihood-ratio chi-square was 566.46 for satisfied couples and 709.51 for dissatisfied couples, with 196 degrees of freedom. Thus, the first-order model cannot be rejected; that is, the first-order model provided a better fit to the data than zero-order (no sequential dependency). A subsequent test comparing the first-order model to the second-order model was nonsignificant. This suggests that there was no evidence that additional information could be gained by considering triads of events. Her analysis, then, was based on a first-order model.

Stationarity.   Stationarity refers to the assumption that the transition probabilities are the same across the observation period. Intuitively, it should be apparent why this assumption is posited. If behavior can be predicted based on some regular relationship between antecedent conditions and consequence events, then one way to assure predictability is make that relationship constant over time (Hewes, 1980).

Viewed another way, stationarity refers to the consistency of transition probabilities for the entire sample across time, whereas homogeneity refers to transition probability consistency across subjects. Thus these two assumptions are similar conceptually, hence they use the same type of statistical test. Examples of tests for stationarity can be found elsewhere (Hawes & Foley, 1976; Krokoff et al., 1987; Manderscheid et al., 1982).

All of these tests are general omnibus tests of the stochastic parameters of the population; as such, they fail to provide specific information about the data. For example, they do not assess stationarity for specific sequences. For information about other options that extract much more specific details the reader is referred to Gottman and Roy (in press). As others (Gottman, 1987; Hewes, 1980) have noted, these tests (and accompanying assumptions) should not be viewed as a restriction on the investigator, or a fault with the data. Instead, the tests provide the investigator with a better grasp of the data, and hopefully, a better understanding of the phenomena being studied.

Log-Linear Models

To understand log-linear analysis, it is first necessary to understand the concept of a model. Models are essentially estimates of the expected cell frequencies of a transition matrix. These estimates reflect the effect of the parameters of the categorical variables (Knoke & Burke, 1980). By providing an estimate of fit to the observed data, models permit a test of how much the estimated cell frequencies differ from the observed cell frequencies, and hence a measure of how specific variables contribute to the observed behavior. For a single set of data, multiple models are developed, each reflecting different estimates for the various single variables and the interaction between variables. For each model, a $LR\chi^2$ is calculated.

In the log-linear approach, a model consists of a mean (or constant) and the parameter effects. For a two parameter design with no interaction, this can be illustrated in its multiplicative form as:

$$F_{ij} = \gamma \; \delta_i^{(A)} \; \delta_j^{(B)} \qquad (6)$$

where F_{ij} represent the number of cases in cell ij given a true model, and γ (gamma sign) is the geometric mean of the number of cases in each cell in the table, and terms $\delta^{(A)}$ and $\delta^{(B)}$ represent the parameter effects on cell frequencies (Knoke & Burke, 1980). By taking the natural logarithms of all the terms in Equation 6, an additive logarithmic form can be written as:

$$\ln F_{ij} = \ln \gamma + \ln(\delta_i^A) + \ln(\delta_j^B)$$

or

$$\ln m_{ij} = \mu + \lambda_i^{(A)} + \lambda_j^{(B)} \qquad (7)$$

These two forms are mathematically equivalent. As can be seen in Equation 7, the estimate of the model is a function of a constant plus the effect of each parameter. The magnitude of the effect is measured as a departure from the value of 0, as it is added to μ. If the cell count for a parameter is greater than the expected cell count, the parameter effect exceeds 0; conversely, a parameter effect of 0 indicates that the cell count does not exceed that expected by the

TABLE 6.4
The 19 Possible Models for a Three-Way Table

Defining Set of Parameters	μ	A	B	C	AB	AC	BC	ABC
{ABC}	*	*	*	*	*	*	*	*
{AB}{AC}{BC}	*	*	*	*	*	*	*	
{AB}{AC}	*	*	*	*	*	*		
{AC}{BC}	*	*	*	*		*	*	
{BC}{AB}	*	*	*	*	*		*	
{A}{BC}	*	*	*	*			*	
{B}{AC}	*	*	*	*		*		
{C}{AB}	*	*	*	*	*			
{BC}	*		*	*			*	
{AB}	*	*	*		*			
{AC}	*	*		*		*		
{A}{B}{C}	*	*	*	*				
{A}{B}	*	*	*					
{A}{C}	*	*		*				
{B}{C}	*		*	*				
{A}	*	*						
{B}	*		*					
{C}	*			*				
{μ}	*							

constant, or simply, adds nothing to the constant. Viewed differently, λ (parameter effect) reflects the amount of skewness of cases across a variable's categories (Knoke & Burke, 1980).

The objective behind using multiple models for a data set is to find a single, simple model which fits the data. Although it is not necessary, most models used in log-linear analysis are hierarchical. That is, they are built up from simple models to increasing more complex ones. As a result of the hierarchical structure, models containing the higher-order relationships contain the simpler, lower-order models. This arrangement simplifies testing the fit of a model.

An example of the hierarchical structure of models in a 3 parameter design is illustrated by Table 6.4. Note that there are 19 testable models in this three way table. Models are denoted by brackets { }, and by virtue of their hierarchical structure, the model AB, an interaction term, implies all the lower order relationships. In this case, {AB} subsumes {A}{B}. At the top of the model hierarchy is the saturated model, it contains all the parameters, and as such, reflects the observed data. The objective of model testing is to find a model which, like the saturated model, has a nonsignificant $LR\chi^2$, yet has fewer parameters (Gottman, 1987).

For smaller, less complex experimental designs (e.g., 2×2), cell estimates can be generated by hand, however for complex designs, maximum likelihood estimates (MLE) of expected cell frequencies must be generated by algorithms developed for this purpose. Two are most common, the Newton-Raphson algorithm used in Bock and Yates' (1973) MULTIQUAL program, and the simpler, more commonly used iterative proportional fitting algorithm (IPF), also called the Deming-Stephan algorithm. With these algorithms it is possible to estimate cell counts once a model is specified. Degrees of freedom for a given model can be determined by counting the number of categories in the variables in each effect in the model, subtract one from each number, and multiply the set.

Model Fitting

Recall that a $LR\chi^2$ is generated for each model, the larger the $LR\chi^2$ relative to the available df, the more the expected cell count departs from the observed cell entries. If the difference between df and $LR\chi^2$ is large, we can conclude that the model does not fit the data well, and should be thought of as an inaccurate representation of the variable interrelationships. Remember the objective is to find a simple model that is not rejected (nonsignificant $LR\chi^2$); that is, a model which fits the data with the fewest parameters. Such a model provides a good approximation of the saturated model. In fact, hypotheses generated for log-linear analyses are essentially comparisons between alternative models and the saturated model (Knoke & Burke, 1980).

Probably the most common method of finding the "fitted" model is to begin with the simplest model, and systematically build the model term-by-term until a reasonable fit is obtained. As each new term is added, it is possible to evaluate the effect of the added term by subtracting the $LR\chi^2$'s for the two models and their respective df. This difference is asymptotically distributed as chi-square, with degrees of freedom equal to the difference in the **df**s for the respective models. This ability to test the difference is an important feature in the log-linear approach.

For example, consider a three-factor {ABC} design testing a model that includes A, B, and AB. If for this model, the $LR\chi^2$ is 49.40 with 20 df and the $LR\chi^2$ for the model less the interaction term (i.e., {AB}) is 212.70 with 36 df, then the $LR\chi^2$ for the AB interaction term is $(212.70 - 49.40) = 163.30$ with $(36 - 20) = 16$ df. In this example, the term {AB} produces a model that is significantly different, and should be included in the model.

The earlier example illustrates how this procedure is used to determine differences in models as you progressively add terms. Differences between two $LR\chi^2$s can also be used to determine the significance of a term in the full model. For example, in a two-dimensional table, if the {A}{B} model holds (fits the data)

$$\ln \hat{m}_{i,j} = \hat{\mu} + \hat{\lambda}_i^{(A)} + \hat{\lambda}_j^{(B)}$$

yields $LR\chi^2 = 12.6$ with $1 =$ df and the submodel (A) holds

$$\ln \hat{m}_{i,j} = \hat{\mu} + \hat{\lambda}_i^{(A)}$$

yields $LR\chi^2 = 51.2$ with $2 =$ df, then the difference in the $LR\chi^2$ evaluates the $\lambda^{(B)}$ term as $51.2 - 12.6 = 38.6$ with df $= 2 - 1 = 1$. Like the previous example, the result would suggest that the $\lambda^{(B)}$ term be kept in the model.

Although systematically adding terms to a simple model is a common method of determining the fitted model, other procedures have been proposed that can help in this process. For example, Brown (1974) suggested a procedure called screening to decide whether to include each parameter in the final model. For each term, Brown suggested obtaining two estimates of significance. One estimate, called a test of *marginal association,* compares two simple models. In a four-factor table, for example, it compares {AB} with {A}{B}. A second estimate, called a test of *partial association,* compares two complex models; one model includes the term of interest (e.g., {AB}) whereas the other does not. Although each method compares the same term, each also yields a different value for the same term. Thus the investigator has a range of significance values that can be used to decide whether to include a particular term in the final model. Even if the investigator uses this method, or simply adds term-by-term to a simple model, or removes term-by-term from the saturated model, the objective—a simple and interesting model—should guide all decisions. As Goodman (1972) wrote:

> By including additional λs in the model, the fit can be improved; and so the researcher must weigh in each particular case the advantages of the improved fit against the disadvantages of having introduced additional parameters in the model. Different researchers will weigh these advantages and disadvantages differently. (p. 41)

Contrasts

After finding a model which fits the data, it is possible to determine which sequences within the data contribute to the observed effects. This can be done by comparing cell counts within the table. Comparisons are made using a standardized λ (Goodman, 1971), where

$$S(\hat{\lambda}) = \frac{\hat{\lambda}}{\sqrt{v(\hat{\lambda})}}$$

(8)

and is approximately normally distributed with zero mean and unit variance (hence, a Z score). Where λ is

$$\hat{\lambda} = \sum_{i,j,k...} a_{i,j,k...} \ln(\hat{m}_{i,j,k...})$$

and $v(\hat{\lambda})$ is

$$v(\hat{\lambda}) = \sum_{i,j,k...} \frac{(a_{i,j,k...})^2}{\hat{m}_{i,j,k...}}$$

where $a_{i,j,k...}$ are the linear constrasts and $\hat{m}_{i,j,k...}$ are the $\log_e$ of the estimated cell frequencies. If $S(\hat{\lambda})$ is significant then the cell differences for the contrasted categories are significantly different.

TABLE 6.5
Example of a Lag 1 Contingency Table Across Occupational Status
and Marital Satisfaction

Group	Antecedent Affect	Consequent Affect					
		H+	Ho	H-	W+	Wo	W-
White collar	H+	0	12	0	8	11	12
	Ho	8	0	29	33	509	168
	H-	2	30	0	3	87	54
Unhappy	W+	7	32	5	0	15	2
	Wo	15	506	75	17	0	70
	W-	11	162	67	1	64	0
	H+	0	24	2	34	49	15
	Ho	23	0	31	96	873	133
	H-	5	36	0	4	43	16
Happy	W+	27	79	13	0	41	5
	Wo	57	894	40	28	0	24
	W-	11	121	18	4	39	0
Blue collar	H+	0	19	1	11	17	5
	Ho	15	0	46	53	520	93
	H-	1	41	0	23	142	97
Unhappy	W+	13	43	22	0	26	5
	Wo	21	524	134	19	0	62
	W-	3	99	100	4	54	0
	H+	0	17	13	30	58	25
	Ho	27	0	40	72	729	108
	H-	8	50	0	24	123	54
Happy	W+	31	70	16	0	48	6
	Wo	54	725	146	40	0	61
	W-	24	117	44	7	62	0

This entire log-linear process can be better understood if we step through an example. Table 6.5 represents a full 2×2 factorial design study of marital interaction in a blue collar/white collar population (Krokoff et al., 1987). This contingency table illustrates the frequency transitions across the two factors: (a) blue or white collar, and (b) happy or unhappy. In each cell, there is a 6×6 matrix. The coded states were husband positive, H+; husband neutral, HO; husband negative, H-; wife positive, W+; wife neutral, WO; and wife negative, W-.

Table 6.6 shows the results of the hierarchical log-linear analysis. Let P = the prior or antecedent code; R = the result, or consequent code; S = satisfaction; and C = class. The model with all three-way interactions fits the data well (df = 19, $LR\chi^2 = 23.1$). The model with the RPC term dropped is only marginally significant ($LR\chi^2 = 55$, df = 38, P = .04). However the RPS and RPC terms are of greatest interest theoretically. They suggest that the Markov matrix varies with marital satisfaction and social class, with marital satisfaction having a much larger effect than social class. For this example we focus on sequences of extended conflict (negative affect). The diagnostic value of these conflicts has been discussed elsewhere (Gottman, 1979; Noller, 1984).

TABLE 6.6
Hierarchical Log-Linear Analysis of the Data in Table 6.5

Effect	DF	Partial Association		Marginal Association	
		Chi-Square	Probability	Chi-Square	Probability
R	5	10223.8	.000		
P	5	10247.8	.000		
S	1	194.6	.000		
C	1	5.9	.015		
RP	19	1642.4	.000	1746.9	.000
RS	5	183.7	.000	204.4	.000
RC	5	136.3	.000	108.7	.000
PS	5	181.2	.000	203.1	.000
PC	5	137.5	.000	110.0	.000
SC	1	0.3	.585	3.6	.057
RPS	19	50.5	.000	44.1	.001
RPC	19	31.9	.032	27.3	.097
RSC	5	43.6	.000	31.1	.000
PSC	5	46.4	.000	31.4	.000

TABLE 6.7
Cell Frequencies, Conditional Probabilities, and Contrasts in the
Reduced Model (RPC Term Dropped)

Groups	H—→W—	S (λ)	W—→H—	S (λ)
Blue collar	140.9 (.25)	4.26	143.5 (.28)	5.23
White collar	82.1 (.29)		87.5 (.17)	
Satisfied	71.0 (.19)	5.59	63.0 (.14)	7.07
Dissatisfied	152.0 (.31)		168.0 (.29)	

Table 6.7 shows the expected cell frequencies in the reduced model and proportions (cell frequency divided by the total number of the specified antecedent). Although the S(λ) terms are quite large, the proportions are moderate, and thus suggest caution in interpreting these contrasts. Nevertheless, these data indicate that (a) that blue-collar husbands are more likely than white-collar husbands to reciprocate wives' negative affect, irrespective of marital satisfaction, and that (b) regardless of class, dissatisfied couples (husbands and wives), are more likely than satisfied couples to reciprocate their partner's negative affect. In short, these results suggest that blue-collar husbands, especially those in an unhappy marriage, are the most likely to reciprocate negative affect. More importantly, for this illustration, these results show that it is possible to measure the relative influence of specific factors (in this case, occupational status, marital satisfaction) on an interaction sequence.

This example illustrates the utility of log-linear analysis with pooled data. Obviously, this was only a brief excursion into log-linear models, and the interested reader is encouraged to read additional, more comprehensive works (see Bishop et al., 1975; Davis, 1974; Gottman & Roy, in press).

TIME-SERIES ANALYSIS

Important individual and family interactions often become apparent only when viewed over time, and unfortunately, most statistical methods fail to address the temporal structure of behavior (a notable exception is Event-History Analysis, see Griffin & Gardner, 1989; Gardner & Griffin, 1989). Moreover, patterns in time-series data usually cannot be detected by visual inspection, hence a method of statistical analysis is necessary.

Although many family investigators collect time-series data, most fail to utilize the temporal information that is inherent in this type of data. Unlike lag-sequential analysis, and its emphasis on extended sequences of behaviors, the time-series approach focuses on a single important behavior (or behavioral index) and monitors the behavior over time. This unique feature of the time-series approach allows the investigator to watch the behavior as it changes during the observation period. In fact, many questions that family interactionalists ask can be answered only with time-series data.

Time-series data are simply data collected over some time period at regular intervals. Although time-series analyses typically require noncategorical data, the categorical data usually collected by family researchers can be converted, using forethought and ingenuity, to a time-series format (see Gottman, 1981).

Researchers that study social interaction often comment on the seemingly cyclical nature of behavior, and frequently express the need for analytic methods that could detect the patterns. In the past, investigators have attempted to summarize and convey their impressions of behavioral patterns by relying on colorful, yet nonquantitative metaphors. Condon and Ogston (1967), for example, commenting on their impressions from 15 minutes of microanalysis of a family's dinner interaction, wrote:

> We are dealing with ordered patterns of change during change, which exhibit rhythmic and varying patterns in the temporal sequencing of such changes. Metaphorically, there are waves within waves within waves, with complex yet determinable relationships between peaks and the troughs of the levels of waves, which serve to express organized processes with continually changing relationships. (p. 224)

These metaphors are an example of an attempt to describe the intricacies of social interaction. Yet, there is still a need to quantify these impressions if they are to be studied scientifically. Currently, time-series methods are available that permit researchers to quantify the peaks and troughs described by Condon and Ogston.

Advantages of Time-Series Data

For investigators who collect categorical data, there are several advantages to creating time-series data. For instance, because data are collected over the period of observation, time-series data *provide a visual picture* of the interaction. A visual representation of the interaction can be useful in understanding how behaviors unfold over the observation period. Consider as an illustration Gottman's (1979, p. 172) time series data obtained from marital interaction (see Fig. 6.2). The variable was the cumulative "total-positive interaction" minus the "total-negative interaction." Gottman found that couples characterized as being high in reciprocating negative affect, produced graphs (both husband and wife) that were quite negative. On the other hand, couples having one partner that typically gave in to the other's complaints produced graphs showing one partner negative and the other positive. Still, couples whose graphs were flat at the start of an interaction tended to have social skill deficits in listening, whereas couples whose graphs were flat at the end of an interaction tended to have social skill deficits in

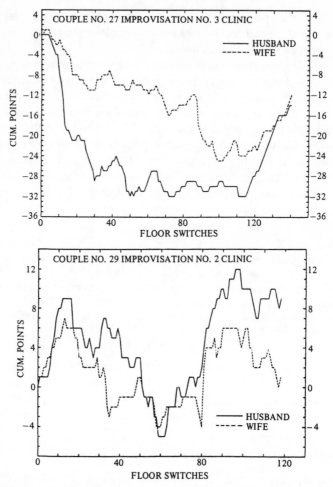

FIG. 6.2.   Time-series data to used to visually illustrate distinct pattern differences across couple types.

negotiation. Thus, from the time-series graphs, Gottman developed a classification of interactional skills that related to response deficits. In effect, the graphs became a useful diagnostic tool for studying and classifying couples' behavior.

Time-series data also provide a mechanism for *discovering the limitations of a coding system*. Because time-series data produce a visual trace of the interaction, abrupt shifts in slope or level could indicate a rare, and possibly important event. It is possible that rare events may not get noticed, or coded, or just as likely that the coding system may not have an appropriate code. An example of time-series data providing this type of information comes from a videotape of couple interaction that Ted Jacob had coded using a version of the Marital Interaction Coding

System (MICS). Using a single index score to summarize the interaction, the couple's interaction began in a very negative way but changed dramatically in the middle and became increasing positive for the duration of the observation period. Subsequent review of the tape indicated the couple's interaction improved after the husband summarized the wife's complaint, and then accepted responsibility for the problem. Gottman (1987) has referred to this use of time series as Gödeling because, like Kurt Gödel's work, it is concerned with using a system to view itself and to discover its own limitations (Gödel, 1932).

Creating Time Series Data

As noted,the investigator that gathers categorical data can create time-series data. There are several options available when creating this type of data. Each option produces a set of time-series for each variable created, and for each person in the interaction unit. Below is an overview of the three options:

Moving Probability-Window.   The object here is to compute the proportion of times an event was observed within a particular block of observations, and then slide the window forward in time. As larger and larger time units are used, the data are smoothed. Although not useful for many frequency domain time-series procedures, it is a useful procedure for graphical display.

Interevent Interval.   As the name implies, this involves graphing the time between specified events over time. Cardiovascular psychophysiologists for example, plot the average time between the R waves of the EKG within a time block of sufficient size. Interevent intervals can be computed with very simple data. For instance, time series data can be created by very crude diary data. Bakeman and Gottman (1986, p. 178) illustrate how interevent intervals can be used to create a time-series from daily records of cigarettes smoked.

Univariate Scaling.   This involves creating, from multiple codes, a critical index of the interaction and plotting it. Consider as an illustration the use by Brazelton, Koslowski, and Main (1974) of a total positive-engagement score in mother-infant face-to-face interaction. Their manner of creating an index score exemplifies the potential for creating time-series data from the type of categorical data usually collected by family interaction researchers.

Cycles in Time-Series Data

Some cycles are extremely regular. Their periods of oscillation (peak-to-peak) are more or less fixed; this is called deterministic cyclicity. This type of a cycle can be illustrated by imagining a well-constructed oscillating pendulum, with a pen attached, marking on a uniformly moving sheet of paper. The motion of the

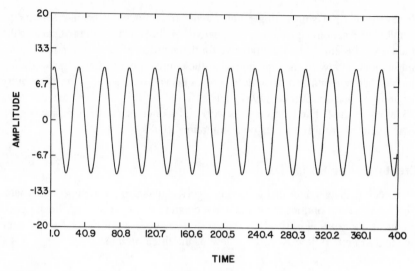

FIG. 6.3.   A sine wave.

pendulum would produce the sine wave illustrated by Fig. 6.3. By attaching a second pendulum to the base of the first, more complex deterministic oscillations are possible. Figure 6.4 illustrates the beat pattern that can be obtained by superposing two sine waves. Although, at first glance the pattern looks menacing, it's not; it's just that in the beat pattern, a faster wave oscillates within the envelope of a slower wave. It should be apparent for this example that extremely elaborate patterns are possible by adding more cycles.

When viewing these elaborate patterns, two variables need to be kept in mind regarding how they were created. Again, consider the case of two pendulums attached to one another. First, each pendulum was shoved to start the movement, how hard it was shoved is the *energy* of the pendulum. This energy is proportional to the square of the amount each pendulum swings; the amount of the swing is called the amplitude of the oscillation. Here amplitude refers to how large the magnitude of the change is from peak to valley.

The second variable is called the *phase* of each pendulum's oscillation, and is where in its arc each pendulum is shoved. Phases for the pendula can be synchronous, opposite (180° out of phase), or somewhere in between. By altering the parameters of these two variables, very complex patterns are possible.

Although the cycles illustrated in Figs. 6.3 and 6.4 are deterministic, most data are not made up of deterministic cycles. In fact, rather than being deterministic, most data are made up of cycles that meander randomly in amplitude or phase around some mean values and with some statistical distributions. In essence, the period of oscillation is a random variable, with a distribution. This is a very important point to remember when analyzing time-series data; moreover, it

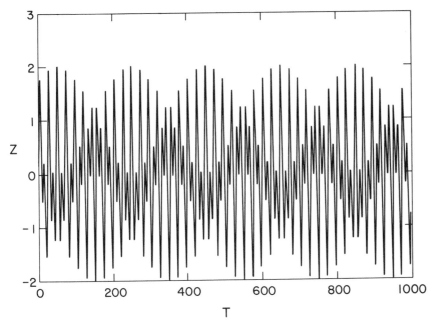

FIG. 6.4.   Beat pattern created by the superposition of two sine waves.

should be noted that this shift from thinking of cycles as deterministic to probabilistic has occurred only in the past century (Gottman, 1981).

Spectral Density Function

Spectral density function is a mathematical tool that allows the investigator to analyze cycles in time-series data. It does so by measuring the amount of energy in each cycle. The usual way to represent this is by a graph. The X axis of the graph measures the frequency of the potential cycles in the data. Frequency refers to how rapidly cycles repeat themselves. The frequency is the reciprocal of the period of oscillation, or stated differently, it is the number of cycles per unit of time. Consider as an illustration a graph with a set of time points, the fastest frequency is one that goes above the mean and then immediately below the mean, thus it repeats every two time points. Hence the fastest frequency is $\frac{1}{2} = 0.5$, and the slowest frequency, obtained by a cycle of infinite period, is 0.0. The range along the X axis for a graph of a the spectral density function goes from 0.0–0.5.

On the Y axis is a plot of density for each frequency, which is related to the amount of energy in each cycle. Remember that this is related to how hard each pendulum was shoved, which is proportional to the square of the amplitude of its oscillation. Figure 6.4 contains a beat pattern that has component cycles of equal

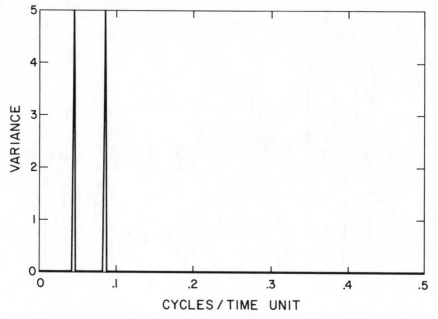

FIG. 6.5.   Spectral density function of the beat pattern. Note the sharp spikes, characteristic of deterministic cycles.

amplitude. The spectral density of the beat pattern is illustrated in Fig. 6.5. These were simulated data, hence the two sharp spikes which characterize deterministic oscillations.

Nondeterministic oscillations, on the other hand, have a band of cycles represented so that their spectral density functions do not have spiked peaks. They are rounded out a bit around the peak. This is illustrated in a subsequent example.

Some important information was given in the previous paragraphs. It might be important to summarize several of the major points that were made. First, most cycles are nearly periodic (stochastic), not deterministic. Second, frequency tells how rapidly things repeat themselves (i.e., cycle). In time-series a cycle implies regular repetition over a fixed time, called the period; the period refers to the peak to peak transition. And finally, the spectral density function tells us which frequencies are present and to what degree. Or stated differently, it tells us how much variance each frequency accounts for in the given time series.

There are two realms of time-series analyses: frequency domain and time domain. Spectral density is found in the frequency domain. This initial review of some terms and concepts was provided so that the reader could understand the examples that follow. However, this is only a very brief synopsis, and an extended review of time series techniques is beyond the scope of this chapter. However, a complete and readable introduction for social scientists is available in Gottman (1981), together with 10 computer programs (Williams & Gottman, 1981). These computer programs have simplified the analysis and interpretation of times series data, and are now available for mainframe or micro-computer applications. Two examples follow, which illustrate the utility and ease of time-series analysis with family interaction data.

Univariate Time-Series

It is often impossible to estimate the effects of rare or unusual events without pooling subjects. Yet for family interaction researchers, rare events, especially those that alter subsequent interaction, are important. However, if we take a subject (e.g., dyad, family) and create a time-series variable that can serve as an index of the interaction, the problem can be solved using interrupted time-series analysis.

First, a single index variable that is theoretically relevant and interesting needs to be created. This variable should be a meaningful measure of the process in the interaction. An example of an index variables was given earlier in the section on Univariate scaling. Figure 6.6 illustrates how the time-series data for this option might look.

Suppose the data in Fig. 6.6 represents a point graph of the wife's negative affect, and at time 30 the husband referred to a relationship he had prior to the marriage. Did this event have any impact on the interaction? The Gottman-

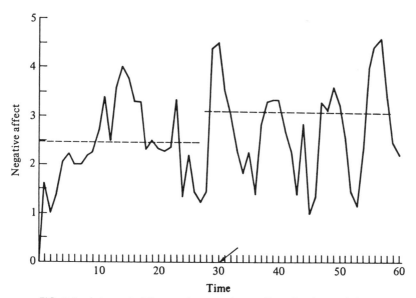

FIG. 6.6.   Interrupted time-series experiment. Note the change in level at time = 30.

Williams program ITSE (Interrupted Time-Series) used a sixth-order auto-regressive model to fit the data. The t test for change in slope was not significant (t = −.13, df = 44), but the t test for change in level was significant (t = 2.15, df = 44). If the situation were real, these results indicate that the event at time 30 did have an impact of the couple's subsequent interaction.

Multivariate

Often investigators of family interaction are interested in questions of synchronicity, reciprocity, and bidirectionality (Gottman & Ringland, 1981). These terms, of course, imply that the individuals interacting may have an influence on each other. By tracking multiple individuals simultaneously using time-series data, these questions can be addressed. The following example of mother-infant interaction was taken from Gottman, Rose, and Mettetal (1982), where additional details can be found. For the mother, 6 nonverbal codes were summed to form a single time-series for the mother, and 7 codes were summed to form a single time-series for the baby. The summed time-series for both mother and infant represented the affective and attentional involvement toward each other. Data were analyzed for two time periods—when the infant was 9-weeks-old, and again at 13 weeks. We review only the findings for the data at 13 weeks.

First it was necessary to determine if the behavior of either individual was cyclical. Spectral density functions for the mother and infant are plotted in Figs. 6.7a and 6.7b. These spectral density functions were calculated using the Williams and Gottman (1981) CRSPES computer program. The horizontal line of dots represent the theoretical spectral density if the data were noise. If the confidence interval (dashed line) around the estimated spectral density function (solid line) rises above this horizontal line, then the peak is statistically significant at $p < .05$. For both mother and child, there is wide band of frequencies for which the spectral density function is significant. It should be apparent that these data are not deterministically periodic. For the baby the significant frequencies extend from 0 to .097, and for the mother it extends from 0 to .80. Both the baby's and the mother's behavior are significantly cyclic, and their cyclicities overlay. If the mother and infant frequency bands did not overlay the two time-series would be statistically independent, and there would be no need to continue.

The next step is to determine if frequency bands are synchronous. For this two additional functions need to be examined: the *coherence spectrum* and the *phase spectrum*. *Coherence* assesses the maximum amount of linear association, and *phase* measures the lead-lag relationship. Both are assessed at each frequency. The coherence is like the square of the correlation coefficient (r^2), and it varies between 0 and 1 (Chatfield, 1985). Moreover, if the coherence is not significant, and large (magnitude determines the confidence interval), then there is no need examine the phase.

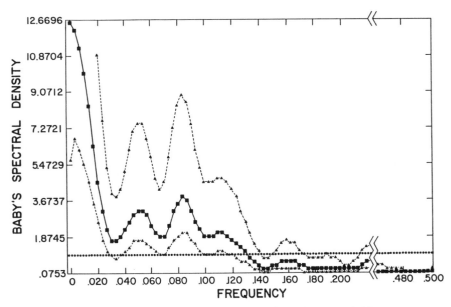

FIG. 6.7a. Spectral density estimates for baby at week 13.

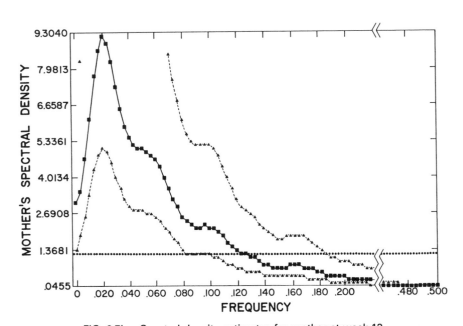

FIG. 6.7b. Spectral density estimates for mother at week 13.

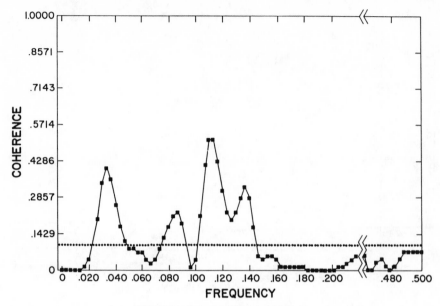

FIG. 6.8.   Coherence at week 13.

Coherence and phase are important only across frequency bands that are statistically significant, and only those bands that overlap between mother and infant; that is, for Fig. 6.8 it would be from .027 to .047. Since the coherence is significant within this band (above the dotted line), the phase spectrum can be examined. The phase may be positive or negative, if it is negative the mother leads the baby, or viewed differently, the baby is able to respond to her mother. A negative phase simply means that the first series entered in the analysis (the x series) leads the second, although the order of entry is arbitrary. Time lag is calculated as minus the phase divided by 2π times the frequency (see Fig. 6.9). For example, at frequency of maximum coherence, .033, the phase is $-.48$, so that the estimated time lag is $+.48 / 2\pi (.033) = 2.32$ seconds at the frequency. These analyses suggest that at 2-months-of-age the baby and mother are coherent, and that the baby is responding to the mother.

Although measures of coherence and phase indicated that the mother and baby demonstrated synchronous behavior, an additional test for autocorrelation (predictability within each time series) must be performed before we can state confidently the behavior of the pair is related. Spurious relationships between two time series can be obtained simply because each of the time series is predictable, to some extent, from its past. This point has been made repeatedly in both the social interaction (Sackett, 1980) and time-series literature (Jenkins & Watts, 1968). This autocontingency must be removed from the data before any causal relationship can be assumed. Relative to this example, the relevant question is:

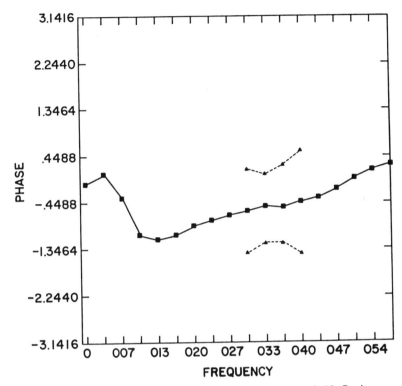

Fig. 6.9.   Phase spectrum for mother and baby at week 13. Dashes with arrows indicate the confidence interval.

Does the mother's data account for variance in the baby's data over and above the variance accounted for by the past of the baby's data?

This question leads to the basis for developing two equations for the possible relationships between the two time series. In the first equation, the mother's past is controlled in an attempt to test the inference B→M (baby influences mother). And in the second equation, the baby's past is controlled in an attempt to test the inference M→B. Using the Williams and Gottman (1981) BIVAR program these equations can be tested. The rationale underlying the tests is as follows: In testing the inference B→M, for example, the objective is to account for as much of the variance in the mother's series by knowledge of her past, and then determine how much we can increase explained variance by adding knowledge of the infant's past. If little or no information is gained by including the infant's past then it can concluded that the infant had minimum influence on the mother's behavior. Alternatively, the process is reversed for testing M→B. Statistical details of these tests are discussed in Gottman (1981) and Gottman and Ringland (1981).

TABLE 6.8
Analysis of Bidirectional Influence for the Mother-Infant Dyad
at 13 Weeks

Model	A	B	SSE	T LN (SSE/T)
1	10	10	1023.202	365.635
2	9	5	1030.747	367.766
3	9	0	1086.913	383.153
4	10	0	1086.835	383.123
5	0	0	451182.000	2131.426
1 vs. 1	Q = 2.131		6 = DF Z = -1.117	
[2 vs. 3	Q = 15.387		5 = DF Z = 3.285] (B→M)	
3 vs. 4	Q = .021		1 = DF Z = -.692	

Model	C	D	SSE	T LN (SSE/T)
1	10	10	869.980	318.591
2	8	1	894.658	326.703
3	8	0	921.930	335.411
4	10	0	913.874	332.866
5	0	0	341648.000	2050.780
1 vs. 2	Q = 8.112		11 = DF Z = -.6.6	
[2 vs. 3	Q = 8.708		1 = DF Z = 5.450] (M→B)	
3 vs. 4	Q = 2.545		2 = DF Z = .272	

Table 6.8 summarizes the two tests of directionality for these data. The important statistic to examine in this Table is the comparison of Model 2 with Model 3. Look at the upper half of Table 6.8, it summarizes the B→M inference. Model 2 has nine autoregressive mother terms (under column A) and five cross-regressive baby terms (under column B); Model 3 has only the nine auto-regressive terms. In "2 vs. 3" on the Table the statistic Q is distributed as chi-square with 5 degrees of freedom. The Z statistic is the standard normal deviate for this chi-square. If this Z score is greater than 1.96, the result is probably significant at $p < .05$. Since for this analysis Z = 3.44, it can be concluded that B→M. Similarly, by examining the lower half of Table 6.8, we can conclude that M→B. Thus at 13 weeks, this dyad demonstrated bidirectional influence.

Before leaving this section on time-series analysis two points need to be made. First, time-series data must be stationary. Stationarity in time-series is conceptually similar to the Markov stationarity discussed in the log-linear section. Time-series data must vary about a fixed mean and have constant spectral density function throughout the data. It is not unusual for time-series data not to be stationary. However, because there are several ways to remedy nonsta-tionarity, this is not usually a serious problem. But again, how this is done is beyond the scope and intent of this chapter. Readers are directed to Gottman (1981) and Gottman and Ringland (1981) for additional details.

A final point. Although a disproportionate amount of this section was devoted to cycles, data do not need to be cyclical in order to be analyzed using time-series methods. Any set of time series data can be approximated accurately by a set of sine and cosine functions (see Gottman, 1981). This implies that investigators can examine the relationship between two time-series irrespective of whether or not cyclicity exists within the data.

Like the sections on lag-sequential analysis, and log-linear models, this section on time-series analysis is intended only to introduce the concepts of this method of data analysis, and to illustrate how this approach is applicable to family interaction data. For greater depth, interested readers are directed to Chatfield (1984), Gottman (1981), and Kendall (1973). Gottman's (1981) text is directly related to the social interaction perspective, and the other books provide the breath needed to fully understand the analysis of time-series data.

SUMMARY

To assess the relevant temporal structure in sequential data requires an initial decision of whether to pool subjects, or to analyze subject-by-subject. If the latter option is taken, and there are sufficient data to warrant confidence in the stability of the statistics, the investigator can use either lag-sequential analysis or time-series analysis. If the investigator elects to pool the data, then log-linear models offer an array of procedures for examining the data's temporal structure. Regardless of the option selected, each data-analytic method provides the investigator with an array of well developed techniques suitable for analyzing family interaction data.

Moreover, advanced statistical packages containing these methods are now available for the micro-computer (e.g., SPSS-PC+, (Nie, 1986)), as are specialized programs like the Williams and Gottman (1981) time series program, and Bakeman's ELAG (1983). As a result, the cost of calculating and the ease of interpreting the results of these approaches are within the capacity of most researchers. Clearly this chapter was written to illustrate these methods, but more importantly, it was written to encourage family interaction researchers to utilize these powerful methods as a means of analyzing behavioral patterns.

ACKNOWLEDGMENTS

The authors wish to acknowledge the support for preparation of this manuscript by NIMH grant MH18262-02 to the first author and by NIMH Research Career Development Award K00257 and NIMH Grant 1R01MH42722-01 to the second author.

The editors gratefully acknowledge the assistance of David Baldwin in reviewing the more technical material in this chapter.

REFERENCES

Allison, P. D., & Liker, J. K. (1982). Analyzing sequential data on dyadic interaction: A comment on Gottman. *Psychological Bulletin, 91*, 393–403.

Altmann, S. (1965). Sociobiology of the rhesus monkey. II. Stochastics of social communication. *Journal of Theoretical Biology, 8*, 490–522.

Anderson, T. W., & Goodman, L. A. (1957). Statistical inference about Markov chains. *The Annals of Mathematical Statistics, 28*, 89–110.

Arundale, R. B. (1982). *User's guide to SAMPLE and TEST: Two Fortran IV computer programs for the analysis of discrete state time-varying data, using Markov chain techniques.* Fairbanks: University of Alaska.

Attneave, F. (1959). *Applications of information theory to psychology.* New York: Henry Holt.

Bakeman, R. (1983). Computing lag sequential statistics: The ELAG program. *Behavior Research Methods & Instrumentation, 15*, 520–535.

Bakeman, R., & Gottman, J. (1986). *Observing interaction: An introduction to sequential analysis.* New York: Cambridge University Press.

Barker, R. G. (1963). *The stream of behavior.* New York: Appleton-Century-Crofts.

Bishop, Y. M. M., Fienberg, S. E., & Holland, P. W. (1975). *Discrete multivariate analysis: Theory and practice.* Cambridge, MA: MIT Press.

Bock, R. D., & Yates, G. (1973). *MULTIQUAL, loglinear analysis of nominal and ordinal qualitative data by the method of maximum likelihood: A FORTRAN program.* Chicago: National Educational Resources.

Brazelton, T. B., Koslowski, B., & Main, M. (1974). The origins of reciprocity: The early mother-infant interaction. In M. Lewis & L. A. Rosenblum (Ed.), *The effect of the infant on its caregiver.* New York: Wiley.

Brown, M.B. (1974). Identification of the sources of significance in two-way contingency tables. *Applied Statistics, 23*, 405–413.

Cairns, R. B. (1979). *The analysis of social interaction: Methods, issues, and illustrations.* Hillsdale, NJ: Lawrence Erlbaum Associates.

Chatfield, C. (1985). *The analysis of time series: An introduction* (3rd ed.). New York: Chapman and Hall.

Condon, W. S., & Ogston, W. (1967). A segmentation of behavior. *Journal of Psychiatric Research, 5*, 221–235.

Davis, J. A. (1974). Hierarchical models for significance tests in multivariate contingency tables: An exegesis of Goodman's recent papers. In H. L. Costner (Ed.), *Sociological methodology, 1973–1974.* San Francisco: Jossey-Bass.

Gardner, W., & Griffin, W. A. (in press). Methods for the analysis of parallel streams of continuously recorded social behaviors. *Psychological Bulletin.*

Gardner, W., & Hartmann, D. P. (1984). On Markov dependence in the analysis of social interaction. *Behavioral Assessment, 6*, 229–236.

Gödel, K. (1932). *On formally undecideable propositions of Principia Mathematica and related systems.* London: Oliver & Boyd.

Goodman, L. A. (1971). Partitioning of chi-squares analysis of marginal contingency tables and estimation of expected frequencies in multidimensional contingency tables. *Journal of American Statistical Association, 66*, 339–344.

Goodman, L. A. (1972). A modified multiple regression approach to the analysis of dichotomous variables. *American Sociological Review, 37*, 28–46.

Goodman, L. A. (1983). A note on a supposed criticism of an Anderson-Goodman test in Markov chain analysis. In S. Karlin, T. Amemiya, & L. A. Goodman (Ed.), *Studies in econometrics, time series, and multivariate statistics* (pp. 85–92). New York: Academic Press.

Gottman, J. M. (1979). *Marital interaction: Experimental investigations.* New York: Academic Press.

Gottman, J. M. (1980). Analyzing for sequential connection and assessing interobserver reliability for the sequential analysis of observational data. *Behavioral Assessment, 2,* 361–368.

Gottman, J. M. (1981). *Time-series analysis: A comprehensive introduction for social scientists.* New York: Cambridge University Press.

Gottman, J. M. (1983). *How children become friends.* Monographs of the Society for Research in Child Development, Serial #201, 48, #2.

Gottman, J. M. (1987). The sequential analysis of family interaction. In T. Jacob (Ed.), *Family interaction and psychopathology: Theories, methods and findings* (pp. 453–478). New York: Plenum Press.

Gottman, J. M., & Bakeman, R. (1979). The sequential analysis of observational data. In M. Lamb, S. Suomi, & G. Stephenson (Eds.), *Social interaction analysis: Methodological issues.* Madison: University of Wisconsin Press.

Gottman, J., Markman, H., & Notarius, C. (1977). The topography of marital conflict: A study of verbal and nonverbal behavior. *Journal of Marriage and the Family, 39,* 461–477.

Gottman, J. M., & Ringland, J. (1981). The analysis of dominance and bidirectionality in social development. *Child Development, 52,* 393–412.

Gottman, J. M., & Roy, A. K. (in press). *Sequential analysis: Temporal form in social interaction.* New York: Cambridge University Press.

Gottman, J. M., Rose, F. T., & Mettetal, G. (1982). Time-series analysis of social interaction data. In T. Field & A. Fogel (Eds.), *Emotion and early interaction.* Hillsdale, NJ: Lawrence Erlbaum Associates.

Griffin, W. A., & Gardner, W. (1989). *The analysis of behavioral durations in observational studies of social interaction.* Manuscript submitted for publication.

Hawes, L. C., & Foley, J. M. (1976). Group decisioning: Testing a finite stochastic model. In G. R. Miller (Ed.), *Explorations in interpersonal communication.* Beverly Hills, CA: Sage.

Hewes, D. E. (1980). Stochastic modeling of communication processes. In P. R. Monge & J. N. Cappella (Eds.), *Multivariate techniques for communication research.* New York: Academic Press.

Jenkins, G. M., & Watts, D. G. (1968). *Spectral analysis and its applications.* San Francisco: Holden Day.

Kendall, Sir M. (1973). *Time-series.* New York: Hafner Press.

Knoke, D., & Burke, P. J. (1980). *Log-linear models.* Beverly Hills, CA: Sage.

Krokoff, L. J., Gottman, J. M., & Roy, A. K. (1987). *Expanding the range of marital interaction research: marital happiness, occupational status, and communication orientation effects.* Submitted for publication.

Lamb, M. E., Suomi, S. J., & Stephenson, G. R. (1979). *Social interaction analysis.* Madison: University of Wisconsin Press.

Manderscheid, R. W., Rae, D. S., McCarrick, A. K., & Silbergeld, S. (1982). A stochastic model of relational control in dyadic interaction. *American Sociological Review, 47,* 62–75.

Miller, G. A., & Frick, F. C. (1949). Statistical behavioristics and sequences of responses. *Psychological Review, 56,* 311–324.

Nie, N. H. (1986). *SPSS-PC+.* New York: McGraw-Hill.

Noller, P. (1984). *Nonverbal communication and marital interaction.* New York: Pergamon Press.

Patterson, G. R. (1974). A basis for identifying stimuli which control behavior in natural settings. *Child Development, 45,* 900–911.

Patterson, G. R., & Moore, D. (1979). Interactive patterns as units of behavior. In M. Lamb, S. Soumi, & G. Stephenson (Eds.), *Social interaction analysis: Methodological issues.* Madison: University of Wisconsin Press.

Raush, H. L. (1965). Interaction sequences. *Journal of Personality and Social Psychology, 2,* 487–499.

Raush, H. L., Barry, W. A., Hertel, R. K., & Swain, M. A. (1974). *Communication, conflict and marriage.* San Francisco: Jossey-Bass.

Sackett, G. P. (1974). *A nonparametric lag sequential analysis for studying dependency among response in observational scoring systems.* Unpublished manuscript.

Sackett, G. P. (1978). *Observing behavior Vol. II: Collection and analysis methods.* Baltimore: University Park Press.

Sackett, G. P. (1979). The lag sequential analysis of contingency and cyclicity in behavioral interaction research. In J. Osofsky (Ed.), *Handbook of infant development.* New York: Wiley.

Sackett, G. P. (1980). Lag sequential analysis as a data reduction technique in social interaction research. In D. Sawin, R. Hawkins, L. Walker, & J. Penticuff (Eds.), *Exceptional infant (Vol. 4).* New York: Brunner/Mazel.

Shannon, C. E., & Weaver, W. (1949). *The mathematical theory of communication.* Urbana: University of Illinois Press.

Siegel, S. (1956). *Nonparametric statistics for the behavioral sciences.* New York: McGraw-Hill.

Ting-Toomey, S. (1983). An analysis of communication patterns in high and low marital adjustment groups. *Human Communication Research, 9,* 306–319.

Vuchinich, S. (1984). Sequencing and Social Structure in Family Conflict. *Social Psychology Quarterly, 47,* 217–234.

Williams, E., & Gottman, J. (1981). *A user's guide to the Gottman-Williams time-series programs for social scientists.* New York: Cambridge University Press.

7

Family Environments of Depressed and Well Parents and Their Children: Issues of Research Methods

Marian Radke Yarrow
National Institute of Mental Health

Psychiatric illness in parents intrudes into family life and into the rearing functions that parents perform, and has significant influences on other family members. Continuing issues for research involve the specification of these influences and the mechanisms through which they affect individual outcomes. This chapter focuses on a special problem within this class of problems. Families in which one or both parents have an affective illness and families in which both parents are well and without histories of psychiatric disorder are investigated with respect to parents' behavior in relation to their children's functioning. What are the interpersonal processes and "cultures" within these families and the course of development in their young children? We are using our ongoing research on families of depressed and nondepressed parents as a case through which to discuss research strategies, measurement procedures, and analytic approaches relating to family research. Our focus here is primarily methodological. However, a sampling of empirical data is also presented to illustrate the methods and procedures.

We have chosen issues of methods as an emphasis for reasons that are obvious to researchers in this field: Family research is still an area of study in which problems of theory and measurement abound, although the field has in recent years become active and revitalized. It is benefiting from new concepts and new approaches—some of which have been developed in family therapy and research; some of which have been drawn from scientific advances in general. All in all, however, family research is not yet renowned for its robust research methodology, and certainly it is an area that is full of methodological challenges.

Research on the family is an enterprise that has many different purposes and interests traceable to diverse disciplinary and clinical origins: How does the family function as a system? How is it shaped by the macrocontexts of which it is a part? What is the nature of marital relationships? What are family influences on developmental processes in the offspring? Across these different objectives there are shared concepts, but also concepts unique to the particular questions. And quite probably, too, different methods and procedures are suited to these different questions. This is a particularly opportune time for conceptual and methodological advances because of the current interest in family research from investigators across a range of disciplines. The convergence of these differing perspectives and skills should be of great advantage to this area of research.

RESEARCH OBJECTIVES

The study that I describe is a venture into methods of arriving at a sound base of information on family environments in relation to the behavior of children growing up in them. The research questions that the study is designed to address elaborate this objective:

1. What are the family environmental variables and combinations of variables that make a difference in children's development? What are the mechanisms involved?

2. How do these environmental influences interact with genetic or constitutional variables over the course of development?

These questions take on a specific focus in this study:

3. What are the distinguishing features of the childrearing environments of young children of depressed parents and nondepressed parents?

4. What are the characteristics of the children of depressed and nondepressed parents at successive developmental stages? The child's social relatedness, emotional development, cognitive and mastery skills are our focus.

These questions make various demands on methods: They require varied units of behavior—units that differ in time and in level of abstraction. They call for varied sampling of behavior: There are necessary considerations of the specific situations that are sampled, the adequacy of various amounts of time that are sampled, and the frequency of sampling. Various questions require different methods. In the present research, we have combined experimental, naturalistic and clinical methods. Answers to the research questions we have posed depend ultimately on the integration of related findings. Hence, considerations are needed at the outset concerning the kinds of integrations that will be made.

BACKGROUND OF THE STUDY

In the context of developmental psychology, one might view our study as a longitudinal study of child rearing and child development. In the context of psychiatric research, one might call it an "offspring" study. It is both. The research questions and research planning grow out of these two perspectives, developmental psychology and developmental psychopathology. From a psychiatric point of view, our interest is in the concordance of parental and child psychopathology, and in the processes of transmission of psychopathology, in the interaction of genetic and environmental influences over the course of development. In psychiatric research, there is rather compelling evidence (see review by Beardslee, Bemporad, Keller, & Klerman, 1983) that depression aggregates in families and is transmitted from generation to generation. However, there are virtually no developmental data and relatively little direct information on how depressed adults carry out the functions of parenting and how this process may contribute to impairment in the offspring. From the psychiatric view, we are looking at the child in terms of signs of pathology, of a diagnosis. From the viewpoint of developmental psychology, we are interested in the rearing process, developmental processes, and children's adaptations and maladaptations.

Sample

A number of considerations that relate directly to the research questions determined sampling criteria. I first describe the sample and then return to the purpose underlying the sampling decisions. The sample (Table 7.1) is defined by the diagnoses of the parents. A standard psychiatric interview (SADS-L) (RDC criteria) (Spitzer & Endicott, 1977) was used to screen the families.[1] The mother's diagnosis was the first gateway into the study. Eligibility for the study was determined by the mother's psychiatric status: The mother (a) was without current or past psychiatric disorder, or (b) had a diagnosis of a major affective disorder—unipolar or bipolar depression. Other diagnoses, namely schizophrenia, antisocial personality, or serious drug and alcohol abuse, disqualified the parent. If the mother was eligible, the father was interviewed. Fathers in families of normal mothers had also to be without history of psychiatric disorder. Fathers in families of depressed mothers either had a diagnosis of depression or were without psychiatric disorder. Many other descriptors of parents' illness (severity, age at onset, time of episodes, level of functioning between episodes, treatment, etc.) were also obtained.

Each family had a child of approximately 2-years-of-age and a child between 5- and 8-years-of-age. The mothers in all of the families were the primary caregivers; although many of them were also employed outside the family. Depressed mothers were all community-living, because our purpose was to study women who were responsible for the rearing of their children. Some of the mothers had had periods of hospitalization earlier in their lives. In a few families, mothers had had short hospitalizations in the lifetime of the children.

---

[1]The diagnostic criteria and information on each family are described in detail in Manual of Procedures, NIMH Child Rearing Study.

TABLE 7.1
Parental Diagnostic Status
SADS-L (RDC Criteria)

Family Classification	Number of Participants
Normal Controls -- both parents no diagnosis	38
Unipolar mother, depressed father	25
Unipolar mother, well father	25
Unipolar mother, absent father	6
Bipolar mother, depressed father	16
Bipolar mother, well father	9
Bipolar mother, father absent	4

Most of the sample is middle and upper middle-class, mostly Caucasian, intact families. A small sample is from a very economically deprived, inner-city group, mainly single-parented Black families. The sample of design and the sample of reality are not identical—a condition not uncommon in clinical research. By design, we had planned to have intact families of two distinct social class groups, a middle-class group and an economically disadvantaged group. The realities of lower social class life dictated changes. We were unable to find many intact families in this group fitting criteria for our depressed and nondepressed groups. Father absence, by necessity, became an environmental variable and a genetic unknown. We have had to be satisfied with a small sample of lower SES families.

The bases for these sampling decisions stem from the following considerations: We were interested in the family environment, and the contributions of both mother and father; therefore, we wanted intact families. We hypothesized that the expression and conditions of parental depression are influenced by social class and that the differences could best be identified by selecting distinct class groups. A longitudinal developmental study might, of course, begin with birth or pregnancy. We chose to begin after infancy. Earlier studies (Gaensbauer, Harmon, Cytryn, & McKnew, 1984) of infants and toddlers of severely depressed parents indicated that problems of attachment, emotional regulation, relating to others were apparent in these children by 18 to 24 months. Therefore, we chose these ages as the beginning point. To enable us to investigate both inter- and intrafamily differences, two siblings from each family were studied. The ages of the children were controlled, as were the times of follow-up assessments, in order that (a) the family interactions and child characteristics could be related to developmental stage or period, and (b) siblings could be observed at the same ages (e.g., the toddlers, at the time of the first follow-up, will have reached the age at which we saw their older siblings at the initial assessments).

THE RESEARCH SCHEDULE

The research schedule (see Table 7.2) provides an overview of procedures in time and space. After the parents have been screened and have agreed to partici-

TABLE 7.2
Study Design

Time 1	Time 2	Time 3 (Projected)
Home Visit Laboratory Apartment	Life Events Interview Laboratory Apartment	Life Events Interview Laboratory Apartment
Observations Interviews	Observations Interviews	Observations Interviews
Day 1 Mother, Younger child	Day 1 Mother, Younger Child	
Day 2 Mother, Younger child	Day 2 Mother, Father, Younger and Older Child	
Day 3 Mother, Younger and Older Child		
Psychiatric Assessment	Psychiatric Assessment	Psychiatric Assessment
Mother, Father, Younger and Older Child	Mother, Father, All Offspring	Mother, Father, All Offspring
	Family Psychiatric History	
Family Feedback	Family Feedback	Family Feedback

173

pate, a visit is made to the home by the staff member who becomes the family research link throughout the study. As in the recruiting, the research is described as a study of child development and rearing, including parents who are depressed and those who are not. If the mother has a diagnosis of depression and does not have some form of professional help, contact is established with a mental health worker. Participants are paid at a nominal rate (established by the institution) for time involved in research procedures.

During the home visit, the mother is interviewed about the family demographics and children's developmental histories. This visit is also an opportunity to observe family circumstances. Over the next month, mother and children come to the laboratory apartment where they spend 3 half-days. Here the major data sets on family interaction and individual characteristics are obtained. Time spent in the apartment is described later. On a fourth visit, each child is seen by a psychiatrist, (the younger child in a play interview, the older child in a standard psychiatric interview, The Child Assessment Schedule (CAS), (Hodges, Kline, Fitch, McKnew, & Cytryn, 1981), and the mother fills out the Achenbach Behavior Checklist on each child, (Achenbach, 1979). Approximately a week later, the mother and father are invited to return for feedback on the children, and referrals or interventions are made when necessary.

After an interval of 2 to 3 years when the younger child is 5- to 6-years-old, and the sibling 8- to 11-years-old, the family returns for a series of half-day apartment observation sessions, and individual testing. The father is included. At this time, both parents are reinterviewed on the SADS to obtain data on their psychiatric status in the period between assessments and currently. The children receive a standard psychiatric interview (CAS). Other measures of the child include a cognitive test, a neuropsychological test, and observations of the child with a peer. The mother again fills out the Achenbach Behavior Checklist on each child. Teachers' reports are also obtained (Achenbach & Edelbrock, 1980). Also, at this time, a probing life events interview (Pellegrini, 1987) is conducted in the home. A second interview focuses on psychiatric problems in family histories. The history is a report by each parent on psychiatric problems in first- and second-degree relatives. Reassessments of the families are made 3 years later, mainly to determine the psychological status of the participants.

CONCEPTUALIZATION AND MEASUREMENT OF THE FAMILY ENVIRONMENT OF THE CHILD

Conceptualization and measurement are very much interdependent. Therefore, an initial task was to conceptualize the rearing environment. On the one hand, such a conceptualization should be applicable to any research on child rearing. On the other hand, it must also be tuned to the particular research interest. For example, the fact that we are investigating parental depression in relation to parental functioning makes affective aspects of rearing an evident priority in conceptualization and assessment. That we wish to investigate processes affecting children's social and emotional adaptations also influences the framework in which one views family environment and the specific measurements that one chooses.

The rearing environment has multiple dimensions. A great number of functions, demands, and gratifications converge and develop into patterned interactions and relationships that constitute the rearing environment. We have identified what we consider to be critical dimensions of parenting, namely: (1) providing care and protection of the child, (2) regulating and controlling the child's behavior in line with needs and requirements from internal and external sources, (3) providing knowledge and skills and understanding concerning the physical and social world, (4) giving affective meaning to interactions and relationships, and (5) facilitating the child's self-understanding. Families can be assessed on any of these dimensions singly or on the total pattern; they can be assessed on the content of their interaction and on the methods by which rearing functions are carried out. Family environment is not static. Measurement of family environment at successive periods of assessment must be alert to possible changes in relation to development, parental illness, and life events. If all proceeds well, the rearing environment does change with changing developmental needs of, and contributions from, the child.

In summary, in the research design and measurement, an attempt is made to take into account a multidimensional childrearing environment, and to maintain a developmental perspective. Environment is measured (a) at an intensive microlevel in which parents and children are observed together under controlled, yet reasonably natural conditions, and (b) at a macrolevel that permits a view of the family in the larger space of everyday living and in the deeper space of time.

A sensitive translation of conceptualizations into measurements is a core obligation and challenge in all research. We have tried to obtain informative indicators of parental care, regulation, facilitation, affect, and relationships with the child, opting for observing these behaviors in the semicontrolled but also reasonably natural circumstances that were designed to bring out, or allow for, this range of demands and interactions. Because we assume that parental depression constitutes a significant systematic screen for perceptions, parents' reporting was viewed as not a good (at least not a sole) source of information about the details of parental behavior or child behavior. Parents, whether depressed or not, however, are important reporters. Interview data were used to supplement observations and to obtain data on events over time (see Table 7.2). The interviews and questionnaires are mainly standard instruments, which are not described here.

The direct observations of parents and children are our main data source. We made use of a natural setting in our laboratory, which is a beautiful old house. In a part of the house we created an apartment, using an existing suite of rooms with

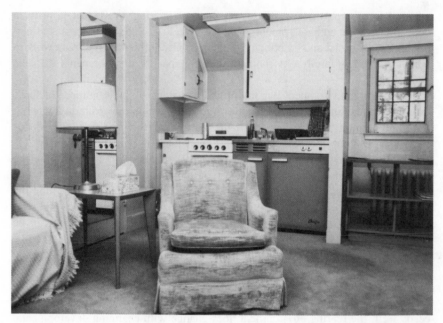

FIG. 7.1a,b. Apartment, suite of rooms with kitchenette and bath-room, used as a natural setting for a laboratory.

kitchenette and bathroom. To it we added viewing walls and a booth for video equipment. The protocol is such that the families come to this apartment over and over again, and it soon becomes "theirs." The physical environment and the time in the apartment are scripted to conform to our conception of rearing dimensions previously outlined. Examples of scripts of physical environment are: a short set of stairs which pose a small potential hazard, a TV, telephone, refrigerator with food, some breakables and temptations on a table, play materials with various potentials for affect, interaction, and mastery, an adjoining room to get away from each other (see Figs. 7.1a and 7.1b). Time in the apartment is planned so as to sample, over the several days, normal routines and events. Certain events are imposed that increase the likelihood of specific kinds of behaviors. Examples of events are: mother prepares lunch, mother and child(ren) eat lunch, mother leaves young child briefly, siblings are left alone while mother is busy in the next room, mother naps, mother reads to child, telephone call interrupts mother, a "doctor" comes to examine the child, an unfamiliar peer and peer's mother come to visit. When father is also present, he has time alone with each child, the whole family eats dinner together, etc. We also make certain that there is unstructured time for parents and children to organize the time for themselves. The various situations are sequenced so as to create a sense of natural flow of events. These situations of intimacy, pleasure, control, stress, and routines are observed and videotaped. Thus, the apartment procedures are intended to provide theoretically relevant samples of family behavior, and in circumstances that are analogous to significant experiences in family life.

For some families, this configuration of events is a reasonable reflection of everyday life; for other families, there is so much chaos and disorganization in their lives, that the apartment may be a spot of peace and an imposed organization. But, for all families, the behavior that we observe is constrained within the limits of time and opportunities provided in the laboratory with the advantages and disadvantages that follow from this constraint. To minimize one disadvantage, the research also includes information on the larger context of family events, especially stressful events in the family (Pellegrini, 1987). Information is obtained also about routine household and family configuration and activities.

Reflecting for a moment on the assessments of family environment before going on to its influences on children, we note that by this approach, we hoped to obtain a base of measures that would permit us to investigate what we believe to be a very important kind of question; namely, *what is the necessary conjunction of critical experiences and variables to produce given effects on children?* The rationale for obtaining the kinds of data, in the kinds of settings, that we have elected is motivated by a variety of interests: (a) to observe behavior in meaningful contexts, (b) to interpret the immediate context and behavior in terms of the broader contexts (i.e., laboratory behavior in terms of contexts of family circumstances), and (c) to observe behavior in relation to the specific situations that have been chosen on theoretical bases. Also, the assessments permit examination of behavior at various levels—relationships, family "culture," and specific interactions.

If one wishes to study the *mechanisms* of influence and change, a truly longitudinal study is perhaps ideal, one in which there is a continuing measurement process. Few such longitudinal studies exist, however. Our study, like many others, is a follow-up study; that is, assessments are made at intervals (in ours, every 3 years). The limitations would appear obvious. Therefore, in order to try to fill-in some of the intervening information, interviews with the parents are used. This, although only a thread of continuing information, serves to form some crucial links.

We have presented the rationale for an approach and strategy for investigating family environment as an influence on children. We now take the presentation further, to translate the approach into specific procedures for assessing family environment and analyses of relations of family variables to child "outcomes." Two areas of family assessment serve as illustrations, (a) maternal methods of controlling and regulating child behaviors, and (b) affect and affect regulation in the family environment (and especially mother's affect). These are important and interrelated areas of parental functioning and they place different demands on measurement.

THE MEASUREMENT OF MATERNAL METHODS
OF CONTROLLING CHILD BEHAVIOR

Maternal methods of controlling child behaviors involve, foremost, the nature of the mother's interventions and interactions in her attempts to influence the child. Maternal methods involve, also, the situations or circumstances that she creates or allows to happen, which contribute to the need for control and the difficulty or ease of control. Here we are concerned with the mother's methods of intervention. The long sessions of interactions in the research apartment provided adequate samples of episodes of mother's control or influence attempts in situations that were similarly varied for all families (Kochanska, Kuczynski, Radke-Yarrow, & Welch, 1987; Kuczynski, Kochanska, Radke-Yarrow, & Girnius-Brown, 1987). Ninety minutes of interactions were sampled. Episodes of control (according to specified criteria) were located and each episode was coded for the occasions and purposes of the mother's attempts, the child's initial responses, mother's subsequent attempts, the child's subsequent responses, and, finally, the ultimate resolution of these confrontations. (See the published articles for details of coding and analyses.) A relatively microscopic analytic system of analysis is used to describe mother and child in relation to each other.

The intent of the coding was to be sensitive to developmental changes and to differences between dyads of depressed mothers and their children and nondepressed mothers and their children. For example, drawing on the articles (cited above), it was found that when children are confronted with adult control, they respond with a variety of strategies; some of which show more emotion regulation, more social competence than others. Children may be passively noncompliant (not "hearing"), may be overtly defiant—with unmanaged anger, may refuse, may negotiate with mother. The frequencies of these strategies change with age during toddlerhood. Passive noncompliance and overt defiance decrease with age (between 1½ and 3½ years); negotiation, involving many cognitive and affective skills, increases in this age period. Here the offspring of severely depressed parents show some impaired mastery skills. Daughters of depressed mothers are less complaint than daughters of well mothers.

There are differences in depressed and nondepressed mothers' attempts to control their children when the children resist. Depressed mothers are more likely than well mothers to step back, to avoid further confrontation with their children.

Except through detailed observation, taking sequences into account, and sampling over considerable time, these distinctions in mothers' behavior and children's responses could not have been captured. Interviews and hypothetical discipline situations would not have revealed the critical data.

At later ages in development, in follow-up assessments, mother's techniques are being reassessed: Have their techniques changed with development? What are the children's techniques of control and influence? What are the associations between mother's and child's approaches? Does the child generalize child-mother interactions to other interactions?

The Measurement of Family Affect.   The second domain chosen as a vehicle for illustrating and discussing measurement of family environment is the affect that parents bring to parenting and the affect in children's functioning. Although maternal nurturance and rejection have been with us in research from the beginning, the effects on the child of the parents' moods and emotions, and the ways in which affect enters into other aspects of rearing are not fully known. Affect in the family can enter into the child's experience in various ways: as the "climate" of family relationships, as a caregiver-model of moods and emotions, as affect directed to the child and underlying the parent-child relationship, and as the child's emotions and the ways in which they are handled by the caregiver.

One measure of mothers' and children's affect was macroscopic in one sense, yet microscopic as well: For the family's time in the apartment, continuous records were made of the expressed moods and emotions of mother and child. Time was arbitrarily divided into minutes. In a period of 1 minute, various emotions can be manifested. The coder's judgment or rating selected the predominant affect, or double affects. A set of conventions determined priorities. Every minute received a code. If a specific emotion (sad, happy, affectionate, anxious-fearful, angry) or an undifferentiated negative mood was not present, the minute was coded neutral. In this way, a consecutive record of affects was obtained. This record of affect across situations, provides a macrolevel index of the mother as a stimulus figure of moods and emotions, and of her affective relationship with her child. This record also provides an index that is sensitive to situational influences (e.g., affect in situations of sociability with her child compared with situations of stress, or mother's affect with younger child compared with older sibling.

Some of the findings based on this index illustrate the nature and functions of affect in the rearing environment. One set of findings deals with the profiles of affect of normal and depressed mothers. These profiles tell us, not too surprisingly, that negative moods and emotions occupy significantly more of the time of depressed than of normal mothers (e.g., on day 1, 27% and 12% of the minutes are coded negative for the depressed and normal mothers, respectively). This finding is replicated on days 2 and 3. Casting the finding solely in group terms does not tell the whole story, however. Differences among mothers are very great—from 0% of the time in negative mood and emotions for some mothers to 80% of the time for others. When mother and child are analyzed as dyads, mother and child are quite concordant in their affects; this is true for both depressed and nondepressed groups. Based on a median split on frequency of negative mood and emotions, 66% of the mothers and children are concordant. When mothers are in the lowest quartile of the group on frequency of negative minutes, 85% of their toddler-age children are below the group median in negative minutes. When mothers are in the highest quartile on negative expression, 79% of their children are above the median (Radke-Yarrow, Richters, & Wilson, 1988). A reasonable conclusion would seem to be that these 2- to 3-year-olds are learning affective patterns of their own as well as experiencing mothers' emotions.

This measure enables one to measure and compare the affective tone of each subgroup (dyad, triad, etc.) within the family. For example, when interaction between mother and either child alone has a high negative affective component, the negative affect between the siblings when they are together without mother present tends also to have high frequency (Radke-Yarrow, Richters, & Wilson, 1988). Mothers do not always have similar patterns of relating affectively with their two children. This measure of affect rather nicely specifies the different experiences of individual children—differences that escape more global conceptualizations of the family.

In yet another way, this record of emotions and moods distinguishes subgroups of depressed mothers. Mothers whose illness is manifested in frequent and evident expressions of sadness and anxiety, compared with mothers for whom these emotions are mixed with many and unpredictable displays of anger, compared with mothers whose major manifestation is apathy, provide quite different learning experiences for their children. Considering these mothers only as "depressed" could obscure what may be critical dimensions of interactions, that have differing consequences for the children. An example that is little more than anecdotal at this stage of analysis is a relation between these specific profiles of emotions of depressed mothers and the nature of the child's attachment. Avoidant attachment appears to be characteristic of dyads in which mothers manifest persisting, anxious sadness. Children of angry, depressed mothers are more likely to show anxious, resistant patterns.

A further microscopic analysis of affect goes beyond noting an expression of emotion in a given minute of time to a detailed coding of the function of the affect in the interactions of mother and child. An example is mothers' use of affection. Although it is possible to evaluate mothers on *amount* of affection and to compare groups (e.g., depressed vs. well, mothers of boys vs. mothers of girls, mothers with secure and insecurely attached children), the blunted value of such an appraisal becomes evident in a microscopic analysis of individual cases. Case study data are suggestive of hypotheses: Mrs. J. rather precipitously becomes physically affectionate when she and her child are confronted with a stressful situation (conceivably interpretable by her child as a signal of stress). Mrs. D. scoops her child into her arms after a fun experience that has left both of them happy and high spirited. Mrs. A. and her 2-year-old cling to each other most of the time. The toddler sits on her mother's lap as her mother anxiously and sadly strokes and kisses her, intermittently.

Just as mothers socialize other behaviors of their children, they also socialize their children's emotions. Our recording of the child's emotions, followed-up by a coding of the mother's specific responses to the child's expression of anger, fear, sadness, joy, etc., captures some of the process of socialization (Radke-Yarrow & Kochanska, in press). Mothers' react variously: by ignoring, explaining, denying, anxiously attending, punishing, consoling, etc. Initial analyses show that mothers' practices show developmental changes. An illustration is mothers' greater tolerance of anger outbursts in younger than in older children (within the very narrow age range of 2 to 3½ years). Mothers' responses also show differences relating to gender of the child: anger in boys more than anger in girls, for example, is likely to bring concern and reward from the mother (i.e., the mother will give or do what the angry child wants).

In the long run, analyses of affective components of the family will need to try to disentangle the contributions of mother and child to each other's affect. Having data over time and from settings and interactions of child and mother with other persons (sibling, father, peer) provides some avenues for disentanglement.

CONFIGURATIONS IN CHILDREARING ENVIRONMENTS

The two domains of environment that have been our illustrations of methods and data have obvious relations to each other and to other domains of rearing. Learning how these domains, singly and in combination, relate to child outcomes is the research objective. As convincing associations appear between specific parental strengths and deficits and specific child characteristics, we have the beginnings of answers, but one can not stop there. Although each of the environmental domains that we have sampled has associations with child properties, each domain considered singly is not a powerful predictor. We stand a far better chance of understanding effects of family on child by considering the interaction of domains within the family.

From the data we have reported here, the environments of children of depressed mothers are distinguishable from the environments of children of well mothers on each of the rearing dimensions: impairments with respect to affective relationships and control practices. Moreover, on dimensions not discussed in this report, such as verbal communications between mother and child, and response to stress, there are further differentiating features. Children of the two groups also show impairments in each of these developmental aspects. These sets of data begin to build a case for a configuration of variables that makes a risk context for a genetic predisposition. We need systematically to search for configurations of environmental dimensions that make critical differences for children, at given developmental stages.

The differences we have discussed in rearing environment and in child characteristics are group differences. But not all families in the depressed or well group fit the model of the significant group difference. Therefore, another phase of research is needed, which is often not pursued. Such a phase involves intensively studying, within families and within individuals, the patterns of deficits and strengths, to attempt to observe (discover) how competent or disordered behavior evolves in the individual family and child, how its development is nurtured by what patterned experiences. The traditional group differences approach via single variables should not be set aside, but it is not the best and only road to discovery of processes. Measurement over time at an individual level is essential.

Developmental theory and empirical and research tools that are now available make it possible to measure family environment and child development at levels of complexity and precision sufficient to materially advance our understanding of family influences on the individual.

CONCLUDING COMMENTS

This has been a case presentation of a research endeavor, an account of the rationale, planning, and part of the implementation of a study of child development in the contexts of well and depressed-parented families. The goal in formulating the study was to conceptualize and measure the rearing environment in a manner that would attempt to do reasonable justice to the complexity but comprehensibility of rearing environments; and would set aside the glib and global measures that often leave environment a relatively weak and erratic variable in predicting child behavior. The sampling of data and findings reported here make this experimentation with methods appear worthwhile. Hopefully, by acquiring substantial systematic data on family environments, it will be possible to perfect critical assessments that will, in turn, bring better understanding of family environment as a contributor to individual development.

ACKNOWLEDGMENTS

Many investigators have contributed to this research: Michael Chapman, Leon Kuczynski, Leon Cytryn, Donald McKnew, Jr., Mark Cummings, Sarah Friedman, Grazyna Kochanska, Tracy Sherman, Frances Bridges-Cline, Editha Nottelmann, John Richters, and David Pellegrini.

This work was supported by the National Institute of Mental Health, Bethesda, Maryland and by the John D. And Catherine T. MacArthur Foundation, Research Network Award on the Transition from Infancy to Early Childhood, Chicago, Illinois.

REFERENCES

Achenbach, T. M. (1979). *Child behavior checklist—for ages 4–16.* National Institute of Mental Health, Bethesda, Maryland.
Achenbach, T. M., & Edlebrock, C. (1980). *Child behavior checklist—teacher's report form.* University of Vermont, Burlington, VT.
Beardslee, W. R., Bemporad, J., Keller, M., & Klerman, G. (1983). Children of parents with major affective disorder: A review. *American Journal of Psychiatry, 140*(7), 825–832.
Gaensbauer, T. J., Harmon, R. J., Cytryn, L., & McKnew, D. H. (1984). Social and affective development in children with a manic depressive parent. *American Journal of Psychiatry, 141,* 223–229.
Hodges, K., Kline, J., Fitch, P., McKnew, D., & Cytryn, L. (1981). The Child Assessment schedule: A diagnostic interview for research and clinical use. *Catalog of Selected Documents in Psychology, 11,* 56.
Kuczynski, L., Kochanska, G., Radke-Yarrow, M., & Girnius-Brown, O. (1987). A developmental interpretation of young children's noncompliance. *Developmental Psychology, 23*(6), 799–806.
Kochanska, G., Kuczynski, L., Radke-Yarrow, M., & Welsh, J. D. (1987). Resolutions of control episodes between well and affectively ill mothers and their young children. *Journal of Abnormal Child Psychology, 15*(3), 441–456.
Pellegrini, D. S. (1987). *Life stress and psychiatric disorders in children of bipolar affective disorder patients and normal controls.* Unpublished manuscript.
Radke-Yarrow, M., & Kochanska, G. (in press). Anger in young children. In N. L. Stein, B. Leventhal, & T. Trabasso (Eds.), *Psychological and biological approaches to emotion.* Hillsdale, NJ: Lawrence Erlbaum Associates.

Radke-Yarrow, M., Kuczynski, L., Belmont, B., Stilwell, J., Nottelmann, E., & Welsh, J. D. (1987). *Affective interactions between normal and depressed mothers and their children.* Unpublished manuscript.

Radke-Yarrow, M., Richters, J., & Wilson, W. E. (1988) Child development in a network of relationships. In R. Hinde & J. Stevenson-Hinde (Eds.), *Individuals in a network of relationships.* Cambridge, England: Cambridge University Press.

Spitzer, R. L., & Endicott, J. (1977). *The schedule for affective disorders and schizophrenia: Lifetime version.* New York: New York State Psychiatric Institute, Biometrics Research.

8

Maternal Depression, Marital Discord, and Children's Behavior: A Developmental Perspective

Hyman Hops
Linda Sherman
Anthony Biglan
Oregon Research Institute

INTRODUCTION

There is no longer any doubt about the deleterious effects of maternal depression on children. What is now required is evidence of the mechanisms by which these effects are executed. This chapter develops several hypotheses about such mechanisms based on the integration of two parallel and somewhat overlapping literatures, clinical and developmental. Data from a study of the family interactions of depressed mothers and matched controls are presented to test these predictions.

Clinical studies increasingly show that the offspring of depressed mothers are at risk for a variety of problems, including depression. The combined clinical and developmental literatures suggest that older girls and younger boys may be most vulnerable and differentially affected. Depressive symptomatology is characterized primarily by *feminine* behaviors, with effects more evident around puberty. Thus, adolescent girls may be particularly at risk for the deleterious effects of depression in mothers. Among boys, conduct disorders account for the plurality of all psychiatric disorders (Rutter, Tizard, Yule, Graham, & Whitmore, 1976), and boys emit higher rates of aggressive antisocial behavior than girls throughout childhood and adolescence (Patterson, 1982; Wells & Forehand, 1985). However, antisocial behavior generally decreases with increasing age. Thus, we would expect younger boys in families with depressed mothers to be uniquely susceptible to such influences.

In a previous study (Hops et al., 1987) we found that (a) compared to normal mothers, depressed mothers displayed higher rates of dysphoric affect and lower rates of happy affect, and (b) compared to children in normal families, those with a depressed mother and maritally distressed parents displayed higher rates of irritable affect. Thus, the study showed that depressed mothers are more aversive in their interactions with family members and that children may be adversely affected, especially in the presence of marital distress. The aim of the present study was to reexamine the children's affective nonverbal behavior (i.e., irritable, dysphoric, and happy) to see whether age and sex account for more variance in children's affect beyond that due to parental depression, marital distress, or their combination. More specifically, we hypothesized that adolescent girls in families with depressed mothers will display higher levels of dysphoric behaviors compared to either younger girls or boys of any age. We also hypothesized that young boys will display the highest rates of irritability, affective behavior characterized by aggressivity. Additionally, we expected to see lower rates of happy affect for each of the sex by age groups within depressed families.

DELETERIOUS CONSEQUENCES OF MATERNAL DEPRESSION

General Effects

It is becoming increasingly clear that parental depression places offspring at risk for various life difficulties including depression (see reviews by Askikal & McKinney, 1975; Beardslee, Bemporad, Keller, & Klerman, 1983; Cytryn, McKnew, Zahn-Waxler, & Gershon, 1986; Rutter & Garmezy, 1983). Weissman et al. (1987) found such children at increased risk for psychological symptoms, treatment for emotional problems, school difficulties, suicidal behavior, DSM-III diagnoses, and health problems (Weissman et al., 1986). In a study of 37 parents with a diagnosis of unipolar depression, 65% of their children received a DSM-III diagnosis, the most frequent of which was major depression (Keller et al., 1986). Of the 72 children in these families with at least one biological parent who was depressed, almost every measure of severity and chronicity of parental depression was significantly related to impairment in their children's adaptive functioning and in the likelihood of a DSM-III diagnosis. Moreover, depression in mothers, but not fathers, was significantly related to children's difficulties.

Disturbances in attachment, academic, and behavior problems have also been found (Gaensbauer, Harmon, Cytryn, & McKnew, 1984; Radke-Yarrow, Cummings, Kuczynski, & Chapman, 1985; Zahn-Waxler, Cummings, McKnew, & Radke-Yarrow, 1984), especially for children of unipolar mothers (Hammen et al., 1987; Winters, Stone, Weintraub, & Neale, 1981). In addition, depressed mothers are more likely to label their children as behavior problems than are nondepressed women (Griest, Wells, & Forehand, 1979), and having aggressive children is associated with a higher incidence of depression (Patterson, 1980).

The outcome of treatment for child behavior problems is improved when depression is also treated (Griest et al., 1982), and improvement in children's behavior is associated with improvements in depression (Patterson, 1980). Taken together, these studies suggest that a clearer understanding of the way that depressed women and their families interact could clarify why these effects occur and might also lead to more effective interventions with such families.

Coercive Processes

A more definitive analysis of the social, interactional context appears to be necessary to more fully understand some of the difficulties depressed people have and to more clearly delineate the mechanisms that may be contributing to the deleterious effect on their children (Biglan, Hops, & Sherman, 1988; Coyne, Kahn, & Gotlib, 1987; Lewinsohn, Hoberman, Teri, & Hautzinger, 1985). A review of the recent literature suggested that aversiveness is rife in interactions with depressed people. consequently, we thought that the conceptualizations of Patterson and his colleagues (e.g., Patterson, 1982; Patterson & Hops, 1972; Patterson & Reid, 1970), about the contributions of coercive processes in the families of aggressive children and maritally distressed partners were particularly germane to the study of depressed mothers within the context of the family.

Three major principles guided our conceptualization of the coercive mechanisms that operate among depressed people. Biglan et al. (1988) review the literature and our own work to provide some evidence for these processes.

1. Depressed individuals exist in aversive environments that are primed for the development of coercive behavior.

2. The behavior of depressed people is aversive to others.[1]

3. The behavior of depressed people is *functional* in that it may (a) reduce the probability of attacks by others, and (b) obtain positive consequences.

Maternal Skill Deficits.   The environments of depressed mothers may be particularly aversive because these mothers may lack the necessary skills to cope with normal stressful events. For example, depressed women may be unskilled in parenting practices, spending less time managing their children's welfare or doing so inappropriately. In a home observation study, Friedman (1984) found that, during interactions with their children, compared to normal mothers, those who were depressed exhibited fewer verbal responses that demonstrated concern

---

[1]In this regard, we have conceptualized two types of aversive behavior, depressive and aggressive. Aggressive behavior includes more directly overt verbal behaviors such as criticism and overt nonverbal behavior such as irritability. Depressive behavior is conceived as more self-focused and includes verbal behaviors such as self-derogation and nonverbal behavior such as dysphoric or sad affect. See Biglan et al. (1988) for more detailed description.

or planning for the future. Maternal depression has also been found to be associated with the use of physical punishment (Ghodsian, Zajicek, & Wolkind, 1984). Such deficits in parenting skills may account for Brown and Harris's (1978) finding that the rate of children's accidents in working-class families with depressed mothers was more than twice as high as that of nondepressed mothers with the same SES. Further evidence for skill deficits in the depressed women was obtained in a study of spousal problem-solving interactions (Biglan et al., 1985). Among normal couples, wives and husbands did not differ in their rates of problem-solving statements. Among depressed couples, wives emitted significantly fewer statements than their husbands; this was especially true when marital distress was present.

Deficits in affectionate responding to children have also been noted among depressed mothers. Reid and Morrison (1983) report that depressed mothers smile infrequently and display less chest-to-chest contact when interacting with their infants. Observed in two analogue situations, unipolar depressed mothers emitted more negative and less positive behaviors to their children than did a control group of low stress mothers (Hammen et al., 1987). Similar findings were reported by Radke-Yarrow (Chapter 7, this volume). The limited affective repertoire of these mothers may have an adverse effect on children's responding. Indeed, normal mothers' simulation of depressive responding increased the probability of negative responding among their 3-month-old children (Cohn & Tronick, 1983). And, daughters of depressed mothers tend to match mothers' affect more than normals (see Chapter 7, this volume). Given that depressed mothers display higher rates of dysphoric affect and lower rates of happy affect (Hops et al., 1987), one would expect their children to behave similarly or in some other restricted fashion.

In examining the conditional responding of one family member to another, we also found evidence for the functional effects of maternal depression. In both the laboratory (Biglan et al., 1985) and the home (Hops et al., 1987), the depressed mothers' depressive behavior lowered the probability that their husbands or children would emit aggressive behavior. We suggested that depressive behavior is functional in providing the women some brief respite from the aversive behavior of other family members. Radke-Yarrow's (this volume) finding that severely depressed mothers are more likely to avoid confrontation when faced with overt child defiance appears consistent with these data. It is possible that the avoidance behavior of her mothers would have been coded depressive in our system, and that the children were being trained to turn off aggressive behavior when their mothers behaved in this way. We also found that family members' aggressive affect would also suppress the mother's dysphoric affect (Hops et al., 1987). Thus, it would appear that all of the family members are contained in an interactive style that promotes aversive interchanges.

Paternal Influences.   The amount of support provided by fathers may mediate the negative impact of the mother. A good relationship with one parent can act as a protective factor (Rutter, 1979) moderating other forms of distress in families (cf. Hetherington, Cox, & Cox, 1978). We found that husbands of depressed wives who had relatively satisfactory marital relationships, displayed higher rates of caring affect towards their children than did those with a depressed spouse and within a maritally distressed relationship or than did those from nondepressed families (Hops et al., 1987).

Taken together, these data suggest that the social context provides important information on the mechanisms by which depressed mothers may adversely affect their offspring, that coercive processes may account for some portion of this negative influence, and that other family members may have a moderating effect. This is entirely consistent with recent studies examining the complex interplay between the marital relationship, parenting, and child development (e.g., Belsky, 1981; Pederson, 1983).

AGE, SEX, AND DEPRESSION IN CHILDREN AND ADOLESCENTS

It is important to examine the influence of maternal depression within a developmental context for several reasons. First, effects that may be attributed to other factors such as maternal pathology or planned interventions, may be simply the result of normal developmental processes (Achenbach, 1979). Second, parental pathology may interact with normal developmental processes such that the effects of maternal depression on children in middle childhood may be quite different from that experienced during the adolescent years. In this section, we review the literature briefly to examine the relative rates of depression reported during childhood and adolescence and identify some possible effects of maternal depression.

Evidence increasingly shows that depressive disorders, defined using standard adult criteria, can and do occur in children and adolescents (Angold, 1988; Lewinsohn, Hops, Roberts, & Seeley, 1988; Puig-Antich, 1982; Puig-Antich & Gittelman, 1982). Although most studies have not used such acceptable criteria, the literature suggests that depressive feelings, if not clinical depression, increase with age. The rates of depression among children are relatively low and equal among boys and girls (Rutter, 1986). A follow-up assessment on the original Isle of Wight sample (Rutter, 1979/1980) showed a tenfold increase in reported feelings of depression from age 10 to age 15 and a fourfold increase in mild to moderate depression. Clinical depression at age 15 increased threefold although the overall rates were quite low. Disproportionate increases in favor of females was noted for both reported feelings and rates of clinical depression. Similar findings were obtained from epidemiological studies of adolescents (Schoenbach, Garrison, & Kaplan, 1984; Schoenbach, Kaplan, Grimson, & Wagner, 1982) in which a disproportionately high number of adolescents had elevated scores on self-report scales of depression compared to adult norms. This has been replicated in recent studies at the Oregon Research Institute; the mean score for almost 2000 adolescents on the CES-D (Radloff, 1977), a self-report instrument of depression, was higher than the cutoff score for clinical depression among adults (Hops et al., 1988; Roberts, Andrews, Lewinsohn, & Hops, 1988). More than one study has noted significantly higher scores for females than males (Kandel & Davies, 1982; Roberts et al., 1988; Whitaker, Davies, Shaffer, Walsh, & Kalikow, 1985). A retrospective study of a sample of 2044 individuals found the hazard rates for depression to be low through age 14, increasing during adolescence and adulthood, and peaking at middle age (45–55) (Lewinsohn, Duncan, Stanton, & Hautzinger, 1986). These rates also indicated an increased incidence for women compared to men, although the average age of initial onset was the same for both ages. Thus, it would appear that depressive symptomatology increases from childhood through adolescence and there is a major shift in reporting for females during that period which coincides with the increased rates noted for adult females.

A wide variety of childhood problems has been associated with maternal depression (see Patterson & Capaldi, in press, for review). However, the studies reviewed above suggest that the specific effects may be determined by the sex of the offspring. For example, effects similar to those displayed by mothers may be seen more frequently in daughters, and especially during adolescence, when the likelihood of depressive symptomatology is greater. Weissman et al. (1987) have provided substantive support for this hypothesis. Boys, on the other hand, may display higher rates of conduct disorders, and perhaps at younger age levels. Patterson and Capaldi (in press) have shown the paths to boys' depressed mood and antisocial behavior to be quite similar. In the next section, we review the literature on the normal development of sex-typed behavior to identify the possible processes that may produce these differential effects.

SEX-TYPED BEHAVIOR AND NORMAL DEVELOPMENT

Male-Female Behavioral Differences

Sex-typed behavior as well as sex segregation has been shown to begin very early in life. Lafreniere, Strayer, and Gauthier (1984) found same-sex play choices for either sex under 18 months was not better than that predicted by chance. By 28 months, however, girls began to show marked same-sex preferences; similar preferences for boys increased linearly with age and were highest at age five. Fagot, Leinbach, and Hagan (1986) showed that sex-typed behavior and segregated play appear to begin at the time that children learn to verbally discriminate one sex from another. At age 2½, only children who were able to apply the labels boy and girl correctly spent more time playing with their own sex. The correct use of gender labels was also shown to be inversely related to aggressive behavior. Thus, as Maccoby (1986) notes, beginning very early on, the social environment of boys and girls becomes markedly different as they grow older.

The behavioral differences that occur among the sexes is also noteworthy. Some of the major ones have been summarized by Maccoby (1986). Boys play more publicly, in larger groups, with more body contact and aggression. Their friendships are also described as more extensive, i.e., primary involvement is through group games or activities. Girls, on the other hand, spend more time indoors, in smaller groups, have one or two best friends, and display much less aggressive behavior. Girls also demonstrate a high probability of turn-taking as opposed to boys. Leadership behaviors also differ among sexes; boys tend to issue direct commands and establish dominance physically, whereas girls attempt to influence others with compliments, asking for advice or favors, or imitation.

How do these differences become established? Although some have argued for a biological component (Maccoby, 1986; Lafreniere et al., 1984), there is also considerable evidence that many of the behavioral patterns are shaped by the adult and peer environments. We review some of these studies next.

Parental Influences

Studies have shown that fathers and mothers respond differentially to boys and girls across the age range (Block, 1983). Parents appear to be more responsive to boys than to girls from infancy, providing more positive and negative feedback (Maccoby & Jacklin, 1974; Margolin & Patterson, 1975). They also provide differential types of stimulation; boys are provided with toys that encourage manipulation and which elicit more explicit feedback. Girls' toys provide less opportunity for such innovation and are less likely to encourage activity and problem-solving behavior. Boys, likewise, are given more opportunity to play and explore, whereas girls are encouraged by their mothers to follow them around the house (Fagot, 1978). Chores, similarly, are differentially assigned to boys and girls. Typically, parents react positively to their children's sex-typical behavior and negatively to cross-sex behaviors (Huston, 1983).

Differential effects of fathers and mothers have also been noted. Fathers have been shown to be more physically rough and use toys less when playing with male compared to female infants (Parke & Suomi, 1980; Power & Parke, 1982). Observations of parent-child interactions also show that fathers exert greater pressure than mothers for sex-appropriate behavior (Maccoby, 1986). Fathers tend to reinforce more instrumental, achievement-oriented behavior in sons and more dependent behavior in their daughters (see Blechman, 1985 for review). And under economic stress, fathers tend to be more rejecting to their daughters (Elder, Van Nguyen, & Caspi, 1985). Mothers contribute to this differential effect as well. Mothers have been observed providing more help to girls during problem-solving situations than to boys, whether or not that help is required (Rothbart & Rothbart, 1976).

It is also important to examine the social contingencies that parents provide to children. Several studies have shown that mothers react differentially to child behaviors of the different sexes, responding to requests for help by sons and to mistakes by daughters (Rothbart, 1971; Rothbart & Rothbart, 1976). Fathers were also shown to encourage their sons' assertiveness and directness while disagreeing more with their daughters (Grotevant & Cooper, 1985). In another study, both parents more frequently interrupted and talked simultaneously with daughters than with sons (Grief, cited in Huston, 1983).

Overall, studies suggest that girls, compared to boys, receive encouragement to display dependency, affectionate behavior, and express tender emotions (Hetherington et al., 1978; Huston, 1983).

Teacher Influences

Evidence is also available suggesting that teachers reinforce and maintain sex-typical behaviors (Serbin, Tonick, & Sternglanz, 1977). While teachers' rates of reinforcement are a function of behavior rather than sex (Fagot, 1985), they provide more positive attention to *feminine* rather than masculine behaviors, i.e., task-oriented achievement as opposed to aggressive behavior (Huston, 1983). This may be due, in part, to situational variables. Girls spend more time in settings with high probabilities of adult contact, e.g., instructional activities, and are likely to receive more positive attention for being compliant (Huston, 1983). Teachers appear to react to boys and girls differently even when their behavior is similar (Etaugh & Harlow, cited in Huston, 1983). Boys may be punished, in part, because of their behavior and, in addition, because of their reputation. Most direct observation studies of teacher behavior in both preschool and elementary school classes have shown that boys receive more punishment from teachers than girls do (Huston, 1983). In contrast, girls' higher ratings on prosocial behavior by teachers and peers is not supported by direct observation in the natural environment (Radke-Yarrow, Zahn-Waxler, & Chapman, 1983).

The findings described above indicate that boys and girls increase in their degree of sex-differentiated behavior with increasing age, differences that have a profound effect on their later lives. These findings also suggest that a significant portion of sex-typed behavior may be attributed to shaping by adults as well as peers. Because adolescence is the period during which sex-differentiated behavior is most likely to be visible, the highest rates of depressive-like behavior would be expected to occur among females during this period.

INTERACTION OF SEX-TYPED DEVELOPMENT AND PATHOLOGY

Studies that have examined sex differences in childhood psychopathology (e.g., see Eme, 1979, for extensive review) have consistently shown that during early childhood, the prevalence rates for boys are consistently higher than those of girls for almost all childhood disorders. Beginning with adolescence, however, the prevalence rates for the sexes reverse, with females higher, particularly in the *neurotic* and affective disorders. The proportionally lower rates of adolescent male psychopathology is localized in personality and gender identity disorders. Where there are precipitating or risk factors, which increase the probability of psychological disorder in children and adolescents, we would predict that males and females would exhibit those disorders associated with their particular sex and age. In general, we would expect to see higher rates of problem behaviors among young boys and adolescent girls.

In addition, specific risk factors may also have differential effects. For example, maternal depression has been shown to produce effects depending upon sex of the offspring (Radke-Yarrow, Chapter 7). Because aggression is primarily associated with boys (Parke & Slaby, 1983), and mothers of aggressive children have been shown to have higher levels of depressive symptoms (Furey & Forehand, 1984; Lewin, Hops, Aubuschon, & Budinger, 1988; Patterson, 1980), we would predict higher levels of aggressive, antisocial, delinquent behavior among young boys.

Girls, on the other hand, would be expected to exhibit higher levels of emotional, unassertive, depressive behaviors, given their shaping history. Thus, depressive-type behaviors should become more discriminable in girls than boys, with increasing age, consistent with the results of epidemiological studies showing higher rates of depression in females during adolescence (e.g., Rutter, 1979/80). Next, we examine data on the behavior of children from the homes of depressed mothers and matched normal controls to test several of the hypotheses presented above.

DESCRIPTION OF THE ORI STUDY

Direct observation data was collected in the homes of 52 intact families with at least one child between the ages of 3 and 16 as part of a study of the family interactions of depressed mothers (Biglan et al., 1985; Hops et al., 1987). Twenty-seven of the mothers met Research Diagnostic Criteria (RDC; Spitzer, Endicott, & Robins, 1978), for clinical depression based on SADS (Endicott & Spitzer, 1978) interviews, were in treatment, and had BDI (Beck, Ward, Mendelson, Mock, & Erbaugh, 1961) scores of 18 or greater. Of the depressed families, 14 were defined as maritally distressed on the basis of mean couple DAS (Spanier, 1976) scores of less than 98. The 25 normal women and their husbands had no history of treatment for any psychological or psychiatric disorder for at least 5 years, presented no evidence of any disorder meeting RDC criteria, and had mean DAS scores greater than 100.

The subjects consisted of the 106 children that were observed in the 52 families. There were 27 girls and 26 boys in the control families, 9 girls and 16

TABLE 8.1
Number of Children in Each Group by Sex and Age

		Control	Depressed	Dep/Dist	
Females	Less than 11	14	5	6	25
	11 or greater	13	4	8	25
Males	Less than 11	16	12	6	34
	11 or greater	10	4	8	22
	Total	53	25	28	

boys in the depressed only families, and 14 girls and 14 boys in the depressed distressed families. Table 8.1 contains the breakdown of the subjects by sex, diagnostic group, and age (below 11 and greater than or equal to 11).

All families were observed in their own homes on 10 1-hour occasions within a maximum period of 4 weeks. Subject families were paid $190 for their participation on a graduated increasing schedule (e.g., $75 after the 10th observation) to reduce attrition. There were no dropouts.

Family interaction was coded using the LIFE coding system (Arthur, Hops, & Biglan, 1982), which was developed specifically for the study of depressed individuals. The coding system contains 37 verbal codes and 7 affect codes. For this analysis we focused on three affect codes which had previously been shown to discriminate between families with depressed mothers and those with normal families. These were dysphoric, irritable, and happy affect. In our previous work, we found that depressed mothers displayed significantly more dysphoric affect and less happy affect than nondepressed mothers, and that children from families with depressed mothers and marital distress exhibited significantly higher levels of irritable affect than did children in any other families (Hops et al., 1987).

Hypotheses

The previous review of the developmental and clinical literature suggested that:

1. The deleterious effect of maternal depression would be noted primarily among young boys and older girls. Specifically, we predicted that in such families:

a. Young boys would display the highest rates of irritable affect.
b. Older girls would display the highest rates of dysphoric affect.
c. Both younger boys and older girls would display the lowest rates of happy affect.

2. Differential effects of sex and age would be seen among both non-distressed and distressed families; the effects would be similar to those specified above but of a lesser intensity.

SUMMARY OF RESULTS

Hierarchical stepwise regression analyses were conducted to predict levels of irritable, dysphoric, and happy affect among the children. Our goal was to see whether age, sex, and their interactions would significantly increase the amount of variance that could be accounted for in children's rates of these three affective behaviors beyond that determined by group membership, that is, having (a) a depressed mother, (b) a depressed mother and maritally distressed parents, or (c) neither. Examining the interaction between age and sex was particularly important because we hypothesized that girls and boys would show differential effects as a function of age.

Dummy variables were created for the presence or absence of maternal depression and marital distress and forced into the equation first.[2] Then, age and sex were allowed to enter to see whether any variance could be predicted from their main effects. Next, the four main effect variables were forced in and the two-way interactions of age, sex, depression, and marital distress were allowed to enter, i.e., age $\times$ depression, sex $\times$ depression, age $\times$ distress, sex $\times$ distress, and distress $\times$ depression. Finally, the four main effects and the five two-way interaction variables were forced in and the three-way interactions of age, sex, depression, and marital distress were allowed to enter the equation.

We predicted the highest levels of dysphoric affect would be seen in the older girls. Each of the steps in the regression analyses are shown in Table 8.2. In the first step, marital distress and not maternal depression accounted for 5.6% of the variance when both were entered simultaneously. Neither age nor sex increased R^2 significantly, although a slight increase overall was noted. However, of the two-way interactions, the interaction of age and depression approached significance, adding 6.4% more to the explained variance for a total of 15%. None of the 3-way interactions was significant.

To more closely examine the contribution of age to dysphoric affect within the context of maternal depression, correlations were computed between age and dysphoric affect independently for the normal and the depressed groups. The correlation was nonsignificant for the normals but highly significant for the depressed, $r = .43$, $df = 51$, $p = .001$. Thus, 18% of the variance in dysphoric affect among the children of the depressed groups could be accounted for by age.

We compared the mean rates of children under 11 with those 11 and older, dichotomizing the sample because children's ages were not spread evenly across the age span within groups and because we were interested primarily in distinguishing between childhood and adolescence. A 3-way ANOVA by age, sex, and group was conducted and, as expected, a significant age $\times$ group effect was

---

[2]Dummy variables rather than the sores on the BDI and DAS were used because the distributions across groups were quite skewed. Normal families were selected with extremely low scores on both these instruments; in contrast, depressed families were selected with extremely high scores on the DAS.

TABLE 8.2
Stepwise Regression of Depression, Marital Distress, Sex, and Age
on Rate of Children's Dysphoric Affect

	R^2	$1R^2$	Beta	F	p
STEP 1	0.056	0.056		3.08	0.050
Distress			0.294	6.05	0.016
Depress			-0.146	1.50	N.S.
STEP 2	0.086	0.030		2.37	0.058
Distress			0.263	4.79	0.030
Depress			-0.128	1.14	N.S.
Age			0.140	2.14	N.S.
Sex			-0.092	<1.00	N.S.
STEP 3	0.150	0.064		3.52	0.006
Distress			0.225	3.67	0.058
Depress			-0.660	8.51	0.004
Age			-0.110	<1.00	N.S.
Sex			-0.103	1.23	N.S.
Age X Depress			0.672	7.52	0.007
STEP 4	No more significant predictors				
STEP 5	No more significant predictors				

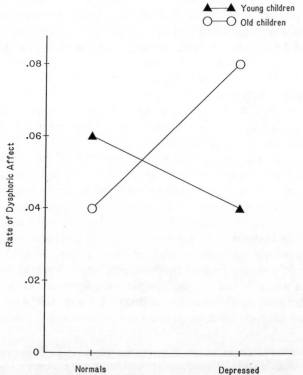

FIG. 8.1. Rates of dysphoric affect by age, sex, and diagnostic group.

obtained, $F(1,98) = 7.05, p < .01$. Figure 8.1 presents the group means graphically. Post-hoc analyses showed no effect of age within the normal group, $M = .06$ and $M = .04$, for the younger and older children, respectively. Among the depressed sample, however, the older children's rates of dysphoric affect were significantly ($p < .05$) higher than those of the younger children, .08 and .04, respectively; they were also significantly higher than the older children in the normal families.

Next, we tested the hypothesis that the highest rates of irritable affect would be exhibited by the younger boys. The results of the hierarchical regression

TABLE 8.3
Stepwise Regression of Depression, Marital Distress, Sex, and Age
on Rate of Children's Irritable Affect

	R^2	$1R^2$	Beta	F	p
STEP 1	0.125	0.125		7.34	0.001
Distress			0.360	9.79	0.002
Depress			-0.012	<1.00	N.S.
STEP 2	0.168	0.043		6.84	0.001
Distress			0.334	8.70	0.004
Depress			0.019	<1.00	N.S.
*Sex			-0.209	5.25	0.024
STEP 3	0.193	0.025		6.02	0.001
Distress			0.313	7.70	0.007
Depress			0.023	<1.00	N.S.
Sex			-0.198	4.79	0.031
*Age			0.160	3.14	0.079
STEP 4	0.238	0.045		6.25	0.001
Distress			0.543	14.05	0.001
Depress			0.004	< 1.00	N.S.
Age			0.166	3.53	0.063
Sex			-0.067	<1.00	N.S.
*Sex X Distress			-0.329	5.97	0.016
STEP 5	0.272	0.034		3.98	0.001
Distress			0.302	<1.00	N.S.
Depress			-0.083	<1.00	N.S.
Age			0.193	1.54	N.S.
Sex			0.145	<1.00	N.S.
*Age X Distress			0.300	<1.00	N.S.
*Age X Depress			0.041	<1.00	N.S.
Sex X Distress			-0.345	4.02	0.048
*Sex X Depress			0.088	<1.00	N.S.
*Age X Sex			0.300	1.79	N.S.
STEP 6	0.301	0.030		4.10	0.001
Distress			-0.059	<1.00	N.S.
Depress			-0.092	<1.00	N.S.
Age			0.072	<1.00	N.S.
Sex			-0.096	<1.00	N.S.
Age X Distress			0.721	3.89	0.051
Age X Depress			0.039	<1.00	N.S.
Sex X Distress			0.249	<1.00	N.S.
Sex X Depress			0.095	<1.00	N.S.
Age X Sex			-0.013	<1.00	N.S.
*Age X Sex X Distress			-0.670	4.04	0.047

*New variables entered

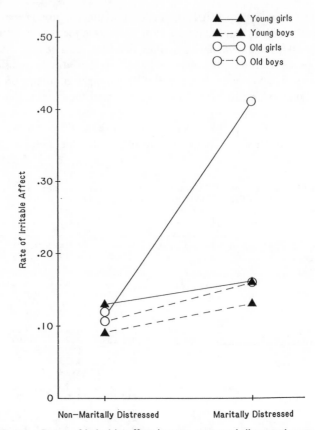

FIG. 8.2.   Rates of irritable affect by age, sex, and diagnostic group.

analyses are presented in Table 8.3. Both two-way and three-way interactions between age, sex, and marital distress, but not depression, added significant proportions to the explained variance, after partialling out the effects due to maternal depression and marital distress. The final R^2 accounted for by all the variables entered was approximately 30%. To examine further the influence of age, sex, and marital distress, correlations were computed between age and rates of irritable affect for each sex for the maritally distressed and non-maritally distressed groups, independently. Only one correlation approached significance; for girls within the maritally distressed group, $r = .50$, $p = .07$, indicating that 25% of the variance in rates of irritable affect could be accounted for by age.

A 3-way ANOVA by age, sex, and group was conducted and the results are graphically presented in Figure 8.2. The group by age by sex interaction was significant, $F(1,98) = 4.73$, $p < .05$. Post-hoc analyses showed that the older girls in the depressed distressed families exhibited significantly ($p < .05$) higher rates of irritable affect ($M = .41$) compared to all other groups. The means for

TABLE 8.4
Stepwise Regression of Depression, Marital Distress, Sex, and Age
on Rate of Children's Happy Affect

	R^2	$1R^2$	Beta	F	p
STEP 1	0.048	0.048		2.61	0.078
*Distress			-0.163	1.85	N.S.
*Depress			-0.079	.43	N.S.
STEP 2	0.080	0.032		2.21	0.073
Distress			-0.163	1.83	N.S.
Depress			-0.062	< 1.00	N.S.
*Sex			-0.140	2.10	N.S.
*Age			-0.125	1.67	N.S.
STEP 3	0.168	0.088		3.34	0.005
Distress			-0.344	5.06	0.027
Depress			0.402	3.19	0.078
Age			0.080	< 1.00	N.S.
Sex			-0.252	5.39	0.022
*Age X Depress			-0.563	5.32	0.023
*Sex X Distress			0.306	4.68	0.033
STEP 4	0.189	0.021		2.49	0.013
Distress			-0.522	2.67	N.S.
Depress			0.502	2.45	N.S.
Age			0.207	1.59	N.S.
Sex			-0.015	< 1.00	N.S.
*Age X Distress			0.230	< 1.00	N.S.
*Age X Depress			-0.732	5.02	0.027
Sex X Distress			0.230	2.73	N.S.
*Sex X Depress			0.057	< 1.00	N.S.
*Age X Sex			-0.310	1.71	N.S.
STEP 5	0.223	0.034		2.73	0.005
Distress			-0.533	2.88	0.093
Depress			-0.937	6.08	0.016
Age			0.403	4.63	0.034
Sex			0.379	1.57	N.S.
Age X Distress			0.276	<1.00	N.S.
Age X Depress			-1.263	9.38	0.003
Sex X Distress			0.259	2.08	N.S.
Sex X Depress			-0.656	2.61	N.S.
Age X Sex			-0.778	5.69	.019
*Age X Sex X Depress			0.829	4.22	0.043

*New variables entered

irritable affect rates were .16, .13, and .16, for younger girls, younger boys, and older boys, respectively, within the maritally distressed families and $M = .13$, .12, .09, and .11, for younger girls, older girls, younger boys, and older boys, respectively, within the nonmaritally distressed families.

We also predicted that younger boys and older girls in families with depressed mothers would show the lowest rates of happy affect. The hierarchical regression analysis showed that the interaction of age, sex, and depression did add significantly to the explained variance, although the 3.4% was only a small proportion of the 22.3% of the total variance accounted for (see Table 8.4). Correlations were computed between happy affect and age for each sex within the depressed and nondepressed groups, independently. Only the correlations for the girls were found to be significant regardless of group. However, the direction of the effect varied according to group; negative in the depressed group, $r = -.57, p < .01$, and positive in the normal group, $r = .42, p < .05$, accounting for 32% and 18% of the variance in happy affect, respectively. For daughters of depressed mothers, age was inversely related to happy affect, whereas the reverse was true in normal families.

The results of the 3-way ANOVA, illustrated in Fig. 8.3, disclosed a significant interaction between age, sex, and group, $F(1,98) = 5.49, p < .05$. Post-hoc analyses showed that the older girls in the normal families had significantly higher rates of happy affect ($M = 1.55$) than did older boys in the normal families ($M = .63$), and older girls ($M = .71$), older boys ($M = 1.02$), or younger boys ($M = 1.08$) in the depressed families. The older girls in the depressed families had significantly lower rates of happy affect than the normal young boys or girls, 1.20 and 1.31, respectively, and young girls in the depressed families ($M = 1.30$).

In summary, the results show that the interaction of age and sex in the presence of maternal depression or marital distress does account for variability in the rates of children's specific affective behaviors. Among the depressed groups,

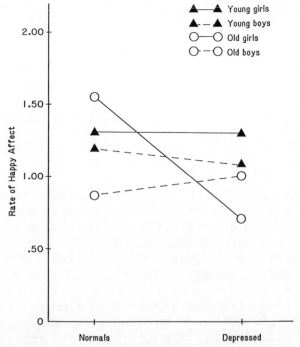

FIG. 8.3. Rates of happy affect by age, sex, and diagnostic group.

older children display the highest rates of dysphoric affect and older girls the lowest rates of happy affect. In the maritally distressed group, the older girls also show the highest rates of irritable affect. In contrast, among the normal families, older girls exhibit the highest rates of happy affect, whereas older boys display the lowest rates. Thus, it is those children aged 11 and over, and especially girls, who appear to be most affected by group membership.

DISCUSSION AND IMPLICATIONS

From our review of the developmental and clinical literature, we hypothesized that the impact of maternal depression would be found primarily among young boys and older girls. No evidence was found in support of the first hypothesis. Young boys did not exhibit either higher rates of negative affect or lower rates of happy affect than their older counterparts. In fact, among the depressed families, age was positively correlated with rates of dysphoric affect for both boys and girls. We did find, however, partial support for the hypothesis that older girls would be more negatively influenced by having a depressed mother in the home. Older girls in both the depressed only and depressed distressed families did display higher rates of dysphoric affect and lower rates of happy affect. Those in the depressed distressed families also showed higher rates of irritable affect. These results may be indicative of a restricted range of affective behavior in these girls, similar to that displayed by their mothers (Hops et al., 1987). They also suggest that as girls enter the adolescent phase of their lives, during which they become more independent and display more adult-like behaviors, they may be more greatly influenced, adversely or positively, by their mother's behavior and level of distress.

These data are consistent with recent results of several studies. The Yale Family Study of Major Depression, (Weissman et al., 1987) has shown that the relative risk of being diagnosed Major Depressive Disorder and the age of onset, increases markedly with adolescence and is higher for girls than boys. Moreover, the age of onset is significantly lower (12–13) for children of depressed parents compared to children of nondepressed parents (16–17). Similarly, Petersen, Ebata, and Sargiani (1987) found that increasingly during adolescence, girls, more than boys, are likely to report depressive moods. Finally, current studies at the Oregon Research Institute show that female high school students not only report significantly more depressive symptomatology (Hops et al., 1988; Roberts et al., 1988) but also show significantly higher rates of diagnosed affective disorder than males (Lewinsohn et al., 1988). Thus, it is not unexpected that the older girls in the present study, who ranged from 11 to 16, had begun to demonstrate rates of dysphoric and irritable affect that were different than those shown by the normal girls. The higher rates of dysphoric affect shown by the older boys in the depressed families is also consistent with Weissman et al.

(1987) and may indicate concurrent or later problems for them as well. The results here provide further support for our conceptualization of two types of aversive behavior, depressive and aggressive (Biglan et al., 1988). The highest rates of irritability were found in families with maritally distressed parents where more overt aggression is more likely to be displayed (Biglan et al., 1985). However, dysphoric and happy affect was related only to maternal depression and not marital distress. Thus, the absence of findings in support of the negative effects of maternal depression on children's overt interactive behavior in two recent studies (Lee & Gotlib, 1987; Webster-Stratton & Hammond, 1987) may have been due to the use of coding systems that did not differentiate between these two types of aversiveness. As did Biglan et al. (1985), we also examined the correlation between dysphoric and irritable affect within the depressed and nondepressed families. These were computed, independently, for the younger and older children.[3] Among the normal families, a significant correlation was found only for the younger children, $r = .75$, $p < .001$, whereas the reverse was true among the depressed families, a significant correlation detected only for the older children, $r = .74$, $p < .001$. The correlations obtained for the normal families are somewhat easier to explain than those obtained for the depressed families. It is expected that younger children have not learned to respond differentially to different stimuli within or across settings. Thus, in conflict situations, they are likely to emit both forms of aversive behaviors that are of interest here, that is, dysphoric or irritable. Older children, on the other hand, with more experience, are more likely to have developed more precise, predictable, and reliable responding patterns, with higher probabilities of responding either aggressively or dysphorically to aversive stimuli. The findings for children within the depressed families, which are the reverse of these found for normal families, are more difficult to interpret. It is puzzling that the younger children did not demonstrate the same lack of differential responding that those in the normal families did. Even young children with depressed mothers have already begun to respond differentially, emitting higher rates of either dysphoric or irritable affect. Yet, the differential responding is not present among the older children in these families. Further research will be required to fully understand the effects discovered here.

We expected to find some differential effects by sex among the normal families as well. Blechman (1985) has argued that the normal socialization of women impairs their ability to function competently. There is considerable evidence in support. Block (1987) reported differential predictors of depression for boys and girls across an 8-year span. Based on teachers' ratings, the preschool predictors of a measure of depression at age 14 for boys were being shy, withdrawn, restricted, and liking to be alone; for girls, they were being helpful of others,

---

[3]Correlations were initially computed separately by sex, but no differences were found.

sharing, giving, excessive compliance, and being oversocialized. If normal adolescent girls are being shaped by the environment to have more psychological difficulties than boys, then higher rates of negative affect should have been evidenced in our sample. To the contrary, we found the *normal* adolescent girls exhibited the highest rates of happy affect. We suspect that we found no support for our hypothesis because our sample may not have been representative of the *normal* population but more representative of competent families. They were selected primarily because neither the parents nor the children had a recent history of any psychological difficulties. Thus, one might conclude that the environmental conditions under which these children were raised may have significantly reduced the likelihood of the older girls or boys becoming depressed or having other psychological problems. The social conditions in families with a depressed mother, on the other hand, may have exacerbated the stresses involved during normal adolescent development. Our previous analyses have shown that depressed mothers are more dysphoric and less happy, and that dysphoric affect is functional in reducing the aggressive behavior of other family members. However, such coercive processes have been shown to increase the overall level of aversiveness among families with a depressed member (Biglan et al., 1985) and among families with aggressive children (Patterson, 1982). This is particularly apparent in families with a depressed mother and a dissatisfied marital relationship, the older girls showing the highest rates of irritability.

Finally, the analyses presented here should be considered to be descriptive and exploratory for several reasons. First, the number of children varies within families; thus, some families may be contributing more of a specific effect than others. We believe, however, that if the effects of age and sex are found to be significant, then presumably, any confounds due to family membership can be considered to be error variance. Second, the numbers of children within each of the diagnostic groups were not distributed equally by age and sex, and the sample size for some of our analyses were quite small. Thus, any significant findings should be considered conservative estimates of those existing in the population at large. Third, no data were collected on other variables which may have provided support for or refuted these hypotheses. These would include pubertal timing (Petersen & Hamburg, 1986), evidence of other psychological difficulties, and academic achievement. Fourth, the design did not control for the possibility that the effects were due to general distress in these families, rather than maternal depression per se, since depression was in part confounded by marital distress. However, as we pointed out in Biglan et al. (1988), this position is not inconsistent with others' findings that deleterious effects on children may not be solely a function of maternal depression, but various forms of familial distress. It is still important to discover, however, what the mechanisms are for the acquisition of dysphoric as opposed to irritable affect among children, and the investigation of the family interactions of depressed mothers seems a good place to begin.

ACKNOWLEDGMENTS

Portions of this chapter were presented at the meeting of the Society for Research in Child Development, Baltimore, 1987. This research was supported by National Institute of Mental Health Grants MH34517 and MH39615, and Biomedical Research Support Grant RR05612. The authors gratefully acknowledge the contributions of Ruth Gibian, Candace Holcomb, Nancy Oostenink, Alan Silverblatt, Scott Smith, Tammy Tengs, and Phil Warner, the observer team, and Barbara Britz and Ginny Osteen for their assistance in preparing the manuscript.

REFERENCES

Achenbach, T. M. (1979). *Child Behavior Checklist*. Bethesda, MD: National Institute of Mental Health.

Akiskal, H. S., & McKinney, W. T., Jr. (1975). Overview of recent research in depression: Integration of ten conceptual models into a comprehensive clinical frame. *Archives of General Psychiatry, 32*, 285–305.

Angold, A. (1988). Childhood and adolescent depression: I. Epidemiological and aetiological aspects. *British Journal of Psychiatry, 152*, 601–617.

Arthur, J. A., Hops, H., & Biglan, A. (1982). *LIFE (Living in familial environments) coding system*. Unpublished manuscript, Oregon Research Institute, Eugene, OR.

Beardslee, W. R., Bemporad, J., Keller, M. B., & Klerman, G. L. (1983). Children of parents with major affective disorder: A review. *American Journal of Psychiatry, 140*, 828–832.

Beck, A. T., Ward, C. H., Mendelson, M., Mock, J. E., & Erbaugh, J. K. (1961). An inventory for measuring depression. *Archives of General Psychiatry, 4*, 561–571.

Belsky, J. (1981). Early human experience: A family perspective. *Developmental Psychology, 17*, 3–23.

Biglan, A., Hops, H., & Sherman, L. (1988). Coercive family processes and maternal depression. In R. DeV. Peters & R. J. McMahon (Eds.), *Marriage and families: Behavioral-systems approaches*. New York: Brunner/Mazel.

Biglan, A., Hops, H., Sherman, L., Friedman, L., Arthur, J., & Osteen, V. (1985). Problem-solving interactions of depressed women and their husbands. *Behavior Therapy, 16*, 431–451.

Blechman, E. A. (1985). Women's behavior in a man's world: Sex differences in competence. In E. A. Blechman (Ed.), *Behavior modification with women* (pp. 3–33). New York: Guilford Press.

Block, J. H. (1983). Differential premises arising from differential socialization of the sexes: Some conjectures. *Child Development, 54*, 1335–1354.

Block, J. H. (1987, April). Longitudinal antecedents of ego-control and ego-resiliency in late adolescence. In J. H. Block (chair), *Longitudinal approaches to adolescent adaptation*. Symposium conducted at the meeting of the Society for Research in Child Development, Baltimore.

Brown, G., & Harris, T. (1978). Social origins of depression: A reply. *Psychological Medicine, 8*, 577–588.

Cohn, J. F., & Tronick, E. Z. (1983). Three-month-old infants' reactions to simulated maternal depression. *Child Development, 54*, 185–193.

Coyne, J. C., Kahn, J., & Gotlib, I. H. (1987). Depression. In T. Jacob (Ed.), *Family interaction and psychopathology* (pp. 509–533). New York: Plenum.

Cytryn, L., McKnew, D. H., Zahn-Waxler, C., & Gershon, E. S. (1986). Developmental issues in risk research: The offspring of affectively ill parents. In M. Rutter, C. E. Izard, & P. B. Read (Eds.), *Depression in children: Developmental perspectives*. New York: Guilford Press.

Elder, G. H., Jr., Van Nguyen, & Caspi, A. (1985). Linking family hardship to children's lives. *Child Development, 56*, 361–375.

Eme, R. F. (1979). Sex differences in childhood psychopathology: A review. *Psychological Bulletin, 86* (3), 574–595.

Endicott, J., & Spitzer, R. (1978). A diagnostic interview: The Schedule for Affective Disorders and Schizophrenia. *Archives of General Psychiatry, 35*, 837–853.

Fagot, B. I. (1978). The influence of sex on parental reactions to toddler children. *Child Development, 49*, 30–36.

Fagot, B. I. (1985). Beyond the reinforcement principle: Another step toward understanding sex role development. *Developmental Psychology, 21*, 1097–1104.

Fagot, B. I., Leinbach, M. D., & Hagan, R. (1986). Gender labeling and the adoption of sex-typed behaviors. *Developmental Psychology, 22*(4), 440–443.

Friedman, L. S. (1984). *Family interactions among children of unipolar depressed mothers: A controlled naturalistic observation study.* Unpublished doctoral dissertation, University of Oregon, Eugene, OR.

Furey, W., & Forehand, R. (1984). An examination of predictors of mothers' perceptions of satisfaction with their children. *Journal of Social and Clinical Psychology, 2*, 230–243.

Gaensbauer, T. J., Harmon, R. J., Cytryn, L., & McKnew, D. H. (1984). Social and affective development in children with a manic-depressive parent. *American Journal of Psychiatry, 141*, 223–229.

Ghodsian, M., Zajicek, E., & Wolkind, S. (1984). A longitudinal study of maternal depression and child behavior problems. *Journal of Child Psychology and Psychiatry, 25*(1), 91–109.

Griest, D., Forehand, R., Rogers, T., Breiner, J., Furey, W., & Williams, C. A. (1982). Effects of parent enhancement therapy on the treatment outcome and generalization of a parent training program. *Behavior Research and Therapy, 20*, 429–436.

Griest, D. L., Wells, K. C., & Forehand, R. (1979). An examination of predictors of maternal perceptions of maladjustment in clinic-referred children. *Journal of Abnormal Psychology, 88*, 277–281.

Grotevant, H. D., & Cooper, C. R. (1985). Patterns of interaction in family relationships and the development of identity exploration in adolescence. *Child Development, 56*, 415–428.

Hammen, C., Gordon, D., Burge, D., Adrian, C., Jaenicke, C., & Hiroto, D. (1987). Maternal affective disorders, illness, and stress: Risk for children's psychopathology. *American Journal of Psychiatry.*

Hammen, C., Gordon, D., Burge, D., Adrian, C., Jaenicke, C., & Hiroto, D. (1987). Communication patterns of mothers with affective disorders and their relationship to children's status and social functioning. In K. Hahlweg & M. J. Goldstein (Eds.), *Understanding major mental disorder: The contribution of family interaction research*. New York: Family Process Press.

Hetherington, E. M., Cox, M., & Cox, R. (1978). The aftermath of divorce. In J. H. Stevens & M. Mathews (Eds.), *Mother/Child, father/child relationships*. Washington, DC: National Association for the Education of Young Children.

Hops, H., Biglan, A., Sherman, L., Arthur, J., Friedman, L., & Osteen, V. (1987). Home observations of family interactions of depressed women. *Journal of Consulting and Clinical Psychology, 55*(3), 341–346.

Hops, H., Lewinsohn, P. M., Andrews, J. A., & Roberts, R. E. (1988). Psychosocial correlates of depressive symptomatology among high school students. In preparation. Oregon Research Institute, Eugene: Oregon.

Huston, A. C. (1983). Sex-typing. In P. H. Mussen (Ed.), *Handbook of child psychology* (4th Ed., Vol. 4, pp. 387–467). New York: Wiley.

Kandel, D. B., & Davies, M. (1982). Epidemiology of depressive mood in adolescents: An empirical study. *Archives of General Psychiatry, 39,* 1205–1212.

Keller, M. B., Beardslee, W. R., Dorer, D. J., Lavori, P. W., Samuelson, H., & Klerman, G. R. (1986). Impact of severity and chronicity of parental affective illness on adaptive functioning and psychopathology in children. *Archives of General Psychiatry, 43,* 930–937.

Lafreniere, P., Strayer, F. D., & Gauthier, R. (1984). The emergence of same-sex preferences among preschool peers: A developmental ethological perspective. *Child Development, 55,* 1958–1965.

Lee, C. M., & Gotlib, I. H. (1987, August). *The effect of maternal depression on child adjustment and mother-child interaction.* Paper presented at the annual meeting of the American Psychological Association, New York.

Lewin, L., Hops, H., Aubuschon, A., & Budinger, T. (1988). Predictors of maternal satisfaction regarding clinic-referred children: Methodological considerations. *Journal of Clinical Child Psychology, 17*(2), 159–163.

Lewinsohn, P. M., Duncan, E. M., Stanton, A. K., & Hautzinger, M. (1986). Age at onset for non-bipolar depression. *Journal of Abnormal Psychology, 95*(4), 378–383.

Lewinsohn, P. M., Hoberman, H., Teri, L., & Hautzinger, M. (1985). An integrative theory of depression. In S. Reiss & R. Bootzin (Eds.), *Theoretical issues in behavior therapy* (pp. 331–359). New York: Academic Press.

Lewinsohn, P. M., Hops, H., Roberts, R. E., & Seeley, J. (November, 1988). *Adolescent depression: Prevalence and psychosocial aspects.* Paper presented at the annual meeting of the American Public Health Association, Boston.

Maccoby, E. E. (1986). Social groupings in childhood: Their relationship to prosocial and antisocial behavior in boys and girls. In D. Olweus, J. Block, & M. Radke-Yarrow (Eds.), *Development of antisocial and prosocial behavior: Research, theories, and issues* (pp. 263–284). New York: Academic Press.

Maccoby, E. E., & Jacklin, C. N. (1974). *The psychology of sex differences.* Stanford, CA: Stanford University Press.

Margolin, G., & Patterson, G. R. (1975). Differential consequences provided by mothers and fathers for their sons and daughters. *Developmental Psychology, 11,* 537–538.

Parke, R. D., & Slaby, R. G. (1983). The development of aggression. In P. H. Mussen (Ed.), *Handbook of child psychology* (4th ed): *Social development* (pp. 605–641). New York: Wiley.

Parke, R. D., & Suomi, S. J. (1980). Adult male-infant relationships: Human and nonprimate evidence. In K. Immelmann, G. Barlow, M. Main, & L. Petrinovitch (Eds.), *Behavioral development: The Bielefeld interdisciplinary project.* New York: Cambridge University Press, 1980.

Patterson, G. R. (1980). Mothers: The unacknowledged victims. *Monographs of the Society for Research in Child Development, 45*(5, Serial No. 186).

Patterson, G. R. (1982). *A social learning approach to family intervention: Vol. 3. Coercive family process.* Eugene, OR: Castalia Publishing.

Patterson, G. R., & Capaldi, D. (in press). A comparison of models for boys' depressed mood. In J. E. Rolf, A. Masten, D. Cicchetti, K. Neuchterlein, & S. Weintraub (Eds.), *Risk and protective factors in the development of psychopathology.* Boston: MA: Syndicate of the Press, University of Cambridge.

Patterson, G. R., & Hops, H. (1972). Coercion, a game for two: Intervention techniques for marital conflict. In R. E. Ulrich & P. Mountjoy (Eds.), *The experimental analysis of social behavior.* New York: Appleton-Century-Crofts.

Patterson, G. R., & Reid, J. B. (1970). Reciprocity and coercion: Two facets of social systems. In C. Neuringer & J. Michael (Eds.), *Behavior modification in clinical psychology.* New York: Appleton-Century-Crofts.

Pederson, F. A. (1983). Differentiation of the father's role in the infancy period. In J. P. Vincent (Ed.), *Advances in family intervention, assessment and theory* (Vol. 3, pp. 185–208). Greenwich, CT: JAI Press.

Petersen, A. C., Ebata, A., & Sargiani, P. (1987, April). Who expresses depressive affect in adolescence. In J. Brooks-Gunn & A. C. Peterson (Co-chairs), *The development of depressive affect in adolescence: Biological, affective, and social factors.* Symposium conducted at the Society for Research in Child Development, Baltimore.

Peterson, A. C., & Hamburg, B. A. (1986). Adolescence: A developmental approach to problems and psychopathology. *Behavior Therapy, 17,* 480–499.

Power, T. G., & Parke, R. D. (1982). Play as a context for early learning: Lab and home analyses. In L. M. Laosa & I. E. Sigel (Eds.), *The family as a learning environment.* New York: Plenum.

Puig-Antich, J. (1982). Major depression and conduct disorder in prepuberty. *Journal of the American Academy of Child Psychiatry, 21,* 118–128.

Puig-Antich, J., & Gittleman, R. (1982). Depression in childhood and adolescence. In E. S. Paykel (Ed.), *Handbook of affective disorders* (pp. 379–392). Edinburgh & London: Churchill-Livingstone.

Radke-Yarrow, M., Cummings, E. M., Kuczynski, L., & Chapman, M. (1985). Patterns of attachment in two- and three-year-olds in normal families and families with parental depression. *Child Development, 56,* 884–893.

Radke-Yarrow, M., Zahn-Waxler, C., & Chapman, M. (1983). Children's prosocial dispositions and behavior. In P. H. Mussen (Ed.), *Handbook of child psychology* (4th ed): *Social development* (pp. 469–545). New York: Wiley.

Radloff, L. S. (1977). A CES-D scale: A self-report depression scale for research in the general population. *Applied Psychological Measurement, 1,* 385–401.

Reid, W. H., & Morrison, H. L. (1983). Risk factors in children of depressed parents. In H. L. Morrison (Ed.), *Children of depressed parents.* New York: Grune & Stratton.

Roberts, R. E., Andrews, J. A., Lewinsohn, P. M., & Hops, H. (1988). *Assessment of depression in adolescents using the Center for Epidemiological Studies Depression Scale.* Submitted for publication.

Rothbart, M. K. (1971). Birth order and mother-child interaction in an achievement situation. *Journal of Personality and Social Psychology, 17,* 113–120.

Rothbart, M. K., & Rothbart, M. (1976). Birth order, sex of child, and maternal helpgiving. *Sex Roles, 2,* 39–46.

Rutter, M. (1979). Maternal depression. *Child Development, 50,* 282–305.

Rutter, M. (1979/1980). *Changing youth in a changing society: Patterns of adolescent development and disorder.* London: Nuffield Provincial Hospitals Trust, 1979. (Cambridge, MA: Harvard University Press, 1980).

Rutter, M. (1986). The developmental psychopathology of depression: Issues and perspectives. In M. Rutter, C. E. Izard, & P. B. Read (Eds.), *Depression in young people.* New York: Guilford Press.

Rutter, M., & Garmezy, N. (1983). Developmental psychopathology. In E. M. Hetherington (Ed.), P. H. Mussen (Series Ed.), *Handbook of child psychology: Vol. 4. Socialization, personality, and social development,* 775–911. New York: Wiley.

Rutter, M., Tizard, J., Yule, W., Graham, P., & Whitmore, K. (1976). Isle of Wight studies, 1964–1974. *Psychological Medicine, 6,* 313–332.

Schoenbach, V. J., Garrison, C. Z., & Kaplan, B. H. (1984). Epidemiology of adolescent depression. *Public Health Review, 12,* 159–189.

Schoenbach, V. J., Kaplan, B. H., Grimson, R. C., & Wagner, E. H. (1982). Use of a symptom scale to study the prevalence of a depressive syndrome in young adolescents. *American Journal of Epidemiology, 116,* 791–800.

Serbin, L. A., Tonick, I. J., & Sternglanz, S. (1977). Shaping cooperative cross-sex play. *Child Development, 48,* 924–929.

Spanier, G. B. (1976). Measuring dyadic adjustment: New scales for assessing the quality of marriage and similar dyads. *Journal of Marriage and Family Therapy, 38,* 15–28.

Spitzer, R. L., Endicott, J. E., & Robins, E. (1978). *Research Diagnostic Criteria (RDC) for a selected group of functional disorders* (3rd ed.). New York: New York State Psychiatric Institute, Biometrics Research.

Webster-Stratton, C., & Hammond, M. (1987). *Maternal depression and its relationship to life stress, perceptions of child behavior problems, parenting behaviors and child conduct problems.* Paper presented at the annual meeting of the American Psychological Association, New York.

Weissman, M. M., Gammon, G. D., John, K., Merikangus, K. R., Warner, V., Prusoff, B. A., & Sholomskas, D. (1987). Children of depressed parents. *Archives of General Psychiatry, 44,* 847–853.

Weissman, M. M., John, K., Merikangus, K. R., Prusoff, B. A., Wickramaratne, P., Gammon, G. D., Angold, A., & Warner, V. (1986). Depressed parents and their children: General health, social, and psychiatric problems. *American Journal of Diseases of Children, 140,* 801–805.

Weissman, M. M., Prusoff, B. A., Gammon, G. D., Merikangas, K. R., Leckman, J. F., & Kidd, K. K. (1984). Psychopathology in the children (Ages 6-18) of depressed and normal parents. *Journal of the American Academy of Child Psychiatry, 23,* 78–84.

Wells, K. C., & Forehand, R. (1985). Conduct and oppositional disorders. In P. H. Bornstein & A. E. Kazdin, *Handbook of clinical behavior therapy with children.* Homewood, IL: The Dorsey Press.

Whitaker, A., Davies, M., Shaffer, D., Walsh, T., & Kalikow, K. (1985, February). *Eating disorders and depression in adolescents: An epidemiological study.* Poster presentation, American Academy of Psychopathology, New York.

Winters, K. C., Stone, A. A., Weintraub, S., & Neale, J. M. (1981). Cognitive and attentional deficits in children vulnerable to psychopathology. *Journal of Abnormal Child Psychology, 9,* 435–453.

Zahn-Waxler, C., Cummings, E. M., McKnew, D. H., & Radke-Yarrow, M. (1984). Affective arousal and social interactions in young children of manic-depressive parents. *Child Development, 55,* 112–122.

9 Initiation and Maintenance of Process Disrupting Single-Mother Families

G. R. Patterson
M. S. Forgatch
Oregon Social Learning Center

This report describes a deviancy-generating process that is often set into motion during the first year of marital separation. For some families, the process continues to unfold over time. Although this process produces increased deviancy for both mothers and their children, the present report is focused primarily on how the process influences the mothers.

In part, this report is highly speculative. The original intent was to present a formulation that could be tested by a longitudinal study designed specifically to test it. The resulting study involved repeated assessment of a sample of single mothers during their first year or two of separation. However, certain limitations in the data set made it impossible to test some crucial aspects of the original formulation. These oversights have been corrected for the new wave of data currently being collected for this sample (Forgatch, 1987). This report outlines the formulation and summarizes the data analyzed thus far.

We can assume that some mothers are more at risk than others for becoming involved in the initiation of the deviancy process. Our findings suggest that massive increases in stress and equally massive losses in social support networks are apparently two of the key factors that start the process. Data are presented that examine this hypothesis. It is also hypothesized that certain personality traits put some mothers at greater risk for experiencing the increased stress and loss of support as disrupting factors.

A formulation about process requires several very different kinds of information. It requires descriptive information about both stability *and* change. For example, the present formulation emphasizes changes in variables such as maternal stress, irritability, support, and depression. Descriptive information is provided describing shifts in mean levels for the indicators for these variables. The study of process also requires some specification of the stability in ordinal rankings among individuals. For example, miniscule changes in measures of irritability across time could be accompanied by profound shifts in ordinal rankings. For this reason test-retest stability correlations are included for the key variables describing single-mother behaviors.

Descriptive data for stability and change in mean levels prepare us for the next question about process: Why is it that some people are at risk for continuing in a given process while others drop out? From a social interactional perspective, one would search within ongoing social exchange patterns for the potential mechanisms that contribute to maintenance.

Our own speculations about these mechanisms are based on more than a decade of attempts to clinically intervene with single mothers with problem children. It seemed that for some of these cases, mothers recovered from the stress of separation rather quickly. These mothers were characterized by only minor depressions; and there were only modest adjustment problems for the children. Other mothers, however, seemed to be caught in a spiral of ever-increasing stressors, increasing depression and major adjustment problems of their youngsters. Our clinical impression was that the mothers most at risk tended to be characterized by highly generalized disruptions in the quality of their social interactions with children, friends, and therapists.

The clinical impression that stress disrupts social-interactional patterns was supported by empirical studies (Patterson, 1983; Wahler & Dumas, 1983). These findings are reviewed in a later section. The essential idea is that for some mothers, marked increases in stress and a loss of social support disrupt basic microsocial exchange processes. Two aspects of the disruption are readily observable. The at-risk mothers seem to be noticeably more irritable in their interactions. As noted by Biglan et al. (see Chapter 5), they are also more likely to display behaviors that would be coded as sad or depressed. The significant increase in single-mother irritable/sad behaviors serves the general function of disrupting social interactions. The present report examines three ways in which such disruptions seem to serve the function of maintaining the deviancy process.

The key to understanding each of the three mechanisms studied lies in the differential reactions of friends and family members to the single-mother irritable/sad behaviors. It is hypothesized that their reactions to the disrupted maternal social patterns determine whether the process is dampened or amplified. As shown in Fig. 9.1, two of the reactions thought to play a central role in maintenance of disruption are provided by friends; the third is provided by the child.

Three Possible Mechanisms

Friends' Reactions. We assume that for some mothers, high levels of stress and loss of support are accompanied by increases in irritable and/or depressive words, irritable or sad facial expressions, and voice tones. They may tend to talk

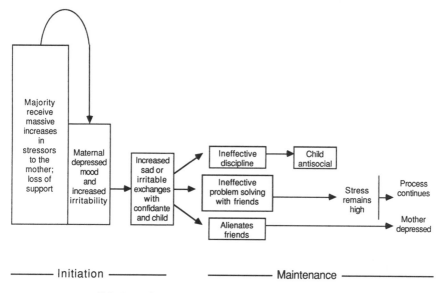

———— Initiation ————   ———— Maintenance ————

FIG. 9.1.   Sequence of steps defining disruption.

too much about their problems, so that their conversations become increasingly unidimensional. Or they may be unable to focus on anything but themselves, which also makes it difficult to have reasonable conversations, thereby causing people to find talking to unhappy people an aversive experience (Coyne, 1976).

It is hypothesized that aversive exchanges with friends can have two unfortunate outcomes. On the one hand, the friends may tend to withdraw from the single mother. On the other hand, when they engage in problem-solving discussions with the mother, the quality of these interactions may doom the effort to failure. Both outcomes are thought to contribute to the maintainence of the deviancy process.

Increased loss of support places the single mother at risk for increases in irritable/sad (aversive) behaviors. But then increased irritable/sad behavior further exacerbates the loss of support. In effect, it is a kind of positive feedback loop that makes a bad situation worse.

Irritable/sad behaviors, when trying to problem solve with a friend, lead to poor problem-solving outcomes. Poor problem-solving outcomes, in turn, place the mother at risk for increasing levels of stress. Increasing levels of stress place the mother at risk for future increases in irritable/sad social-interactional patterns. This general formulation suggests several means by which such a process could be dampened. For example, one could begin by reducing the irritable or sad components of the mothers' interactional style. This could be accompanied by specific training in problem-solving effectiveness and in how to strengthen her support network. Some combination of these interventions might well interrupt this self-perpetuating process.

The Child's Reactions.   The third possible maintenance mechanism presented in Fig. 9.1 pertains to the contribution of the child to the mother's level of present and future stress.

One of the key assumptions in our coercion model relates the irritable/explosive characteristics of the parents during discipline confrontations to the likelihood of actual reinforcement for antisocial child behavior. The child's increasingly skilled use of antisocial behavior when interacting with the parent directly contributes to increasing parental stress. Concomitant problems in school adjustment further exacerbate the situation.

All three hypotheses about maintenance mechanisms are examined later.

Some Further Assumptions and Implications

The general formulation about single mothers is part of a broader set of ideas relating to family process outlined in Patterson, Reid, and Dishion (in press) and Patterson and Bank (1987). It might be helpful to the reader to briefly summarize some of the assumptions implicit in this general approach.

The general idea is that there are minor day-to-day variations in social-interactional patterns for most family members. Negative variations usually do not flourish because they are dampened by the social reactions of significant others in the ensuing days' interactions (Patterson & Bank, 1987). However, in some instances the interactions produce deviant behaviors that are not dampened and the process begins. Presumably, the longer individuals remain in the process, the more likely they are to move on to more extreme manifestations of the deviant behavior.

Each new form of deviancy is thought to constitute a recognizable stage or step in a sequence. For example, in the present report the mother might move from a dysphoric mood that lasts a few days to a second step in which the mood continues over weeks to a third step in which other symptoms are added to dysphoria, and diagnosable clinical depression results.

In such a progression, the movement from one stage to another is a probabilistic one. Individuals at any given stage in a process are at risk for moving on to more extreme forms. The progression is transitive in the sense that most or all of the individuals at an advanced stage have moved through the preceding ones. One assumption implicit in transitive progressions is that there are only a limited number of paths to a given process. If there were a large number of paths to the same outcome, then the use of conditional probabilities to define the movement from one stage to another would not be very informative.

The idea of a progression in stages and the specification of transitional likelihoods for moving from one stage to another has been studied primarily in the development of antisocial behavior in boys (Patterson et al., in press). Similar models have been formulated for alcoholism (Zucker, in press) and substance abuse (Kandel & Yamaguchi, 1985).

There is a second working assumption that should be noted. It seems reasonable to suppose that there may be two kinds of causal variables: immediate (synchronistic) effects and delayed effects. For example, for recently separated mothers, increased stress combined with a loss of support might produce a relatively immediate increase in maternal depressed mood. Another example of synchronous variables would be major disruptions in parental discipline and monitoring followed, rather quickly, by increases in child coercive behavior.

We suspect that there is an important set of causal variables that do not have a synchronous effect; rather the effect manifests itself only over a long period of time (Patterson & Bank, 1987). For example, when mothers undergo a stressful transition like divorce, their friends may tolerate their unpleasant moods for a while. If their mood continues month after month, however, even the best of friends are likely to become intolerant. The resulting loss of support eventually increases the mother's depression. For children, an increase in antisocial behavior is likely to be accompanied by high rates of noncompliant behaviors in the classroom, eventually leading to academic failure.

In that these delayed effects are both products of and eventual determinants for future stages of the process, we have tentatively labeled them as positive feedback mechanisms. If they exist, such variables are of considerable interest because they would probably contribute to our understanding of factors that amplify deviancy processes in families. The report by Patterson and Bank (1987) contains examples of structural equation modeling (Dwyer, 1983; Jöreskog & Sörbom, 1983) for positive feedback loops of this kind. Comparable analyses are planned for a single-parent longitudinal data set, but must await improvements in assessment built into the next wave of data collection.

For the present, the stage models provide a convenient metaphor for thinking about how a major depression might develop for some single mothers but not for others.

PROCEDURES

The sample participated in a 1-year study. The first assessment lasted more than 23 hours. It included: home observations, laboratory problem-solving interactions, face-to-face and telephone interviews, teacher ratings, maternal diaries, and several questionnaires.

The families were briefly reassessed at 6-month intervals over the course of a year. Two abbreviated probes consisted primarily of self-report data, including questionnaires and structured diaries from the mothers 6 months after the first assessment. Twelve months later, teacher ratings were collected, plus diaries from the mothers, and questionnaires and telephone interviews from mothers and sons.

A recently funded proposal makes it possible to carry out an additional full assessment, extending the follow-up to approximately 36 months after the initial assessment. This fourth probe features an intensive effort to supplement the mothers' self-reports for depression, irritability, and support systems with clinical evaluations, observations, and repeated reports by members of her support group.

Sample

The sample consisted of 194 families with sons aged 6 through 12 years whose parents had been separated for 3 to 12 months; 187 completed the study. Families were paid approximately $200 for their participation. The average age of the mothers was 33.0 years; 90% were caucasoid. Even though 72% of the mothers had some training beyond high school, many were living under poverty conditions. Thirty-nine percent were unemployed and 55% reported receiving public assistance.

At the time of the analyses presented here, 146 families had completed the full assessment.

Building a Construct

Wherever possible, we have made an effort to define concepts by more than a single method of measurement and by more than a single agent. The reason for this is based on the reasonable assumption that all methods of assessment for family behavior are distorted in some fundamental sense. Although each measure may be reliable, it presents a biased or incomplete assessment of the latent construct (Bentler, 1980; Pedhazur, 1982; Sullivan, 1974).

Our working assumption is that models based on variables defined by multiple methods and multiple agents will be most generalizable (Patterson & Bank, 1986, 1987). It is often expedient to construct a model of child problem behaviors based only on reports by a single agent, such as the mother. This approach facilitates large survey samples that require inexpensive assessment procedures. Reid, Bank, Patterson, and Skinner (1987) showed that such data can be used to model a statistically coherent account of maternal perceptions of the determinants for child antisocial behavior. However, the model defined by multiple measures based on maternal reports did not relate significantly to the model of child antisocial behavior as defined by other agents. In effect, a model based only on maternal report data was of very limited generalizability. The chapter by Bank, Dishion, Patterson, and Skinner (Chapter 10) provides a more detailed discussion of the role of method variance in model estimation as well as three alternatives for coping with the problem.

In the present study, it was possible to obtain data from multiple agents and methods for many of the constructs. In Waves 2 and 3, most of the data were provided by maternal self-report but were based on different methods: questionnaires, diaries, and telephone interviews. The analyses carried out after the study was completed showed that the use of maternal diary reports and questionnaires in the same model led to discriminant correlations being as large or even greater than the convergent correlations (e.g., created problems of method variance).

Unfortunately, four of our key constructs necessary for the process model of maternal stress were exemplars of the method variance problems created by self-report data. They are: Maternal Depressed Mood, Maternal Irritability, Maternal Support, and Maternal Stress. An extension of the study reported here has made provision for other than maternal self-report in defining these constructs. If the efforts to solve the "glop problem" are successful, then it will be possible to complete structural equation modeling for the formulations presented in this report.

The steps in building these constructs have been described in Forgatch, Patterson, and Skinner (in press), Patterson (1986a), Patterson and Bank (1986), and Patterson et al. (in press). The details of the itemetric, factor, and reliability analyses for each of the constructs are available in Capaldi and Patterson (1988) on request. The following sections give a brief description of the indicators for the constructs used in the present analyses.

Maternal Depressed Mood Construct. This construct was composed of three indicators. One indicator was the widely used CES-D self-report measure of depressive symptoms (Radloff, 1977). The other two indicators were obtained from a structured diary that mothers filled out twice a week over a 3-week interval. A mood rating was obtained twice a day from the mother. The mean of the 12 ratings provided one indicator score. The other indicator was a scale of 7 items from the diary reports describing somatic complaints that are among DSM-3 depression symptoms (e.g., changes in sleep patterns, weight, energy). The mean of six ratings defined that score.

Maternal Stress Construct. The development of this construct was described in the report by Forgatch et al. (in press). The indicators included negative life events (Sarason, Johnson, & Siegel, 1978), recent hassles, financial problems, and family health problems. In this report, the first three indicators were used. A fourth indicator was added—proportion of negative daily events—because the family health problems data had not been collected at all three probes. The new indicator was based on a diary measure summarizing daily pleasant and unpleasant events averaged across 6 days. The score was the mean proportion of negative to total events.

Maternal Irritability Construct. This construct was composed of two indicators, both obtained from the diary. One was a mood rating made twice a day on a 7-point scale from irritable to calm. The mean of the 12 scores was used. The other indicator was a diary measure composed of two items, one rating anger level for the day on a 5-point scale, and the other the sum of five items that made the mother angry that day.

Maternal Social Support Construct. This construct was defined by two indicators for most analyses. The isolation indicator was based on three items from a questionnaire: feeling lonely, without anyone to talk to, and without anyone to share experiences with. The second indicator was the percent of positive contacts. This was adapted from Wahler's insularity measure (Wahler, Leske, & Rogers, 1977). The variable was included in the mother's diary and collected on 6 different days. Mothers rated their contacts with adults (friends, relatives, in-laws, others) as positive, negative, or neutral. The score was the mean proportion of positive contacts to total contacts. For the analysis in Fig. 9.2, the indicator *support network* was composed of 11 items from a questionnaire asking about availability of friends who provide advice.

THE PROCESS BEGINS

The hypothesis is that the high levels of stress and loss of support accompanying separation are variables associated with the initiation disruptions in family process. Data are briefly reviewed that relate to comparisons in levels of stress for separated and nonseparated families. In that the stress and support variables are thought to play a dual function, contributing to the initiation and maintenance of the disruption process, data are presented that relate to these issues. Structural equation modeling is used to model the contribution of stress and support to the initiation of the process. Descriptive data will also examine changes in mean levels over time of support, stress, depression, and irritability.

Maternal Traits and Disruption Effects

A general formulation about the coercion process serves as a background for our speculations on stress-induced disruptions for recently separated mothers Patterson et al. (in press). From that perspective, some single mothers seem to be at greater risk than others for high levels of stress and for loss of support. There are two maternal dispositions thought to be related to such increased risk: antisocial and social incompetence. It is hypothesized that socially incompetent and antisocial single mothers are at greatest risk for stress and for depression. This hypothesis is currently being investigated by Forgatch (1988); at the time of this writing these analyses have not been completed. The analyses that *have* been completed show that socially incompetent and antisocial single mothers are at grave risk for disrupted discipline confrontations with their sons (Patterson & Bank, 1987).

Much of the present report is focused on understanding what the antecedent might be for maternal depression and the attending disruptions in social interactions with friends and sons. The assumption is that maternal depression mediates the impact of stress and loss of support on disrupted social-interactional patterns.

Higher Levels of Stress for Single Mothers?

Most investigators who study single mothers assume that marital separation marks a sudden increment in levels of stress for the mother (Bloom, Asher, & White, 1978; Hetherington, Cox, & Cox, 1978, 1979; Wallerstein & Kelly, 1980). Our contacts with the mothers in the study reported here lead us to concur in labeling the first year or two of separation as the crises years. The accompanying assumption is that these mothers are more stressed than are mothers in intact families (e.g., Forgatch et al., in press; Hetherington et al., 1978, 1979, 1980; Zill, 1978).

There is a methodological problem that must be noted when considering these findings. The likely possibility exists that during the months prior to separation, mothers were embroiled in an intense marital conflict that led to the decision to separate. Initiating a study such as the present one some months after the actual separation means that one is really not studying onset of a process. We are therefore forced to accept the fact that when the study began, the process was well underway. Large-scale longitudinal studies of at-risk (for separation) samples are required that study the condition of the mother and children *prior* to separation. The follow-up study of essentially middle-class families by Block, Block, and Gjerde (1986) is a case in point. They note, for example, that boys in divorced families tended to be more antisocial prior to, as well as following, the separation.

Stress, Support and Depression at Initiation

The hypothesis examined in this section is that the measures of support and stress obtained 3 to 18 months after separation will both contribute significantly to measures of maternal depression. Structural equation modeling was used to examine the coherence of the model. In that the model was based completely on maternal self-report data, it is assumed that the model is of relatively limited generalizability, as shown in the studies by Reid et al. (1987).

The model in Fig. 9.2 describes the assumption that both Stress and Social Support constructs make direct contributions to the Depressed Mood construct. It was also assumed that Stress may also have an indirect effect on Depressed Mood mediated by Social Support. As shown there, Stress contributes directly to Depressed Mood, and indirectly through its contribution to loss of social support. We return to this topic in a later section.

The chi square value of 20.14 ($p = .126$) indicates an acceptable fit between

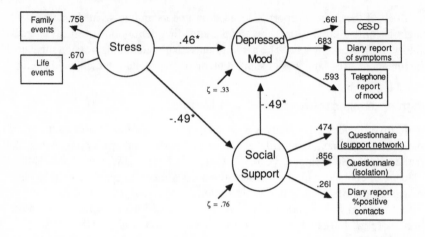

$\chi^2_{(\overline{14})}$ 20.14

p = .126

N = 191

$^*p$ < .01

FIG. 9.2. Concurrent effects of stress and social support on maternal depression.

the data set and the a priori model. The significant path coefficients are consistent with the idea that Stress has both a direct and an indirect effect on maternal Depressed Mood. Taken together, the two variables accounted for 67% of the variance in the measure of maternal depression.

The matrix for correlated residuals suggested opening the model to acknowledge the relations between the family events indicator and the diary support indicator, the diary depression and the questionnaire support indicators and the daily telephone depression and questionnaire support indicators. These modifications were made in the model shown in the figure.

The findings are consistent with the hypothesis that stress and loss of support both contribute significantly to maternal depressed mood.

Stationarity?

Stationarity assumes that the relation between X and Y is independent of trial; the same relation holds regardless of when in the sequence one samples the data. In the present context, this relates to the assumption that stress and support make relatively the same contributions to depressed mood at all three probes. This is of

TABLE 9.1
Regressing Depression on Stress and Support

	Time-1	Time-2	Time-3
Composite Variable	Beta	Beta	Beta
Stress	.37*	.45*	.48*
Social Support	-.34*	-.33*	-.36*
R^2	.28*	.38*	.44*

*$p < .001$

interest because it could be that, while stress and support are significant contributors early in the process, 12 months later one or both variables may no longer be relevant to depression.

A multiple regression analysis was used to provide a preliminary assessment of the relative contribution of the two variables to maternal Depressed Mood at each of the three probes. As shown in Table 9.1, the findings are consistent with the idea of a stationary process in that the pattern of contributions is quite similar at all three points in time.

It is interesting to note that the amount of variance accounted for 12 months later is roughly half again more than that accounted for in the initial testing. It seems that understanding stress and loss of support is even more important in the second crisis year than it was in the first year. The findings emphasize the need to raise the question of why it is that some mothers continue to be stressed and without support while others do not. From the present perspective, it is assumed that the mothers that continue to be stressed and unsupported will continue to be depressed and therefore at risk for disrupted social exchanges.

STABILITIES AND CHANGES OVER TIME

The study of process requires that we examine both stability and changes that occur over time (Sameroff, 1981). This section examines the stability correlations and mean level scores for measures of the maternal Stress, Social Support and Depressed Mood constructs.

Stability

It is assumed that there is a good deal of stability in the process even during the crisis years of separation. For example, those mothers who tend to be highly stressed and depressed during the initial assessment are expected to occupy similar relative rankings on these measures some months later.

The data in Table 9.2 summarize the stability coefficients for all four of the key composite scores. The general findings are consistent with the stability in

TABLE 9.2
Test-Retest Stability Correlations for Constructs[a]

	Time-1 to Time-2 Intake to 6 Mos	Time-2 to Time-3 6 Mos to 12 Mos	Time-1 to Time-3 12 Mos
Determinants			
Stress	.68[b]	.66	.66
Social Support	.58	.42	.49
Outcomes			
Irritability	.61	.65	.58
Depression	.75	.43	.43

[a] N = 146
[b] All values p less than .001.

showing moderate stability for the 12-month interval. There were modest decreases in the stability during the second 6-month interval for two of the composite scores (Depressed Mood and Social Support).

Each of the three retest correlations for the Stress composite score was in the .66 to .68 range, suggesting that this was quite stable. The findings showed somewhat less stability for the Social Support composite score, with a range of .42 to .58. As might be expected, the stabilities for the two outcome variables were about equal in magnitude to the stabilities for the two variables thought to be determinants. The range was from .58 to .65 for maternal irritability and from .43 to .75 for depressed mood.

Changes in Mean Level for Stress

Does the level for maternal stress change during the 12-month interval of the study? The mean scores for the three assessment probes are summarized in Table 9.3 for each of the four indicators that define the Stress construct.

Mothers' reports for negative life events and for recent hassles showed decreases over the 12-month period. For the negative life events measure, the decreases were significant at each follow-up probe. The drop from the initial to the 6-month assessment was significant ($t = 2.85$, $p < .01$) and from the 6- to the 12-month probe ($t = 2.76$, $p < .01$). The recent hassles measure showed no significant change from initial assessment to the 6-month probe, but the decrease from the 6- to the 12-month probe was significant ($t = 6.49$, $p < .01$).

The majority of the mothers were living in poverty at the outset of the study, and they reported no significant change in their status over the first year. They also reported no significant change in the proportion of negative to positive events they experienced on a daily basis. Both stressors were shown to characterize single-parent families in the national probability survey by Zill (1978).

It seems, then, that from the mother's perspective some aspects of stress remain stable while others show modest improvement. Her financial condition

TABLE 9.3
Levels of Maternal Stress at Three Points in Time

| | Initial Assessment | | 6 Months | | 12 Months | |
| | Time-1 | | Time-2 | | Time-3 | |
	Mean	SD	Mean	SD	Mean	SD
Negative life events	5.25	2.91	4.44	3.47	3.66	2.85
Recent hassles	11.10	3.25	11.35	4.69	8.90	4.32
Financial problems	2.17	.48	2.09	.53	2.05	.51
Proportion negative events (Diary)	.353	.135	.346	.161	.347	.161

remains stable and precarious during this 12-month interval. In her daily reports, she continues to report the same high relative incidence of negative events although negative life events and recent hassles abate somewhat. It would seem, however, that as a sample these recently separated mothers remain much more stressed than the sample of mothers from intact families reported in Forgatch et al. (in press).

Changes in Mean Level for Support

Does the mean level of support reported by single mothers change during the 12-month study interval? Two indicators for social support were used to examine this question, the questionnaire measure of maternal self-reported isolation and the diary report of her positive contacts. The mean levels for these two indicators over the course of the year are summarized in Table 9.4.

There was a small but significant improvement in the daily percentage of positive contacts within the first six months ($t = 2.98, p = .003$). This modest increment was maintained from the 6- to the 12-month probe.

TABLE 9.4
Changes in Mean Level of Support at Three Points in Time

| | Initial Assessment | | 6 Months | | 12 Months | |
| | Time-1 | | Time-2 | | Time-3 | |
	Mean	SD	Mean	SD	Mean	SD
Isolation (questionnaire)	8.62	2.36	8.81	2.22	9.03	2.32
% Positive contacts (diary)	.76	.22	.81	.21	.81	.24
Support network (questionnaire)	31.99	4.64	29.55	3.76	28.48	4.08

There was an accompanying (nonsignificant) trend for *increasing* feelings of isolation and a significant decrease in availability of friends who provided helpful advice at each probe ($t = 7.94$; $p < .001$ for the first 6-month period; $t = 3.08$; $p < .002$ for the last 6-month period).

The picture for changes in the mean level of support and stress are consistent with the idea that the first year or two following separation are characterized by high levels of stress and continued reduction in social support. The single mother and her family continue to be at grave risk for disruption. This is in keeping with the long-term follow-up study of separated families reported by Hetherington (1987) that showed some mothers continue to struggle with these problems, and with their children, some years after the separation.

The question is how one identifies which families will remain highly stressed and disrupted and which will not. A later section considers three mechanisms that may be related to these shifts.

Changes in Mean Levels for Depressed Mood and Irritability

It is likely that stressors and loss of support increase both irritable and depressed mood behaviors. As we see later, there are only a few studies that examine this hypothesis. For the time being, we do not know whether stress elicits increases in irritability and depressed mood follows, or is it that maternal irritability and depressed mood are concomitant reactions to stress and loss of support? We lean toward the second sequence, but it is merely a hunch.

Our hypothesis is that maternal irritability and depressed mood are intimately related. This assumption is supported by findings from a study by Watson and Tellegen (1985), who showed significant covariations between self-report scales measuring irritability and depression. The hypothesis is also supported by findings from the daily diary reports collected in the current sample of single mothers. In these structured diaries, mothers rated both sadness and irritability twice a day. The ratings were collected twice a week for each assessment probe. The anchors for the two 7-point scales were depressed versus happy and irritable versus calm, with neutral as a midpoint for each. The data were relatively stable at all three assessments in showing that on any given day, 58% to 61% of the mothers felt *both* irritable and depressed. At any one of the three probes, from 4% to 7% indicated that they were only depressed, and from 11% to 15% indicated they were only irritable. About 20% to 26% said they were neither depressed nor irritable. These reports suggest that, on a day-to-day basis, the majority of the highly stressed single mothers experienced irritability, and this often included an unpleasant blend with sadness.

Changes Over Time. Equivalent data were collected at all three points in time for constructs defining Maternal Depressed Mood and Maternal Irritability.

TABLE 9.5
Changes in Mean Levels of Maternal Depression and Irritability
at Three Points in Time

	Initial Assessment Time-1		6 Months Time-2		12 Months Time-3	
	Mean	SD	Mean	SD	Mean	SD
Depressed mood						
CES-D	18.54	11.81	15.73	11.15	15.92	11.77
Diary rating	4.69	1.0	4.73	1.0	4.85	.98
Symptoms diary	1.16	.34	1.13	.35	1.11	.36
Irritability						
Diary rating	4.5	.09	4.7	.09	4.8	.08

Mean levels for the indicators of these constructs are summarized in Table 9.5. At a global level, mothers reported a modest amelioration in depression over the 12-month interval. The drop in the CES-D measure was significant when comparing initial assessment to 6-month follow up ($t = 2.67, p = .008$). This drop in level persisted through the 12-month assessment. If one accepts the recommended score of 16 or greater on the CES-D measure as a cutting score, then even 12 months after the study began a substantial portion of the sample would be classified as depressed. While the global impression tended toward some improvement this was not supported by data from the mothers' daily diary reports of the occurrence of sadness and depressed symptoms.

The findings for the diary ratings of mood emphasize the fact that on a more molecular day-to-day level, there is little sense of improved status. Overall, most of the mothers report themselves to be quite sad and quite irritable. The stability correlations reported earlier in Table 9.2 imply that there is some shifting about in ordinal rankings for the two variables. Mothers reporting themselves to be most irritable or depressed at one point in time are not necessarily the ones who are most extreme six months later. The following section details the nature of these shifts in outcome variables. Because the measure of depression (CES-D) is better known, it is used as an illustration.

Stayers and Movers

What is the likelihood of changing one's status as depressed or nondepressed from one 6-month interval to another? That is the question explored in this section.

The large scale longitudinal surveys by Aneshensel (1985) and Weissman, Myers, Thompson, and Belanger (1986) both showed marked fluctuations in self-reported depression over time. In the present study, we assumed that the mothers who remained at high levels of depression over the three points in time

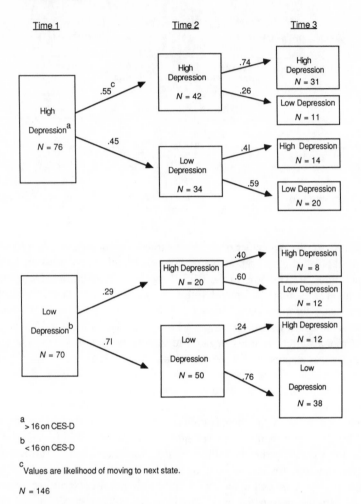

FIG. 9.3. Depressed stayers and movers at three points in time.

(roughly 12 months) would be at greatest risk for both clinical depression and for disrupted family processes.

The scores on the CES-D were used to classify the single mothers as depressed (score 16 or above) or nondepressed at each of the three points in time. The findings are summarized in Fig. 9.3. Our first surprise was that about half our sample of single mothers remained in the same state at all three assessment points. Twenty-six percent were symptom free for all three time points. Twenty-one percent reported themselves to be depressed at each assessment. The finding that over one-fifth of the single mothers were consistently depressed is consistent with the findings by Aneshensel (1985), who also found that adults who stayed in the depressed process were likely to be female and of low economic status. We would assume that the mothers who remained depressed would be most at risk for disrupted social interaction.

If a mother reported being nondepressed at one point in time, the likelihoods ranged from .24 to .41 that she would report being depressed at some later point in time. What is of particular interest is the finding that, of those mothers who reported themselves as nondepressed at the beginning of the study, only 28.9% reported themselves depressed 12 months later. Given a baserate expectation of around .45 for the 12-month probe, this finding is meaningful. Those who start well tend to end well. On the other hand, those who begin badly (depressed) are at grave risk of ending badly. Given a depressed state at the onset of the study, the risk was .59 of being in a depressed state at the 12-month probe.

These descriptive findings suggest several things. We must understand why, of the mothers who start depressed, 40% drop out of the deviancy process. Is this shift accompanied by a large reduction in stress or an increase in social support? If so, what brings about these changes? Why do 59% of the mothers who start badly also end badly? Why do they not drop out, too? It is this latter group that serves as the focus for the remainder of the report. Three mechanisms are examined that may relate to the continuance of these single mothers in the deviancy process. Each of the mechanisms reflects a slightly different outcome of disruptions in the single mothers' social-interactional patterns.

MOTHERS' DISRUPTED SOCIAL INTERACTIONS

From the social-interactional perspective, disrupted patterns of interaction can serve as a type of amplifier for the effects of stress. None of the studies carried out thus far has explored the effect of loss of social support as a disruptor for these patterns. For the present, the assumption is that stress and loss of social support serve similar functions.

As noted earlier, the marker variables signaling a disruption effect include increased rates of irritable and sad behaviors. Some of the studies have used conditionals describing action/reaction patterns (e.g., the likelihood the mother will react in an irritable way even though the prior response of the child had been neutral or positive). Observation data are required in order to measure this disruption; typically the data describe sequences of interactions among family members in the home (Hops, Sherman, & Biglan, see Chapter 8; Reid, 1978; Radke-Yarrow, Chapter 7), or during family problem-solving activities (Biglan, Lewin, & Hops, Chapter 5; Forgatch, in press; Gottman, Chapter 4).

We suspect that the disruptions generalized even to casual contacts. However, we particularly are interested in what happens when the mother interacts with key figures in her social environment. For example, what happens to the quality of social interaction with old friends, relatives, and her children? What happens when the mother brings up her problems while talking to old friends? What happens when she is in a discipline confrontation with her child?

Observation studies show that stress produces dramatic increases in negative behaviors in social interaction sequences (Patterson, 1983; Wahler & Dumas, 1983). Both studies examined the covariation across days between maternal stressors and observed irritability in mother–child interactions. On days when mothers reported higher levels of stressors from outside the home, observations showed that they were more likely to be aversive with their children. Needless to say, not all mothers display this covariation. We assume that irritable parents are most likely to show increased stress-induced irritability (e.g., stress amplifies existing irritability). Although neither the Patterson nor the Wahler studies tested this amplifier hypothesis, this idea has been advanced and supported by the studies of Elder and his colleagues (Elder, Caspi, & Nguyen, in press). The stress amplification studies are discussed in more detail later.

We assume that the effects of stress may be neutral, pathological, or enhancing depending on their effect in altering social-interactional patterns (Patterson, 1983). For example, the careful review by Garmezy and Rutter (1983) showed that negative outcomes for child behavior tended *not* to occur in stable households even under conditions of extreme stress such as floods, wars, or social violence. It is our stance that in so-called stable households the social-interactional patterns are less likely to be disrupted by increases in parental irritability or sadness. There is evidence suggesting that in some families stressors may even enhance positive social exchanges. For example, the longitudinal study by Elder et al. (in press) showed that severe economic stressors arising from the Great Depression actually produced some *positive* outcomes for girls.

Data presented in the following sections are used to examine the relation between composite measures of stress and increased maternal irritability during problem-solving interactions with her confidante. The covariation between maternal stress and irritability are also examined. A still later section explores the covariation between such disruptions and risk for future negative outcomes for single mothers.

Stress-Induced Increases in Irritability

Carefully designed laboratory studies with mice and rats suggest that the threshold for reacting to aversive stimuli may be heritable (Cairns, Gariepy, & Hood, 1988; Knutson & Viken, in press). In the Cairns et al. study, cross-breeding generations of fighting and passive mice produce significant effects within a few generations. It seems that what is altered in the "inhibition" of reactions to aversive stimuli. In this sense, the single mothers' irritable reactions to aversive stimuli (stressors) may have a heritable component. Be that as it may, we assume that the major contribution to variance in measures of observed irritability is environmental experience.

The details of how such connections between external stressors and maternal irritable reactions might be strengthened are detailed in Patterson (1982) and Wahler and Dumas (1983). The key idea is that the reactions of important others may reinforce the occurrence of irritable and sad behaviors. When stressed, these mothers have learned that irritable (or sad) behaviors produce immediate, reinforcing reactions from the social environment. For example, in the short run, her irritable behaviors may elicit soothing reactions from her friends or certain family members, such as daughters. In the short run, her shouted commands may also produce increased compliance from her children, especially her sons. As we shall see, this may increase the risk, in the long run, that the deviancy process will be maintained.

The specifics that describe the manner in which the social environment might train the mother to use high rates of irritable or sad behaviors fall under the rubric of escape-avoidant conditioning (or negative reinforcement) (Hineline, 1977; Patterson, 1982; Patterson et al., in press). The fact is that during social exchanges these contingencies alter the future behaviors for one or both members. Each individual is attending only to maximizing his or her immediate self-interest and in so doing, ignores the fact that the long-term outcome for one or both may be extremely negative. The process is called the *reinforcement trap* and constitutes a key mechanism for training coercive behaviors, Patterson (1982).

Studies of interaction sequences show that in negative exchanges one person is likely to try to react in such a way as to "soothe" the other (a felicitous term suggested by Gottman). Examples of this as it applies to marital conflict are presented in Gottman (see Chapter 4), and for adult depression in Biglan et al. (Chapter 5). The general idea is that whatever works in turning off the other's irritable outbursts is reinforced, and whatever elicits irritable reactions is more likely to be avoided in future exchanges. For example, Radke-Yarrow (Chapter 7) notes that depressed mothers were more likely to give in to the child's noncompliant behavior (submitting is soothing).

Chapter 5 by Biglan et al. outlines how depressed maternal behaviors might also shape the behaviors of family members. For example, their functional analyses showed that wife depressive behaviors may reduce the likelihood of husband hostile verbal behaviors. The idea that irritable and depressive behavioral events may serve some function is not peculiar just to social-interactional theorists. The position taken in the developmental studies of emotion by Izard and his colleagues is also a functional one (Izard & Schwartz, 1986).

Summary

Up to this point,   the data emphasize stability as one of the more salient characteristics for this first year or two of separation. The levels of stress, loss of support, irritability and depressed moods remain quite high over the 12-month interval for the study. The analyses suggested that the high levels of stress and the loss of support may play key roles in producing maternal distress at all three assessment probes in the study.

The data also showed that a substantial proportion of the single mothers remained distressed (depressed and perhaps irritable as well) throughout the three measurement probes. One may say that these mothers continue to be stressed and unsupported during the entire study. Then we must ask why this is so. Why do the levels of stress not drop after a period of some months? Why is the social support network not refurbished and why are new intimacies not developed? The assumption is that there are three mechanisms built into the process for some mothers. The mechanisms serve to keep mothers in the deviancy process. These issues are considered in the following sections.

STAGE 2: THE SOCIAL ENVIRONMENT REACTS

As noted earlier, the second stage in the process is defined by the effects produced by the disruptions in maternal social interactions. The first two effects to be considered involve the interactions of mother and confidante. The third involves the mother and her son. These reactions to the mothers' increased irritable interactions are thought to constitute three mechanisms that serve to keep some mothers in the deviancy process. In each case, correlational data are presented to aid our examination of the issues relating to these mechanisms.

Loss of Maternal Support as a Mechanism

We believe that for some individuals the development of relatively minor devian-cies is followed by a rapidly accelerating drift toward an isolated existence. There are undoubtedly many reasons for such a drift. A social-interactional perspective requires that we search for determinants within the social-interac-tional patterns of the target person. In this section we examine the possibility that irritable and depressed single-mother behaviors function as aversive stimuli that literally drive people away. This, in turn, is accompanied by an increasing risk for a maintenance of depressed moods. A test of this hypothesis requires that disrupted maternal social exchanges at one point in time contribute to a loss of social support as measured at some later point.

The assumption is that factors within the process determine the increment in disrupted social interactions, and that in certain settings the unfortunate outcome is a contribution to maintenance in the process. Conceptually, these relationships define what we mean by a positive feedback loop. Two approaches to a correla-tionally defined feedback loop are discussed; in each case, data are presented by way of illustration.

The studies by Wahler et al. (1977) showed strong support for the hypothesis that irritable and depressed mothers tended to be more isolated. The data also showed that a disproportionate number of contacts the mothers did have were negative in valence. The follow-up study by Hetherington (1983) showed that lack of a support network covaried with maintenance of single-mother depression. She also noted that single mothers living alone were at greatest risk for continued depression, while those who formed new intimate relations and/or had a mother or previous spouse involved were less at risk for depression. In the across-time study mentioned earlier (Patterson, 1983), maternal daily mood ratings also covaried with reports of positive contacts.

The Dawes Approach to Feedback Loops.   We think of the Dawes procedure as a rough screening device to identify candidates worthy of more rigorous evaluation for status as feedback loops. It can be thought of as a crude Litmus test. If the results are positive, then more sophisticated analyses are warranted. A more rigorous test would involve structural equation modeling of cross-lagged relationships that take stability into account. The report by Bank and Stoolmiller (1989) is an example of this application.

The Dawes approach has never appeared as a published article; it emerged in the course of a discussion over lunch. The approach is based on simple bivariate correlations. First calculate the correlation between X (the potential determinant) and Y (the effect variable). Then calculate the X and Y correlation again at Time 2. If the magnitude of the correlation changes significantly when calculated at two different times, it *implies* that over time both variables shift and that they tend to shift in the same way (e.g., if one increases, so does the other). This might mean that the shifts occur because one variable influences the other. There are of course a number of equally plausible competing hypotheses.

In the present case, it is assumed that maternal irritability drives friends away. The X variable consisted of mothers' reported irritability, a composite score measured by the Caprara questionnaire and the daily diary report. The Y variable, support, was measured with two indicators, one that measured parent positive contact with friends and one that measured maternal feelings of isolation.

At the initial assessment, the correlation between maternal irritability and reports of feeling isolated was .31 ($p < .01$). The comparable correlation at the 6-month probe was .48 ($p < .001$). A comparison of the two correlations produced a $t = 2.40$ ($p < .05$). The correlations indicate that certain mothers were becoming more extreme in both their irritability and in their loss of social support. The correlations do not tell us that one thing is causing the other; both variables could be determined by some third variable. But the Dawes litmus test suggests that the irritability-social support relationship may be worth exploring further.

At initial testing, the correlation between maternal irritability and her daily reports of positive contacts with friends was $-.12$ (n.s.). At the 6-month probe, the correlation was $-.38$ ($p < .001$). The comparison of the two correlations produced a $t = 3.71$ ($p < .001$). This relationship also meets the criterion for the Dawes test. In that the measure of daily positive contacts correlates significantly with the reports of being isolated, both will serve as indicators to define the latent construct Social Support for the next stage in the analyses.

Cross-Lagged Model.   The traditional cross-lagged panel design is a more systematic method for examining what might be a delayed causal effect (Pedhazur, 1982). If multiple-method indicators were available for maternal irritability and social support at all three points in time, the structural equation modeling format could be used to examine cross-lagged effects. In the present case, both constructs, Social Support and Maternal Irritability, were defined by multiple methods but they were provided by a single agent, the mother. As pointed out by Bank et al. (Chapter 10), the effect is to create a model in which the method variance *across* constructs exceeds the within-construct convergence. The effect of this was that the model "blew up."

Analyses currently under way suggest that requisite "hetero-agent" indicators may be present in the existing data set and can be used in future analyses of this problem. For example, a small sample of videotapes of mothers and confidantes were scored for observed mother irritability. In keeping with the present hypothesis, the relationship between this measure and mothers' concurrent report of support was $-.25$ ($p < .05$). Confidantes' reports about the extent of the mothers' social support network can provide a second agent indicator for social support. For the present, only the maternal self-report data are complete and will be used in a cross-lagged panel analyses to illustrate the next step of the search for a feedback loop.

For this analysis, illustrated in Fig. 9.4, the measures of friends and isolation were combined as indicators for Social Support. Two measures from the diary, mood ratings and the sum of anger events, defined Maternal Irritability. The hypothesis was that maternal irritability would have both synchronous and delayed effects on social support measures.

The findings are consistent with the hypothesis that Maternal Irritability is a significant determinant for Social Support. The synchronistic paths from Maternal Irritability to Social Support are consistent at all three points in time. Notice, too, that these path coefficients remain significant even when they are calculated (as standard partial betas) *relative* to the stability estimates for Social Support. At any given point in time, maternal Social Support can be accounted for partially by measures of Social Support obtained 6 months previously *and* by the current level of maternal self-reported irritability. Mothers who are currently irritable and previously had little social support will report lower current levels of social support.

It is interesting to note that the modification indices demanded a direct stability path from Time 1 to Time 3 for both composite scores. In fact, the model did not fit until these paths were introduced.

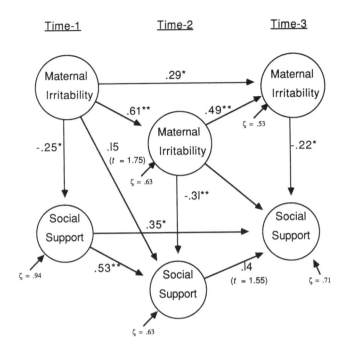

Time-1   Time-2   Time-3

$\chi^2_{(4)}$ 8.78

$p = .067$

$^*p < .01$

$^{**}p < .001$

FIG. 9.4. Path analysis of the maternal irritability–social support mechanism.

The data did not support the idea that levels of maternal irritability at one point in time would account for future levels of social support. Thus, maternal irritability cannot be thought of as a delayed causal variable. The model suggests that the relation is more synchronistic; current levels of irritability determined current levels of support. We plan to repeat the examination of this model using observation-based multiple-agent reports for the two constructs.

Given that the more systematic approach provides data consistent with either the synchronistic or feedback loop hypothesis, then the next step would be to reject the spurious-correlation model described by Dwyer (1983). In this case, a hypothetical construct X is introduced that presumably is a determinant for both Maternal Irritability and Social Support. If the model survived this test, it would signal the need to design an experimental manipulation that would establish the causal status of Maternal Irritability (e.g., random assignment to an experimental procedure that would effectively reduce Maternal Irritability and a placebo that would not).

Poor Problem-Solving Outcome as a Mechanism

The hypothesis is that disrupted maternal social interactions with a confidante leads to poor problem-solving outcomes. Poor problem solving, in turn, contributes to the maintenance of high levels of future stress. The associated hypothesis is that irritable/sad single mothers will tend to select, or be selected by, confidantes who match them in this disposition. Presumably, it is the joint contribution of irritable friend and irritable mother that is most disruptive of the problem-solving process.

The hypothesis is based on the general formulation presented by Forgatch (in press). Her findings showed that when family members expressed high levels of irritable behavior during problem-solving discussions, the outcome tended to be limited. Problem-solving outcome was defined in terms of problem definition, quality of proposed solutions and extent of resolution. Poor outcome for family problem solving correlated significantly with measures of child antisocial behavior.

There are three hypotheses that are of central issue in this model. The first hypothesis is that problem-solving outcome would covary with reports of maternal stress. Two studies have been based on problem-solving exchanges involving parents and their children discussing their own problems. Both studies showed a nonsignificant correlation between current stress and problem-solving outcome, but there was a significant correlation found between outcome and later reports of stress. One study involved intact families (Patterson et al., in press); the other used data from the single-mother sample described in the present report.

These findings led to the hypothesis that future levels of stress would also relate significantly to problem-solving outcome in interactions between the single mothers and their confidantes.

As a pilot test of this possibility problem-solving discussions were coded for the first 41 videotapes collected for single mothers and their confidantes. The remaining cases will be coded in the next year.

The first hypothesis was that irritable mothers would be likely to select, or be selected by, irritable confidantes. In keeping with this, the correlation between coders' scores for mother irritability and that of her confidante during problem solving was .57 ($p < .001$).

The second hypothesis required a significant correlation between future measures of maternal stress and the single mother-confidante problem-solving outcome score. Initial assessment of outcome correlated $-.13$ with current maternal stress and $-.19$ with maternal stress 6 months later. The covariation between initial problem-solving outcome scores and maternal stress reported 12 months later was $-.33$ ($p < .05$).

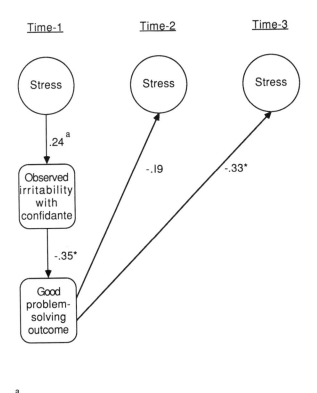

$^a p < .10$

$^* p < .05$

FIG. 9.5. A bivariate study of problem-solving outcome with confidante and later stress.

The relation between problem-solving outcome and later stress level could be artifactual. The coding of the remaining tapes will tell its own story. On the other hand, the data suggest that the causal effect may be delayed for as much as 12 months. Using McNemar's (1969) conservative test for differences between correlations from the same sample, the increase in the strength of the correlation from Time 1 to Time 3 approached significance. For the small sample of 41 on which the mother-confidante problem-solving data have been scored, the one-tailed t score was 1.508 ($p < .10$). It is also reassuring to note that a similar lagged correlation has been obtained in the longitudinal study of at-risk families. Here too, current levels of problem solving relate to future levels of stress.

The model stipulates that the effect of stress on problem-solving outcome is mediated by the disruption of mother-confidante social interactions. It can be seen from the bivariate correlations in Fig. 9.5 that both of these hypotheses were supported. Mothers who reported high levels of concurrent stress tended to have more irritable exchanges during problem solving. These negative exchanges correlated with poor outcomes, and thus replicated the earlier findings by Forgatch (in press). The relationship between stress, irritability, and problem solving is complex. There is not a direct relationship between current stress and problem-solving outcome; the relation is mediated by irritability. But there is a lagged effect of outcome on future stress.

Summary

We have made a case for moderate stability in the single mothers' reports of stress, depression, irritability, and social support over a 12-month interval shortly following their separation. While the mean levels and stability correlations both attest to the relative constancy of these experiences, it is also true that a significant number of mothers were dropping in and out of the depression process during this time. Maternal reports of stress and social support functioned as significant covariates at all three points in time.

The stage model introduced here assumes that if one can explain why some mothers remain stressed and without social support, then one understands the problem of maintenance in the depression process. Two dynamic mechanisms were examined that might relate to the maintenance of the process. The first was that the irritable behavior of stressed mothers might lead to the selection of confidantes characterized by high levels of negative behavior and negative affect. Such behaviors occurring during maternal efforts to solve difficulties would lead to unsuccessful outcomes and a long-term increase in stress levels. The other traced the relation between maternal irritability and increased loss of social support over time. The data were consistent with both hypotheses.

The following section traces out the steps leading to yet another potential contributor to the mothers' continuing high level of stress. This time the contributor is the child. The section briefly traces the effects of disruptions in mother-child interactions to adjustment difficulties for the child. These difficulties increase the maternal level of stress.

Deviant Child Behavior as a Mechanism

Two hypotheses are examined in this section. It is assumed that single-mother irritable behavior during discipline confrontations places the child at significant risk for learning antisocial behavior (as well as for school failure, depressed mood, and peer rejection). The second hypothesis is that the son's adjustment problems contribute directly to future levels of maternal stress. Both hypotheses are examined using structural equation modeling.

The Hetherington Effect. Two longitudinal studies found that during the first years of separation, boys from essentially middle-class families were significantly more antisocial (Hetherington et al., 1979, 1980; Wallerstein & Kelly, 1980). A large-scale probability survey by Zill (1978) surveyed families with children 7 through 11 years. Those children from separated and divorced families were described by both teachers and parents as more aggressive.

In the study by Hetherington et al. (1979, 1980), the increase in teacher- and parent-reported aggression was significant for both boys and girls during the first year of separation. In the second year, some boys continued to maintain their increased aggressiveness, but many of the boys and most of the girls returned to a more normal range of functioning. Six years after the divorce, a significant number of the mothers were still having difficulty with antisocial sons (Hetherington, 1987). Hetherington et al. speculated that boys' increases in antisocial behavior were due to the disrupting effect of stress on parenting practices. The model presented in Fig. 9.6 arose from discussions with her about the precise means for examining this series of assumptions. We have come to label the resulting model as the *Hetherington effect*. The model examined the general

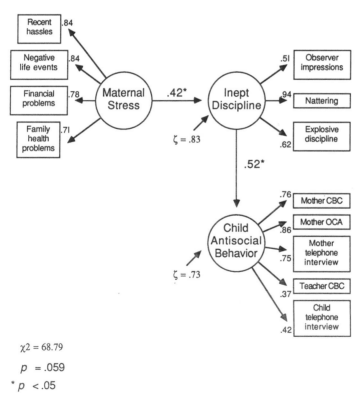

$\chi2 = 68.79$

$p\ = .059$

$^{*}p\ < .05$

FIG. 9.6. Mediational model for the Hetherington effects. From Forgatch, Patterson, and Skinner (in press).

relation between single-parent stress, disrupted discipline, and the sons' antisocial behavior.

Observations collected in the home during discipline confrontations defined the mothers' disrupted social interactions. There were three indicators for the Inept Discipline construct. Given the mother was interacting with her son, the likelihood of maternal irritability that occurred regardless of what the child was doing defined the indicator, *nattering*. Given the child was deviant, the likelihood of a maternal abusive reaction (threat, humiliate, hit) defined the indicator, *explosive discipline*. Observer global ratings of failure to provide discipline follow-through and consistency formed the third indicator, *observer impressions*.

The first test of the model was made by Forgatch et al. (in press). The data were collected from 64 single–mother families. The two key path coefficients were both significant. They provide strong support for the mediational model required to support a Hetherington effect. As shown in the figure, the effect of Maternal Stress on Child Antisocial Behavior is mediated by maternal Inept Discipline.

The chi-square analysis showed there was a fit between the obtained and the hypothesized covariance structures. The model also accounted for a modest 27% of the variance in Child Antisocial Behavior. Our confidence in this general model was increased by the fact that Viken (1988) was able to replicate it using data from the longitudinal studies of high-risk families.

The writers assume that in the model, the construct Maternal Depression could be substituted for the Stress construct. The effect of single-parent maternal depression on child behavior would be mediated by the disruptions in discipline or other family-management practices. In keeping with this assumption, Radke-Yarrow (Chapter 7) showed that clinically depressed mothers were significantly more likely than nondepressed mothers to be negative in their interactions with their children. Forgatch (1987) is currently testing this model using data from single-parent families. However a study by Patterson and Dishion (1988) showed that for *intact* families maternal depression was not significantly related to discipline practices.

Child Deviancy and Concurrent Maternal Stress.   The findings in the preceding section showed that the irritable behaviors of highly stressed single mothers covaried with discipline confrontations, and these disruptions were related to antisocial behaviors. The hypothesis we examine in this and the following section is that antisocial behavior, and probably other forms of child deviancy as well, contribute to increased maternal stress.

One implication of this hypothesis is that the relation between maternal stress and child adjustment problems is a *bidirectional* one. Maternal stress contributes indirectly to child adjustment problems; and child adjustment problems contribute directly to maternal stress. This position is in keeping with the transactional effects emphasized in the developmental literature (Sameroff, 1981).

The modification indices from the Hetherington effect model emphasized the fact that the model could be strengthened by a simple alternative. The modification suggested was a new path from the Child Antisocial Behavior construct in the Maternal Stress construct.

In order to identify the model, the path from Inept Discipline to Child Antisocial Behavior was dropped. Structural equation modeling showed that the path from Child Antisocial Behavior to Maternal Stress was .49 ($p < .05$). This is consistent with the idea that rising levels of child deviancy may contribute to maternal stress. In fact, this variable accounted for 24% of the variance in the current measures of Maternal Stress. The chi-square value of 64.39 ($p = .099$) showed a good fit for the predicted and obtained covariance structures.

Child Deviancy and Future Levels of Maternal Stress. The hypothesis examined in this section is that rising levels of antisocial behavior contribute to *future* levels of single-mother stress.

One can perhaps easily understand why living with a problem child might contribute to maternal reports of stress. What is not so apparent is why there might also be a long-range contribution to increasing levels of stress. Our hunch is that it relates in part to the increasing frequency of negative reports about the problem child from relatives, neighbors, teachers, principals, and eventually from the juvenile court. The daily round of family conflict would be another stressor. However, it should be noted that this variable (family conflict) is not included as an indicator for our measure of stress.

An earlier study showed that child deviancy makes unique contributions to a construct measuring parental rejection of the child (Patterson, 1986b). One might assume that over a period of a year or two, such consistent negative feedback from community agents might also contribute to increases in parental levels of stress.

The matrix of correlations summarized in Table 9.6 were based on data from the single-parent sample collected during the initial assessment and during the 12-month follow-up probe. The indicators for the Child Antisocial Behavior construct and Maternal Stress at Time 1 were obtained during the initial assessment. Maternal Stress indicators at Time 3 were assessed at the 12-month follow-up probe.

The convergence for the indicators defining Maternal Stress seemed rather borderline at both assessment probes (median of .23 and .30). The convergence for the Child Antisocial Behavior construct seemed somewhat stronger (median of .31) but not quite as robust as has been the case for older samples of boys (Patterson et al., in press).

The potential problem for modeling lies in the fact that three of the indicators for the Child Antisocial Behavior construct were based on maternal self-report (Mother CBC, Mother OCA, and Mother telephone report variables). Two of the Maternal Stress measures (the recent hassles and negative life events variables) were also heavily loaded on maternal self-report. This creates the likelihood that

TABLE 9.6

Convergent and Discriminant Correlations for Stress Maintenance Model

	Stress at Time 1				Stress at Time 3				Child Antisocial					
	Recent hassles	Negative life events	Financial problems	Family health problems	Recent hassles	Negative life events	Financial problems	Family health problems	Mother CBC	Mother OCA	Mother telephone report	Teacher CBC	Child interview	Child telephone report
Recent hassles	1.00													
Neg life events	.519	1.00												
Financial problems	.391	.228	1.00											
Family health	.235	.143	.108	1.00										
Recent hassles	.593	.413	.251	.069	1.00									
Neg life events	.349	.460	.267	.151	.356	1.00								
Financial problems	.353	.258	.604	.066	.307	.348	1.00							
Family health	.214	.200	.188	.166	.179	.106	.286	1.00						
Mother CBC	.332	.282	.116	-.013	.330	.159	.164	.106	1.00					
Mother OCA	.289	.144	.207	-.014	.264	.154	.170	.171	.679	1.00				
Mother telephone	.432	.280	.069	-.048	.250	.175	.068	.094	.525	.568	1.00			
Teacher CBC	.076	-.019	-.074	-.004	.046	.119	-.040	.103	.183	.218	.166	1.00		
Child interview	.095	.128	.095	-.040	.109	.091	.088	.046	.205	.308	.284	.063	1.00	
Child telephone	.183	.124	.069	-.009	.247	.076	.107	.101	.315	.384	.401	.204	.361	1.00

238

some portion of the relation *between* the Child Antisocial Behavior and Maternal Stress constructs will reflect method variance. It is also likely that the stability measures for the Maternal Stress construct will also reflect a substantial contribu- tion of method variance as discussed by Bank et al. (see Chapter 10).

In keeping with discussions by Dwyer (1983) and others, we followed the procedure of allowing the error terms to covary for the same indicators measur- ing Maternal Stress at the two points in time (e.g., the residual for each of the four Maternal Stress indicators assessed at Time-1 were allowed to correlate with each of the corresponding indicators at Time-3). Finally, based on data in the modification index, the mother telephone interview variable was allowed to correlate with mother report of recent hassles variable collected at Time-1.

When discussing lagged causal relationships, it has been traditional to calcu- late the correlation between, say, Child Antisocial Behavior at Time-1 and Maternal Stress at Time-2. The correlation between Maternal Stress at Time-1 and Child Antisocial Behavior at Time-2 is also calculated. If the former is greater than the latter, then one might attribute a delayed causal effect to Child Antisocial Behavior on Maternal Stress. There are many difficulties with such an approach (see Dwyer, 1983; Kenny, 1975; Rogossa, 1980).

In our view, the cross-lagged correlation between Child Antisocial Behavior at Time-1 and Maternal Stress at Time-2 should take into account the stability of Maternal Stress. This is in keeping with the more general point raised by Gollob and Reichardt (1987) that a precise estimate of either synchronistic or delayed effects must be made relative to the stability estimate for the dependent variable. For example, Maternal Stress scores that were either extremely stable or unstable could have major implications for a cross-time correlation with Child Antisocial Behavior. If the score were completely unstable, then by definition one would not obtain a cross-lagged correlation with Child Antisocial Behavior. On the other hand, if earlier measures of Child Antisocial Behavior explain some of the reasons for the stability in Maternal Stress, then the cross-lagged path will be significant and accompanied by a commensurate reduction in the stability coeffi- cient for Maternal Stress.

Now, the question is, how much of the variance in the dependent variable measured at Time-2 (Maternal Stress) is accounted for by knowledge of the Maternal Stress measured at Time-1 relative to the amount accounted for by knowing the scores for the assumed causal variable at Time-1 (Child Antisocial Behavior)? In other words, the variance accounted for at Time-2 is a relative function of both stability and so-called causal variables. If the measures for Child Antisocial Behavior and Maternal Stress are correlated at Time-1 (and they are), and both are correlated with the Maternal Stress measures at Time-2 (they are), then as one contributes more the other contributes less. If Child Antisocial Behavior and Maternal Stress were uncorrelated (not interconnected in the same process), then the former would add variance to whatever is accounted for by knowing the stability of Maternal Stress alone. In one sense, variables for the

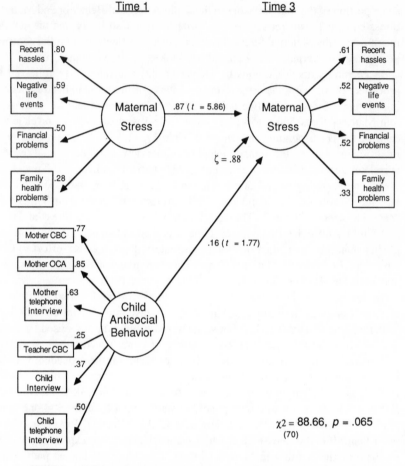

FIG. 9.7. Child antisocial behavior as a possible maintenance variable.

Child Antisocial Behavior construct that are products earlier in the process of something like Maternal Stress can take variance away from stability coefficients when tested for a delayed causal connection.

The outcome of the attempt to model these ideas are summarized in Fig. 9.7. In general the model provides only modest support for the idea that earlier measures of Child Antisocial Behavior contribute significantly to later measures of Maternal Stress.

The hypothesized delayed effect would require a significant path from Child Antisocial Behavior at Time-1 to the Maternal Stress construct at Time-2. The path coefficient, expressed as a standardized partial beta of .16, was of only borderline significance. This value is relative to the stability coefficient for

Maternal Stress of .87. Most of the variance in Maternal Stress is accounted for by the stress measures obtained 12 months earlier.

The chi-square value of 88.66 showed a reasonable fit of the model to the data ($p = .065$). The data offer marginal support for the hypothesis that child problem behaviors may function as feedback loops serving to maintain the stress-induced process.

SOME IMPLICATIONS

Separation-induced stress can set in motion a process that moves through a sequence of steps or stages. Not all single mothers move into this process, but early in the separation period a majority do slip into a depressed mood for at least brief interludes. About 40% were characterized by depressed moods that persisted through the three test probes. We believe this group is at risk for major clinical depression and, simultaneously, for antisocial problems with their sons. We are currently exploring these two hypotheses in studies now underway.

During the first and second years following separation, stress and loss of social support seem to be two of the significant contributors to maternal depression. The findings also suggested that these two variables might be key determinants at all three points assessed in the study reported here. This pointed to a kind of stationarity for the process, and raised a new question. Why is it that some mothers remained at high levels of stress and without support while others did not?

Maternal irritability seems to be a constant companion to single-mother depression and stress. The present report emphasizes the special function of single-mother irritability (and perhaps sadness too) in disrupting social-interactional patterns with her confidante and her son. Three facets of the disruptions were thought to serve as mechanisms contributing to the long-term maintenance of the process.

Over a period of time, maternal irritable/sad behaviors are thought to increase the mothers' loss of support; this in turn serves to maintain maternal depression. The irritable behaviors are also thought to disrupt mother-confidante problem-solving exchanges; this in turn is thought to contribute to the future high levels of stress. Irritable exchanges with the son, especially during discipline confrontations, set in motion a secondary process. This one moves the child into increases in antisocial behavior, which over time contribute marginally to the maintenance of future levels of maternal stress.

Each of the three mechanisms is defined by disruptions at the microsocial level. In keeping with our general social-interactional stance, we assume that changes in the microsocial level serve the important function of driving many forms of social behavior, both prosocial and deviant in form. As used here, the term *driving mechanism* refers to the reinforcing contingencies embedded in these social exchanges. It is these contingencies that actually bring about the changes in social behavior. The point is, to understand what happens to families during separation, one must actually observe the mothers' interactions with members of her primary group (e.g., friends, children, relatives). Repeated observations would provide the information necessary to understand how these processes unfold over time.

The formulation about mechanisms for maintenance also focused our attention on another set of questions that are crucial in understanding this process. What are the relations among maternal stress, irritability and sadness? Is stress a stimulus that controls both these maternal reactions? To what extent are maternal sadness and irritability elicited by stress and to what extent are they shaped by the reactions of key persons in the mother's social environment? Future studies that explore the process model outlined in the present report will have to address these questions.

The original study was designed to contribute to our understanding of the antisocial and depressed reactions of *sons* during the first years of separation. The data set functioned very well in explicating that problem. In designing the study, maternal depression was of sufficient interest to lead to the inclusion of multiple measures of depression (CES-D, daily diary, telephone contacts). At the time, it seemed that each of these represented different methods and could therefore function as separate indicators in defining the latent construct Depression. We took a similar perspective on the problem of defining the stress, support, and irritability constructs. It was only later that we learned that all of these measures are a variation on a theme of self-report and, indeed, they were not separate indicators but a single one.

The current study by Forgatch (1987) is an attempt to correct these problems. If she is successful, then it will be possible to use structural equation modeling to model many of the mechanisms discussed in the present report. In either case one thing is very clear, and that is that the study of maternal depression is characterized by some extraordinarily complex problems of measurement. What is startling about this is that in an area so heavily researched, these problems of method variance have been largely neglected or simply ignored.

ACKNOWLEDGMENTS

The writers gratefully acknowledge the support provided by MH 38318 (Family Mental and Policy Research Branch) for the collection and analyses of the data. We wish to thank Karen Gardner and her staff for the care with which these data were collected and to Martie Skinner and her colleagues who carried out the statistical analyses.

REFERENCES

Aneshensel, C. S. (1985). The natural history of depressive symptoms: Implications for psychiatric epidemiology. *Research in Community and Mental Health, 5,* 45–75.

Bank, L., & Stoolmiller, M. (1988). *Effects of antisocial behavior on preadolescent boy's self esteem.* Paper for SRED annual conference. Oregon Social Learning Center, Eugene, Oregon.

Bentler, P. M. (1980). Multivariate analysis with latent variables: Causal modeling. *Annual Review of Psychology, 31,* 419–455.

Block, G. H., Block, J., & Gjerde, T. F. (1986). The personality of children prior to divorce: A prospective study. *Child Development, 57,* 827–860.

Bloom, B. L., Asher, S. J., & White, S. W. (1978). Marital disruption as a stressor: A review and analysis. *Psychological Bulletin, 85,* 867–894.

Cairns, R. B., Gariepy, J. L., & Hood, K. E. (1988). Dual genesis and the puzzle of aggressive mediation. *Report from the Social Developmental Laboratory, 1*(4), 1–18. Department of Psychology, University of North Carolina, Chapel Hill, NC.

Capaldi, D., & Patterson, G. R. (1988). *Psychometric properties of fourteen latent constructs from the Oregon Youth Study.* New York: Springer-Verlag.

Coyne, J. C. (1976). Depression and the response of others. *Journal of Abnormal Psychology, 85,* 186–193.

Dwyer, J. H. (1983). *Statistical models for the social and behavioral sciences.* New York: Oxford University Press.

Elder, G. H., Caspi, A., & Nguyen, P. V. (1986). Resourceful and vulnerable children: Family influences hard times. In R. K. Silbereisen & K. Eyferth (Eds.), *Development as action in context: Problem behavior in normal youth development* (pp. 167–186). Berlin: Springer.

Forgatch, M. S. (1987). Family process model for depression in mothers. *Grant Proposal 2 RO1 MH38318-04.* Rockville, MD: National Institute of Mental Health, Child and Family and Prevention Subcommittee.

Forgatch, M. S. (in press). Patterns and outcome in family problem solving: The disrupting effect of negative emotion. *Journal of Marriage and the Family.*

Forgatch, M. S., Patterson, G. R., & Skinner, M. (1988). A mediational model for the effect of divorce on antisocial behavior in boys. In M. Hetherington (Ed.), *The impact of divorce, single parenting, and stepparenting on children* (pp. 135–154). Hillsdale, NJ: Lawrence Erlbaum Associates.

Garmezy, N., & Rutter, M. (Eds.). (1983). *Stress, coping, and development in children.* New York: McGraw Hill.

Gollob, H. F., & Reichardt, C. S. (1987). Taking account of time lags in causal models. *Child Development, 58,* 80–92.

Hetherington, E. M. (Ed.). (1983). *Handbook of child psychology: 4. Socialization, personality, and social development.* New York: Wiley.

Hetherington, E. M. (1987, June). *Divorce and remarriage.* Paper presented at the second annual Family Consortium conference, "Understanding Family Life Transitions," Santa Fe, NM.

Hetherington, E. M., Cox, M., & Cox, R. (1978). Aftermath of divorce. In J. H. Stevens, Jr., & M. Matthews (Eds.), *Mother-child, father-child relations.* Washington, DC: National Association for the Education of Young Children.

Hetherington, E. M., Cox, M., & Cox, R. (1979). Family interaction and the social, emotional, and cognitive development of children following divorce. In V. Vaughn & T. Brazelton (Eds.), *The family: Setting priorities.* New York: Science and Medicine.

Hetherington, E. M., Cox, M., & Cox, R. (1980). *Stress and coping in divorce: A focus on women.* Unpublished manuscript. University of Virginia, Charlottesville.

Hineline, P. (1977). Negative reinforcement and avoidance. In W. Honig & J. E. Staddon (Eds.), *Handbook of operant behavior* (pp. 364–414). Englewood Cliffs, NJ: Prentice-Hall.

Izard, C. E., & Schwartz, G. M. (1986). Patterns of emotion in depression. In M. Rutter, C. Izard, & P. Read (Eds.), *Depression in young people: Developmental and clinical perspectives* (pp. 33–71). New York: Guilford Press.

Jöreskog, K. G., & Sörbom, D. (1983). *LISREL VI: Analysis of linear structural relationships by maximum likelihood and least squares methods* (2nd ed.). Chicago: Natural Education Resources.

Kandel, D. B., & Yamaguchi, K. (1985). Developmental patterns of the use of legal, illegal, and medically prescribed psychotropic drugs from adolescence to young adulthood. In C. L. Jones & K. J. Battjes (Eds.), *Etiology of drug abuse: Implications for prevention* (NIDA Research Monograph 56). Washington, DC: U.S. Government Printing Office.

Kenny, D. A. (1975). Cross-lagged panel correlations: A test for spuriousness. *Psychological Bulletin, 82,* 887–903.

Knutson, J. F., & Viken, R. J. (1984). Animal analogues of human aggression: Studies of social experience and escalation. In D. C. Blanchard, K. J. Flannelly, & R. J. Blanchard (Eds.), *Biological perspectives on aggression* (pp. 75–94). New York: Alan R. Liss.

McNemar, Q. (1969). *Psychological statistics (4th ed.).* New York: Wiley.

Patterson, G. R. (1982). *A social learning approach: 3. Coercive family process.* Eugene, OR: Castalia Publishing Co.

Patterson, G. R. (1983). Stress: A change agent for family process. In N. Garmezy & M. Rutter (Eds.), *Stress, coping and development in children* (pp. 235–264). New York: McGraw Hill.

Patterson, G. R. (1986a). The contribution of siblings to training for fighting: A microsocial analysis. In D. Olweus, J. Block, & M. Radke-Yarrow (Eds.), *Development of antisocial and prosocial behavior: Research, theories, and issues* (pp. 235–261). Orlando, FL: Academic Press.

Patterson, G. R. (1986b). Maternal rejection: Determinant or product for deviant child behavior? In W. Hartup & Z. Rubin (Eds.), *Relationships and development* (pp. 73–94). Hillsdale, NJ: Lawrence Erlbaum Associates.

Patterson, G. R., & Bank, L. (1986). Bootstrapping your way in the nomological thicket. *Behavioral Assessment, 8,* 49–73.

Patterson, G. R., & Bank, L. (1987, October). *Some amplifying and dampening mechanisms for process in families.* Paper presented at the Minnesota Child Psychology Symposium, "Systems and Development," Minneapolis, MN.

Patterson, G. R., & Dishion, T. J. (1988). Multilevel family process models: Traits, interactions, and relationships. In R. Hinde & J. Stevenson-Hinde (Eds.), *Relationships within families: Mutual influences* (pp. 283–310). Oxford: Clarendon.

Patterson, G. R., Reid, J. B., & Dishion, T. J. (in press). *A social learning approach: 4. Antisocial boys.* Eugene, OR: Castalia Publishing Co.

Pedhazur, E. J. (1982). *Multiple regression in behavioral research.* New York: Holt, Rinehart and Winston.

Radloff, L. S. (1977). The CES-D Scale: A self-report depression scale for research in the general population. *Applied Psychological Measurement, 1,* 385–401.

Reid, J. B. (1978). *A social learning approach: 2. Observations in the home setting.* Eugene, OR: Castalia Publishing Co.

Reid, J. B., Bank, L., Patterson, G. R., & Skinner, M. L. (1987, April). *The generalizability of single versus multiple methods in structural equation models of child development.* Paper presented at the meeting of the Society for Research in Child Development, Baltimore, MD.

Rogossa, D. A. (1980). A critique of cross-lagged correlations. *Psychological Bulletin, 88,* 245–258.

Sameroff, A. J. (1981). Development and the dialectic: The need for a systems approach. In W. A.

Collins (Ed.), *Minnesota Symposium on Child Psychology* (Vol. 15, pp. 83–103). Hillsdale, NJ: Lawrence Erlbaum Associates.

Sarason, I. G., Johnson, J. H., & Siegel, J. M. (1978). Assessing the impact of life changes: Development of the life experience survey. *Journal of Consulting and Clinical Psychology, 46*(5), 932–946.

Sullivan, J. L. (1974). Multiple indicators: Some criteria of selection. In H. M. Blalock (Ed.), *Measurement in the social sciences* (pp. 93–156). Chicago: Aldine.

Viken, R. J. (1988). *Relation of stress to maternal discipline practices.* Manuscript in preparation. (Available from the author, Department of Psychology, Indiana University, Bloomington, IN 47405.)

Wahler, R. G., & Dumas, J. E. (1983, June). *Stimulus class determinants of mother-child coercive exchanges in multidistressed families: Assessment and intervention.* Paper presented at the Vermont Conference on Primary Prevention of Psychopathology, Bolton Valley Winter/Summer Resort, VT.

Wahler, R. G., Leske, G., & Rogers, E. (1977). *The insular family: A deviance support system for oppositional children.* Paper presented at the Banff International Conference on Behavior Modification, Alberta, Canada.

Wallerstein, J. S., & Kelly, J. B. (1980). *Surviving the breakup: How children and parents cope with divorce.* New York: Basic Books.

Watson, D., & Tellegen, A. (1985). Toward a consensual structure of mood. *Psychological Bulletin, 98*, 219–235.

Weissman, M. M., Myers, J. K., Thompson, W. D., & Belanger, A. (1986). Depressive symptoms as a risk factor for mortality and for major depression. In L. Erlenmeyer-Kimling & N. E. Miller (Eds.), *Life-span research and the prediction of psychopathology* (pp. 251–260). Hillsdale, NJ: Lawrence Erlbaum Associates.

Zill, N. (1978, February). *Divorce, marital happiness, and the mental health of children: Findings from the FCD National Survey of Children.* Paper presented at the NIMH workshop, "Divorce and Children," Bethesda, MD.

Zucker, R. (1987). The four alcoholisms: A developmental account of the etiological process. In P. C. Rivers (Ed.), *Nebraska Symposium on Motivation, 1986: Vol. 34. Alcohol and addictive behaviors* (pp. 28–83). Lincoln: University of Nebraska Press.

10 Method Variance in Structural Equation Modeling: Living with "Glop"

L. Bank
T. Dishion
M. Skinner
G. R. Patterson
Oregon Social Learning Center

In the past 10 years there has been a marked increase in the use of structural equation modeling (SEM) in the study of family processes and their outcomes. As articulated by Martin (1987), SEM is not a panacea for the ambitious investigator, and of course, does not alleviate interpretive problems resulting from poor quality data, sampling biases, or internal validity problems resulting from faulty study design. On the other hand, SEM has a number of clear and far-reaching advantages. It does not require that error terms be uncorrelated among the independent and dependent variables. In fact, with SEM the question can be addressed statistically. In addition, both the measurement and causal models can be estimated simultaneously, thereby increasing our understanding of both aspects of model building and how they might interact. Thus, a more thorough understanding of the data as they relate to the confirmation or disconfirmation of theoretical hypotheses is possible. Furthermore, relatively complex theoretical structures can be posited and tested, while in a very real sense maintaining experiment-wise alpha levels at known and acceptable rates.

The analytic versatility of SEM also provides an opportunity to examine issues that have long haunted psychological researchers, such as the issue of how measurement method determines the outcomes to a research enterprise. For example, if one defines both the independent and dependent variable with a common measure (e.g., observer impressions or self-report) in a structural model, the estimated effect coefficient is much higher than when the variables are defined by nonoverlapping indicators. For example, reviews by Rutter (1979) and Emery (1982) showed consistent correlations between reports of marital discord and child adjustment problems. However as pointed out in a later study by Emery and O'Leary (1984), in most of these studies the same person (usually the mother) reported on both variables. In their study, they found significant correlations between mothers' reports and marital discord and child adjustment problems and between parents' and teachers' reports of child behaviors. However, the correlation between mothers' reports of marital discord and teachers' ratings of child behavior were essentially zero.

In the context of SEM, overlapping methods in defining constructs can lead to impossible empirical results such as negative variances or correlation estimates that exceed 1.0. (See Harman, 1967, on Heywood cases and Dillon, Kumar, and Mulani, 1987, for a current review of these problems in the modeling context.) In the more serious case, coefficients are within interpretable bounds, yet they are the likely products of shared methods across constructs. We have come to call results yielding such biased estimates the *glop* problem.

SEM affords an opportunity to reconsider the role of measurement method in our research practices and findings. The primary aim of this chapter is to cast attention to the method variance issue in the context of current research on families and their outcomes. We provide four specific, meaningful, and practical *solutions* for handling method variance. Each is applied to data sets from developmental models that illustrate the advantages and disadvantages for a given approach.

We have come to believe that the more representative sampling of methods and agents will lead to more generalizable models than will sampling of monomethod indicators. Presumably, models positing structural linkage, but tested with the same *method* or same *agent* across constructs, are in a sense confounded by the method variance explanation. These issues are addressed in several of the examples presented in this paper, and explored in detail by Reid, Patterson, Bank, and Dishion (1988) and Patterson, Ramsey, and Bank (1988). Issues of generalizability of models are not a focus for the present report. The following discussions center on the problem of method variance in measurement. After a brief historical review of the problem, we illustrate the four procedures we have examined thus far.

HISTORICAL CONTEXT

We see the development of the method variance problem as inevitable in behavioral science investigations. It is best understood in the historical context of psychologists' quest for reliable and valid data. For example, in the late 19th century, Wundt used only professional subjects in his laboratory because of the concern for reliability of responses. These subjects were trained to make fine gustatory, olfactory, and tactile discriminations so that they could meet a high standard of reliability. Although this strategy for generating data had some clear advantages (e.g., known reliability, ease of gathering data), it was obviously limited in utility to testing hypotheses of human perception. Furthermore, even trained, professional respondents could have a distorted response set. By the beginning of the 20th century, this method was being replaced by the experimental method applied to animal learning. The contributions of Pavlov and Thorndike captured the attention of a new generation of psychologists. This excitement was paralleled by developments in mental tests during World War I that laid the foundation for much of what is now modern measurement theory. The growth of measurement strategies and techniques over the first half of this century was, indeed, prodigious, and as good hindsight now suggests, it was only natural for MacCorquodale and Meehl (1948) and others (Carnap, 1956; Cronbach & Meehl, 1956; Fiegl, 1956) to formalize the distinction between hypothetical constructs and operational definitions and to introduce the idea of a nomological network.

It was the Campbell and Fiske (1959) publication that constituted an important watershed in the development of measurement theory. They pointed to the need for the validity of hypothetical constructs to be demonstrated beyond a single-measurement domain. They also provided a kind of litmus test for this demonstration: the multitrait–multimethod matrix. Construct validity, according to the classic Campbell and Fiske paper, could be demonstrated when two or more methods are used to measure two or more traits (see Fig. 10.1; after Campbell & Fiske, 1959). For example, traits A, B, and C, could each be operationally defined using methods 1, 2, and 3; then, it should follow that convergent correlations (A1, A2, and A3; B1, B2, and B3; and C1, C2, and C3) are statistically significant *and* exceed "discriminant" correlations (all other pairings of the nine variables). It is possible to be even more specific in that, among discriminant correlations, same-method correlation magnitudes (A1–B1, A1–C1, B1–C1, A2–B2, A2–C2, etc.) should exceed different method correlation magnitudes (A1–B2, A1–C2, A1–B3, A1–C3, A2–B3, etc.). As the number of traits and methods increases, this test becomes very difficult to satisfy.

Cattell's (1957) approach to this problem was to collect data using three different methods: physiological, behavioral, and self-report/questionnaire data. He hypothesized that all of these data types, when incorporated into personality measurement devices, would be significantly related. Campbell and Fiske (1959) would add that those converging relationships would also have to be greater than each of those measure's interrelationships with other measures using the same method, but constructed to measure an unrelated dimension (discriminant validity).

In the 3 decades since the formulation of the method variance problem, there has been at best limited success when applying the Campbell and Fiske yardstick to various constructs (e.g., Kazdin, Esveldt-Dawson, Unis, & Rancurello, 1983; Patterson & Bank, 1986; Saylor, Finch, Baskin, Furey, & Kelly, 1984). Studies have been unable to obtain consistent convergent and discriminant validities in defining trait structure or find that method variance accounts for the majority of

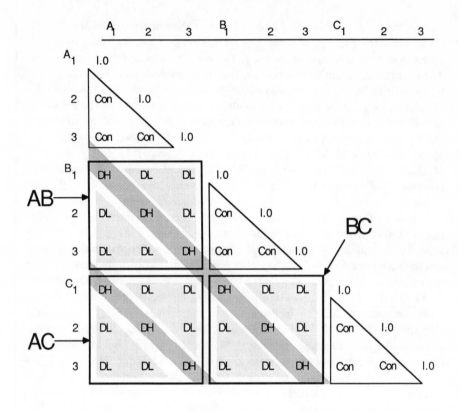

Con = Convergent validities

DH = "High" (same method) discriminant validities

DL = "Low" (different method) discriminant validities

FIG. 10.1. The Campbell and Fiske (1959) multitrait-multimethod matrix.

variance in their data, or both. The present authors believe that the reason for this lies largely in the heavy reliance on a very limited data base. Most of the studies have used global judgments based on reports from only one or two agents. The assumption is that most global ratings of self and others essentially sample a general negative–positive set (see Dawes, 1985).

PRELIMINARY STRATEGIES IN SETTING UP OSLC LONGITUDINAL STUDIES

NIMH support was given for a 3-year planning study as a basis for designing a longitudinal study of families at risk for producing delinquent boys. The planning study was used to develop a battery of indicators that would define key constructs for a general model that encompassed family and peer group as primarily involved in training for antisocial behavior (Patterson & Dishion, 1985). The first problem encountered in planning the assessment battery was how to cope with the Campbell and Fiske problem. Following Nunnally (1978) and other psychometric theorists (Cronbach, 1970), we would agree that psychological measures must serve three functions:

1. *content validity* (i.e., represent the substantive content of each of the concepts from the general model),

2. *construct validity* (i.e., each concept in the model must be defined by converging measures). To this we added the proviso that they must also sample reports by at least two agents and at least two different methods of assessment, and

3. *predictive validity* (i.e., in the context of model building it would also be required that each construct relate significantly to the pattern of constructs defined a priori as being related).

The general model also required that certain key constructs measured at one stage would predict/correlate with specific outcome variables at later stages of development (Patterson, Reid, & Dishion, in press).

We see these three functions as hierarchically related, in that the conclusions we draw concerning the predictive validity between two constructs entirely depends on the degree the measure reflects the appropriate content (content validity) and seems to uniquely define a psychological trait within a nomological network of other psychological traits (construct validity) (Cronbach & Meehl, 1956; Nunnally, 1978; Patterson & Bank, 1987).

To determine the validity of a measure of a given trait, it is necessary to include multimethod assessments of at least two traits (Campbell & Fiske, 1959). In keeping with the assumptions underlying SEM, the current writers believe that *all* assessment procedures introduce some measure of bias or distortion in the data (Bentler, 1980; Sullivan, 1974). For example, parents introduce their own biases and response sets when reporting on the behavior of their child (Reid, Baldwin, Patterson, & Dishion, in press). Thus, from a single measure of child aggression we are unable to determine to what extent, across subjects, the score we obtain reflects systematic variance due to the parents' perceptual biases. Bias might also be introduced by faulty wording of the items or by the assessment context itself (e.g., clinical versus research). Content validity, then, does not only refer to the items included in the measure but also the measurement method itself. For this reason, Campbell and Fiske (1959) stated the imperative that has guided our approach to measure development and sampling: *diverse methods and traits are needed to assess validity.*

Observation data may be less susceptible to method variance related to perceptual biases, but more susceptible to other sources of method variance. For example, observation data cannot efficiently sample such low baserate events as fire setting or stealing. The behavior sampled by observation code systems may be specific only to the setting where the data is collected (e.g., the home).

The studies reviewed in Reid (1978) and Patterson (1982) showed that the molecular data collected by observers was relatively impervious to experimenter bias. However, some of the same studies showed significant effects of experimenter bias reflected in observers' *global* ratings. If we ask observers to make global judgments—that is, observer impressions—we find great difficulty in distinguishing separable parenting traits (e.g., positive parenting, discipline, parent rejection). In fact, in the context of SEM we first encountered the glop problem when we attempted to analyze two or more parenting dispositions when each was defined on the basis of observers' global impressions. There are obviously many possible reactions to this problem, the first being to question the very assumptions underlying a particular research question. Are the independent variables we define (within a set) really different or representative of an underlying single dimension?

It is also tempting to minimize this method influence by simply taking out overlapping measures for different constructs and rerunning the model. This latter strategy raises another interesting question: To what extent is method variance theoretically relevant? For many questions the definition of a construct provides a theoretical hierarchy for selecting the appropriate method for a construct of interest. For example, in the research by Dishion (1988), parenting behavior was measured by a combination of home observation data, the child's social disposition by global impressions of parents, teachers and the child, and peer relations by sociometric items from peer nominations. Patterson and Capaldi (in press) also delineate a model of depression that relates home characteristics to the child's relations in the school setting to depression. In this way, the three types of validity are fundamentally interrelated from the beginning stages of construct definition, to content sampling, the determination of construct validity (convergent and discriminant validity), and finally, to predictive validity.

The method variance issue quickly turns into the glop problem when, on a theoretical basis, we suspect that our estimates of predictive validity are systematically inflated because of shared method variance between two constructs. There are several things that can be done about this. First, it is possible to form a factor based only on method variance. We could remove the contribution of this factor to each of the constructs and then reexamine the residual model. Second, given a large set of indicators for each construct, we could employ nonoverlapping indicators across constructs.

Thus, when we find that two constructs are indistinguishable, a full range of analyses exist to address the measurement question to determine construct validity and predictive validity. In general, we are developing a systematic procedure for model building that proceeds through the three hierarchical questions addressed above: content validity, construct validity and predictive validity. We think these steps create a systematic process useful for generating and analyzing data that can address the full range of issues surrounding predictive validity.

MODEL BUILDING AND TESTING

The first step in model building and testing requires a well-articulated (a priori) theoretical model. The general model then determines what measures to collect on what constructs, and formulates the foundation for collecting multiagent and multimethod data on the key theoretical constructs. Careful work in construct building does not preclude method variance problems (Patterson & Bank, 1987). But with some procedures for working with the problem, a critical examination of the glop can be quite informative. For example, it might lead to reconsidering the original hypothesis with a more sophisticated understanding of the measurement issues. When appropriate, it may lead to a shift in the analytic strategy.

Given that the constructs are adequately defined, the next and last stage in our premodeling strategy is to carry out a confirmatory factor analysis to demonstrate that one can, in fact, differentiate one construct from another. Thus, the confirmatory factor analysis provides a test of the measurement model. The last step in our strategy is to apply SEM as a means of confronting the Campbell and Fiske test.

We now turn to each level in the modeling enterprise and discuss the considerations we have found to be useful.

Theoretical Foundation

An explicit theoretical model plays a critical role as a vehicle for organizing one's thinking on a complex developmental theory and also as a tool in setting out logical steps for the analysis of data. The fact that many hypotheses can be tested with SEM is a very substantial bonus, and the use of SEM is central to testing the general hypotheses summarized in Fig. 10.2. The relationships suggested by Fig. 10.2 can, however, also be tested via factor analysis, multiple regression and path analysis—albeit less elegantly than with SEM. Figure 10.2 illustrates the big picture, the "grand model," which cannot be tested except in smaller, theoretically meaningful chunks. Studying this general model, however, suggests a progression of much simpler and very straightforward hypotheses.

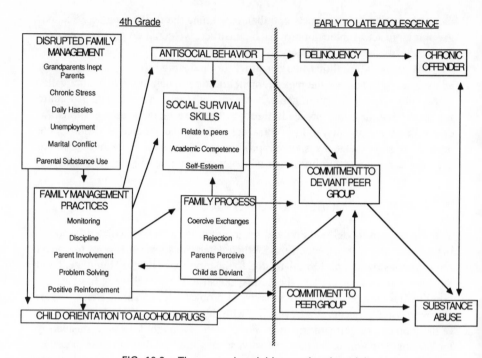

FIG. 10.2.   The general social interactional model.

The general model dictates the constructs to be sampled in a measurement strategy. Note that in our research program, consistent with the social interactional approach (Patterson & Reid, 1984; Patterson et al., in press), there has been a concerted effort to build models including family-management constructs, which are clinically malleable. In the current context, we are interested in the role of family-management practices in the etiology of child antisocial behavior, depression, substance use, and poor peer relations. Similarly, in research on maternal depression, Forgatch has examined the role of problem-solving skills in determining future episodes of maternal depression (Forgatch, Patterson, & Skinner, in press; Patterson & Forgatch, this volume). Both the general model for child antisocial and for maternal depression are being examined in a longitudinal context. Both problems are thought to unfold in a prespecified series of steps (Patterson & Bank, 1987).

Thus, testing of more specific theory-driven predictions will follow the hypothesized process of the general longitudinal models. In agreement with Meehl's (1978) highly critical stance on social science, we see hypothesis testing as proceeding through a number of increasingly rigorous tests:

1. parametric models that examine both the measurement and process assumptions simultaneously;

2. testing specific predictions about cause and effect, which can be valuable even without random assignment or systematic intervention (e.g., developmental shifts in the independent variable should be followed by accompanying shifts in the dependent variable);

3. experimental manipulation, actively intervening on the independent variables hypothesized as determinants.

Construct Building

The approach to building constructs has been described as bootstrapping (Patterson & Bank, 1986). This metaphor, originally introduced by Cronbach and Meehl (1956), defines a process of formulating the assessment of constructs that proceeds from the conception of the construct to its measurement, from its measurement to validation, from validation back to redefinition and reconceptualization of the construct, and then returning to improving the measurement once again. At the present time, there is no definitive end to this process of successive approximation, simply a gradual, increased measurement fidelity.

The first step in building a construct is to identify a priori variates (often scales) developed to measure a given construct. Often five to six scales are available for each construct, each based on different methods of assessment and/or reports from different agents (see Fig. 10.3).

The next step is to analyze the items within each scale for internal consistency. Individual items that generate item-total correlations of less than .20 are dropped from the scales. Scales that produce alphas (Cronbach, 1951) of less

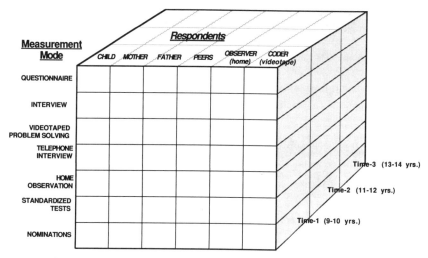

FIG. 10.3.   Multiagent and multimethod strategy for sampling indicators for theoretical constructs.

than .60 are excluded from further analyses. In keeping with the aggregation principle (Epstein, 1979), each indicator represents an aggregate of information across items and/or behaviors. These indicators must then show convergent validity in order to be considered useful in further analyses.

Another important aspect of construct building is the choice of methods of data collection for a particular latent variable. The indicators that define the constructs could be ordered along a continuum from molar to molecular. The term *molar* implies a broad-spectrum assessment (e.g., global judgments that sample across time and settings). The term *molecular* describes judgments about more restricted time intervals (e.g., behavior occurring in one day) or descriptions of action-reaction sequences. For example, the Child Peer Relations construct is entirely molar in its measurement. It is designed to sample the child's as well as significant others' global impressions about this trait across two settings, home and school. Given that the objective is to establish the most general model possible, then it seems reasonable to begin with a set of indicators that sample peers and teachers, as well as mother, father, and child.

As indicated by Cairns and Green (1979), there are assets and liabilities associated with using both molar and molecular measures. As these authors point out, molecular measures are ill-suited for sampling low baserate, but perhaps extremely meaningful, events; they also do not provide a broad spectrum synthesis sampling across settings and time. However, they are uniquely suited to describing interactional sequences that slip by the casual observer (e.g., the parental and child reactions during discipline confrontations).

Given a group of potential indicators for a construct, we then proceed to examine its factor structure. Our general theoretical expectation when construct development begins is that it will be unidimensional. As Bentler (personal communication) has pointed out to us, however, if a construct is actually multidimensional, and we summarize it with a single factor, we might end up leaving our "corners" (in the factor analytic space) untouched. Although we generally begin by carrying out a forced one-factor solution, this analysis is followed by an exploratory solution that allows the same number of factors to be extracted as there are eigenvalues greater than 1.0.

Confirmatory Factor Analysis (Campbell and Fiske Revisited)

For the purposes of this discussion, let us assume that a single-factor solution is satisfactory and superior to any multidimensional solution. The next step is to check convergent and discriminant validities. Presumably there is reasonable convergence among the indicators in order to arrive at the one-factor solution, but the question still remains as to whether the convergent validities *exceed* the discriminant validities with indicators from all other constructs in any given model. To satisfy the requirements of the Campbell and Fiske (1959) multitrait–

multimethod matrix, this condition must exist. No matter how correct the a priori model is, structural equation models are very unlikely to fit a data set if the Campbell-Fiske hierarchy of convergent/discriminant validity magnitudes is not met.

In actual practice in the OSLC modeling studies, discriminant validities typically range from 0 to .2 or .3. For those constructs that are strongly related in theory, some of the discriminant validities may be as high as in the .4 to .5 range. Again, this condition can only be acceptable in the presence of commensurately high convergent validities. Even higher discriminant validities occasionally exist. Usually, but not always, the two indicators that reflect the high discriminant validity are drawn from the same agent or same method. For example, when peer nomination data are used to build indicators for both the Antisocial Behavior and for the Peer Relation constructs, the discriminant validities will be very high. Such a finding leads us to rework the indicator scale (removing more ambiguous items) or possibly not use a particular indicator for a specific model. This strategy leaves us at times with a construct's indicator network changing somewhat from one model to another.

Although this selective employment of indicators is less than perfect, it has been extremely helpful as a practical solution for dealing with the method/agent variance problem. Interestingly enough, we find very good stability of constructs across time even when using mutually exclusive indicator sets. For example, the stability for the Antisocial Behavior construct was .8 from Wave 1 to Wave 2 using different sets of methods and agents for the two points in time.

RELIABILITY

Reliability of constructs is an interesting concept. Basic psychometric theory tells us that fallible reliability of any measure reduces the maximum observed validity possible. Constructs whose indicators demonstrate poor reliability would presumably suffer from the same problem, and in the worst case scenario, it would be impossible to demonstrate hypothesized paths in a model. The matter becomes somewhat more complex with the use of multiple indicators because theoretically latent variables are "infallible" (that is, they are measured without error). Huba and Bentler (1982) demonstrated algebraically that the use of true scores to assess theories yields more accurate estimates of causal influence than using observed scores. Thus, the potentially confounding influences of measurement error in observed variables can be eliminated through using structural equation models with latent variables.

Clearly, one must begin with well-conceived measurements. As pointed out succinctly by Martin (1987), latent variable models cannot create meaning from an unsatisfactory data set, no matter how wonderful the theoretical model may be. As already noted, our experience thus far with current data sets suggests good stability of constructs at least over periods of 1 and 2 years. The design of the project also permitted a retest for each indicator over a period of two to six weeks for a randomly selected subset of the sample. In this fashion, indicator reliability can be estimated for short- and long-term intervals.

CONSTRUCT VALIDITY

Obviously, a construct may be reliable but of little use in modeling because of its limited validity. There is a series of steps involved in demonstrating construct validity. The first step, confirmatory factor analysis, demonstrates that the construct is discriminable from some other related construct. The second step requires that the construct be statistically significantly related to other constructs as demanded by the theory-driven model.

Differentiating One Construct from Another

An example demonstrating the first kind of validation is reported in a study by Patterson and Bank (1987). In this analysis, it was found that a two-factor measurement model was superior to a single-factor model for a set of indicators hypothesized to measure parental monitoring and discipline practices. Thus, it was concluded that the discipline and monitoring indicator clusters formed two related but distinguishable constructs.

A different outcome, however, was reported by Forgatch et al. (1988), for the Stress and Negative Affect constructs. When submitted to a similar confirmatory factor analysis, it was found that the single-factor model was a better fit than the two-factor model. In fact, the standardized estimate of covariation between Stress and Negative Affect yielded by LISREL VI (Jöreskog & Sörbom, 1986) exceeded 1.0. This obviously spurious coefficient is likely to have occurred because of excessively high discriminant validities as compared to the convergent validities.

There are many reasons why one may fail to demonstrate construct validity in this exercise, all of which have been carefully enumerated by Cook and Campbell (1979, pp. 64–68). Because both Stress and Negative Affect were defined exclusively on each mother's subjective assessment, it seemed necessary to test for what Cook and Campbell refer to as a monomethod bias. Before alternative hypotheses could be examined concerning the poor construct validity of these two constructs considered together (such as construct confounding), one would need to examine the possibility of monomethod bias. We feel it is extremely important to fully address the methodological question of construct validity before we can estimate the statistical relation between two constructs.

Our recent efforts strongly emphasize the need to devote much time to developing multiagent/multimethod assessment procedures *prior* to model testing. In the case of Negative Affect and Stress, we had not anticipated these as major foci for modeling; for this reason very little effort was made to develop indicators from other than self-report measures. The oversight led to the failure of such constructs to pass the first requirement for construct validity.

Construct Validity in a Theory-Driven Model

The next question was whether the Discipline and Monitoring constructs fulfilled the function predicted by the a priori model. It was required that they significantly predicted the antisocial behavior of the target child. The dependent variable described antisocial child behaviors at home and at school. The SEM analyses supported these contributions (Patterson & Bank, 1986).

Construct validity has often been demonstrated in another way (e.g., Cronbach, 1970). For example, constructs that have a predictive function could be said to be valid. However, if this relationship is due to a shared method/agent, the results would be *spurious*. Even a priori attempts at establishing construct validity that correlate a new measure with other existing valid measures would have the same logical difficulties if shared methods and/or agents were used.

The assumption driving our strategy of construct development is that the constructs will be more complete and more informative when subjected first to confirmatory factor analysis and then subsequently analyzed for predictive validity in process models. To this end, SEM provides a statistical method for converging on *less biased estimates* of predictive validity, by providing the capability of simultaneously distinguishing between method variance, random error variance, and true construct variance (Dwyer, 1983). The estimates of predictive validity always approximate the actual value, depending on preliminary work in construct definition and the quality of data. As discussed earlier and more extensively by Cook and Campbell (1979), one mistake is to rely exclusively on one assessment method in construct definition. The practical implication of monomethod bias in the context of SEM is the inability to distinguish the "true" relation between two constructs from the shared variance due to a common method of assessment for both constructs—most commonly self-report. In a later section, however, we describe a strategy for testing whether content other than method is present even when only one method or agent has been used (see *Yoked Method, Random Content* section).

ANALYTIC STRATEGIES

Other than Cattell's work, *no one* we are aware of has systematically set out to deal with the method variance problem in a programmatic way. In fact, because efforts to deal within the multitrait-multimethod matrix have uniformly been less than clear successes, investigators have apparently removed the method-bias problem from the scientific agenda. Certainly, this has been true in the personality literature. In the experimental literature, there exists some evidence of the same kind of problem; for example, Patterson and Hinsey (1964) noted that in classical conditioning studies (Humphreys, 1943) and instrumental learning as well (Pubols, 1960), time-dependent and time-independent measures of response strength cannot be assumed to be equivalent. Time-dependent and time-independent measures of response strength were controlled by different parameters.

Since the 1970s, the ideas of multivariate analyses have spread with relative rapidity through psychology with the explicit need for multiple independent and dependent variables (i.e., multiple indicators). Given that this view has been generally embraced by the field, it is all the more interesting that relatively few investigators have focused significant attention on the method-bias issue.

Given the multiagent and multimethod data required, we have developed four analytic strategies with which we can examine the potential informant/concept and method/concept confound. We emphasize, at this juncture, that these strategies do not solve the method problem. They do, however, provide the researcher with tools and options for analyzing multiagent and multimethod data. All four strategies have been constructed within the SEM format and can be summarized as follows.

Nonoverlapping Agents and Methods

In this approach, mutually exclusive or nonoverlapping methods and agents are used for adjacent constructs in a model. This approach is likely to be useful only when a small number of constructs (i.e., two to four) are used in a model. With greater numbers of constructs that are all specified as interrelated, finding the necessary number of mutually exclusive methods and agents for the various constructs becomes a most challenging task. Even though our goal has been to develop from four to eight indicators for each of the key constructs in our general model, this may still be insufficient for the task.

With four constructs, we have been able to use this nonoverlap-indicator strategy by defining each construct with just two indicators (Patterson & Capaldi, in press). The benefit of neatly sidestepping the method variance problem was, therefore, paid for by a loss of flexibility in using the collected data. This, of course, makes use of only a relatively small subset of the available measures for each construct; in a sense one is throwing away costly data.

The Risk Factor Strategy

In this approach, each participant is scored for the presence ($+1$) versus absence (0) of a particular symptom or life event. The total score, therefore, is a sum between 0 and the total number of items. Note that the risk factor scores collapse across indicators (regardless of agent or method) to arrive at a single number. We have found this technique especially helpful in dealing with measures of stress.

The various indicators of stress (e.g., employment status and financial problems, physical ailments, perceived difficulties) did not converge well. The solution was to form a single "risk factor" that summed the exposure to stress for each individual across all the indicators; that is, a cut score for each indicator was set, and individuals were determined to be at risk or not for each item. Thus, a single indicator construct has been used for stress.

The Method Factor

Our third strategy was initially suggested by Jöreskog (1974), who used a measurement model to simultaneously observe factor loadings on both method and concept dimensions. Due to occasional difficulties in identifying some of these models, we have modified Jöreskog's method somewhat when necessary. First we obtain agent/method factor loadings in a preliminary analysis, then use those loadings as "fixed" parameters to test the entire measurement model including the content dimensions (for details see the following section).

This strategy allows testing in many situations in which we would otherwise have inadequate degrees of freedom. Estimating the measurement agent/method factors before analyzing the concept factors is a conservative test. The concept constructs are defined by the residual variance remaining after the agent/method variance portions have been removed. Thus, valid concept variance may be "confused" with method variance in that sequence of analyses. It is highly probable that some of the method/agent factor variances would be shared with the substantive factors in a "simultaneous" analysis.

When sufficient degrees of freedom permit, the method factor approach should be conducted in one step as Jöreskog suggests. Rudinger and Dommel (1986) provide an excellent example of construct validation using this strategy with the Jackson Personality Research Form (Jackson & Paunonon, 1980), although we find parts of the interpretation of their results questionable. Our illustration (later, this section) of this technique is also accomplished in one step per confirmatory factor analysis, though some of our conclusions differ markedly from those of Rudinger and Dommel.

A subset of the method factor strategy is to allow same method or agent uniquenesses to covary. If a small number of paired uniquenesses can be specified a priori, then this strategy allows more complex process models to be undertaken. Care must be taken, however, to avoid adding and/or deleting the estimation of these covariances ("theta-deltas" when using the LISREL program) to improve goodness of fit. When such parameters are estimated as a post hoc model fitting procedure, replication of the final model on an independent data set is essential if there is to be confidence in the solution.

Dawesian Selection of Indicators

This approach was generated by Robyn Dawes (personal communication). He posed the question in a slightly different way:

If there is an informant/concept confound, then a measurement model containing indicators with the precise combination of agents and methods used in the desired model, but using a random assortment of concepts, should not be significantly poorer than the initial measurement model.

In many ways, this is a very appealing notion. A single test could allow an investigator to go ahead testing a process model with evidence that there is significant content variance, above and beyond any method variance. Unfortunately, the initial measurement model and the Dawesian alternative will have precisely the same number of degrees of freedom (by definition), and, therefore, goodness of fit comparisons cannot be evaluated statistically. There is another potential drawback with this method in that successfully passing the Dawesian alternative test does not guarantee the absence of method variance, only the presence of "true" construct content. Thus, in the context of a process model, it is still possible that structural relationships are at least partially built on method variance.

TOOLS FOR EXAMINING GLOP

Factors with Nonoverlapping Indicators

The method variance confound is logically resolved when one specifies models with constructs that are defined uniquely by divergent methods. The most theoretically meaningful approach in specifying such models is to sample methods that are integral to the construct definition.

As an example of this approach to model development and testing, we discuss the research by Dishion (1988) on a social-interactional model of the child's development of peer relations outside the home. The primary hypothesis to be tested was that peer rejection was a product of the child's poor academic performance and antisocial behavior. Presumably both of these are seen as an outcome of disrupted parenting (Patterson et al., in press). The model was developed and tested combining the two cohorts of the Oregon Youth Study. The study procedures, details of construct development, and the theory underlying this model are included in Patterson et al.

Data were available on peer relations and child antisocial behavior from peers, parents and teachers. A cursory examination of Table 10.1 shows that the correlations between measures of different constructs using the same method are often higher than the convergent validities within constructs. In the context of a confirmatory factor analysis, these two constructs merged into one indistinguishable dimension. For some research questions these findings might be the last step in a confirmatory analysis testing the dimensionality of a given set of measures. However, on the question of peer relations and child antisocial behavior, there is considerable evidence indicating that the child's problem behavior

TABLE 10.1
Convergent-Discriminant Correlation Matrix (N=206)

	Child Antisocial			Peer Relations		
	Parents	Peers	Teachers	Parents	Peers	Teachers
Child Antisocial						
Parents	1.0					
Peers	.42***	1.0				
Teachers	.43***	.64***	1.0			
Peer Relations						
Parents	-.64***	-.33***	-.39***	1.0		
Peers	-.33***	-.71***	-.49***	.32***	1.0	
Teachers	-.39***	-.48***	-.71***	.42***	.49***	1.0

and the peers' reaction to the child were two distinguishable processes. For example, about one-quarter of the rejected children are not particularly antisocial (Coie & Koeppel, in press). These other children seem to include hyperactive, physically handicapped, withdrawn, or shy youngsters. We view these findings as essentially an outcome of inappropriate measurement selection of indicators for the two constructs.

It was assumed that all three agents (parents, teachers, and peers) were not clearly equal in terms of informants on each construct, and that the perspective of each agent carried a unique bias that contributed to confounding these two constructs. In pursuing this question, Dishion (1988) redefined both constructs using indicators that were especially relevant to the content of each construct (see Fig. 10.4). For example, peer nominations were used to define each child's peer relations, using positive nominations (likability and acceptance) as one indicator and rejection as the second indicator.

Note that this approach to sampling measures is not arbitrary. The use of peer nominations as the exclusive indicator to define peer relations is consistent with this vast developmental literature, as well as theoretically coherent. Who else, if not peers, are able to report on how accepted a child is among peers at school? It is also important to include positive and negative sociometric nominations as separate indicators of the child's peer relations. The reason for this is that much of the literature on sociometric status reveals that these two (moderately correlated) dimensions are additive in defining peer relations (Coie, Dodge, & Coppotelli, 1982; Peery, 1979).

Reports of parents and teachers obviously carry considerable weight in the measurement of the child's antisocial behavior, as these are agents that are primarily concerned with child management. The child might also be included as an informant in terms of reporting on antisocial acts committed out of the purview of supervising adults. Combining the reports of these three agents is consistent with the hypothesis to be tested, namely, that it is the child's antisocial *disposition* that determines rejection.

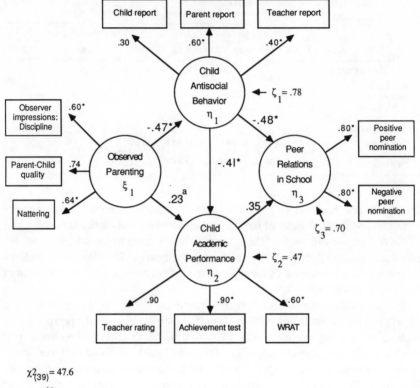

$$\chi^2_{(39)} = 47.6$$

$p = .16$

$N = 101$

$^{a}p < .10$

$^{*}p < .05$

FIG. 10.4.   Indirect effects of parenting on peer relations model with nonoverlapping indicators.

Theoretically, this hypothesis is an important complement to developmental research in that often the measurement of the child's behavior is restricted to the school setting. The next step, then, is to relate this disposition to parenting practices. Note that in this model, Dishion (1988) used an operational definition of parenting practices (observed parenting) that relied exclusively on the observed behavior of the parents with the child in the home setting. This strategy is consistent with the work within this research group demonstrating the importance of actually observing parenting practices rather than relying on interview reports (Patterson, 1982, 1986; Patterson & Bank, 1986; Reid, 1978).

The measurement of the Child Academic Performance follows the same logic. Reliance is placed on tests of academic achievement *and* the teachers' ratings;

both measurement sources are highly pertinent to this construct. Note that both Child Antisocial Behavior and Child Academic Performance are defined by teacher ratings. In the present case, this does not seem to present a problem in the testing of the model.

As can be seen in Fig. 10.4, it was found using SEM that both Academic Skills and Antisocial Behavior contributed to the child's poor Peer Relations at school. Using this nonoverlapping measurement strategy, these two constructs accounted for 30% of the variance in Peer Relations in school. This is a respectable amount given the paucity of method variance in this estimate. The effect coefficients from the Academic Skills and Antisocial Behavior constructs were both statistically significant. The chi-square goodness-of-fit test revealed that the indirect model provided an adequate fit to the observed correlations. This model was also compared to a contrasting model which consists of an alternative socialization model for the child's development of peer relations.

We see this approach to engineering measurement models with nonoverlapping methods as particularly important for those models where such a strategy yields a theoretical contribution. In the above model, for example, it was found that the child's general antisocial disposition across settings covaried with poor peer relations. This adds information to previous findings that rely on either peers or observed behavior in the school to account for a child's relations with peers. We also see this measurement strategy as providing a more conservative estimate of the relation between constructs, and therefore a more rigorous approach to model testing. Third, the strategy remains consistent with the multiagent and multimethod measurement imperative now challenging social science. The methods should be selected on a theoretical basis, and the constructs accordingly labeled.

The Risk Factor: The Problem Lies in the Construct

In the foregoing example, the method variance confound was primarily due to poor measurement. But the problem sometime lies not so much in the measurement process as in the construct itself. Some things are more difficult than others to define.

We think Family Stress is such an example. As a tentative solution to such a problem, we propose the use of a simple, additive risk score. Such a single score would presumably estimate the extent to which a family is exposed to a variety of stressors. This example is discussed in detail in Patterson et al. (in press, Chapter 6). For the purposes of illustration, analyses from Cohort 1 of the Oregon Youth Study sample ($n = 104$) are presented here.

The notion examined in the model shown in Fig. 10.5 is that parental use of monitoring practices was codetermined by the parents' social advantage/competence as well as their level of stress impinging on the family. The parents' social advantage was seen as a modulator variable where it significantly

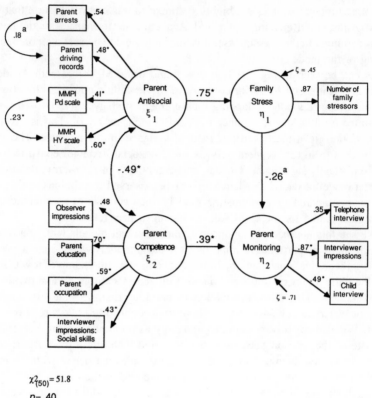

$\chi^2_{(50)} = 51.8$

$p = .40$

$N = 101$

$^a p < .10$

$^* p < .05$

FIG. 10.5.   Stress as a risk factor predicting parental monitoring.

modulated the impact of stress on the disruption of parenting. The central notion here is that the antisocial parent generates a certain level of stress for his or her family through frequent bouts of unemployment, contacts with social agencies, family conflict leading to divorce, etc.

This hypothesis does not contradict the stress amplification hypothesis introduced by Elder, Van Nguyen, and Caspi (1985). They showed that the effect of catastrophic disruptors, such as the Great Depression, exacerbated negative traits such as father irritability. The model in Fig. 10.5 might be seen as providing the complimentary hypothesis that certain traits tend to have their own products, and for the antisocial parent, an increased level of stress is presumed to be one.

In our initial examination of this model, we defined Stress by six independent indicators: Parent report of negative life events (Holmes & Rahe, 1967); Daily Hassles Scale (Family Event Checklist) (Oregon Social Learning Center, 1985);

the parent report of family medical problems; unemployment; the number of children per parent in the family; and family income divided by the number of family members. The convergent-discriminant validity matrix, however, revealed high correlations among parent-report indicators across the Parent Antisocial and Family Stress constructs. The relatively low convergent correlations for indicators in the Family Stress construct means that this model will probably not work. These data, as might be expected, lead to SEM estimates linking parent antisocial behavior and family stress that exceed 1.0. The parent report method was apparently accounting for more variance than the construct variance. Was this an occasion of poor measurement or poor construct definition?

We decided adjustments in both the construct definition and the measurement strategy were necessary. One of the key assumptions underlying the Campbell and Fiske (1959) paradigm is that one is measuring a coherent trait or disposition. We began to question whether the measurement of family stress was indeed a trait or circumstances that are often only moderately interrelated. The problem, then, seemed to be an inappropriate acceptance of the trait measurement assumptions for a factor that consisted of loosely associated processes. One way of addressing this issue is to redefine family stress as a risk factor: the more stress you are under, the more likely it is that you will be disrupted. The additive risk approach counts each stress indicator as indicative of stress or not. The approach was previously used by Rutter (1979), where the number of risk factors a child was exposed to in the family environment was examined in respect to his or her mental health. In deriving a total score for individuals for stress across indicators, a median split was used as a global measure of stress on each variate. Thus, a person's total score across indicators summarized the level of stress the family was under. Note that this scoring is a significant departure from the usual scaling technique, where low scores on a subset of stress indicators can offset high scores on other indicators, yielding an average total score. We think that the effect of stress on human performance better conforms with the assumptions underlying the additive risk model, where it is the number of sources of stress that impede performance.

Inspection of Fig. 10.5 reveals that this redefinition of Family Stress, and consequent revised measurement strategy, seemed to function adequately in a SEM model, minimizing the method variance problem and providing a multi-agent/multimethod definition of stress that was theoretically important and practically manageable. This model provided a close fit to the data, and resulted in a statistically superior fit to two alternative models. The modulating model was only partially supported with these data, as we expected both Family Stress and Parent Social Advantage/Competence to produce statistically reliable SEM effect coefficients to Parent Monitoring. Current work is underway to replicate this model in Cohort 2 of the Oregon Youth Study, and then to rerun the entire model with combined cohorts to provide a better estimate of actual effect coefficients and model fit indices.

Theoretically, these results are interesting as they raise the point that there are characteristics of parents that underlie parenting practices, and that the function of stress on parenting is best considered in conjunction with these parent traits. Patterson and Dishion (1988) take up this issue in more detail, with special reference to parental discipline practices.

Methodologically, the additive risk approach to scaling multiple indicators on a theoretical construct is very promising for variables such as stress, which reflects a range of experiences to which a person is exposed. Other constructs that may also fit the bill are Social Support and Child Stress, where both constructs are only partially determined by the actions of an individual. Although this strategy provides a method for managing the method variance problem, it does not necessarily alleviate the problem. For example, if all indicators are defined on the same method, risk scoring would not undo the obvious method bias.

Method Factors

As noted in the introduction of this section, Jöreskog's (1974) method-factor strategy appears to be the very best technique available for teasing apart content and method variance; unfortunately, it is most difficult to move with confidence from such an analysis to the next step of testing a process model (except in the case of a no-method-factor demonstration). As an example of the use of this technique with our own work, we will consider the relationships among three constructs: Maternal Stress, Support, and Depression. These data are taken from the OSLC longitudinal study of separated/divorced mothers ($N = 87$) with young sons (aged 6 to 12 at wave 1). All data in this set of analyses were maternal self-report. Table 10.2 is the correlation matrix for the 11 indicators used for the three constructs. Four alternative confirmatory factor analysis models were tested representing one, two and three content factors as well as a fourth factor analysis that indicated a mother-report factor in addition to the three content factors. The logic of such a sequence of tests is discussed in Patterson and Bank (1987). The notion is that not all theoretical constructs are necessarily discriminably different from one another, yet this empirical demonstration is essential if any particular set of constructs is to be used in the correct specification of a model. In the present case, it was thought that Stress and Depression might easily collapse into a single factor, and very possibly all three of the hypothesized constructs could best be statistically summarized in a single factor.

The confirmatory factor analysis most consistent with our theoretical position would appear to be a three-factor solution with Stress, Support, and Depression factors all allowed to intercorrelate with one another, but with no complex loadings (i.e., each indicator is permitted to load only on the factor it was designed to measure and is forced to have a zero loading on the other two factors). That analysis yielded a solution with all loadings statistically significant, as expected, but with no significant intercorrelations among factors. The

TABLE 10.2
Convergent and Discriminant Validities for Stress, Support, and Depression

	Negative Life Events	Current Finances	Daily Hassles	Family Medical History	Supportive-ness of Friends	# Contacts with Friends	CESD[a]	Telephone Report: Mood	Happiness Rating	Lubin[b]	Diary
Negative life events	1.0										
Current finances	.60	1.0									
Daily hassles	.56	.60	1.0								
Family medical history	.35	.34	.43	1.0							
Supportiveness of friends	.19	.07	.13	-.01	1.0						
# Contacts with friends	-.22	-.22	-.32	-.12	.24	1.0					
CESD	.15	.13	.12	.20	-.05	-.28	1.0				
Telephone report: mood	-.03	-.15	.01	-.05	.05	.10	.46	1.0			
Happiness rating	.16	.00	.03	.18	-.10	-.26	.41	.30	1.0		
Lubin	.07	.07	.10	-.13	-.04	-.12	.28	.52	.37	1.0	
Diary	.27	.24	.36	.21	-.14	-.21	.30	.28	.20	.27	1.0

[a] See Radloff (1977)

[b] See Lubin (1967)

Support-Depression relationship approaches significance ($r = -.30, p < .10$). The goodness of fit measures for this model were chi-square = 85.35 ($df = 42, p < .001$), GFI = .863 (adjusted GFI = .784), and RMSR = .112. The two-factor solution also resulted in all significant factor loadings, and the stress-depression intercorrelation with support reached statistical significance ($r = .52, p < .01$); chi-square = 125.46, ($df = 44, p < .001$), GFI = .765 (adjusted GFI = .647), and RMSR = .105. Clearly, the three-factor solution is superior to the two-factor solution (chi-square difference = 40.11, $df = 2$). The single-factor solution, as hypothesized, was poorest: four of the eleven indicators failed to even load on this one general factor, and the chi-square was significantly poorer than that of the two-factor solution. In each of these analyses the factor loadings for the two stress indicators were set equal to one another so that the model would be identified.

There is, however, a final logical step in this sequence of analyses. Because all indicators were based on maternal self-report, it is appropriate for the investigator to be concerned about a monomethod bias. It was, therefore, hypothesized that the best alternative model would have four factors, the three hypothetical constructs *plus* a maternal "frame of reference" method factor. To test such a model, all indicators are allowed to load twice, once on the intended content factor and then again on the method factor. In this analysis, all factor intercorrelations were set equal to 0. As in the three-factor solution, all indicators loaded significantly on their content factors, and eight of the eleven indicators also loaded significantly on the method factor. It was necessary to fix the error variance for the mother's telephone report of mood to .20. Goodness-of-fit measures for the model were: chi-square = 51.77 ($df = 35, p > .03$, GFI = .911, adjusted GFI = .833), and the RMSR = .069. The chi-square difference between the three-factor and three-plus-method-factor solutions is 33.58, with $df = 7, p < .001$. It was essential that the method factor be included.

The factor intercorrelations were set to 0 because there were no significant correlations in the three-factor solution, and the method factor was not expected to relate to the substantive factors. It should be noted that alternative solutions, including estimates for the factor intercorrelations, either failed to converge or resulted in improper solutions. Wothke (1987) cites similar problems in modeling multiple traits and methods, and he believes that the *trait-method model* is overparameterized. The current solution, however, appears statistically and interpretationally correct. When theoretically acceptable, constraining some or all factor intercorrelations to 0 may resolve the overparameterization problem.

With a successful method-factor solution, the investigator is left with the very difficult problem of how to formulate any process model given the demonstrated importance of the method factor. In many instances, it may be impossible to continue without an expanded or new data set. In some situations, it will be possible to use one or more of the other strategies outlined in this chapter. It should be noted that in many instances simply allowing the indicator residuals (i.e., thetas in LISREL) to covary for pairs of variables that share the same method or agent provides a practical solution for working with process models.

Another alternative when appropriate is to use the method factor as a substantive construct. As noted earlier, maternal self-report data can be considered the mothers' frame of reference (Reid, Bank, Patterson, & Skinner, 1987) and as such may have significant predictive power for phenomena taking place at home.

RANDOM CONTENT/YOKED METHOD FACTORS

Two theoretically related constructs, Academic Performance and Peer Relations, were selected for use as an illustration of the Dawesian alternative test. The data were drawn from 101 families participating in the Oregon Youth Study, Cohort I, Wave 1. For this example, each construct was intentionally defined with indicators that have method, agent, and context overlaps: teacher CBC, parent CBC, and peer nomination defined Peer Relations, while Academic Performance was defined by parent and teacher CBC and standard school test scores. Note that *within* each construct there are similar methods (CBC) and contexts (teachers and peers; teachers and school tests), and method, agent and content are shared *across* the two constructs. Clearly, any process model including paths between these two constructs would be suspect. How important a role would the shared methods play in any relationship observed between Academic Performance and Peer Relations operationally defined in this way?

Before attempting to answer this question, it was important to first assure ourselves that each construct contained content variance above and beyond the shared methods, agents and contexts. The correlation matrix in Table 10.3 shows convergent validities that are acceptable for Peer Relations and very good for Academic Performance. Note that there are a number of discriminant validities that are as large or larger than some of the convergent validities.

TABLE 10.3
Convergent-Discriminant Validities for Correct Content Indicators of Peer Relations and Academic Performance Constructs

	Peer Relations			Academic Performance		
	Parent CBC	Teacher CBC	Peer Nomin.	Parent CBC	Teacher CBS	School Tests
Peer Relations						
Parent CBC	1.0					
Teacher CBC	.30	1.0				
Peer Nomin.	.29	.48	1.0			
Academic Performance						
Parent CBC	.11	.28	.30	1.0		
Teacher CBC	.17	.43	.47	.76	1.0	
School Tests	.02	.12	.21	.50	.52	1.0

TABLE 10.4
Convergent-Discriminant Validities for Random (Cross) Content Indicators with
Same Method/Agent as Indicators of Peer Relations and Academic Performance

| | Peer Relations | | | Academic Performance | | |
	Parent CBC	Teacher CBC	Peer Nomin.	Parent CBC	Teacher CBC	School Tests
Peer Relations						
Parent CBC (depression)	1.0					
Teacher CBC (peer relations)	.22	1.0				
Peer Nominations (social skill)	-.24	-.34	1.0			
Academic Performance						
Parent CBC (antisocial beh.)	.62	.32	-.33	1.0		
Teacher CBC (anxiety)	.18	.46	-.17	.28	1.0	
School Tests (academic perf.)	-.14	-.12	.22	-.03	-.13	1.0

The Dawesian test would have us approach these constructs by sampling from indicators with different content while controlling for method and/or agent. Two of the three indicators for each construct were replaced in the required fashion, resulting in the correlation matrix shown in Table 10.4. Parent CBC for Peer Relations was replaced by parent CBC for Depression, and peer nominations for Peer Relations was replaced by peer nominations for Social Skill. For Academic Performance, parent CBC was replaced by the parent CBC for Child Antisocial Behavior and teacher CBC was replaced by the teacher CBC on Child Anxiety. As can be observed, convergent validities for the cross-content Peer Relations construct are only slightly poorer than in Table 10.3, while the drop in convergent validity for Academic Performance is very substantial. The discriminant validities appear to be of similar magnitude across the two matrices with the single exception of parent CBC (for Child Depression and for Child Antisocial Behavior) being correlated $r = .62$. The parallel discriminant validity in Table 10.3 is only .11.

Forced one-factor solutions for each of the four constructs (that is, Peer Relations and Academic Performance with and without original content) resulted in very similar solutions for the two Peer Relations constructs and dramatically different ones for the Academic Performance constructs. Table 10.5 contains the indicator loadings for each of the four factors. Note that the cross-content Peer Relations factor loadings are all lower than the corresponding substantively related indicators, but the magnitudes are not markedly different.

On the other hand, cross-content Academic Performance does not form a

TABLE 10.5
Factor Loading for Two Correct Content and Two Random (Cross) Content Factors

Peer Relations

	Correct content	Cross content
Parent CBC	.425	.389 (depression)
Teacher CBC	.697	.554 (peer relations)
Peer Nominations	.688	-.618 (social skills)

Academic Performance

	Correct content	Cross content
Parent CBC	.858	.282 (antisocial)
Teacher CBC	.872	.976 (anxiety)
Peer Nominations	.579	-.123 (academic performance)

factor at all, but the original proper content indicators form a very tight factor, as we might expect. Incidentally, all loadings were statistically significant for the three factors that hang together, and none of the loadings even approached statistical significance for the cross-content Academic Performance factor. There is little doubt that Academic Performance contains significant content above and beyond any converging method, agent, or context variance, but we cannot be so confident of Peer Relations.

Next, a confirmatory factor analysis was performed using the six original indicators defined above to define Academic Performance and Peer Relations. All loadings were statistically significant and the correlation between the two constructs reached $r = .63$. Clearly, a substantial relationship exists between the two constructs, and the fit is satisfactory, chi-square $= 8.24$, $df = 8$, $p = .41$.

When the cross-content factors are used in a parallel confirmatory factor analysis, the fit is not acceptable (chi-square $= 25.83$, $df = 8$, $p < .001$) and worse still, the relationship between the two constructs is $r = 1.37$. As noted earlier, we have dubbed such events as "exploding models." The pattern of poorly converging relations and powerful same-method discriminant validities is extremely likely to produce similar results in a consistent fashion.

It would appear, then, that we have returned to the original Campbell and Fiske methodology. In fact, we are able to go at least one step further. Counting up hits and misses in the classic multitrait–multimethod matrix is typically inadequate for assessing the *degree* of method variance bias. Only in the most extreme cases is interpretation clear. That is, when the hierarchy of correlation magnitudes is exactly—or not at all—as expected, the conclusion is obvious, but in most instances we are left somewhere between those two extremes.

The confirmatory factor analysis format provides one way to assess *severity* of the method variance bias when content and cross-content parallel constructs are subjected to the same tests. Will the model with appropriate theoretical content fit? How will the cross-content alternative model compare? Unfortunately, this procedure for generating alternative, yoked method/random content constructs will produce structures with equal numbers of degrees of freedom, and it is impossible to test for significant differences in chi-square magnitudes. Nonetheless, the comparisons of content and cross-content constructs that share the same method biases may be very helpful to an investigator in reaching a "go" or "no go" decision with a particular set of indicators when there is concern about method variance in a data set. Hayashi and Hays (1987) have recently completed a program that also helps evaluate the relative biases in a multitrait–multimethod matrix. Their method works within the Campbell and Fiske framework, producing summaries of convergent and discriminant validities and t tests based on the numbers of hits and misses within each portion of the matrix.

Because random- (or cross-) content indicators may or may not have a substantive relationship with other indicators in these alternative models, it is strongly recommended that several sets of alternative random indicators be selected, and the same comparisons described in this section be made several times. Similar findings for each comparison construct would go a long way toward dispelling concerns that correlations from alternative contents might be clouding the method bias comparisons. It might also be instructive to subject the original and cross-content correlation matrices to the Hayashi and Hays program described earlier.

DISCUSSION

Dealing with method/agent variance is an important methodological issue for behavioral scientists that has been, at best, fraught with difficulties. Working with structural equation models has provided some new opportunities for (1) crudely teasing apart method from content variance (using Jöreskog's 1974 strategy, including some modifications and additions), (2) establishing techniques that clearly avoid the problem (i.e., nonoverlapping indicators and risk factors), and (3) providing a test assuring the presence of substantial content variance (i.e., the Dawesian random content/yoked method approach). These strategies have only been tested in a limited context in our work, and undoubtedly require further development. One purpose of this chapter is to invite other investigators to take on the method variance problem using some of these newly available tools.

There is no one correct approach to this problem, and an investigator's choice of strategy will depend on the theoretical basis of the process model (e.g., are the hypothetical constructs believed to be independent or nearly so), the number of constructs of interest, the number of indicators in a particular model sharing the same method or agent, and the number of indicators available in defining a construct. In some instances, the strongest case can be made by using two or more of these approaches as alternative models presented in conjunction with an initial process model that is believed to contain some unknown percentage of method variance.

For example, we have a number of large data sets with similar variables in each; thus, the Dawesian strategy makes good sense for us to use early on as an alternative measurement model. Problems at this stage would stop further work because operationally defined constructs would appear to contain no substantial content variance. One could go back to the drawing board as far as the development of operational definitions; it is possible that there might be no immediate "cure" for this unhappy state of affairs. The particular hypothesis of interest could be untestable with the offending data set. On the other hand, given a satisfactory Dawesian test, the happy investigator would be assured and be able to assure others that the hypothetical constructs under study are comprised largely of content variance. In testing an hypothesized process model and alternatives to it, however, shared methods/agents across factors might best be dealt with by allowing the appropriate paired uniquenesses to covary; failure to estimate these "correlated errors" would, in our experience, make a satisfactory fit of the model to the data much less likely.

Practically speaking, we have made the most use thus far of nonoverlapping indicators and estimates of covariances of shared method/agent uniquenesses. We are currently at work on the Dawesian "litmus test," and, ironically, have been unable to make much use of Jöreskog's method-factor approach. It is Jöreskog's technique that holds the most promise for actually teasing apart method from content variance, and we are still working in this area; the method-factor strategy may prove too unwieldy to be useful in the actual testing of process models, but may provide the most precise examples of content versus method variance in constructs. In our work, the most useful strategies for dealing with method variance are those that can direct or inform our efforts with structural models; that is, once the predictive component is added to the measurement model, informed statements concerning method bias must still be possible.

Final Thoughts

An obvious implication of the accumulated work on the method-variance issue is that monomethod research is biased to varying degrees in any given data set. Reid, Patterson, et al. (1987) have explored a series of competing models that pit self-report (as the single most common measure in psychological research) against more generalizable networks of multimethod-multiagent indicators. Results thus far suggest that in the prediction of child antisocial behavior, maternal self-report (even with multiple self-report indicators) predicts relatively little criterion variance (13%) when the child's antisocial behavior is measured with multiagent-multimethod indicators; in contrast, in a model using multiagent-multimethod indicators across the criterion as well as all predictor constructs, approximately 40% of the variance was accounted for. When maternal self-report was used for all indicators (i.e., criterion as well as predictor constructs), there was a strong fit of the model to the data and substantial criterion variance (approximately 40%) was again accounted for. This result was consistent with expectations.

Taken together, this series of analyses was interpreted as illustrating several major points: first, in terms of external validity—and we mean across dependent measures as well as across populations—constructs defined by multiagent and multimethod indicators are far more likely to continue to demonstrate predictive validity than constructs defined by single methods and agents; and second, at least with self-report data, monomethod operational definitions can provide models with good internal validity. This second point carries greater import than may be initially obvious. For example, although a mother's self-report may be distorted (see Dawes, 1985), her "life portrait" is likely to be a coherent one. A mother's view of her child's behavior is bound to influence the child, regardless of whether or not others share her view. In the clinical arena, the mother's perspective may indeed be what needs to be addressed. Her view may be of overriding importance for the family.

There is much work yet to be accomplished in this area, but for the first time since Campbell and Fiske introduced the multitrait-multimethod matrix, there appears to be a growing number of technical tools to help in understanding the impact of method variance on our work as social scientists.

ACKNOWLEDGMENTS

Support for this project was provided by Grant No. HD 22679, NICHD Center for Research for Mothers and Children; Grant No. MH 38318, NIMH Mood, Anxiety and Personality Disorders Research Branch; and Grant No. MH 37940, NIMH Center for Studies of Antisocial and Violent Behavior.

The writers gratefully acknowledge the helpful comments by P. M. Bentler, R. Dawes, M. Stoolmiller, and J. Tanaka on previous drafts of this manuscript.

REFERENCES

Bentler, P. M. (1980). Multivariate analysis with latent variables: Causal modeling. *Annual Review of Psychology, 31*, 419–455.

Cairns, R. B., & Green, J. A. (1979). How to assess personality and social patterns: Observations or ratings? In R. B. Cairns (Ed.), *The analysis of social interactions: Methods, issue, and illustrations.* Hillsdale, NJ: Lawrence Erlbaum Associates.

Campbell, D. T., & Fiske, D. W. (1959). Convergent and discriminant validation by the multitrait-multimethod matrix. *Psychological Bulletin, 56*, 81–105.

Carnap, R. (1956). The methodological character of theoretical concepts. In H. Feigl & M. Scriven

(Eds.), *Minnesota studies in the philosophy of science: 1. The foundations of science and concepts of psychology and psychoanalysis.* Minneapolis: University of Minnesota Press.

Cattell, R. B. (1957). *Personality and motivation, structure and measurement.* Yonkers-on-Hudson, New York: World Book Co.

Coie, J. D., Dodge, K. A., & Coppotelli, H. (1982). Dimensions and types of social status: A cross-age perspective. *Developmental Psychology, 18,* 557–570.

Coie, J. D., & Koeppl, G. E. (in press). Adapting intervention to the problems of aggressive and disruptive rejected children. In S. R. Asher & J. D. Cole (Eds.), *Peer rejection in childhood.* New York: Cambridge University Press.

Cook, T. D., & Campbell, D. T. (1979). *Quasi-experimentation: Design and analysis issues for field settings.* Boston: Houghton Mifflin.

Cronbach, L. S. (1951). Coefficient alpha and the internal structure of tests. *Psychometrika, 16,* 297–334.

Cronbach, L. S. (1970). *Essentials of psychological testing.* New York: Harper and Row.

Cronbach, L. J., & Meehl, P. E. (1956). Construct validity in psychological tests. In H. Feigl & M. Scriven (Eds.), *Minnesota studies in the philosophy of science: 1. The foundations of science and concepts of psychology and psychoanalysis.* Minneapolis: University of Minnesota Press.

Dawes, R. M. (1985). *The distorting effect of theory-based schemas on responses to questionnaire items eliciting summaries or global judgment based on retrospective memory.* Unpublished manuscript. (Available from the author, Dept. Social Science, Carnegie-Mellon University, Pittsburgh, PA 15213.)

Dillon, W. R., Kumar, A., & Mulani, N. (1987). Offending estimates in covariance structure analysis: Comments on the causes of and solutions to Heywood cases. *Psychological Bulletin, 101,* 126–135.

Dishion, T. J. (1988). *A developmental model for peer relations: Middle childhood correlates and one-year sequelae.* Unpublished doctoral dissertation, University of Oregon, Eugene.

Dwyer, J. H. (1983). *Statistical models for the social and behavioral sciences.* New York: Oxford University Press.

Elder, G. H., Van Nguyen, T., & Caspi, A. (1985). Linking family hardship to children's lives. *Child Development, 56,* 361–375.

Emery, R. E. (1982). Interparental conflict and the children of discord and divorce. *Psychological Bulletin, 92*(2), 310–330.

Emery, R. E., & O'Leary, K. D. (1984). Marital discord and child behavior problems in a non-clinical sample. *Journal of Abnormal Child Psychology, 12*(3), 411–420.

Epstein, S. (1979). The stability of behavior: I. On predicting most of the people much of the time. *Journal of Personality and Social Psychology, 37,* 1097–1126.

Fiegl, H. (1956). Some major issues and developments in the philosophy of science of logical empiricism. In H. Feigl & M. Scriven (Eds.), *Minnesota studies in the philosophy of science: 1. The foundations of science and concepts of psychology and psychoanalysis.* Minneapolis: University of Minnesota Press.

Forgatch, M. S., Patterson, G. R., & Skinner, M. L. (1988). A mediational model for the effect of divorce on antisocial behavior in boys. In E. M. Hetherington, & J. D. Arasteh (Eds.), *Impact of divorce, single parenting, and step-parenting on children.* Hillsdale, NJ: Lawrence Erlbaum Associates.

Harman, H. H. (1967). *Modern factor analysis* (2nd ed.). Chicago: University of Chicago Press.

Hayashi, T., & Hays, R. D. (1987). A microcomputer program for analyzing multitrait-multimethod matrices. *Behavior Research Methods, Instruments, and Computers, 19,* 345–348.

Holmes, T. H., & Rahe, R. H. (1967). The social readjustment rating scale. *Journal of Psychosomatic Research, 11,* 213–217.

Huba, G. J., & Bentler, P. M. (1982). On the usefulness of latent variable causal modeling in testing theories of naturally occurring events (including adolescent drug use): A rejoinder to Martin. *Journal of Personality and Social Psychology, 43,* 604–611.

Humphreys, L. G. (1943). Measures of strength of conditioned eyelid response. *Journal of General Psychology, 29,* 101–111.

Jackson, D. N., & Paunonon, S. V. (1980). Personality structure and assessment. *Annual Review of Psychology, 31,* 503–551.

Jöreskog, K. G. (1974). Analyzing psychological data by structural analysis of covariance matrices. In R. C. Atkinson, D. H. Krantz, & P. D. Suppes (Eds.), *Contemporary developments in mathematical psychology* (Vol. 2). San Francisco: W. H. Freeman.

Jöreskog, K. G., & Sörbom, D. (1986). *LISREL VI: Analysis of linear structural relationships by maximum likelihood, instrumental variables, and least squares methods* (4th ed.). Mooresville, IN: Scientific Software, Inc.

Kazdin, A. E., Esveldt-Dawson, K., Unis, A. S., & Rancurello, M. D. (1983). Child and parent evaluations of depression and aggression in psychiatric inpatient children. *Journal of Abnormal Psychology, 11,* 401–413.

MacCorquodale, K., & Meehl, P. E. (1948). On a distinction between hypothetical construct and intervening variables. *Psychological Bulletin, 55,* 95–107.

Martin, J. A. (1987). Structural equation modeling: A guide for the perplexed. *Child Development, 58,* 33–37.

Meehl, P. E. (1978). Theoretical risks and tabular asterisks: Sir Karl, Sir Ronald and the slow progress of sift psychology. *Journal of Consulting and Clinical Psychology, 66,* 239–242.

Nunnally, J. C. (1978). *Psychometric theory* (2nd ed.). New York: McGraw-Hill.

Oregon Social Learning Center. (1985). *Family event checklist.* (Available from OSLC, 207 E. 5th, Suite 202, Eugene, OR 97401.)

Patterson, G. R. (1982). *A social learning approach to family intervention: 3. Coercive family process.* Eugene, OR: Castalia Publishing Co.

Patterson, G. R., & Bank, L. (1986). Bootstrapping your way in the nomological thicket. *Behavioral Assessment, 8,* 49–73.

Patterson, G. R., & Bank, L. (1987). When is a nomological network a construct. In D. R. Peterson & D. B. Fishman (Eds.), *Assessment for decision* (pp. 249–275). New Brunswick, NJ: Rutgers University Press.

Patterson, G. R., & Capaldi, D. M. (in press). A comparison of models for boys' depressed mood. In J. E. Rolf, A. Masten, D. Cicchetti, K. Neuchterlein, & S. Weintraub (Eds.), *Risk and protective factors in the development of psychopathology.* Boston, MA: Syndicate of the Press, University of Cambridge.

Patterson, G. R., & Dishion, T. J. (1985). The contribution of families and peers to adolescent delinquency. *Criminology, 23,* 63–79.

Patterson, G. R., & Dishion, T. J. (1988). Multilevel family process models: Traits, interaction, and relationships. In R. A. Hinde & J. Stevenson-Hinde (Eds.), *Relations between relationships within families.* Oxford: Clarendon Press.

Patterson, G. R., & Hinsey, W. C. (1964). Investigations of some assumptions and characteristics of a procedure for instrumental conditioning in children. *Journal of Experimental Child Psychology, 1,* 111–122.

Patterson, G. R., Ramsey, E., & Bank, L. (1988). *A monomethod model for deviant peers: You can't get there from here.* Manuscript in preparation. (Available from the authors, OSLC, 207 E. 5th, Suite 202, Eugene, OR 97401.)

Patterson, G. R., & Reid, J. B. (1984). Social interactional processes within the family: The study of moment-by-moment family transactions in which human social development is embedded. *Journal of Applied Development Psychology, 5,* 237–262.

Patterson, G. R., Reid, J. B., & Dishion, T. J. (in press). *Antisocial boys.* New York: Cambridge University Press.

Peery, J. C. (1979). Popular, amiable, isolated, rejected: A reconceptualization of sociometric status in preschool children. *Child Development, 50,* 1231–1234.

Pubols, G. H. (1960). Incentive magnitude, learning, and performance in animals. *Psychological Bulletin, 57,* 89–115.

Reid, J. B. (1978). A social learning approach to family intervention: 2. Observation in home settings. Eugene, Oregon. Castalia Publishing Company.

Reid, J. B., Baldwin, D. V., Patterson, G. R., & Dishion, T. J. (in press). Some problems relating to the assessment of childhood disorders: A role for observational data. In M. Rutter, A. H. Tuma, & I. Lann (Eds.), *Assessment and diagnosis in child and adolescent psychopathology.* New York: Guilford Press.

Reid, J. B., Patterson, G. R., Bank, L., & Dishion, T. (1987, April). *The generalizability of single versus multiple methods in structural equation models of child development.* Paper presented at the meeting of the Society for Research in Child Development, Baltimore.

Rudinger, G., & Dommel, N. (1986). An example of convergent and discriminant validation of personality questionnaires. In A. Angleitner, & J. S. Wiggins (Eds.), *Personality assessment via questionnaires: Current issues in theory and measurement* (pp. 214–224). New York: Springer-Verlag.

Rutter, M. (1979). Protective factors in children's responses to stress and disadvantage. In M. W. Kent & J. E. Rold (Eds.), *Primary prevention of psychopathology: 3. Social competence in children.* Hanover, NH: University Press of New England.

Saylor, C. F., Finch, A. J., Jr., Baskin, C. H., Furey, W., & Kelly, M. M. (1984). Construct validity for measures of childhood depression: Application of multitrait-multimethod methodology. *Journal of Consulting and Clinical Psychology, 52,* 977–985.

Sullivan, J. L. (1974). Multiple indicators: Some criteria of selection. In H. M. Blalock (Ed.), *Measurement in the social sciences* (pp. 93–156). Chicago: Aldine.

Wothke, W. (1987). *Multivariate linear models of the multitrait-multimethod matrix.* Paper presented at the American Educational Research Association, Washington, DC.

11 Reflections: A Conceptual Analysis and Synthesis

Irving E. Sigel
Educational Testing Service

Elaine Blechman
Albert Einstein College of Medicine

This chapter attempts a synthesis of the papers in this volume. The papers represent different models of research directed at a common problem of interest—the study of depression and aggression in families. The fact that different models for research exist poses some critical problems for both research and practice. Because the goal of research in this area is to seek answers to questions about the pervasive impact of depression on family members, and hence develop treatment programs to alleviate the potential risks to members of families with depressive parents, there is good reason to create a coherent model of the illness and its consequences. The variety of contexts, constructs, mechanisms, and methods listed in Table 11.1 show the diverse areas of interest.

Searching for commonalities among the diverse models is, we believe, a step toward more extensive and inclusive construction of models guiding research and practice dealing with the role of depression in the family context, particularly if we can systematize the relationships among the relevant variables.

As is well known in the physical sciences and often in medicine, researchers build on the shoulder of the predecessors. There is, overall, a continuous growth process where the accumulation of knowledge results in building a relatively integrated edifice. To be sure, this may be an idealized notion of how other scientific endeavors work, but nevertheless it seems clear that the physical and biological sciences develop common procedures and share a somewhat agreed upon notion of method that lead to replicable results of experiments. The behavioral sciences are not so blessed—at least not at this time. Investigators have greater license to develop their own theories, their own sets of procedures, and their own analyses resulting in considerable diversity. Further, there is not too much sharing of procedures and methods and there is relatively little replication

TABLE 11.1
Contexts, Constructs, Mechanisms, and Methods

Contexts

Chronic Unmanageable Stress
Parent-Child Interaction
Marital Interaction

Mechanisms

Negative Reinforcement
Punishment
Diffuse Physiological Arousal

Constructs

Family Structure
Child Academic Competence
Child Social Competence
Depression
Antisocial Behavior
Aggression
Marital Conflict
Stress
Social Support
Parental Monitoring
Parental Discipline
Childrearing Techniques
Family Violence

Data Types

Direct Observation of Interpersonal Behavior
Physiological Measurement
Ratings by Natural Observers
Self-Report
Expert Ratings

Methods of Data Collection

Survey Research
Epidemiologic Research
Longitudinal Research
Laboratory Research
Clinical Research

Methods of Data Analysis

Multiple Regression and other Multivariate Methods
Structural Equation Modeling and other methods of
    testing causal models
Methods of Sequential Analysis such as Time-Series
    Analysis, Log-Linear Analysis

of experimental findings. In fact, there is relatively little experimental work in the strict sense of the word. Rather, our research is much more descriptive where investigators select variables that fit into their own conceptual mode and invent their own methods. The end result is a considerable amount of descriptive data providing a variety of information regarding the phenomenon under study. Because of this diversity it periodically becomes necessary to take stock of and seek the common denominators among the various research reports.

One consequence of the diversity among behavioral scientists is that they go their separate ways and do not become acquainted with the relevant research which on the surface is distal from their own conceptual and empirical approach.

This volume represents the efforts of a group of outstanding investigators and methodologists to transcend their differences and learn from each other. The contributors were selected because they share a common target—depression and aggression in the family. They were also selected because they each view this target through different conceptual and methodological lenses.

The assumption underlying the selection is that sharing such diversity will help the general understanding of the common problem of interest. It may be that we shall conclude that a multidisciplinary and multiperspective approach will be needed to deal with the complex problems.

A further aim here is to reflect on this body of diverse information with the hope that by reviewing it in all of its complexities and diversities, the opportunity will present itself to highlight disagreements, complementarities, and agreements. Finally, we hope to identify future research directions.

In the process of seeking coherence among the chapters, we shall analyze the various models and thereby come to devise a rationale for systems development expressed, perhaps, in a structural modeling approach (SEM), which will move us toward a greater understanding of the interactions among relevant variables which play a significant role in determining the outcomes of parental depression for family members.

To generate points of contact among the papers we describe paths from parental depression to children's pathology. We proceed to a conceptual discussion of the prerequisites for developing a systems approach to a comprehensive research program for family studies by emphasizing the role of causality in the context of developing an SEM strategy. We conclude with an identification of questions that must be addressed to fill in critical gaps in our knowledge base.

PATHS FROM PARENTAL DEPRESSION AND AGGRESSION TO CHILD PSYCHOPATHOLOGY: THE CONTRIBUTORS' VIEWS

Many of the papers in this volume raise questions, and some provide answers, about the pathway from parental mood disorders (particularly maternal depression) to child mental health via family interaction. There seems to be agreement among the contributors (as in the field at large) that chronic, clinically severe maternal depression increases the risk (by some unknown factor) of subsequent child psychopathology. Maternal depression seems to often precede the emergence of aggression and depression in sons, and depression in daughters.

The chapters can be grouped into two broad categories: center focused and method focused. The chapters by Radke-Yarrow; Hops, Sherman, and Biglan; Biglan, Lewin, and Hops; and Patterson and Forgatch focus on the within-family interactions as sources of pathology, while the chapters by Kellam, Anthony, and Ensminger; and Gottman emphasize the role of the school. The remaining chapters by Banks, Patterson, Dishion, and Skinner; Gottman; Gelles; and

Griffin and Gottman describe methodologies relevant to family research. Their essays provide approaches to the topics addressed in this volume as well as family studies in general.

CONTENT-FOCUSED CHAPTERS

Radke-Yarrow. We begin with the chapter by Radke-Yarrow as her work reflects a point of view that comes from the traditional child developmental perspective, where family relationships are often viewed in terms of the child-rearing model, using five characteristics of parenting as basic to her research program. These are:

> . . . provide care and protection of the child, regulating and controlling the child's behavior in line with the needs and requirements from internal and external sources, providing knowledge and skills and understanding concerning the physical and social worlds, giving affective meaning to interactions and relationships and finally being invested in and facilitative of the child's development.

Working from these dimensions as virtual determinants of the subsequent research plan, she proceeded to set up a longitudinal research program which involved interviews, assessment observations of children and their parents in homes, in a created home-like laboratory situation in order to determine the effects of parents' pathology on child development. The developmental perspective was manifest in the longitudinal nature of the study. The general outlines of the study are depicted in Fig. 11.1.

The Radke-Yarrow model investigating the consequences of family pathology should yield an understanding and subsequent explanation of the phenomena under study. Her report describes the procedures employed and it can be seen that she has a broad spectrum operating since both psychological, social, and contextual (social and physical) factors are inherent in the work. The perspective also considers development as involving transformational processes—and this can best be done by using a longitudinal design. The report does provide some results suggesting that parental pathology does in fact impact the children—a finding we shall have occasion to see reiterated in almost all of the studies.

Hops, Sherman, and Biglan. They begin with a developmental point of view different from Radke-Yarrow. Radke-Yarrow uses a process conceptualization, asking what the process changes are that are involved in parental interaction as well as in the nature of the child to answer questions about children's development. Hops et al. present a specific age-based model, which implies that age changes and developmental changes are one and the same, i.e., age changes

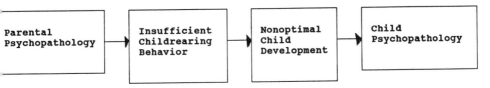

FIG. 11.1. Radke-Yarrow. Path

reflect developmental changes. However, using age as a criterion of development is using a score to reflect change rather than the process(es) as indicator(s)
of change. This is a conceptual difference that allows for explanation, because
age is a denotative variable, not an explanatory one. Age, like social class,
defines a sample but does not explain much about the phenomena in question.
The family in this study is characterized in terms of the coercive model, one
described by Patterson (1982).

The Hops team focuses on the mother as the significant target in the familial
context. By comparing families of pathological and nonpathological family
members, a comprehensive view of the family variables is presented, which is
hypothesized as influencing the development of sex typed behavior among girls
and boys. The theorizing in this chapter is based on a behavior model wherein
primary explanations of outcomes are couched in behavioral terms. Although the
macro–micro dimensions are clearly stated, the conceptualization provided does
not specify particular sets of expected relationships. The theory guiding this
project is in fact a broadly conceived conceptual framework encompassing both
macro- and micro-variables (see Fig. 11.2). This leaves the model open-ended
with opportunities to explore the variety of variable relationships. The study is
both hypothesis generating and hypothesis testing.

The quality of the mother-father relationship, as well as the depressed state of
a parent, serve to effect children's mental health. Marital harmony mitigates
childhood depression and/or aggression, while marital discord relates to pathological development. The girls seem to be more influenced by maternal depression, and as they get older, more girls manifest depressive symptoms. Boys, on
the other hand, show more aggressive antisocial behavior.

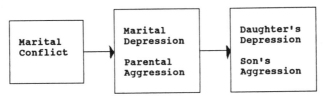

FIG. 11.2. Hops, Sherman, and Biglan. Path

Biglan, Lewin, and Hops.   These writers use contextualism as a prime organizing principle. Pepper (1967) has identified contextualism as a "world view hypothesis" which holds that every factor influences every other factor. In other words, there is an ongoing set of natural influences. Because every author in this volume considers the context to be critical, the question is, is Biglan et al.'s strategy different from the others? The defined context of interest specifically deals with the act of aggression, which is considered aversive. The implicit causal agent is this particular aversive event in the context in which it occurs. Behavior of individuals is effected by the reinforcement patterns used in these contexts. S–R models are the examples of context, since influence of particular defined variables, to wit S and consequently R's, generate linkages. In this case aversive behaviors → aggression.

Biglan et al., as contextualists, enlarge their contextual construct to include social forces that maintain, or at least generate, certain classes of aversive events. Remedial or preventive strategies can be applied to identify the relationships of the aversive event to other consistently relevant variables. In essence, these authors seek to define a set of coherences with the aversive event as the target.

This model can then be characterized as an S–R approach within a linear interactive setup. Using Structural Equation Modeling-type (SEM) analyses instantiates the linear behavioral model as well as allowing for contextual analysis. These technical and schematic developments help set directions for subsequent efforts at unraveling the complexities inherent in understanding the antecedents, consequences, and amelioratives regarding the development of depression and aggression.

Patterson and Forgatch.   Patterson and Forgatch study mothers' stress as one antecedent to children's antisocial behavior at home (see Fig. 11.3). The model is interactive and cyclical placed in a developmental context. Here development is conceptualized in terms of interdependence of events, since "each stage defines subsequent stages so events are not ahistorical nor independent of their history."

Of particular importance in this study is the use of an amplification process integrated in SEM, that is, significant variables are selected (in this case, stress),

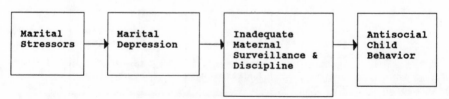

FIG. 11.3.   Patterson and Forgatch. Path

which provide a broader net by which to identify sources of influence on the dependent variable(s). Patterson (1985), is an advocate of SEM and his chapter with Forgatch is a prime example. First, the particular variables that are influenced by maternal stress are identified, particularly ineffective discipline strategies; the authors' basic argument is that ineffective discipline leads to an increase in antisocial behavior. A feedback process occurs in which participants are "trapped" or habituated in their response patterns. A second characteristic of the model can be described as amplification—stress factors explicated to demonstrate the multidimensionality of stress (e.g., negative life events, family health, family finances). These are the multidimensionalities of stress which increase in its influence. The sequence of events identified by Patterson and Forgatch stresses:

$$\text{induced description} \rightarrow \text{depressed mood} < {\text{mo} \atop \text{ch}} > \text{negative feedback.}$$

The process can be reduced to an interactive model where effects are enlarged as the feedback process continues. The model becomes more extensive as new variables are plugged into the SEM.

What is new about the Patterson–Forgatch path is a recognition that women's lives outside the home influence their behavior at home with their children. This recognition is consistent with Patterson's depiction of mothers as the eye of the domestic tornado, highly influential and highly victimized by parent-child strife. This recognition is also consistent with Wahler's work on the stressors impinging on socially insular mothers and their childrearing behavior (Wahler, 1980). For Patterson and Forgatch, stress impairs the mother's affect, behavior, and cognition so that she acts, thinks, and feels depressed. Her depression, in turn, limits her abilities to monitor and to influence child behavior in an effective manner.

Patterson and Forgatch's path, consistent with Patterson's own coercion hypothesis, involves deviance-amplification processes which operate concurrently and sequentially. The more combative a child, the more ineffective the mother. And presumably, the more depressed the mother, the more unresolved problems mount up to exacerbate her daily dose of stress.

Patterson and Forgatch take the traditional child development concept of stage and define it idiosyncratically as "a sequence of experiences that are connected in a probabilistic manner" (Patterson and Forgatch, this volume). In traditional developmental psychology, a "stage" invariably emerges in the same place in the sequential scheme of growth propelled by endogenous factors. Variations in rate of emergence of stages are due to exogenous inhibitors. Probably the best known stages are Piaget's levels of cognitive competence. In contrast to such traditional usage, Patterson and Forgatch portray stages of functioning which are likely to emerge given the presence of exogenous antecedents and consequences. The traditional child development conception of stage envisions a preprogrammed unfolding of the developing organism which can only be inhibited by the interference of adverse conditions such as ineffective parenting. For Patterson and Forgatch, the course of normal child development is preprogrammed by the culture which prepares most parents to rear their offspring in remarkably similar ways. Deviant parents who do not conform to the norms of their culture can rear exceptionally limited-or talented-children.

The previous four studies report remarkably consistent findings linking maternal depression to child outcomes. Setting the three paths (as we've sketched them) side by side, makes us wonder how much of the variance in child outcome is influenced by the contexts each group selected for study (childrearing, marital relationships, stress). Do we need all three to account for significant variance in child outcomes? Or, is there one critical context and which is it? We also wondered whether processes described for mothers by Radke-Yarrow and Patterson and Forgatch, operate in a similar manner for fathers. For example, does extrafamilial stress influence paternal aggression (borrowing a step from Hops' path) as it does maternal depression? Placing the three paths side by side made us realize that social support, especially the extrafamilial kind obtained at work and with friends, is not included as a buffering or moderating variable by any of the investigators. Furthermore, none of the three groups explains under what conditions (including adverse ones) children emerge as competent.

Finally, each of the previous models sought essentially familial determinants of depressive behavior, minimizing extra familial experiences, e.g., peer relations, school experiences. Peer relations, for example, may exacerbate or instigate depression and aggression. In fact, the classroom may function as a reinforcing context. Empirical testing of the role of the school is described from an epidemiological perspective by Kellam, Anthony, and Ensminger.

Kellam, Anthony, and Ensminger.   Using an epidemiological approach, Kellam, Anthony and Ensminger broaden our understanding of the social consequences, as well as social forces influencing the expression of depressive and aggressive behaviors in children. Kellam's et al. use the *social field concept* as the unit of analysis, in contrast to the studies described in this volume, which limit the social field to the family in its psychological and physical environments (simulated or natural). Kellam et al. include the school as part of the child's social field. The overarching concept guiding Kellam et al. is the interactive process between natural rates, "i.e., individuals who define social tasks and rate adequacy of performance." They map the developmental paths "leading to later depression and aggression . . ." Focusing on school variables and teacher ratings, they identify antecedents of depression and other symptoms in males and females and relate them to children's failure to learn. What Kellam et al. have demonstrated is that school ratings regarding learning and temperament relate differentially to later depression, aggression, and antisocial behavior (delinquency, substance abuse).

What is important and novel in family studies is the use of the classroom as a

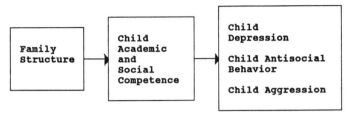

FIG. 11.4. Kellam. Path

critical social field contributing to long-term maintenance and psychological dysfunction of the children's symptomology originating in the family. In effect, the family sets the stage; the school perpetuates or enhances the symptomology.

The question arises—Is there the linear relationship: types of family structure → child's classroom adjustment → depressive outcome? Kellam et al. point out that these obtained relationships do describe the connection between family and school. The robust nature of these results makes the next level of analysis crucial; namely, the *specification of developmental processes*.

Some of the preceding studied by Radke-Yarrow, Hops et al., and Biglan et al. provide some of the specific details of family interaction that amplify Kellam's et al. findings. One word of caution, however, Kellam's sample consists of low-income urban Blacks, whereas other samples consist of Caucasians from an urban environment. The demographics for the other samples are not often specified, and we are not informed of the role these factors play in determining the reported child outcomes. If we are to take Kellam's perspective into account in a broad contextual view, it becomes clear that community school characteristics may be critical factors for amplifying children's problems. In fact, it may be the case that the school eventually can function autonomously from the family and become the primary source of the difficulty. Of course, the opposite is possible; the school experience can mitigate or neutralize family effects. The school-home relationship is an important area for further study for all classes of children.

Kellam's et al. epidemiology perspective provides a broadening framework which can incorporate each of the other models since they vary along a macro-micro dimension.

METHOD-ORIENTED CHAPTERS

The next group of papers provide the methods needed to test causal models linking the family to child and parent mental-health outcomes.

Bank, Patterson, Dishion, and Skinner. Structural Equation Modeling (SEM) is well represented in this volume, in this chapter, and in the one by

Patterson and Forgatch. To be sure, each of the previous chapters employs statistical analyses, but does not use such an articulated preordained model. The contrast between the Bank's et al. essay and the data-based papers in terms of conceiving of method may be instructive in their complementarity.

The Bank et al. paper, a methodological chapter, describes in great detail the various technical steps required to effect a reliable and valid body of data. By highlighting sources of "glop," as they refer to noise in the data gathering system, they describe procedures for determining the reliability and validity of their measures.

Bank et al. describe the complex process in model building—a prerequisite to identifying critical relationships among predefined variables. The argument is that model building will provide a basis for confidence in developing generalization. The steps outlined by Bank et al. are: (1) development of a theoretical foundation, that is, construct building; (2) development of reliable measures; (3) engaging in construct utilization which leads to (4) construct validation. There steps are necessary for the creation of structured equations which are precise quasi-mathematical statements of relationships. The particular steps to develop such models with particular attention to the "dangers" or sources of error are outlined in this chapter.

The descriptions of the processes linking the constructs are not articulated, leaving open the level of explanation of how these variables interdigitate conceptually. It is this lacunae that requires explication. We address this in part in a later section.

Gottman, focusing on the marital conflict, offers a potentially powerful prototype for refocusing and broadening the perspective of the experiential-based thinkers by entering psychophysiological constructs into his conceptualizations.

Gottman.   In Gottman's paper he offers the DPA construct, *Diffuse Physiological Arousal,* which is a physiological construct incorporating autonomic and endocrine systems which effect cognitive and social behavior. The explication of his theory is schematized in the chapter by Gottman.

The significance of this model is its incorporation of biological systems as sources for control of behavior. The data Gottman supplies for the importance of DPA in the context of marital conflict is such that it might be incorporated into the models dealing with depression and aggression. Is it not possible that enlarging the experimental models to include DPA variables will inform us as to sources of arousal or maintenance of patterns of interaction among family members? The research perspectives need not, hopefully, become polarized. The time has not yet arrived when truth is owned by anyone. Rather, our goal as scientists is to extend our horizons, to incorporate those variables that experimentally and/or conceptually enhance our explanatory and predictive focus, not only for ongoing actions, but as bases for intervention.

Accepting the simple fact that humans are creatures whose actions are not independent of their biology is to ignore the type of data reported by Gottman. Some may contend that the plea for greater extension of our model building to incorporate physiological variables where possible is creating a straw man. The evidence to the contrary can be found in the dearth of conceptualizations that consider the variables described by Gottman in new model building.

Griffin and Gottman.   A micro-analysis is exemplified in the Griffin and Gottman chapter on "Social Interaction." Its significance rests in its presenting both a logic and methodology for studying social interaction in dyads. Describing family interactions is a complex and difficult task. Griffin and Gottman focus on social interaction sequences which mirror interpersonal communications among family members. They describe three procedures for analyzing social interaction so that their effect can be assessed: log linear, log sequential, and time series. Each of these procedures allows for different sets of analyses to discover the effect particular interaction sequences have on the participants. Common to all three procedures are the following:

1. What are the behaviors (social interactive behaviors) that will be coded?
2. What level of molar-molecular distinctions will be required or used?
3. What is the most productive unit of analysis in a dyadic analysis?
4. What theory guides the selection of categories and their relationships?
5. How many variables can be used in a system created for any of the three approaches described: log linear analysis, log sequential analysis, and time series.

Answers to these questions are suggested by the authors, but procedures are not discussed. Yet procedures are needed in order to proceed to use any of the systems (Bakeman & Gottman, 1986).

At this stage of the game our increasing sensitivity to the complexity of family interactions and dynamics precludes our excluding any reliable and valid method of data collection.

Gelles.   In this chapter a new construct—family violence—and a new method—survey research—are added to our list. The construct of family violence is both important and hard to define. It incorporates different acts (e.g., physical and sexual abuse) and different agents and victims (e.g., husbands and wives, parents and children). Measurement of the construct is difficult since informants are reluctant to admit activities that are at best embarrassing and, at worst, felonious. The measurement and ethical problems with which Gelles struggles in respect to the construct of family violence cloud the study of every aspect of family life. Problems with biased parental reports of their childrearing behavior hinder our understanding of how depressed mothers, as well as aggressive fathers, influence child mental-health outcomes. It is for this reason, that Radke-Yarrow relies on direct observation of the parent-child interactions of mothers varying in levels of depression.

Gelles contends that despite the inherent bias in self-reports of family violence, survey research relying on self-report data is a useful tool. A multistage study would convince us all of its usefulness. In Stage 1, survey research relying on self-report data might yield a pool of informants with a broad range of self-reported characteristics who do, or do not, admit to family violence of a specific sort (e.g., wife beating). In Stage 2, these informants would participate in a series of emotionally challenging interpersonal, laboratory tasks, during which their behavior is directly observed, their physiological arousal monitored, and their self-ratings regarding the experience collected. Husbands and wives might have such data collected during the right after discussion of a topic that they agree often provokes arguments at home ("How much beer you drink every night." "How much you nag me"). We would anticipate that among these couples denying wife beating, some would evidence threatening and extremely hostile husband behavior in the lab. Working backward, we would want to know what surface characteristics manifest in Stage 1 responses predict Stage 2 lab violence among couples denying wife beating. Working forward, we would want to follow these couples, repeatedly measuring couple self-report and lab behavior, in order to predict which Stage 1 and 2 characteristics predict the onset of self-reported violence. Such a study combines macro-survey analysis in Stage 1 with micro-direct observation of couple interaction in Stage 2, and epidemiologic research in subsequent follow-up stages. In the following section we address such questions as we come to reflect on where we have been and where we are going.

These papers, however, exciting and in some cases, ground breaking, also force us to realize how many important conceptual, methodological, and phenomena-based questions still remain unanswered and are not even clearly stated.

We now turn our attention to some critical research conceptual, methods, and content questions.

RELEVANCE OF CAUSE, EXPLANATION
TO THE STUDY OF FAMILIES

Each of the studies and methods described seeks to establish lawful relations among the variables of interest. Implicated in the search is the unstated goal of specifying on a probability level the cause for outcome, e.g., maternal depression causes depression in daughters. Of course, we do not say that because of a number of reasons such as: "There is no evidence that the causal links are that clear cut "; or "There are other sources for childhood depression other than maternal depression." In spite of such caveats, as well as our awareness that many of our statistical procedures are statements of relationships and not cause (zero order correlation), there is still the underlying search for cause—hence the preoccupation on philosophical as well as on empirical, scientific grounds of causal inference. Path modeling and SEM are statistical attempts in the behavioral sciences to create precise statements of hypothesized relationships, thereby providing reasonable bases for making predictions. "The prediction paradigm of science interprets all scientific assertions of valid causal relations" (Rappaport, 1968, p. xiii).

The goals of the research studies reported in this volume are expressed in prediction paradigms which imply causal explanations of relationships. One of the practical outcomes of this approach is that intervention strategies can be mapped onto these predictive paradigmatic studies.

Requisite to these efforts is the conceptual requirement to clarify such concepts as cause, causal inference, and explanation. In the course of such an effort, it is also necessary to identify variables precisely and then proceed to specify relationships among them. In this way, a system can be built expressed in a structural equation or a path model. Hopefully, such an overarching strategy will enable us to accomplish three purposes: (1) identify variables relevant to the effects of family psychopathology; (2) order these variables in terms of intercausal connections as a systems perspective; and (3) generate linear and/or reciprocal models of social interactions among family members.

The introduction of the concept of *cause* probably will generate some disagreement because there are those who eschew the term "cause" for philosophical or scientific reasons. The philosophical reasons do not concern us at this point. The interested reader is referred to Bunge (1959), Cook and Campbell (1979), and Wallace (1972, 1974). This represents those empirically oriented investigators who search for explanations of social and behavioral phenomena. Once the search for explanation of events is targeted, causal considerations arise. The use of SEM and path modeling highlights the need to develop conceptions of causal relations. Once we proceed on the track, it becomes necessary to develop a theory. How else can one construct meaningful structural equations and/or path models? So, we shall first come head on to a discussion of *cause* and its relation to explanation. This then leads us directly to a consideration of developing systems which can be expressed in SEM.

Cause and explanation are intertwined since cause is a necessary basis for explanation.

Cause can be defined loosely . . . as being either a necessary condition or a sufficient condition or both. More precisely, the cause of a given event (its effect) can be defined either as (1) that set of conditions, among all conditions that occurred, each of which was necessary and the totality of which was sufficient for occurrence of the event in question or (2) some one or more conditions within that set which were novel or unusual controllable. (Rollins, 1967).

The search for cause entails the definition of variables and relationships among them, in order to move to produce predictions or explanations. In building a model in addition to defining a variable, it is necessary to determine the level of definition. A good example of the definitional problem is described by Griffin and Gottman. The possible levels of variable definition range from the molecular to the molar. A concrete example is the definition of emotion. An individual's emotional expression is observed and can be rated in a number of ways. It can be rated on a global level, e.g., the individual is angry, happy, etc.; or the emotion can be described in terms of molecular level, e.g., the lips are curled (even that can be interpreted as gross). However, for our purposes think of the difference between identifying the shape of the mouth as an expression of emotion in contrast to a holistic reference. Now to be sure, Ekman and his colleagues have identified the components of a particular emotion so that they can identify the signal for a particular emotional state (Ekman, Friesen, & Ellsworth, 1972). The investigator has to decide on the level of choice and has the subsequent problem of explaining and predicting what caused the behavior change. The choice is a function of the predilection of the investigator which may stem from a personal interest to an empirical base. It may be the case that the micro-level variables are expected to be less predictive than more global ones and hence to get results one is forced to combine the bits into much larger wholes, thereby returning to the global rating. If this is the case, why not start at the global level?

In view of that, in the following section we present a systems perspective for developing an explanatory approach which will address the macro–micro relationship.

Concepts of Explanation: A Systems Paradigm

Explanation in science is not of one cloth. Meehan (1968) makes a persuasive case for shifting from a deductive paradigm of explanation—an approach characteristic of physical scientists wherein it is assumed "that scientists search for general laws that will 'cover' particular cases" (p. 4). Meehan (1968) argues that:

> The conception of scientific inquiry . . . asserts that scientists seek intellectual instruments that permit understanding and control of the phenomena—that *control* is the central factor in the scientific enterprise. This conception is not wholly compatible with the deductive paradigm, for the emphasis on use and purpose (to control events) that follows from it leads to criteria of adequacy that cannot be met when the deductive paradigm is used. (p. 4).

Meehan proposes a systems paradigm which seems most appropriate for family research. A systems approach has been defined by Meehan (1968) as "a complete, self-contained set of variables; nothing moves into or out of the system and the notion of an 'external' influence is a contradiction in terms since the system would then be open'' (p. 54). A system is a set. Variables identified and evaluated in the systems paradigm have empirical referents. However, there is no empirical or natural system. Rather, the relationships among variables are logically constructed. In effect, a systems paradigm involves the fusion of logical and empirical, following three steps: identification of the phenomenon embedded in an empirical description that is dynamic, that stipulates change; the phenomenon has to be defined wherein sets of relationships are hypothesized to generate exceptions; and finally, the variables need to have empirical meaning. "If the system is isomorphic to the situation in which the phenomenon occurs, the system provides an explanation of the event" (p. 57). To be sure, it is not possible to identify every variable, and that may not be of moment, since variables in the empirical world are not all of the same strength. The choice of variables is the decision of the investigator.

The suggestion for a systems paradigm is not to say there is one system. Rather, it is to say that there may be various levels of variables used to build a system, ranging from a macro- to a micro-level. For example, in political science the variables may be the nation whereas in anthropology, it may be folk societies, or in sociology of the family and/or in psychology, behaviors are the particulars chosen. In the research reported in this volume, the units of measurement tend to be particular behaviors.

The systems paradigm proposed here seems to be compatible with recent developments in model building using structural equation and/or other path models. Each model is a closed system working with selected variables. The selection of variables and the ordering of relationships reflects the "bias" of the investigator. However, the models can vary in extensiveness, as well as in degree of embeddedness in the empirical world. Whether each model can be encapsulated so that a grand model will emerge seems problematic, even desirable. The studies in this volume reflect different levels of breadth to create an isomorphism with the empirical world.

One of the critical advantages of a systems approach is control. To control events requires an empirical base with minimal certainty of causal relations. The search for explanation is a necessary requirement. To be sure, as Meehan (1968) asserts, it is possible to "control events without understanding. Explanations are herein conceptualized as linked to control events in the empirical world; an explanation is an instrument that suggests ways in which man might in principle intervene in an empirical situation to alter the course of events" (p. 21). The control aspect is particularly appropriate in the context of those studies which provide intervention possibilities (either clinical or constitutional) to deal with the consequences of family pathology. In a systems paradigm variables are identified with an empirical referent (not necessarily behavioral, e.g., school organizations). Once relationships for explaining effects of each on the other are determined, procedures for intervention become possible.

Providing explanation, however, is not sufficient. What is needed is a determination of "how" the modification of the particular activity should proceed. An explanation informs us "what to control." A mother controlling her feelings of depression is critical to reduce aggression in her son. Now, the *how* to deal with that brings us to another phase of the systems paradigm.

Causal Modeling is Statistical

Each of the models describing family factors as related to the development of aggression and depression essentially employs an experiential model. Whether the model focuses on maternal, familial, or community experiences, the outcomes for the child are explained in terms of experience, be they parent, teacher, or peer interacting with the target child. Such a level of explanation can be attributed to either the implicit environmental-learning models we as psychologists work with or to an acknowledgement that no other explanatory model is available. It seems more likely that the former rationale is the more probable since an experiential model can work as a guide for positive therapeutic outcomes. This may be one reason why behavioral scientists eschew a biologically driven model.

The causal model that seems to derive from this approach is a focus on behavior variables and surface characteristics of subjects. This is characteristic of much of current psychology. The concepts are translated into quantitative relationships because

> in psychological science, statistical explanation is the preferred mode of seeking explanation/cause. Statistical explanations are explanations containing lawlike statements based on observations of statistical regularities and/or on the statistical theory of probability. It is generally accepted that probabilistic statements, as interpreted in the sciences, cannot be finally confirmed or even disconfirmed by observational evidence. It is also accepted that we cannot deduce from any statistical generalization a statement to the effect that any particular event *must* occur. (Morgenbesser, 1968, p. 121; italics added)

Confidence in the findings presented is based on statistical criteria, leading to acceptance of the constructs built into the model. Thus it seems that the first step in seeking explanation is to accept the findings because of their theoretical relevance as a basis of a scientific generalization.

Scientific generalizations derive from conceptual and empirical bases. This is the deductive model described by Meehan (1968). Examining the arguments from Meehan's systems analysis we can come to a conceptual base for guiding the use of SEM as an explanatory approach, transforming SEM into a system.

However, to use the systems approach as a model (an implicit goal in preparing this chapter) some additional activities are needed.

Prerequisites to Model Building

We begin with the primary proposition that all constructs employed in a study are the constructions of the investigator. Constructs are inventions derived from experiences or beliefs of the investigators. Even selections of conceptual systems are constructions. These choices set the direction for the subsequent model building and research strategy in general. So, for example, when an investigator elects to study antisocial behavior, he or she constructs a set of ideas, creates variables, which in his or her mind are events that will, in the short- and long-run, (whichever temporal focus is chosen) contribute to antisocial behaviors. For example, it is reported that the mother's nonresponsiveness to her child's aggression connects to the child's increased antisocial behavior. In other words, is it the fact that given A (mother's behavior) the result is B (child's behavior)? The $A \rightarrow B$ relationship suggests a causal connection; namely, it is A that determines B. But, why should this be the case? What is there about A that will cause B? Is it inevitable? What are the factors that will prevent $A \rightarrow B$? If on the one hand this relationship obtains in empirical tests, a causal statement need to be drawn. The next step is to ask, *How* $A \rightarrow B$. Replication will only confirm the relationship, but elaboration by introducing variables that reflect the mechanism(s) of influence might be called for. In seeking a systems-type approach, the search is on for other factors that converge to help specify those factors that in their wholeness contribute to the child's aggression. This is not an easy task and we do not presume to suggest at this time how this should be done, but it needs to be done to explain the connection.

Again, we turn to our constructive mind and try to identify C or D that determines the connection $A \rightarrow B$. We come back to our initial question: What is there about A that influences what of B? The basic indivisible unit, i.e., the molecular unit in behavioral science is likely to be a composite, i.e., inclusive of a number of aspects. For example, the child of a depressed mother refuses to comply when given a command. Thus what is observed is the parent's action Ac. If it is a phrase, e.g., "Stop doing that," we have an utterance which is classified as a directive (D), *but* it is embedded in the context of *voice tone* (VT), *temporal locus* (TL). The E of the three can also be incorporated into a single category of the mother's action (AC); VT + TL, i.e., CT + T + TL. Which of these does one enter into the equation? Or is D entered? If so, then the relative effect of VT on TL is lost. How does one decide? Does each variable have to be entered and a pretest done, or can a logical answer be used to create the variable?

Sigel (1982) in a study of parents' teaching strategies identified parents' verbal messages of use the cognitive demand quality of the message as the organizing principle. For example, in a statement such as, "What color is your father's car?,'' the demand of the message is to "label." The type of response the child gives indicates whether he or she understands the question or whether there is doubt that he or she did. In any event the child's response to the message is also coded. It was found that directive teaching strategies relate negatively to children's verbal IQ. The finding was obtained with two different samples (Sigel & McGillicuddy-DeLisi, 1984). Now this result was for content, ignoring voice tone, temporal locus, and child response. Are these data sufficient to allow the generalization that middle-class parents' teaching strategies have psychological significance? The finding does *not* tell us what element of the utterance determines the effect. Does this analytic approach put us in the position of infinite regress in experimentation to tease out each innuendo, each attribute of the event? It depends on the level of variable explanation that is desired. Confidence in the answer depends on one of two possibilities: (1) A predetermined prediction of a relationship was made and the finding confirms it, or (2) A replication of the study is done. Since the relationship was predicted on the basis of theory, and since the finding was replicated, there is reason to be confident in the results, but still aware that this finding, like so many of our psychology results, is at a relatively low level. But as Simon (1968) puts it, the causal connection between the two variables depends on the context provided by scientific theory. It is a causal ordering of variables and not the values of the variables that might be significant. If this is the case we become concerned with both the magnitude and how variables are ordered.

Bank et al. provide another example of definitional issues when they tell us how to avoid the glop problem (false moves) in technical terms. Their perspective has to be implemented by a theory because "in order to explain an event we often must redescribe it in terms of a given theory: moreover two events in ordinary life can be classified under the same term, may for purposes of explanation have to be described differently and explained by different theories" (Morgenbesser, 1968, p. 122).

For each term, then, in any SEM model, each construct has to go through similar processes of refinement. Once this task is resolved, the conceptualization of relationships among the constructs becomes the next step. Having resolved the molar-molecular issue relative to a construct, the next task is to define for predictive/explanatory purposes the relative interactive significance of the constructs as they pertain to the outcome. Thus in the study of depressive mothers relative to the effects on their children, what else has to be entered into the equation to test what hypothesis is generated? Hops includes age and sex of children as factors. Radke-Yarrow has included a broad band of constructs which when entered into regression models demonstrate the effect of depression in mothers with adjustment and mental health status of children.

It is clear from the papers in this volume that the determinants of the mental health status of children is determined by a number of specified familial factors. Readers may quarrel with the term determined here. In the context of the structural equation model building that we have seen in the aforementioned chapter, it is evident that when entering related constructs into the equation, the relationships are consistent and significant. These findings fit the scientific notion of determinism since causal explanation is intrinsically deterministic—i.e., give events a, b, c, . . . or, the combined effect of these is X, where X is the mental health status of the child. It is not a or b, or c which create the effect, but it is a × b × c that does. If one removes any one of the listed factors, the results change and the relationships no longer hold. If each of the investigators confirmed that "a," "b," and "c" alone did not produce results, nor did a combination of any two, then one is fairly well assured that there is something significant about the relationship among the three. However, it can be the case that the obtained significant relationships between independent composite variable(s) do not exhaust all possible causes of the outcome. Thus, it is important to indicate that the obtained variables allow for approximation of causal relations.

It is fortunate at this time that SEM and its companion path analysis are available to us in family research. The reason may be obvious in that family research requires multivariate and multidimensional approaches. The days of simplistic univariate approaches is passe. We are knowledgeable about the complexities of family interaction. In addition, the technology, both hard- and software, enable such complex analyses to take place.

The papers in this volume exemplify different models of explanation. Yet, even though the investigators are interested in causal connectives, they leave out an array of potential sources of "cause" relative to children's mental health outcomes. The results of the research provide a set of approximations. The addition of additional variables may enhance the outcome, e.g., including background or genetic variables.

Little emphasis was placed on biogenetic factors. It would seem that the biology-environmental intersect, and relative weight attributed to each, would influence the direction the research might take. In this volume the environmental emphasis appears predominant. Even causal linkages are attributed to environment where causal linkages between maternal depression and depressive symptoms in daughters are correlated and the relationship becomes stronger as the children age. Although one author (Radke-Yarrow) places the emphasis on the nature of daughters' social interactions, implying an exogenous factor determination, alternative genetic explanations are possible. For example, depression may be a family trait which may be sex linked and may emerge when changes in hormonal balance and body changes occur. Hence high incidence of depression occurs among adolescent girls. We are not suggesting that this is a *fact,* but it is a demonstration of how one might search for a more biologically centered approach.

Aggression can also be conceptualized relative to the weight of biological/environmental influence. Although the target of expression of aggression is external in contrast to depression which is internally directed, there is reason to believe that acting out behavior is not just a response to prior frustration, but rather is a "selective" coping strategy determined in part by predisposing temperamental/genetic factors. It is these biological features for both depression and aggression that account for individual differences in frequency of either of these behavioral factors.

The point is that the investigator has choices as to *how* to conceptualize the etiology of either of these syndromes. In our view a necessary step in the data analysis program is to develop a number of variables to understand the complex set of relationships functioning here.

The studies reported here regarding outcomes are in agreement. However, because the results have come about through different models and different measures, the commonalities are on a relatively abstract level and the determinants of the outcome may be different. It may be another instance of the classic problem of similar phenotypes stemming from different genotypes.

The next phase of necessary conceptualization is to seek an appropriate intervention strategy. This is best accomplished in psychology by creating a second level of experimentation based on explanations derived from the systems generated to explain outcomes.

Flowing from such understanding is a greater probability for discovering appropriate intervention strategies. Studies like those of Radke-Yarrow, Hops, Patterson and Forgatch, dramatically demonstrate that the development of depression and aggression depends on maternal interaction and marital discord, as well as on the sex of the target child. This being the case, what is the optimal point of entry into the stream of family functioning to alter the course of the potential for agonistic behavioral development among the children?

The point of entry relative to intervention in family processes to mitigate the effects of ongoing pathology or as a preventive measure depends on how the family as an agent of influence is conceptualized. None of the papers articulated a comprehensive developmental view of the family. Blechman, however, demonstrates how she did it prior to her creation of a path model for her intervention research project (Blechman & McEnroe, 1985).

Assumptions of the Path Model. The path depicted in Fig. 11.5 involves the following assumptions, many of which remain to be tested. When a couple marries, the partners' communication and problem-solving skills determine the style of marital communication they initially adopt with each other. Their overt style of marital communication together is paralleled by their covert experiences of the marital relationship. If their style of marital communication involves reciprocation of good communication and problem solving, partners are likely to experience high levels of social support in the relationship. If their style of marital communication involves low levels of good communication and problem solving, partners are likely to experience high levels of stress in the relationship. The support and stress they experience can be gauged not only by self-report but

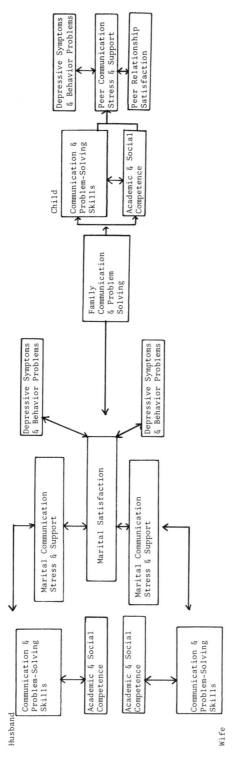

FIG. 11.5. Pathway to child competence, depression and behavior problems via family interaction.

also by direct measurement of physiological arousal during marital interaction. Marital communication, stress, and support are processes which characterize the burgeoning marital relationship. Marital satisfaction, on the other hand, is a product of these processes. It is the sum global rating which partners provide when asked, in one way or another, "How satisfied are you with this relationship?" "If you had the choice, would you do it over again?" Much of the variance in marital satisfaction can be accounted for by the processes of marital communication, stress, and support.

These are but some of the consequences of conceptualization of the problems or levels. Seeking the relationships between micro- to macro-levels and vice-versa is a thing of the future.

Conceptual and Methodological Issues as Bases for Explanation

The number of issues that are addressed in this section begin with the initial definitional identity of the phenomenon or phenomena.

Given the identification of the phenomena and the delineation of variables, the next step is to create some appropriate measures. The procedure in part is described by Patterson and Bank (1986). There is no need to dwell on the formal properties of developing measures. However, it is necessary for there to be a linkage between concept and method. This relationship should be tight, allowing for minimal slippage between concept and measurement. A major problem is that psychological variables are not only complex events, but some are unstable. As to the first point, what level of variable is to be measured? Then we ask, *Can it conceptually stand alone?* Even so we make choices of aspect or emphasis of a particular variable. For example, McGillicuddy-DeLisi and Sigel (1989) in their study of birth order and child spacing made arbitrary decisions of spacing, 2-years is near and 3-years is far spacing. Is 3-year spacing more or less important than 2- or 4-year spacing? To be sure we can work out statistical solutions provided large samples can be obtained, but the rationale still has to be articulated. We often, even too often, make decisions of this type on unstated assumptions. Another issue involves level of variable definition, a topic we touched on before.

Griffin and Gottman (this volume), in their description of social interactions, operate on a molecular level analyzing statements made by one participant to another. However, even these molecular statements have to be categorized. By what criteria?

Let us illustrate the issues using our projects since we are familiar with them. Sigel and McGillicuddy-DeLisi (1984) investigated the relationship between parents' teaching strategies and children's cognitive functioning. The experimental task was to have parents teach their children a particular task. The teaching context was a dyadic one which involved one parent teaching his or her child a paper-folding task (origami). The interactions were videotaped. The first decision was how to code the teaching strategies. A coding system was developed identifying 42 teaching strategies—yes, with excellent reliability (Sigel & McGillicuddy-DeLisi, 1984). However, the frequencies of particular behaviors posed a problem in that some behaviors occurred only a few times and other behaviors occurred more often. But, in doing the coding, two issues arose: (1) What should the unit of behavior be? We could have set up codes on the basis of time—an utterance every 5 seconds, for example, and a response within that, or we could code continuously—mother speaks, child responds, with no allowance for sampling within time units. The latter approach reflects the sampling argument in the context of the interaction and further, it is a nonprobabilistic approach. Time samples within contexts, e.g., 5- or 10-second intervals assume that the sample will be representative of all utterances and responses. The choice of this approach can be justified on practical grounds, in that coding every utterance is time consuming and actually really not be any better than time sampling. Regrettably we did not test the efficacy of these two approaches. Rather, we proceeded to code every utterance because we wanted to stay close to the ongoing behavior minimizing the sampling in this arena. We elected to sample in terms of minutes of continuous interaction. So, we selected a time sample of continuous interaction within a larger time frame (10 minutes). We used the first 2 minutes, the middle 2 minutes, and the final 2 minutes, yielding a total of 6 minutes out of 10. Admittedly, this choice was arbitrary, not based on empirical methodological comparisons. But still, every other time unit of 2 minutes could be coded as follows in terms of *structure, content, affect* or *tone, function*. The 6 minutes were combined for statistical purposes to yield the total time. Then the child's responses can be coded in terms of acceptance/rejection of message, accompanying behavior (action) and verbal (behavior). In each instance the event is complex and contains a number of elements, each of which is part of the whole and can influence the response. A comment uttered in a friendly voice might undo the command quality which leads to a noncompliance utterance. The same utterance in a firm and friendly tone can get compliance. Will the tone without the message have any effect leading to the assumption that tome is significant? Bugental and Shennum (1984) reported such an analysis, asserting that tone without a verbal message does have an effect on the child's response.

What then defines not only the particulars of the coding system, but the particular aspects that are used in data analysis? My colleagues and I (Sigel, McGillicuddy-DeLisi, & Johnson, 1980) chose the message in the form of cognitive demands because in our theory the content carried the demand which was central to the theory. The outcome of theses studies yielded moderate levels of significant correlations. If we were able to tease out the effects of "tone," would the findings have been different? Or if another coding scheme were used, would the results have been stronger? We do not know. Practical considerations kept us from doing all of those micro-analyses. Unfortunately, too often these exogenous, practical constraints such as funds, limit our efforts.

Blechman et al. used a quite different observational approach which is direct observation of family behavior. Molecular observational measures of communication and problem-solving skill (BLISS) allow testing of assumptions about what constitutes good communication and problem solving. At this point, these skills are equated with high levels of the following strings of molecular behavior: facilitative listening, self-disclosure, descriptive praise, selective attention, request, compliance, problem solving. The assumption is that effective therapists and members of effective families often demonstrate communication and problem-solving skill, defined in this manner. The facilitative listening string is central to our concept of communication skill. Facilitative listening involves attention to a speaker's self-disclosures and problem solving, including questions and comments which serve to encourage the speaker into further self-disclosure and autonomous problem solving.

In general, we all need to be concerned with the sampling of social interactions, irrespective of the procedure. Observational data, irrespective of codes, often makes two probabilistic assumptions depending on the particular techniques employed: (1) If 5-second intervals were used and only one utterance fitting the system is coded, it is assumed that the sampling procedures is okay. Rarely is this notion tested by using a continuous coding system and (2) the broader time sample is representative of the participants' interactions. Sampling is often determined arbitrarily and unreflectively. It should be made patently clear in reports of observation data *why* particular sampling procedures are used and the degree to which there is confidence in assuming that the sampling procedures are justified. This is not an issue of reliability, but of validity. Reliability data do not answer the question posed above. Reliability analyses reveal only that observers agree on the appearance and coding of behavior. To assume anything other than this is to go beyond the data. To engage in such methodological studies is to get involved in labor-intensive and hence extensive operations. Hence we fall back on justifying sampling on the basis of probabilistic theory which, actually, undergirds most of our measurement.

Any type of social interaction observational data using discrete markers for behaviors also is in danger of decontextualizing the behavior. For example, to count frequencies of a particular category of behaviors, ignoring what preceded it or what followed it, yields a kind of census of the event but limits our understanding of it. To count the number of times a parent asked a question without knowing what led up to it or what the response of the other is, to learn only that n questions were asked. The likelihood that such information will in itself serve the cause of understanding is dubious. It is the case that it does serve a useful, but limited purpose.

Of course, the assertion that frequency counts of utterances are decontextualized derived from a basic premise that an individual's actions are not random events, but rather emerge from a context and are used to achieve some objective. The types of analyses proposed by Griffin and Gottman deal with this question when they describe the statistical analyses in terms of conditional probabilities and create a unit which is the behavior *A* and the other individual's response, *B*. But this is not to say one cannot enlarge *A* and include an event prior to *A* which extends the unit, but takes into account a direct antecedent. Regularity of the sequence can be empirically determined given the coding sequences. Thus, the unit may be (pre *A, A* and *B*). How to manipulate these constellations is a statistical issue and the reader is referred to the references cited by Griffin and Gottman.

Here again the investigator has a number of choices regarding how to code these social interactions. Fortunately, there have been significant developments in this area beginning with Markow chaining which enables the investigator to make predictions of behaviors. Bakeman and Gottman (1986) and Gottman have provided extensive procedures for statistically analyzing dyadic interactions. These approaches provide a considerable set of techniques describing how molecular behaviors can be used in statistically meaningful ways.

Of course, the investigator has the choice to decide on the level of categorization. However, investigators should realize the imitations of his or her particular approach. The bottom line is that there is a tradeoff for every procedure. The role should be to select those variables considered to be central to the issue. For example, in Sigel and McGillicuddy-DeLisi (1984) the critical communication strategy of interest is the degree of autonomy the parent allows the child in decision making. However, they have not dealt with development of grammar comprehension because it can be argued that the grammatical-type of analysis is not relevant. Rather, they are guided by their theory which focused on communication relevant to logical reasoning (Sigel & McGillicuddy-DeLisi, 1984).

Because a major objective of research in the papers presented seek to identify the consequences of parental depression, the research procedures are essentially descriptive-correlational. Notable exceptions are the work of Patterson and Forgatch and Gottman. By increasing the number of variables in their equation, they were able to demonstrate more powerful predictions of consequence. This enhancement of the equation's predictive power was not due to an treatment effect; rather, it was increasing only as number of variables. Had they been able to manipulate one or more of the variables among their population, they could be carrying out what might be classified as a quasi-experimental investigation. *Quasi-experimental* because they would be "experiments that have treatments, outcome measures, and experimental units, but do not use random assignment to create comparisons from which treatment-caused change is inferred" (Cook & Campbell, 1979, p. 6). None of the studies in this volume fit that quasi-experimental model, yet causal influence is made, that is to say, by using SEM there is an implication of causation. However, since the outcomes in all of the studies are nonexperimental, what can be said about cause? Our contention is that these studies are probably as close as we can get to experimentation in a clinical setting because of ethical and practical considerations. What is to be done?

One strategy that is expressed in a number of the papers is to work out a theory clearly stating direction of the relationships between and among variables. A second approach is to carry out contrast studies using different populations which should confirm the previous findings or provide counter-examples by working with contrasting populations. Sigel and McGillicuddy-DeLisi did their initial study with families varying only in spacing and number of children (Sigel et al., 1980). Later they investigated a set of families, one-half of them with a communication handicapped child. In each case the theoretical model was the same. The results form these studies with contrasting populations predicted similar results.

The implications of this is that here is some generalizability of these results to a large representation of the population. The results are not psychological laws, nor can they be considered to be universal. The studies do not produce scientific laws because the level of generality is restricted. Thus they cannot be universal. Nevertheless, the consistency in the findings lends support to basic theory with the constraints of family size, SES, and sex of the child. The point here is that even though experimental approaches are circumscribed, use of them in subsequent quasi-experimental research designs or the use of repeated studies on related populations may be timely.

The answers to these questions are to be discovered by a function of the research design. Correlational studies are the most frequent. The strengths and weaknesses of correlational studies of the experimental method in the behavioral sciences are well known and do not to require a detailed exposition at this time (Cook & Campbell, 1979). But, in the work of Patterson and his colleagues experiments were done. This demonstrated that under some conditions clinical experimentation is possible. At this point the practical aspects of conducting experiments require a clinical center where participation in the clinic involves mandatory involvement in the experimental program. Others may argue that experimental procedures are inimical to these types of problems. The issue cannot and will not be resolved here.

There was much discussion of context in these papers (see Hops, Biglan et al., Radke-Yarrow). Patterson and Forgatch build context into their very definition of model, ''The network of variables and accompanying product defines what is meant by model'' (Patterson & Forgatch, this volume). This being the case, concern with content is not at issue. Rather, attention is drawn to the network of variables (see Fig. 11.5 for the network). Note the network lists behavior and events which in their totality influence maternal stress. Of course, there may be other factors that could be entered into the model such as mother's behavior toward siblings, or marital conflict. Incorporation of these additional variables may reduce the unaccounted for variance. But, are such additions necessary? That decision of course rests with the investigator, depending on the level of understanding, explanation and predictability sought. What Patterson and Forgatch have demonstrated is the utility of model building as a tool for identifying relevant stages of change and the network that is involved.

In addition to descriptive methods (including surveys) and experimental methods, case histories provide another approach; they are not reflected in this volume. That it is not included is not to reject it as a potentially useful approach. The pros and cons of case histories have been discussed for years and no doubt the usual criticisms are well known. In the context of this volume, however, it might be worth mentioning the potential values. If family case studies are used which focus on the multiple sources of influence in the family context, there is an opportunity to examine how particular variables interact. In a way certain themes or patterns of variables can be traced over the course of time. The types of analyses done will depend of course on the kind of data that are available. For example, the types of social interaction analyses described by Griffin and Gottman or by Gottman provide a corpus of data which can be used to trace interaction patterns over relatively long time frames. The argument is that such analysis is too labor intensive to make it worthwhile since single cases preclude generalizations. Cases can be accumulated using similar analytic strategies and by using consistent procedures for each case. This method allows for replication. In this way single case replication studies can provide the basis for generalizing about family interactive patterns.

In sum, then, conceptual and methodological issues about the articles in this volume provide an excellent sample of the types of research au courant. Let us turn now to some questions still waiting to be addressed and hopefully such a perspective allows for setting directions for future research.

Before proceeding to do this, let it be made clear that we are not proposing a "grand theory" of depression and/or aggression. It may be that the time is not right for such a complex undertaking. Perhaps it may not be possible at all. But, using the previous chapters as a source, we shall structure the remaining remarks to focus on what direction do each of the chapters suggest either by omission of certain relevant areas or by commission pointing to implications of the research for future research and current practice.

Issues Not Addressed but Relevant. As indicated earlier there are a number of issues that, we believe, must be addressed if we are to continue to untangle the depression-aggression problem. First, as indicated in the discussion of conceptualization, the etiology of depression has to be considered. The research of other investigators attending to etiology should be made more relevant. One of the major questions is the etiology of unipolar versus bipolar depression. Although both are under the rubric of depression, are there differences in their origins as well as in their manifestations?

A second issue has to do with the characteristics of depressive episodes. Most of the studies reported here have focused on depression as a static variable. However, there is variation in the duration and intensity of a depressive episode. Do fluctuations in the temporal state and depth make a difference in terms of family interaction patterns? The frequency and quality of mood swings create another source of variation and the potential for generating differential outcomes of the marriage and the children.

Concomitantly, further studies of the psychophysiological characteristics of depression may be relevant, and especially so because of the pharmacological treatment of depression. If it is possible to alleviate depressive mood swings by taking drugs, then a type of intervention is possible. Further, we are informed in this way about a physiological basis for depression. That is to say that if drugs can alleviate depressive symptomology and their withdrawal results in a return to the depressive state, does this not suggest that the etiology of the depression resides in the biochemical structure of the person? It may well be the case that subsequent behaviors are reactive since the person knows that only by using drugs can he or she hope for a relatively comfortable state. Is this not a different category of depressive character structure from those whose depression seems more actually determined—e.g., the parent having difficulty with his or her marriage.

Most of the studies found the course of the development of depression to differ with the sex of the child. Daughters of depressive mothers were found to be more vulnerable to depression. Why? Sons were found to be more apt to become aggressive and/or antisocial. Why? Findings of this sort are not only found in studies of families, but also in classrooms in urban public schools. In the latter instance, the sample was made up of poverty-level Blacks and the other sample predominantly consisted of middle-class White families. The similarity of the findings is sticky. What needs to be developed is a theory of gender differences in outcome for children of depressed mothers.

The theory will of course depend on the proclivity of the investigator. A neo-Freudian approach, for example, would focus on the daughter's identification with the mother as a way of attracting the mother's interest and love. Because depressive mothers are distant and anergic, identifying (unconsciously, of course) with the mother is a way of redirecting the mother's attention from self to the child.

Each of these interpretations still focuses on dyadic relationships with the family. How about looking at the family as a unit, an organizational unit whose central characteristics can be described in patterned terms, yielding a typology. Is this approach feasible when there are so many combinations of interactions? Is it worth the effort to seek such a conceptual model? Are the analytic methodologies available?

The answer may be a qualified yes, using Bank et al. as a point of departure. Such models allow for developing a complex set of within-family interactions. The outcome of this is a statistical way of testing the model. Of course, it may appear trite. This suggested approach may be possible only for some problems.

Heretofore, all of the studies have focused on pathology—pathology of the parents, of the marriage, of the children. Yet, is it not the case that not every daughter in the family developed depressive symptoms, or that every boy became an acting out delinquent? Why? Focusing on health and resilience is not of interest apparently. Yet, it seems reasonable to conclude that if we could discover the source of such resilience and strength, we would be en route to identifying coping strategies for the children of depressed mothers. We are not minimizing the difficulty in undertaking such research, but it is a necessary redirection since our data to date and our generalizations do not reveal the simple fact that these findings only refer to a relatively small number of children and *not* to every child in the family. Is it not of interest to know that the studies reported here do not focus on *all* of the children in the family?

Although most of the studies involved more than one child in a family, none analyzed the data in terms of birth order and spacing of births. For some reason these variables have been relegated to irrelevant by many researchers, judging by their inclusion in research design other than Zajonc and Markus (1975). Yet, McGillicuddy-DeLisi and Sigel (1989) found birth order and spacing effects relevant for cognitive development. Of particular importance is that the finding that birth order and spacing effects vary with socioeconomic status. In addition to this empirical finding, it stands to reason that the family constellation should be of moment for determining the kinds of interactions that are possible. Age and sex differences, variation in temperament and parental experience in childrearing are just some of the variables omitted in many studies of families.

Although a set of linkages of family members is a direction that is needed, there is also another set of linkages that these papers have minimized, that is, relationship of the family to the community. The study by Kellam et al. reveals the relationship between the home and the school. Schools, to be sure, play a dominant role in the lives of children and families. This approach is a prototype for beginning research into family connections with extended family and community networks. For example, networks can serve both healthy and unhealthy interests, e.g., neighborhood gangs can exacerbate proclivities for antisocial acting-out behaviors. Opportunities for such activities may be counter to the role of the school. Not only are there sources of negative influences, but also opportunities for support systems for maintaining or enhancing social constructive actions. Here as in the discussion of intra-family member resilience, the same issue arises: How is it that some children are not tempted by the allure of quick money or drugs and are able to stay aloof in spite of peer pressure?

In the final analysis research in the family field can be conceptualized and studied at different levels and with different connectors. Thus, studies of families on an epidemiological level, using surveys to get an incidence of particular types of values, beliefs and values, represent a level of investigations far removed from the assessment of individual face-to-face situations. Such differences are evident in this volume. At what level an investigator elects to enter is, of course, a matter of personal prediction. There is no dearth of questions to address. However, the overall responsibility for all investigators is to keep the big picture in mind so that in time some of the pieces can fit and our knowledge base is secured and broadened. That knowledge is always tentative is not a new idea, *but,* that the knowledge base in these studies reveals so much commonality is heartening.

Throughout this volume the perspective of the family as a developing unit has been minimized. To be sure, age differences have been defined and stages described *but* not in terms of the family as a unit. There have been attempts at such characterization, e.g., stages defined in terms of the presence of children or of governance. However, there may well be other ways to characterize the family—e.g., in functional terms such as *coherence* versus diversive, or inner- versus outer-directed. The point here is that the family is a dynamic, changing unit whose type and rate of change must be built into our conceptualization irrespective of its pathological state.

Another important consideration for the future is an emphasis on comparative family studies. Although this volume tended to focus on families with pathologies, there is still the need to undertake comparative studies of family coping and managerial strategies to provide a broad base for understanding the family which is embedded in a series of difficulties. The need for normative coping as a basis of comparison can only strengthen the overall contribution of the types of families described in this volume.

In time, no doubt, there will be a distillation of our newly found information and it is toward such a distilled, clarified, and simplified knowledge base that we are all striving. Gathering of information such as reflected in this volume is a step toward such coherence.

Unanswered Questions about the Paths to Child Psychopathology

The contributors in this volume could not be expected to address every pertinent question. We end the chapter by posing specific questions that derive from our more general discussions of the issues:

1. By what path do children of depressed mothers (or angry fathers) travel toward psychiatric disability and social deviance? How much of the variance in childhood psychopathology at Time 2 can be explained by maternal depression at Time 1? Are there other antecedent, potentially causal variables (such as paternal aggression) which explain as much or more variance in child outcome?

2. Do we need three contexts (parental stress, parent-child interaction, marital interaction) to account for significant variance in child outcomes? Or, is there one critical context? Which is it?

3. Does each context affect maternal and paternal behavior in the same way? With the same effect on children?

TABLE 11.2

Some Classes of Variables Employed in Parent-Child Research

Family Demographics	Psychological Characteristics/States	Parent Behaviors/Actions	Child Outcomes
Parents	Parents	Teaching Strategies	Intellectual-Cognitive
Education	Values	Teaching Strategies	IQ
Occupation	Beliefs	Discipline-Management	Problem-Solving Skills
Age	Attributions	Strategies	(Social-Nonsocial)
Sex	Attitudes	Verbal Interactions - Social	Attributions
Family Size	Temperament	Physical Contact	Cognitive Styles
Ethnicity	Knowledge Level		Moral Judgment
Area lived in	Cognitive Level		Knowledge
Characteristics of home	IQ		Language Usage -
Birth Order	Personal-Social Character		Comprehension
Child	Child		Academic
Age	"Normal"		Achievement - math,
Sex	Mentally Retarded		Science, Reading
Educational Level	Emotionally Disturbed		Achievement Motivation
Birth Order	Gifted and Talented		Personal-Social Character-
	Learning Disabled		istics
	Premature Birth		Self-Concept
			Impulse Control
			Social Behavior (pro/anti)
			Temperament
			Emotional Expressiveness
			(Control)
			Social Interaction (Peers)
			Ego Development

311

4. What role does social support from extra-familial sources play in buffering extrafamilial or intrafamilial stressors?

5. Under what conditions do competent children emerge from families burdened with high levels of extra- and intrafamilial stress?

6. Do the three contexts interact with SES in their impact on family members? Why?

7. Does interaction between parent and target child differ significantly from interaction between parent and all children? How is marital interaction altered by the presence of children?

8. What is the relationship between self-report, natural rater, expert rater, and direct observation measures of the same constructs?

9. Does family interaction, child outcome, and the intervening causal pathway differ between groups in which: the parent reports depressive symptoms in the clinical range but has not earned a DSM-III psychiatric diagnosis, the parent has earned a DSM-III psychiatric diagnosis. Does it differ between diagnostic groups?

Table 11.2 is an idealized model of the various factors that interact in the nuclear family context. The complexity is self-evident. However numerous as the variable are that we identify as sources of potential influence on the different family members, there are still major formidable tasks awaiting us. One is the determination of which of these variables is relevant and to what degree. This decision, however, is dependent on conceptual and empirical development. The challenge then is to develop a comprehensive family system model, subject to empirical testing. Various research strategies are being developed to advance our knowledge, some of which are described in this volume. In this way advances can be made in this complex area.

ACKNOWLEDGMENTS

Part of the research reported by Sigel and McGillicuddy-DeLisi in this paper was supported by the National Institute of Child Health and Human Development Grant No. R01-HD10686 to Educational Testing Service, National Institute of Mental Health Grant No. R01-MH32301 to Educational Testing Service, and Bureau of Education of the Handicapped Grant No. G007902000 to Educational Testing Service.

Thanks to Linda Kozelski for her skillful assistance.

REFERENCES

Bakeman, R., & Gottman, J. (1986). *Observing interaction: An introduction to sequential analysis.* New York: Cambridge University Press.

Blechman, E. A., & McEnroe, M. J. (1985). Effective family problem solving. *Child Development, 56,* 429–437.

Bugental, D. B., & Shennum, W. A. (1984). "Difficult" children as elicitors and targets of adult communication patterns: An attributional-behavioral transitional analysis. *Monographs of the Society for Research in Child Development, 49*(1, Serial No. 205).

Bunge, M. (1959). *Causality.* Cambridge, MA: Harvard University Press.

Cook, T. D., & Campbell, D. T. (1979). *Quasi-experimentation: Design & analysis issues for field settings.* Boston: Houghton Mifflin.

Ekman, P., Friesen, W., & Ellsworth, P. (1972). *Emotion in the human face.* New York: Pergamon.

McGillicuddy-DeLisi, A. V., & Sigel, I. E. (1989). Family environment and children's representational thinking. In S. Silvern (Ed.), *Development of literacy* (Vol. 6). Greenwich, CT: JAI Press.

Meehan, E. J. (1968). *Explanation in social science: A system paradigm.* Homewood, IL: Dorsey Press.

Morgenbesser, S. (1968). Scientific explanation. In *International encyclopedia of Social Sciences* (pp. 117–122). New York: Crowell, Collier & MacMillan.

Patterson, G. R. (1982). *Coercive family process.* Eugene, OR: Castalia.

Patterson, G. R. (1985). *Family process: Loops, levels, and linkages.* Paper presented at the SRCD Study Group on "Interacting Systems in Human Development," Ithaca, NY.

Patterson, G. B., & Bank, L. (1986). Bootstrapping your way in the nomological thicket. *Behavior Assessment, 88,* 49–73.

Pepper, S. C. (1967). *World hypotheses: A study in evidence.* Berkeley, CA: University of California Press. (Original work published 1942)

Rappaport, A. (1968). Forward in W. Buckley (Ed.), *Modern systems research for the behavioral scientist* (p. xiii). Chicago, IL: Aldine.

Rollins, C. D. (1967). Causation. In P. Edwards (Ed.), *The Encyclopedia of Philosophy* (Vol. 2). New York: Macmillan.

Sigel, I. E. (1982). The relationship between parents' distancing strategies and the child's cognitive behavior. In L. M. Laosa & I. E. Sigel (Eds.), *Families as learning environments for children* (pp. 47–86). New York: Plenum.

Sigel, I. E., & McGillicuddy-DeLisi, A. V. (1984). Parents as teachers of their children: A distancing behavior model. In A. D. Pellegrini & T. D. Yawkey (Eds.), *The development of oral and written language in social contexts* (pp. 71–92). Norwood, NJ: Ablex.

Sigel, I. E., McGillicuddy-DeLisi, A. V., & Johnson, J. E. (1980). *Parental distancing, beliefs and children's representational competence within the family context* (ETS RR 80-21). Princeton, NJ: Educational Testing Service.

Simon, H. (1968). Causation. In *International encyclopedia of Social Sciences.* New York: Crowell, Collier & MacMillan.

Wahler, R. (1980). The insular mother: Her problems in parent-child treatment. *Journal of Applied Behavior Analysis, 13,* 207–219.

Wallace, W. (1972). *Causality and scientific explanation* (Vol. 1). Ann Arbor: The University of Michigan Press.

Wallace, W. (1974). *Causality and scientific explanation* (Vol. 2). Ann Arbor: The University of Michigan Press.

Zajonc, R. B., & Markus, G. B. (1975). Birth order and intellectual development. *Psychological Review, 82,* 74–88.

Author Index

Numbers in *italics* indicate pages with complete bibliographic information.

Subject Index

A

Abuse, child, 109
  as aversive behavior, 107
  definition, 51–52
  incidence estimates, 56–59
  laws, 54
  rate estimates, 58, 60–61
Abuse, spouse
  as aversive behavior, 107
  definition, 52
  laws, 54–55
Acetylcholine (ACh), 85
Achenbach Behavior Checklist, 174
Additive risk model, 267–268
Adjustment problems, child's, 236
Adrenal endocrine processes, 87
Adrenal glands, 83
Affect, 106
  age differences, 202
  child's, 195–202
  depressed mothers, 108, 194
  and depression, 108
  family patterns, 180–181
  in rearing environment, 179–181
  relationships, 182
  self rating, 79
  self report, 80–81
Affect, angry, 106
Affect, dysphoric
  and age, 195, 201

in children, 195–196, 201–203
in family process, 194, 203, 212
and maternal depression, 108, 184–186,
  188, 197
response to, 106
Affect, happy, 185–186, 188, 194, 199–203
Affect, irritable, 108, 186, 194, 197–199,
  201–202
Affect, negative, 106, 201, 203
  and Diffuse Physiological Arousal (DPA),
  75, 87
  and health, 97
  and marital conflict, 98–99
  and marital satisfaction, 81, 83, 88–90
  and soothing, 92, 96
Affect, positive, 83, 99
Affect, sad, 106
Aggressive behavior, 188, 202–203
  aversive control, 111
  aversively stimulated, 113–114
  of children, 107–108, 186–187, 234–235
  and chronic pain, 109
  definition, 105–106, 187
  and depression, 108–109
  and marital distress, 202
  negative reinforcement, 112
  response to, 106
American Association for Protecting Children,
  54
American Association for the Protection of
  Children, 56–57